THE INCENSE
and
THE GLORY

Golden Censer Ministries

ISBN 978-1-64515-697-0 (paperback)
ISBN 978-1-64515-698-7 (digital)

Copyright © 2019 by Golden Censer Ministries

All rights reserved. No part of this publication may be reproduced, distributed, or transmitted in any form or by any means, including photocopying, recording, or other electronic or mechanical methods without the prior written permission of the publisher. For permission requests, solicit the publisher via the address below.

Christian Faith Publishing, Inc.
832 Park Avenue
Meadville, PA 16335
www.christianfaithpublishing.com

Golden Censer Ministries can be contacted at:
www.goldencenserministries.org and by
Email at: js@goldencenserministries.org

Printed in the United States of America

The biblical symbols that we are going to be studying about in this book and their application to us today can ONLY be spoken or written ABOUT…the true speaking and writing that brings about the manifestation in living reality of what THOSE symbols are pointing us to can ONLY be done supernaturally by God.

It is for this reason that this book is dedicated to the Glorious Church without spot or wrinkle or any such thing and to the Lord Jesus Christ, Emmanuel, who alone is worthy and who alone is able to restore each and every member of that church to the fullness of His image and likeness.

CONTENTS

Preface..7
Introduction...9

Part 1 Approaching the Throne 15
Chapter 1:   The Veil and the Porches 17
Chapter 2:   The Throne of God..33
Chapter 3:   The Incense and the Atoning Blood 55
Chapter 4:   Approaching the Throne 73
Chapter 5:   The Veil and the Covenant.............................87
Chapter 6:   The Covenant of Circumcision 95

Part 2 The Holy of Holies 123
Chapter 7:   The Atonement Sacrifices............................125
Chapter 8:   Perfect and Imperfect Sacrifices 147
Chapter 9:   The Contents of the Ark 165
Chapter 10: The Throne of Mercy and Judgment 189
Chapter 11: The Beginning of Judgment 201
Chapter 12: Righteous Judgment.......................................215
Chapter 13: When Judgment Is Set 225

Part 3 The Holy Place 243
Chapter 14: Reflections from the Holy of Holies 245
Chapter 15: The Olive Oil for the Lamps 257
Chapter 16: Lighting the Holy Place..................................273
Chapter 17: The Lamps and the Ten Virgins.....................287
Chapter 18: The Oil in the Extra Vessel.............................309

Chapter 19: The Table and the Feasts 323
Chapter 20: Righteous Seed and the Promise of Harvest 341
Chapter 21: The Basket of Sacrifices 359
Chapter 22: The Architect's Master Plan 391

Part 4 The Outer Court 403
Chapter 23: The Basket and Wave Offerings 405
Chapter 24: The Sea of Brass and Washing 431
Chapter 25: Change of Garments and the Anointing Oil 443
Chapter 26: Burnt Offerings 455
Chapter 27: The Red Heifer and the Water of Purification 461
Chapter 28: Examining the Sacrifice 469

Epilogue 473

Appendix 1: Understanding the Law 487
Appendix 2: The Birthright 501
Appendix 3: The Kinsman Redeemer 515
Appendix 4: God Being Misunderstood 533
Appendix 5: The Son of Man 561
Appendix 6: Understanding the Timepiece of God 579

PREFACE

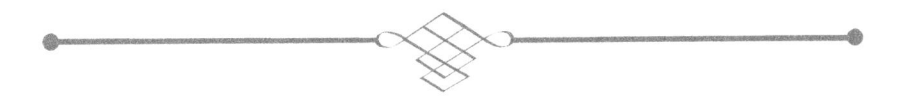

Based upon the following scripture, it is the author's firm belief that all truly supernatural faith is based upon the Word of God.

Rom. 10:17 "So then faith cometh by hearing, and hearing by the **word** of God."

John 1:1 "In the beginning was the **Word**, and the **Word** was with God, and the **Word** was God."

John 1:14 "And the **Word** was made flesh, and dwelt among us (and we beheld his glory, the glory as of the only begotten of the Father), full of grace and truth."

Heb. 4:12 "For the **word** of God is **living**, and powerful, and sharper than any two-edged sword, piercing even to the dividing asunder of soul and spirit, and of the joints and marrow, and is a discerner of the thoughts and intents of the heart." **(1833 Webster Bible)**

The **Word** of God has a human name (given **among** men, **Acts 4:12**), and His Name is the Lord Jesus Christ. All **true** knowledge, understanding, wisdom, and power come from Him and from Him **alone**.

Since it is the heartfelt desire of the author for the reader to fully attain a divinely inspired and supernaturally empowered faith in God and in the Word of God, this book uses a unique writing style that makes extensive use of quotations from the Holy Bible—the Word of God.

Unless otherwise noted, all scriptural references are made from the 1906 edition of the King James Version of the Bible.

It is also the profound yearning of his heart that every reader be so blessed by God that He can begin in them the fulfilling of His proclamation…

>   **Num. 14:21** "But as truly as I live, all the earth shall be filled with the glory of the LORD."
>
>   **Hab. 2:14** "For the earth shall be filled with the knowledge of the glory of the LORD, as the waters cover the sea."

INTRODUCTION

The Incense and the Glory
(The Seven Levels of Kingdom Power and Manifestation)

The question was once asked, "How do you solve the world's problems?" It was asked not with the expectation of an answer but as though it was an unanswerable question. But it **does** have an answer.

To understand the answer, it is important to understand that the answer is not a thing or even a concept, but a person, and His name is the Lord Jesus Christ.

While this may sound like an oversimplification of a complex problem, this is only because of underestimating the person that we are talking about and the cause of the problem.

It is safe to say that if the first man, Adam, had never fallen in sin, we would have none of the problems in the world that we see today. Adam fell from a position of being created in the image and likeness of God and of continual intimate relationship with Him. That fall is the origin of all of the problems that exist and have existed in the world.

In order to solve the world's problems, it is necessary to come back to that original position and relationship. Any resolution of the world's problems that is attempted without **that** restoration can only result in a continuation and perpetuation of the problems, instead of a resolution.

This Bible study addresses exactly this point of restoration and identifies the pattern that God has established in His Word for it to be possible.

The majority of the problems that exist in the world on a planet-wide scale are problems between nations (Table 2). If the problems between nations could be resolved, then there would be harmonious cooperation between the nations to resolve the few remaining problems.

Many of the problems between nations spring from internal conflicts within the nations. The majority of the problems within each nation arise because of the problems that exist between states or provinces. If these problems were resolved, then there would be harmonious cooperation between the states or provinces to resolve the few remaining problems.

Most of the problems within states or provinces come from conflicting attitudes and opinions that are prevalent in communities or cities. If these attitudes and opinions were brought into conformity to the will and desire of God, then the conflicting attitudes and opinions would disappear, and instead of conflict…again there would harmonious cooperation to resolve the few remaining problems.

The cause of most of the conflicting attitudes and opinions between communities or cities originates from the failure of the churches to catch the vision that God wants to impart and shoulder the responsibility of having the kind of impact for God in their surroundings that God wants them to have. If the churches caught this vision and faced the responsibilities that the vision requires, then the conflicting attitudes and opinions would simply vanish away under the impact of the presence of God in the community.

However, many of the churches do not catch that vision or face their responsibilities because of being overly occupied in resolving conflicts between "cliques" and family problems that continually threaten to tear the churches apart. However, if the problems between "cliques" and families were resolved, then there would be greater purpose, resolve, and vision to impact their communities. If each person in each ministry and leadership position felt secure in their service and that there was a continual atmosphere of respect—consideration and unified purpose to achieve the common goal of reaching the world for Christ—then there would be a unity of heart and mind that would please God to dwell in the midst of.

But the origin of the problems between "cliques" and families come from internal personality differences between the members of the groups or families. If these internal conflicts in groups and families were resolved, then the harmony in each group and home would overflow into a multiplication of edification and building-up in the church.

In order for those personality conflicts to be resolved, it is necessary that there comes a transformation in each person from being self-centered and self-seeking into being Christ-centered and Christ-seeking. This requires (individual/personal) responsibility to learn from the Lord Jesus…"His meekness and humility of heart," just as He said in **Matthew 11:28–30**.

It is by learning the divine humility that was in Christ that we can cast aside every vain reasoning and every high thing that exalts it's self against the knowledge of God and bring every thought into subjection to Him by not leaning to our own understanding, but instead, by trusting in Him with all of our hearts. In this, there is expressed a profound faith, love, and humility that will change not only ourselves and our families, but also our churches, communities, and even the world.

But what does real humility "look" like? We desperately need to catch the vision of it.

Please consider the following contrast (Table 1).

Satan does not have anything original. Everything that he does is just a perverted imitation of something that was originally created by God.

Because of his pride (**Eze. 28:17**), Satan rebelled against God and vainly imagined that he could devise a better way of doing things than God who created Him. The result of that vanity was rebellion, and the automatic fruit produced by that rebellion was disobedience, and the definition of sin is…the transgression (disobedience) of the laws of God (**1 John 3:4**).

In contrast, when we humble ourselves to God, we recognize that His way is "always" the best way. That humble recognition will produce subjection instead of rebellion, and that subjection will produce obedience instead of disobedience, and when that obedience is the supernaturally empowered manifestation of the character of God in us, it is called holiness. But notice, just as the humility is the divine humility that was in Christ, so also the subjection is His subjection to the will of the Father. Just as He was faithful to the heavenly vision that He had of the will of the Father, and just as that vision was given because of His relationship with the Father, so also the obedience is that divinely empowered persecution, enduring heavenly vision following obedience that was in Him. Because without Him, we can do "nothing" (**John 15:5**), but with Him, "all" things are possible (**Matt. 19:26; Mark 9:23, 10:27; Luke 18:27**).

The following Bible study, therefore, is about the specific biblical instructions and patterns that God has established, to learn from the Lord Jesus His humbleness of heart. So that as He leads us and instructs us in His ways, we can be transformed from glory to glory and faith to faith as we walk in His light, and His precious blood (and the power of the life that is in the blood) cleanses us from all sin **and** sinful way.

This intimate relationship with God at the personal level (Table 2) is the foundation that every subsequent level of kingdom power and manifestation is based upon. Therefore, the solution to the world's problems is not so much what we **have** as much as it is what we **become**…and we become that solution as **He** produces the living reality of His image and likeness anew in us and thereby erases **every** negative effect of the fallen condition.

I trust that you also will be filled with the glory, wonder, love, and passion that He so desires to impart to every member of the Church body that is becoming, not just a Bride…but Wife, a glorious Church without spot or wrinkle or any such thing (**Eph. 5:23**), the Wife of the Lamb (**Rev. 19:7**).

The Seven Levels of Kingdom Power and Manifestation

God	Devil
Humility	Pride
Subjection	Rebellion
Obedience	Disobedience
Holiness	Sin
Life	Death

Table 1

1) **Personal**
2) Family
3) Church
4) City/Community
5) State/Province
6) National
7) World Wide

Table 2

PART 1

Approaching the Throne

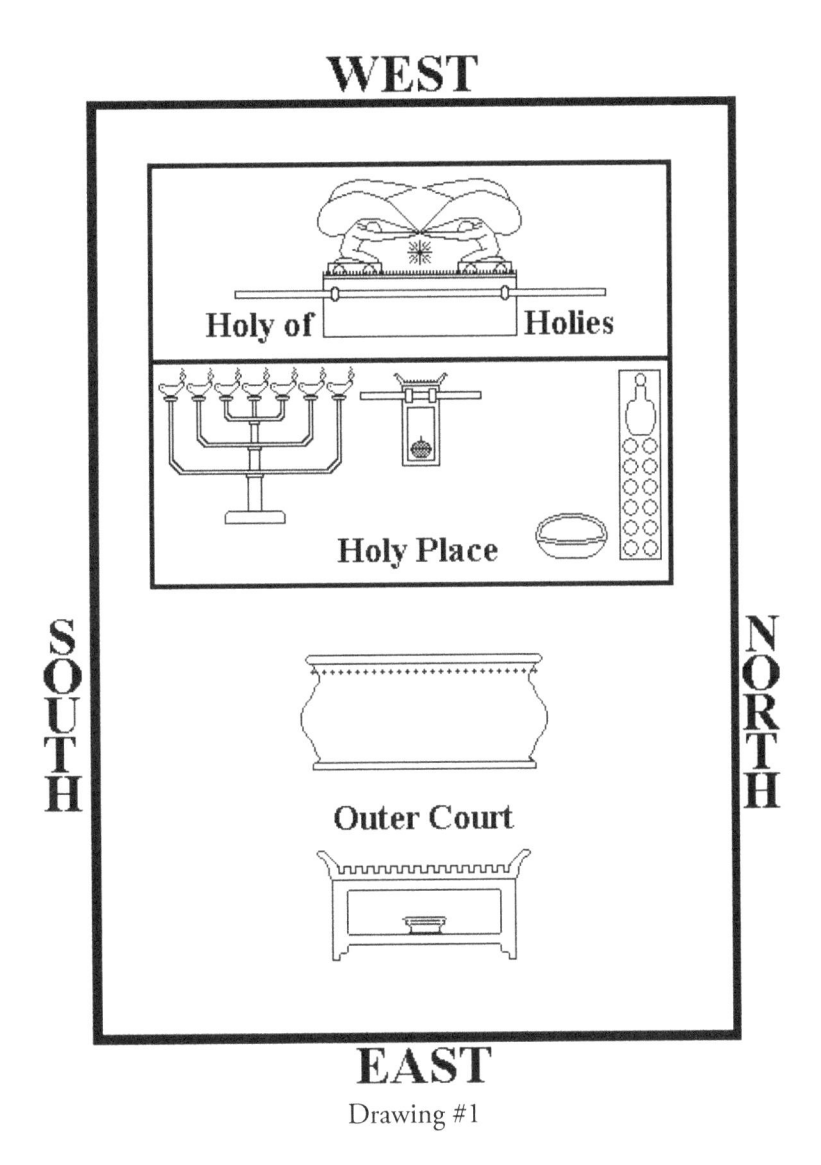

WEST

Holy of Holies

Holy Place

SOUTH **NORTH**

Outer Court

EAST

Drawing #1

Identifying How the Porches of the Temple Apply to Us Today

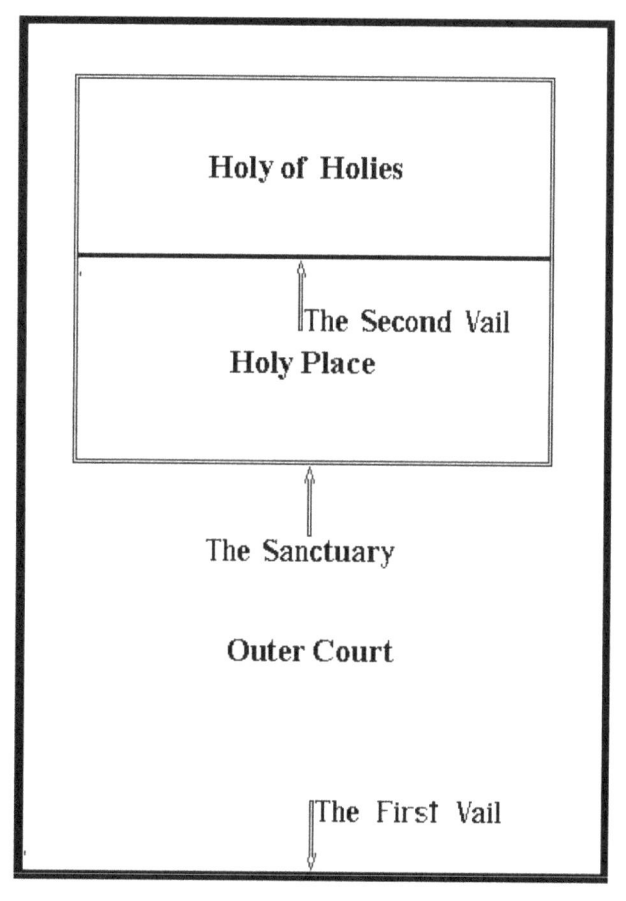

Holy of Holies

The Second Vail
Holy Place

The Sanctuary

Outer Court

The First Vail

Drawing #2

CHAPTER 1

The Veil and the Porches

The Apostle Paul taught the symbolic parallel between the Temple or Tabernacle and our bodies. This is a theme that can be seen throughout his ministry, and it even had an impact on the teachings of the other apostles as they wrote their parts of the New Testament.

> **1 Cor. 3:16** "Know ye not that ye are the temple of God, and that the Spirit of God dwelleth in you?"

In order to understand how this comparison works, it is first necessary to establish how the three porches of the Temple apply to different aspects of our being (**ref.** drawings #1 and #2). The first form that the Temple had was called the Tabernacle. The word *tabernacle* literally means "tent" and was made out of different kinds of cloth and animal skins. It had two primary areas which were called the court and the sanctuary. The sanctuary was literally a second tent inside of the tent of the outer court.

The sanctuary was also divided into two parts by a veil or curtain which was also referred to as the veil of covering, inner veil, or the second veil. In this way, we can identify that there were three porches—the Outer Court, the Holy Place or inner court, and the Holy of Holies. It is important to note that the outer limits of the court, or Outer Court, were defined by a veil or tent of hanging cloth. Therefore, there were two veils or tent cloth hangings that were mentioned by the Apostle Paul, and this is a key detail when searching out biblical symbols about the veil, and it is necessary to correctly discern which and where each of these two veils apply. This distinction helps us to keep a clear picture of how the porches apply to our being.

Not only was the Apostle Paul extremely knowledgeable about the Temple and Tabernacle, he was also a tentmaker by trade.

> **Acts 18:1** "After these things Paul departed from Athens, and came to Corinth."
>
> **Acts 18:2** "And found a certain Jew named Aquila, born in Pontus, lately come from Italy, with his wife Priscilla; (because that Claudius had commanded all Jews to depart from Rome:) and came unto them."
>
> **Acts 18:3** "And because **he was of the same craft**, he abode with them, and wrought: **for by their occupation they were tentmakers**."

Therefore, the Apostle Paul had an intimate understanding about the Tabernacle in multiple different ways.

The fact that there were **two** veils that were mentioned by the Apostle Paul is demonstrated by the use of the term "second veil" and noting that we cannot have a "second veil" without having a "first veil."

Paul, when he spoke about the sanctuary, said:

> **Heb. 9:1** "Then verily the first covenant had also ordinances of divine service, and a worldly **sanctuary**."
>
> **Heb. 9:2** "For there was a tabernacle made; the first, wherein was the candle-

stick, and the table, and the showbread; which is called the sanctuary."

Heb. 9:3 "And after the **second veil**, the tabernacle which is called the Holiest of all."

Note that the use of the word *sanctuary* speaks about the sanctuary *only* (the tent within the tent of the Outer Court), not about the entire Temple or Tabernacle.

Therefore, when the phrase "*first*, wherein was the candlestick" is used in this verse, it is talking about the first part of the "Sanctuary (the Holy Place)" and not about the Outer Court. However, when the term "second veil" is used, it is a passing reference that was made to the "first veil" which *is* the Outer Court. Also note that "after the **second veil**, the tabernacle which is called the Holiest of all."

We can conclude this from the following scriptures that show even more the locations of both the second veil and the first veil.

2 Cor. 3:14 "But their **minds** were blinded: for until this day remaineth the same **vail** untaken away in the reading of the old testament; which vail is done away in Christ."

2 Cor. 3:15 "But even unto this day, when Moses is read, the **vail** is upon their **heart**."

2 Cor. 3:16 "Nevertheless when it shall turn to the Lord, the **vail** shall be taken away."

With this, we can see that the veil that is being spoken about is the second veil, but it is mentioned in terms of being between the mind and the heart instead of in terms of being between the Holy Place and the Holy of Holies. The conclusion, therefore, is that the

Holy Place is symbolic of the mind, and the Holy of Holies is symbolic of the heart. In this, we can see that **2 Cor. 3:14–16** is the New Testament application of the following verse:

> **Exo. 26:33** "And thou shalt hang up the vail under the taches, that thou mayest bring in thither within the vail the ark of the testimony: and **the vail shall divide unto you between the holy place and the most holy**."

In this Bible study, discussion about the terms *spirit* and *soul* will be purposefully avoided, because to properly address the application of these terms would require another entire book. However, the terms of *mind* and *heart* as they are used in the scriptures will be faithfully followed. We can also see that when the heart "turns to the Lord," the veil of separation that divides between the heart and mind is taken away. We see that the significance of this veil being removed is that, when the heart turns to the Lord, the divine light of His presence comes into our hearts to dwell (**1 Cor. 3:16** "…and that the Spirit of God **dwelleth** in you."). Therefore, with the light of His presence in our hearts and the veil of separation being removed from between our hearts and minds, there is an overflowing of His divine light into our minds, and the following scripture is also fulfilled.

> **John 16:13** "Howbeit when he, the Spirit of truth, is come, he will **guide** you into all truth: for he shall not speak of himself; but whatsoever he shall hear, that shall he speak: and he will **show** you things to come."

Not only will we understand the scriptures "guide you into all truth," but this overflow is also prophetic, "will show you things to come," and He shows us things to come so that we can be a people that are "prepared for every good work" (**2 Tim. 2:21**). It is also important to notice that in **2 Cor. 3:14–16,** the reference to the veil being "done away in Christ" is a direct reference by the Apostle Paul to the Temple veil being torn when Christ was crucified (**Matt. 27:51**; **Mark 15:38; Luke 23:45**).

Rom. 12:2	"And be not conformed to this world: but be ye transformed by the renewing of your **mind**, that ye may prove what is that good, and acceptable, and perfect, will of God."

This overflow is what transforms and renews our minds, but it can only happen when the veil is torn. This brings our hearts into subjection to God and our minds (thoughts) into that same subjection. The result of this veil being taken away is that hypocrisy is done away, and the will of God as it is in heaven begins to be done in earth by and through the naturally resulting obedience.

Rom. 8:6	"For to be carnally **minded** is death; but to be spiritually **minded** is life and peace."
Rom. 8:7	"Because the carnal **mind** is enmity against God: for it is not subject to the law of God, neither indeed can be."

This overflow makes us to be spiritually minded and removes the enmity against God, and thereby produces subjection to God. It is the veil of separation that divides between the mind and the heart that makes the difference. As long as the veil remains, then the mind is carnal; when the veil is removed (by Christ), then the mind becomes a spiritual mind.

Rom. 8:9	"But ye are not in the flesh, but in the Spirit, if so be that the Spirit of God **dwell** in you. Now if any man

have not the Spirit of Christ, he is none of his."

Rom. 8:27 "And he that searcheth the **hearts** knoweth what is the **mind** of the Spirit, because he maketh intercession for the saints according to the will of God."

1 Cor. 1:10 "Now I beseech you, brethren, by the name of our Lord Jesus Christ, that ye all speak the same thing, and that there be no divisions among you; but that ye be **perfectly joined together** in the same **mind** and in the same judgment."

This overflow will bring us to "be perfectly joined together."

1 Cor. 2:16 "For who hath known the **mind** of the Lord, that he may instruct him? But we have the **mind** of Christ."

If the divine light that is in the heart *is* Christ, then the overflow is the mind of Christ coming into *our* minds.

Eph. 4:23 "And be renewed in the spirit of your **mind**."

Eph. 4:24 "And that ye put on the new man, which after God is created in righteousness and true holiness."

As that renewal happens, it will create in us "righteousness and true holiness." True holiness proclaims every jot and tittle of the word of God to be true, and not in word only, but in power and demonstration (**1 Cor. 2:4**). By the veil being removed, the enmity between the fallen condition and God is removed. All of the rebellion and disobedience that are the natural and automatic manifestations of that enmity, therefore, also cease to exist.

> **Php. 2:2** "Fulfil ye my joy, that ye be **like-minded**, having the same love, being of one accord, of one **mind**."
>
> **Php. 2:3** "Let nothing be done through strife or vainglory; but in lowliness of **mind** let each esteem other better than themselves."
>
> **Php. 2:4** "Look not every man on his own things, but every man also on the things of others."
>
> **Php. 2:5** "Let this **mind** be in you, which was also in Christ Jesus."

Just as Christ was humble and concerned for us, so also will that overflow make us to be humble of mind and concerned for each other's well-being on every level—spiritually, emotionally, and physically.

> **Col. 1:21** "And you, that were sometime alienated and enemies in your **mind** by wicked works, yet now hath he reconciled"

If being enemies in our minds produces wicked works, then being conformed in our minds will produce the righteous works of His righteousness in us. This overflowing is part of Him reconciling us to Himself and removing the alienation and enmity that came into the human race because of the fall.

2 Tim. 1:7	"For God hath not given us the spirit of fear; but of power, and of love, and of a sound **mind**."

This overflowing is the sound mind of Christ making our minds to be sound (healed) also, and it provides the power to do the works of **His** righteousness.

Heb. 8:10	"For this is the covenant that I will make with the house of Israel after those days, saith the Lord; I will put my laws into their **mind**, and write them in their **hearts**: and I will be to them a God, and they shall be to me a people."

This overflowing is part of Him fulfilling His promise of giving the New Covenant and is therefore a **fundamental part** of everything that the New Testament was given for.

Heb. 6:19	"Which hope we have as an anchor of the soul, both sure and stedfast, and which entereth into that within the **veil**."
Heb. 6:20	"Whither the forerunner is for us entered, even Jesus, made an high priest for ever after the order of Melchisedec."
Heb. 9:1	"Then verily the first covenant had also ordinances of divine service, and a worldly sanctuary."
Heb. 9:2	"For there was a tabernacle made; the first, wherein was the candlestick,

	and the table, and the showbread; which is called the **sanctuary**."
Heb. 9:3	"And after the second **veil**, the tabernacle which is called the **Holiest of all**."
Heb. 9:4	"Which had the golden censer, and the ark of the covenant overlaid round about with gold, wherein was the golden pot that had manna, and Aaron's rod that budded, and the tables of the covenant."
Heb. 9:5	"And over it the cherubims of glory shadowing the mercyseat; of which we cannot now speak particularly."
Heb. 9:6	"Now when these things were thus ordained, the priests went always into the first tabernacle, accomplishing the service of God."
Heb. 9:7	"But into the second went the high priest alone once every year, not without blood, which he offered for himself, and for the errors of the people."
Heb. 9:8	"The Holy Ghost this signifying, that the way into the **holiest of all** was not **yet** made manifest, while as the first tabernacle was yet standing."
Heb. 9:10	"Which was a **figure** for the time then present, in which were offered

both gifts and sacrifices, that could not make him that did the service perfect, as pertaining to the **conscience**."

Heb. 9:11 "Which stood only in meats and drinks, and divers washings, and carnal ordinances, imposed on them **until** the time of **reformation**."

Heb. 9:12 "But Christ being come an high priest **of good things to come**, by a greater and more perfect tabernacle, not made with hands, that is to say, not of this building."

Heb. 9:13 "Neither by the blood of goats and calves, but by his own blood he entered in once into the holy place, having obtained eternal redemption for us. For if the blood of bulls and of goats, and the ashes of an heifer sprinkling the unclean, sanctifieth to the purifying of the **flesh**."

Heb. 9:14 "How much more shall **the blood of Christ**, who **through the eternal Spirit** offered himself without spot to God, purge your **conscience** from dead works to **serve** the living God?"

Heb. 9:15 "And for this cause he is the mediator of the **new testament**, that by means of death, for the redemption of the transgressions that were under the first testament, they which are called might receive the promise of eternal inheritance."

Through the offering of His flesh (the first or outer veil) referred to in **Heb. 10:20**, the way has been consecrated for us to be able to enter in behind the **second veil** into the Holiest of all.

Heb. 10:19	"Having therefore, brethren, **boldness** to enter into the **holiest** by the blood of Jesus."
Heb. 10:20	"By a **new and living way**, which he hath **consecrated** for us, through the **veil**, that is to say, his **flesh**."
Heb. 10:21	"And having an high priest over the house of God."
Heb. 10:22	"Let us draw near with a true heart in full assurance of faith, having our **hearts** sprinkled from an evil **conscience**, and our **bodies** washed with pure water."
Heb. 10:23	"Let us hold fast the profession of our faith without wavering; (for he is faithful that promised;)"
Heb. 10:24	"And let us consider one another to provoke unto love and to good works."

By carefully considering the context in which the word *veil* is used in each of the above three scripture passages, we can conclude that the Outer Court is the flesh, the Inner Court or the Holy Place is our minds, and the Holiest of all, or the Holy of Holies, is our hearts.

Also, it should be noted that the Inner Veil is removed (**2 Cor. 3:14–16**) and that the reference to (v. **14**) "untaken away" means "unlifted," but the references to (vv. **14** and **16**) "done away" and "taken away" mean a "complete removal" or "casting away."

Therefore, the reference to the Inner Veil in **2 Cor. 3:14–16** is not speaking in every detail about the "veil" in **Heb. 10:20**.

> **Heb. 10:20** "By a new and living way, which he hath consecrated for us, through the **veil**, that is to say, his flesh."

The ONLY similarities between the two are that they were both "broken" or "torn." but the "veil" of His flesh was not entirely done away with or cast off because THAT veil STILL continues on until this day.

> **Rom. 8:27** "And he that searcheth the hearts knoweth what is the mind of the Spirit, because **he maketh intercession for the saints** according to the will of God."

> **Heb. 1:3** "Who being the brightness of his glory, and the express image of his person, and upholding all things by the word of his power, when he had **by himself** purged our sins, **sat down** on the right hand of the Majesty on high."

> **Heb. 10:12** "But **this man**, after he had offered one sacrifice for sins for ever, **sat down** on the right hand of God."

For this reason, we can see that the physical body of the Lord Jesus was NOT done away with or "cast away," but rather, it is seated "on the right hand of the Majesty on high" and is still making "intercession for the saints **according to the will of God**." So the first veil of His flesh was torn on the cross in order for Him to completely remove (destroy) the second veil.

It is necessary that these parallels and distinctions be clearly understood before we continue with the details of the furnishings of the Temple and in order for us to understand how those details apply to us today.

Through all of these details, we can now understand that the "sanctuary" is the same thing as the "inner man" that is spoken about in the following scripture.

> **Eph. 3:16** "That he would grant you, according to the riches of his glory, to be strengthened with might **by his Spirit** in the **inner man**."

And "the promise of the Father" that the Lord Jesus spoke about in:

> **Luke 24:49** "And, behold, I send **the promise of my Father** upon you: but tarry ye in the city of Jerusalem, **until ye be endued with power from on high**."

> **Acts 1:4** "And, being assembled together with them, commanded them that they should not depart from Jerusalem, but wait for **the promise of the Father**, which, saith he, ye have heard of me."

> **Acts 2:33** "Therefore being by the right hand of God exalted, and having received of **the Father the promise** of the

> Holy Ghost, he hath shed forth this, which ye now see and hear."

This is something much more than only the giving of the Holy Ghost. We can also see that "the promise of the Father" is not ONLY to give the gift of the Holy Ghost, but that it is given for the specific purpose of writing the Law of God (descriptions of how His character behaves) in our hearts (Holy of Holies) and minds (Holy Place) in giving us the New Covenant (**Jer. 31:31–33**; **Heb. 8:10**, **10:16**). Not only is it given upon the sanctuary (inner man, both heart and mind) but to also wait until that power (of His life, **John 1:4**) also manifests its self through the Outer Court (of our flesh, **Luke 24:49**).

Acts 1:8 "But **ye shall receive power, after that the Holy Ghost is come upon you**: and ye shall be witnesses unto me both in Jerusalem, and in all Judaea, and in Samaria, and unto the uttermost part of the earth."

We will be His witness as living epistles (**2 Cor. 3:2–3**), temples filled with the glory of His presence (in all three porches), and manifesting the power of His life for all men to see through the surrender of our flesh (the Outer Court).

The Golden Altar for Burning Incense is the Key to Identify that the Mercy Seat and the Throne of God are the Same and Where the Throne of God is Today.

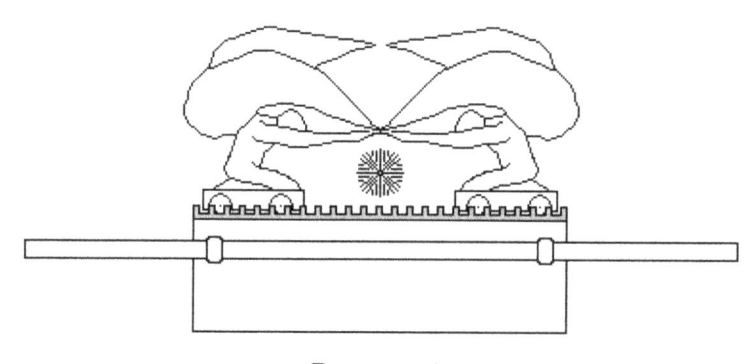

Drawing #3

CHAPTER 2

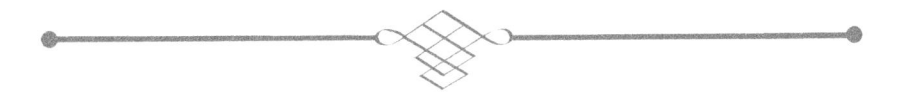

The Throne of God

There are many people that believe that the throne of God is in the heart of man. This same thing has also been taught extensively. However, nearly every attempt to prove it scripturally has usually been done in a very indirect way. In order for true supernatural faith to arise, it is necessary for the foundation of that faith to be firmly and clearly established in the word of God.

> **Rom. 10:17** "So then faith cometh by hearing, and hearing by the **word** of God."

In order to prove in a direct way that the throne of God is in the heart of man, it is necessary to understand:

1) The porches of the Temple and how they apply to our being.
2) The position of three items in the Temple and how they relate to each other.

The three items are:

1) The Ark of the Covenant.
2) The Mercy Seat.
3) The golden altar for burning incense.

The key to proving that the throne of God is in the heart of man is the golden altar for burning incense. But first, it is necessary that we understand how the scriptures use the word *testimony*.

The Testimony

A curious detail exists in the Bible about "the testimony."

Exo. 12:37	"And the children of Israel journeyed from Rameses to Succoth, about six hundred thousand on foot that were men, beside children."
Exo. 13:17	"And it came to pass, when Pharaoh had let the people go, that **God led them** not through the way of the land of the Philistines, although that was near; for God said, Lest peradventure the people repent when they see war, and they return to Egypt."
Exo. 13:18	"But **God led the people** about, through the way of the wilderness of the Red sea: and the children of Israel went up harnessed out of the land of Egypt."
Exo. 13:20	"And they took their journey from Succoth, and encamped in Etham, in the edge of the wilderness."
Exo. 13:21	"And **the LORD went before them by day in a pillar of a cloud**, to **lead** them the way; and **by night in a pillar of fire**, to give them light; to go by day and night."

Exo. 13:22	"He took not away the pillar of the cloud by day, nor the pillar of fire by night, from before the people."

Before the children of Israel even came to the Red Sea, the pillar of fire was already leading them. Even though it is obvious to us *now* that God was with Moses, as evidenced by the plagues in Egypt, God wanted to give further **testimony** that He was with Moses and Israel in a different way. He did so by appearing in the form of the pillar of fire to show His love for them, not just by bringing plagues upon their enemies, but also in protecting, blessing, leading, and providing. It was a continual witness that was constantly visible and gave them shade by day and light at night in addition to all of the other provisions. It was also a **testimony** to the surrounding peoples that could see the **testimony** of God's presence with Israel from far off.

After crossing the Red Sea and after the well of Marah (**Exo. 15:22–26**), but before they came to Mount Sinai (**Exo. 19:1–2**), God gave them manna to eat (**Exo. 16:1–30**)—divine provision.

Exo. 16:31	"And the house of Israel called the name thereof Manna: and it was like coriander seed, white; and the taste of it was like wafers made with honey."
Exo. 16:32	"And Moses said, This is the thing which the LORD commandeth, **Fill an omer of it to be kept for your generations**; that they may see the bread wherewith I have fed you in the wilderness, when I brought you forth from the land of Egypt."
Exo. 16:33	"And Moses said unto Aaron, **Take a pot, and put an omer full of manna therein, and lay it up**

	before the LORD, to be kept for your generations."
Exo. 16:34	"As the LORD commanded Moses, so **Aaron laid it up before the Testimony, to be kept**."

At this point in the journey, they still had not arrived at Mount Sinai (**Exo. 19:1–2**). It was on Mount Sinai that God gave to Moses the pattern and design of the tabernacle and all of its furnishings (**Exo. 25:1–31:18**). Therefore, the stone tablets of the Ten Commandments had not been made yet (**Exo. 31:18**), the ark of the testimony and the tabernacle did not exist yet (**Exo. 35:1–40:38**), but Aaron took some of the manna and "laid it up before the **Testimony**" (**Exo. 16:34**).

So, where and what was the "Testimony?"

Remember that when the tabernacle was made and all of the sacrifices were made and the blood of the atonement was offered, there was a specific response from God (in addition to allowing the high priest to come out of the Tabernacle alive) that He gave as a **testimony**, showing that He had accepted the atonement. That response was that the pillar of fire came down, first upon the mercy seat, and then filled the entire tabernacle. That same pillar of fire gave **testimony** both to the children of Israel and also to the Egyptians (**Exo. 14:19–20**) that God was with Moses and that God accepted the atonement.

Therefore, when Aaron laid up the manna "before the Testimony," he set it in front of the place where the pillar of fire was located.

The Ark of the Covenant

Two terms that are used in the Bible are synonymous for the same thing—the Ark of the Covenant and the Ark of the Testimony.

The Ark of the Covenant was a box made out of acacia (shittim) wood and gold. It was only referred to as the box (ark) *until* the articles of testimony were placed inside of it.

> **Exo. 25:16** "And thou shalt put into the **ark** the **testimony** which I shall give thee."
>
> **Exo. 25:21** "And thou shalt put the mercy seat above upon the **ark**; and in the **ark** thou shalt put the **testimony** that I shall give thee."

Now we see that the "testimony" was not **only** the pillar of fire but also consists of the things that were provided by God as a witness and as signs of the covenant. It is for this reason that the "Ark of the Covenant" and the "Ark of the Testimony" are synonyms for the same thing. In God's way of doing things, there is never a covenant without a witness or testimony that gives evidence to the living reality of the one who gave the covenant. Therefore, the first item of testimony, besides the pillar of fire, was the manna (**Exo. 16:34**). The next item of testimony that God gave to Moses was the stone tablets of the Ten Commandments as can be seen in the following verses:

> **Exo. 31:18** "And he gave unto Moses, when he had made an end of communing with him upon mount Sinai, two **tables of testimony**, tables of stone, written with the finger of God."
>
> **Exo. 32:15** "And Moses turned, and went down from the mount, and the two **tables of the testimony** were in his hand: the tables were written on both their sides; on the one side and on the other were they written."

> **Exo. 34:29** "And it came to pass, when Moses came down from mount Sinai with the two **tables of testimony** in Moses' hand, when he came down from the mount, that Moses wist not that the skin of his face shone while he talked with him."

It was only after the articles of witness which included the Tablets of the Testimony (**Exo. 32:15**) were placed inside of the ark that the ark was called the Ark of the Testimony. It was about the same time that the stone tablets were placed into the ark that the manna was placed inside also.

> **Exo. 40:20** "And he took and put the **testimony** into the **ark**, and set the staves on the ark, and put the mercy seat above upon the ark."

> **Exo. 40:21** "And he brought the **ark** into the tabernacle, and set up the **veil of the covering**, and **covered** the **ark of the testimony**; as the LORD commanded Moses."

While it is commonly thought that the "testimony" was only the stone tablets, at this point the items of "testimony" consisted of **both** the stone tablets **and** the golden vessel of manna. At the same time that the ark became known as the Ark of the Testimony, it also became known as the Ark of the Covenant. It was called that when the stone tablets were placed inside and not when the scrolls of the law (the written covenant) were put inside of it.

The scrolls of the law (Torah) were not completed until the death of Moses, and even though the scrolls began to be written (**Exo. 20:1–31:18**) before the stone tablets were given by God to Moses (**Exo. 31:18**), the scrolls were *completed* much later. Therefore, the

Ten Commandments are the brief summary of all of the laws, but those laws contain details that cannot be expressed fully in a brief summary. Also note that in **Exo. 40:21,** the second veil or inner veil was also called "the **veil of the covering** (see also **Exo. 35:12, 39:34; Num. 4:5; Isa. 25:7**). When the Tabernacle was made, there were two cherubims that covered the Ark of the Covenant (**Exo. 25:18–22, 37:7–9**), and when the temple of Solomon was built, there were also two cherubims that guarded the entrance into the Holy of Holies (**1 Kings 6:23–28; 2 Chr. 3:10–13**). However, there is a mention of a fifth cherubim in **Eze. 28:14** and **16** as a **covering** cherub, but *that* cherubim was in a fallen condition (**Eze. 28:15–19**).

It is for this reason that when the heart is converted to the Lord, the **veil of covering** is removed (**2 Cor. 3:14–16**) together **with** its cherubim. As long as the heart is unconverted, the mind remains in spiritual darkness and under subjection to demonic influences (the fallen fifth cherubim that was in Eden—the garden of God, **Eze. 28:13**, the dragon—**Rev. 12:9** and **20:2**). But when the light of God (**John 1:4**) comes into the heart, all darkness has to flee away, and even the mind is illuminated by the glory of the presence of God. When that happens, the thoughts of our minds will proclaim that every jot and tittle of the Word of God is true.

As long as any thoughts (or actions) remain that contradict any part of the Word of God, there are still remnants of the demonic influence of the fallen "covering" cherubim. But when the heart is converted to the Lord, the **covering veil and cherubim** is removed (**2 Cor. 3:14–16**), and the glorious light of the presence of God can illuminate not only our hearts, but also our minds, and even bring our bodies into subjection in the obedience of Christ (**2 Cor. 10:5**). When the **covering veil** is removed, not only are all demonic influences taken away, but also, our self-will is transformed from being an obstacle (because of the rebellion of pride and vanity of the fallen cherubim, **1 Sam. 15:23**) to the light of God into being subject (by humility) to God to **transmit** His divine light (**John 1:4**).

Deut. 10:8   "At that time the LORD separated the tribe of Levi, to bear the **ark of**

	the covenant of the LORD, to stand before the LORD to minister unto him, and to bless in his name, unto this day."
Deut. 31:9	"And Moses **wrote** this **law**, and delivered it unto the priests the sons of Levi, which bare the **ark of the covenant** of the LORD, and unto all the elders of Israel."
Deut. 31:26	"Take this **book of the law**, and put it in the side of the **ark of the covenant** of the LORD your God, that it may be there for a witness against thee."

The Holy of Holies is symbolic of the heart, and the Ark of the Covenant was in the Holy of Holies. The Book (scroll) of the Law was placed inside of the Ark of the Covenant, and the very act of putting it there was symbolic of the **promise of the Father** to send the New Covenant to be written in our hearts and minds (**Jer. 31:31–33; Luke 24:49; Acts 1:4, 2:33**) by the Spirit of God.

2 Cor. 3:3	"Forasmuch as ye are manifestly declared to be the epistle of Christ ministered by us, **written** not with ink, but **with the Spirit of the living God;** not in tables of stone, but **in fleshy tables of the heart.**"
1 John 3:18	"My little children, let us not love in word, neither in tongue; but in deed and in truth."

1 John 3:19	"And hereby we know that we are of the truth, and shall assure our hearts before him."
1 John 3:20	"For if our heart condemn us, God is greater than our heart, and knoweth all things."
1 John 3:21	**"Beloved, if our heart condemn us not, then have we confidence toward God."**
1 John 3:22	"And whatsoever we ask, we receive of him, because we **keep** his commandments, and **do** those things that are pleasing in his sight."
1 John 3:23	"And this is his commandment, That we should believe on the name of his Son Jesus Christ, and love one another, as he gave us commandment."
1 John 3:24	"And **he that keepeth his commandments dwelleth in him, and he in him. And hereby we know that he abideth in us, by the Spirit which he hath given us.**"

We know that He is living in us by the Spirit of His Life, supernaturally fulfilling His Word in us in ways that we are unable to do without Him, making **all things** possible.

Num. 10:33	"And they departed from the mount of the LORD three days' journey: and the **ark of the covenant of the**

LORD went before them in the three days' journey, to search out a resting place for them."

The same stone tablets that were called the "tables of testimony" (in **Exodus 31:18**) were also called the "tables of the covenant" as can be seen in the following verses:

Exo. 34:28   "And he was there with the LORD forty days and forty nights; he did neither eat bread, nor drink water. And he wrote upon the **tables** the words of **the covenant**, the ten commandments."

Deut. 9:9   "When I was gone up into the mount to receive the tables of stone, even the **tables of the covenant** which the LORD made with you, then I abode in the mount forty days and forty nights, I neither did eat bread nor drink water."

Deut. 9:11   "And it came to pass at the end of forty days and forty nights, that the LORD gave me the two tables of stone, even the **tables of the covenant**."

Deut. 9:15   "So I turned and came down from the mount, and the mount burned with fire: and the two **tables of the covenant** were in my two hands."

Heb. 9:4   "Which had the golden censer, and the ark of the covenant overlaid round about with gold, wherein was the golden pot that had manna, and Aaron's rod that budded, and the **tables of the covenant**."

If we want the divine inspiration of God to move among us in prophetic utterance to instruct us in the way that we should walk ("search out a **resting** place for them," **Num. 10:33**), to give us true **rest** in Him and prophetic vision so that we will not perish (**Prov. 29:18**), then we must recognize that His covenant must be hidden within our hearts (**Psa. 119:11**). Even though it is written in the fleshly tables of the heart, it is to be as unchangeable as though it was written in stone.

Jer. 31:33	"But this shall be the covenant that I will make with the house of Israel; After those days, saith the LORD, I will put my **law** in their inward parts, and write it **in their hearts**; and will be their God, and they shall be my people."
Eze. 11:19	"And I will give them one heart, and I will put a new spirit within you; and **I will take the stony heart out of their flesh, and will give them an heart of flesh**."
Eze. 11:20	"That they may walk in my statutes, and keep mine ordinances, and do them: and they shall be my people, and I will be their God."
Eze. 36:25	"Then will I sprinkle clean water upon you, and ye shall be clean: from all your filthiness, and from all your idols, will I cleanse you."

Eze. 36:26	"A new heart also will I give you, and a new spirit will I put within you: and **I will take away the stony heart out of your flesh, and I will give you an heart of flesh.**"
Eze. 36:27	"And I will put my spirit within you, and cause you to walk in my statutes, and ye shall keep my judgments, and do them."
2 Cor. 3:3	"Forasmuch as ye are manifestly declared to be the epistle of Christ ministered by us, written not with ink, but with the Spirit of the living God; **not in tables of stone**, but **in fleshy tables of the heart.**"

What does God use to remove the stony heart?

1 Kings 18:37	"Hear me, O LORD, hear me, **that this people may know** that thou art the LORD God, and **that thou hast turned their heart back again.**"
1 Kings 18:38	"Then **the fire of the LORD fell, and consumed** the burnt sacrifice, and the wood, **and the stones**, and the dust, and licked up the water that was in the trench."

It is the fire of the Life of God that burns up the stony heart and makes it to be a tender heart of flesh that can receive the writing of the Word of God and make us to be living epistles of testimony of the New (marriage) Covenant.

The Mercy Seat

The Mercy Seat was an altar that was made of pure gold without wood and was placed upon the Ark of the Covenant and was literally the lid for the ark; therefore, the ark and all of its contents were the basis or foundation upon which the Mercy Seat rested. The items of witness, testimony, and covenant, and also the wood and gold, are all the foundation for the Mercy Seat.

The golden Mercy Seat with the blood of atonement was the seal and lid over the Ark of the Covenant and all of the witness and testimony that are contained within it.

Exo. 25:17 "And thou shalt make a **mercy seat** of **pure gold**: two cubits and a half shall be the length thereof, and a cubit and a half the breadth thereof."

Exo. 25:21 "And thou shalt **put the mercy seat above upon the ark**; and in the ark thou shalt put the testimony that I shall give thee."

Exo. 25:22 "And there I will meet with thee, and I will commune with thee from above the mercy seat, from between the two cherubims which are upon the ark of the testimony, of all things which I will give thee in commandment unto the children of Israel."

It is upon this altar that the blood of the yearly sacrifice for atonement (Kippur) was to be put. This blood upon the Mercy Seat covered the sins of the people for one year. At the end of a year, another covering of blood had to be put upon it for the sins of the people to continue to be covered. If the blood of the yearly sacrifice was not put upon the Mercy Seat, then the sins of the people were not covered. For the process of the atonement to be possible, the Ark of the Covenant had to be in its proper place in the Tabernacle.

Words that are used nearly synonymously with atonement are redemption (what the atonement does pays the price to redeem us back to God), justification (the condition, position, and relationship that the atonement brings the worshipper into), and remission (what happens to the sins because of the blood being on the Mercy Seat).

Redemption, justification, and remission are all part of the work that the atonement does for us. It is important to notice that the Mercy Seat had the same size as the Ark of the Covenant.

Exo. 25:17		"And thou shalt make a **mercy seat** of pure gold: **two cubits and a half shall be the length thereof, and a cubit and a half the breadth thereof**."
Exo. 25:10		"And they shall make an **ark** of shittim wood: **two cubits and a half shall be the length thereof, and a cubit and a half the breadth thereof**, and a cubit and a half the height thereof."
Exo. 37:1		"And Bezaleel made the **ark** of shittim wood: **two cubits and a half was the length of it, and a cubit and a half the breadth of it,** and a cubit and a half the height of it."

Therefore, the Mercy Seat literally was the lid for the Ark of the Covenant. Also, everything that was inside of the sanctuary was made out of acacia (shittim) wood and gold or of pure gold without acacia wood. The furnishings that were in the outer court were made out of acacia wood and brass or solid brass without acacia wood.

Gold is symbolic of deity, and brass is symbolic of judgment, and the wood is that which proceeds, grows, or is made out of earth.

Therefore, the acacia wood is used in all of the furnishings for the temple with the exception of a few things. The exceptions are the laver in the outer court which was made entirely out of brass, the lamp stand in the Holy Place was made entirely out of gold, and both the cherubims over the Mercy Seat and the Mercy Seat in the Holy of Holies were made entirely out of gold.

It is in this Holy of Holies (the heart) that the (earthly) acacia wood is covered with gold (deity) and then filled with the witness, testimony, and covenant of God and sealed with the pure gold Mercy Seat that the blood of the atonement cleanses and prepares us for an encounter with God. It is the promise of God to meet with us in that secret place that is consecrated and set aside for His **exclusive** habitation.

Exo. 26:34 "And thou shalt put the mercy seat **upon** the ark of the testimony in the most holy place."

Exo. 40:20 "And he took and put the testimony into the ark, and set the staves on the ark, and put the mercy seat **above upon** the ark."

Exo. 25:22 "And **there I will meet with thee**, and I will commune with thee **from above the mercy seat, from between the two cherubims** which are upon the ark of the testimony, of all things which I will give thee in commandment unto the children of Israel."

Exo. 29:43	"And **there I will meet with the children of Israel**, and the tabernacle shall be sanctified by my glory."
Num. 17:4	"And thou shalt lay them up in the tabernacle of the congregation before the testimony, **where I will meet with you**."

How do we get into this place of intimate communion, relationship, and encounter with God and for His throne to be established in our hearts? How do we get into this position where the entire tabernacle that we are can be entirely filled with the glory of God and sanctified in and by His presence? It is by the incense.

The Golden Altar for Incense

The golden altar for incense was made out of acacia (shittim) wood and covered with gold. It was located in the Holy Place just outside of the Holy of Holies, right in front of (or before) the Ark of the Covenant.

Exo. 30:1	"And thou shalt make an altar to burn incense upon: of shittim wood shalt thou make it."
Exo. 30:2	"A cubit shall be the length thereof, and a cubit the breadth thereof; foursquare shall it be: and two cubits shall be the height thereof: the horns thereof shall be of the same."
Exo. 30:3	"And thou shalt overlay it with pure gold, the top thereof, and the sides thereof round about, and the horns

	thereof; and thou shalt make unto it a crown of gold round about."
Exo. 30:4	"And two golden rings shalt thou make to it under the crown of it, by the two corners thereof, upon the two sides of it shalt thou make it; and they shall be for places for the staves to bear it withal."
Exo. 30:5	"And thou shalt make the staves of shittim wood, and overlay them with gold."
Exo. 30:6	"**And thou shalt put it before the veil that is by the ark of the testimony, before the mercy seat that is over the testimony, where I will meet with thee**."
Exo. 30:7	"And **Aaron shall burn thereon sweet incense every morning**: when he dresseth the lamps, he shall burn incense upon it."
Exo. 30:8	"And when Aaron lighteth the lamps **at even, he shall burn incense upon it**, a **perpetual incense** before the LORD **throughout your generations**."
Exo. 30:9	"Ye shall offer no strange incense thereon, nor burnt sacrifice, nor meat offering; neither shall ye pour drink offering thereon."

> **Exo. 30:10** "**And Aaron shall make an atonement upon the horns of it once in a year with the blood of the sin offering of atonements**: once in the year shall he make atonement upon it **throughout your generations**: it is most holy unto the LORD."

Identifying the Throne of God

Now we are ready to identify that the throne of God is in the heart of man. Please notice that the term that applies in the following scripture is "mercy seat."

> **Exo. 30:6** "And thou shalt put **it** before the veil that is by the ark of the testimony, **before the mercy seat** that is over the testimony, where I will meet with thee."

The "it" that is referred to in the first part of the verse is the golden altar of incense. However, when reference is made to the **same** altar for incense (but in the heavenly pattern) and is spoken about in the book of Revelations, a different term is used for the Mercy Seat.

> **Rev. 8:3** "And another angel came and stood at the altar, having a golden censer; and there was given unto him much **incense**, that he should offer it with the prayers of all saints upon the **golden altar** which was **before the throne**."

Therefore, because the Ark of the Covenant was inside the Holy of Holies, which is symbolic of the heart, and because the mercy seat was upon the Ark of the Covenant, we can see that when the "good things to come" (**Heb. 9:11**) are made manifest, the throne of God is in the heart of man, because the mercy seat and the throne are the **same** thing. It is also important to note that when it is mentioned in **Rev. 8:3**, there is no mention about the veil, because by the time that John saw the revelation, the veil had already been removed.

Col. 2:16 "Let no man therefore judge you in meat, or in drink, or in respect of an holyday, or of the new moon, or of the sabbath days."

Col. 2:17 "**Which are a shadow of things to come**; but the body is of Christ."

Heb. 9:11 "But Christ being come an high priest of **good things to come**, by a greater and more perfect tabernacle, not made with hands, that is to say, not of this building."

Heb. 10:1 "For the law **having a shadow of good things to come**, and not the very image of the things, can never with those sacrifices which they offered year by year continually make the comers thereunto perfect."

If the throne of Almighty God, the creator of the heavens and the earth, is in our hearts, then how great are the promises that He has given us!

2 Pet. 1:2 "Grace and peace be multiplied unto you through the knowledge of God, and of Jesus our Lord."

2 Pet. 1:3 "According as his divine power hath given unto us **all things** that pertain unto life and godliness, through the knowledge of him that hath called us to glory and virtue."

2 Pet. 1:4 **"Whereby are given unto us exceeding great and precious promises: that by these ye might be partakers of the divine nature, having escaped the corruption that is in the world through lust."**

By the promises of God that He fulfills, we become partakers of the divine nature, just like Adam was in the beginning before the fall. Therefore, through God being seated on the throne of our hearts, we have access to the fullness of atonement and everything that it does—redemption, justification, and remission of sins—and *that* work will fill the entire temple that we are; thereby, He is sanctifying it, just as completely as the Shekinah filled *that* temple which was so filled with His divine light that there was no room for darkness or shadow anywhere in His temple. Just as the following scripture describes:

Exo. 29:43 "And there I will meet with the children of Israel, and the **tabernacle** shall be **sanctified** by my **glory**."

Isa. 6:1 "In the year that king Uzziah died I saw also the Lord sitting upon a throne, high and lifted up, and **his train filled the temple**."

Isa. 6:2 "Above it stood the seraphims: each one had six wings; with twain he covered his face, and with twain he covered his feet, and with twain he did fly."

Isa. 6:3	"And one cried unto another, and said, Holy, holy, holy, is the LORD of hosts: the whole earth is full of his glory."
Isa. 6:4	"And the posts of the door moved at the voice of him that cried, **and the house was filled with smoke**."

If we are the temples of His habitation, and His train—or the robes of His righteousness—**fill** the temple, then we will be **filled** with His righteousness so much that there no longer is any room for the shadow or darkness of *any* sin or unrighteousness in us.

Matt. 5:6	"Blessed are they which do hunger and thirst after **righteousness**: for they **shall** be **filled**."

They will be filled with what? His righteousness!

Rev. 19:7	"Let us be glad and rejoice, and give honour to him: for the marriage of the Lamb is come, and his wife hath made herself ready."
Rev. 19:8	"**And to her was granted that she should be arrayed in fine linen, clean and white: for the fine linen is the righteousness of saints**."
Rev. 19:9	"And he saith unto me, Write, Blessed are they which are called unto the marriage supper of the Lamb. And he saith unto me, These are the true sayings of God."

The Blood of the Atonement Works Together with the Incense to Provide Entrance into the Holy of Holies.

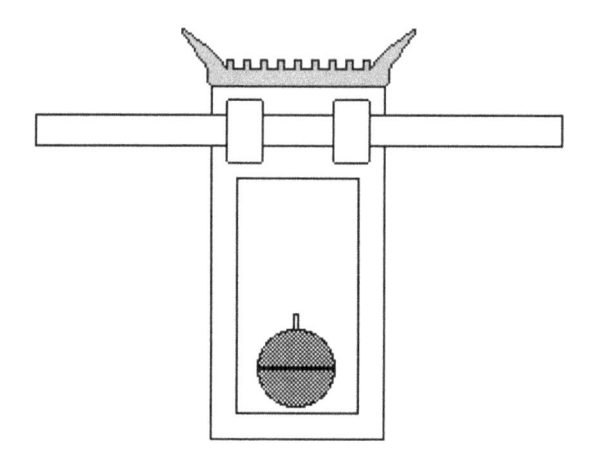

Drwaing #4

CHAPTER 3

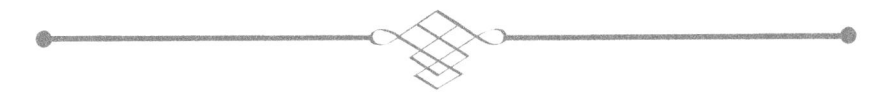

The Incense and the Atoning Blood

Now that we have identified how the porches apply to our being and where the throne of God is and that the key to identifying the throne of God is the golden altar for incense, we will now see how to use the key to obtain access into the Holy of Holies, obtain the promised encounter with God, and be holy tabernacles that are sanctified exclusively for and by His habitation.

The Atoning Blood and the Golden Altar for Incense

When speaking about the golden altar for the incense, the scripture says:

Exo. 30:6	"And thou shalt put it before the veil that is by the ark of the testimony, before **the mercy seat** that is over the testimony, where **I will meet with thee**."
Exo. 30:10	"And Aaron shall make an atonement upon the horns of it once in a year **with the blood of the sin offering of atonements**: once in the year shall he make atonement upon it throughout your generations: it is most holy unto the LORD."

Lev. 16:17 "And there shall **be no man in the tabernacle of the congregation** when he goeth in to make an atonement in the holy place, until he come out, and have made an atonement for himself, and for his household, and for all the congregation of Israel."

Lev. 16:18 "And he shall go out unto **the altar that is before the LORD**, and make an atonement for it; and shall take of the **blood** of the bullock, and of the **blood** of the goat, and put it upon the horns of the altar round about."

Lev. 16:19 "And he shall **sprinkle** of the **blood** upon it with his finger **seven times**, and cleanse it, and hallow it from the uncleanness of the children of Israel."

When the blood was put upon the horns of the altar "round about," it literally means "all four" of the horns of the altar. The blood was then also sprinkled upon the altar seven times to cleanse it. It is essential to notice that everything that was done in the Temple was done upon the basis of the blood of the atonement. The altar for incense had to be cleansed with the **same** blood of the yearly sacrifice of atonement. If the blood of the atonement was not upon the altar **before** the fire and the incense were placed upon it, then the incense would have no meaning and it would **not** have provided access into the Holy of Holies.

There are four details that were necessary for the incense to be accepted. The blood of the atonement that the altar of incense had to be cleansed with is the first item. The second item is that there was to be no strange incense offered upon this altar.

Exo. 30:9	"Ye shall **offer no strange incense thereon**, nor burnt sacrifice, nor meat offering; neither shall ye pour drink offering thereon."

The third item was that no strange fire was to be offered upon the altar.

Lev. 10:1	"And Nadab and Abihu, the sons of Aaron, took either of them his censer, and put fire therein, and put incense thereon, and offered **strange fire** before the LORD, which he commanded them not."
Lev. 10:2	"And there went out fire from the LORD, and devoured them, and they died before the LORD."
Lev. 10:3	"Then Moses said unto Aaron, This is it that the LORD spake, saying, I will be sanctified in them that come nigh me, and before all the people I will be glorified. And Aaron held his peace."
Num. 3:4	"And Nadab and Abihu died before the LORD, when they offered **strange fire** before the LORD, in the wilderness of Sinai, and they had no children: and Eleazar and Ithamar ministered in the priest's office in the sight of Aaron their father."
Num. 26:60	"And unto Aaron was born Nadab, and Abihu, Eleazar, and Ithamar.

Num. 26:61 "And Nadab and Abihu died, when they offered **strange fire** before the LORD."

Strange fire was any fire that was kindled by the hand of man. If the fire was not started by God Himself and was actually the fire that He **is**, then everything that was being offered by fire was not accepted.

Deut. 4:24 "For the LORD thy **God is a consuming fire**, even a jealous God."

Deut. 9:3 "Understand therefore this day, that the LORD thy **God is he which goeth over before thee; as a consuming fire** he shall destroy them, and he shall bring them down before thy face: so shalt thou drive them out, and destroy them quickly, as the LORD hath said unto thee."

It is the fire of God that goes before us into battle, gives us the victory, and brings us in to possess the land of blessings and promises that He has promised to us.

Heb. 12:28 "Wherefore we receiving a kingdom which cannot be moved, let us have grace, whereby we may serve God acceptably with reverence and godly fear."

Heb. 12:29 "For our **God is a consuming fire**."

This consuming fire is God Himself who destroys all sin and unrighteousness by the divine light of His presence. If He has come into our hearts and has taken His rightful place in the throne of our hearts as the King that He truly is, then every shadow and darkness of sin will be purged out of our entire being (all three porches) by the light of the glory of His presence (Shekinah). However, this fire will not destroy who we are in Him, because we will be like the burning bush that was on fire but was not consumed or destroyed.

Exo. 3:1 "Now Moses kept the flock of Jethro his father in law, the priest of Midian: and he led the flock to the backside of the desert, and came to the mountain of God, even to Horeb."

Exo. 3:2 "And the angel of the LORD appeared unto him in a flame of **fire** out of the midst of a bush: and he looked, and, behold, **the bush burned with fire, and the bush was not consumed**."

Exo. 3:3 "And Moses said, I will now turn aside, and see this great sight, why the bush is not burnt."

Exo. 3:4 "And when the LORD saw that he turned aside to see, God called unto him out of the midst of the bush, and said, Moses, Moses. And he said, Here am I."

Exo. 3:5 "And he said, Draw not nigh hither: **put off thy shoes from off thy feet, for the place whereon thou standest is holy ground**."

Exo. 3:6 "Moreover he said, I am the God of thy father, the God of Abraham, the

God of Isaac, and the God of Jacob. And Moses hid his face; for he was afraid to look upon God."

It will only consume and destroy all of the effects that being in a fallen condition has in our being, which prevents us from manifesting His character and nature (image and likeness).

Dan. 7:9 "I beheld till the **thrones were cast down**, and **the Ancient of days** did sit, whose garment was white as snow, and the hair of his head like the pure wool: **his throne was like the fiery flame, and his wheels as burning fire**."

Dan. 7:10 "**A fiery stream issued and came forth from before him**: thousand thousands ministered unto him, and ten thousand times ten thousand stood before him: the judgment was set, and the books were opened."

When it says that "the thrones were cast down," it means "*humbled* to be placed in their rightful or correct position." Several other versions of the Bible state "until the thrones were *placed*."

If we try to offer a kindled fire of carnally produced exuberance and think that it will be accepted by God, we are running a tremendous risk. We must wait upon the Lord in reverent expectation, inviting Him to kindle His holy fire within us (**Lev. 9:24; Num. 9:15–16**). We should not accept or be deceived by false imitations and substitutes for the true consuming fire of the presence of God. The true fire **will** produce supernaturally empowered obedience. False imitations do not have the power to produce the living reality and will even try to make excuses for that lacking by twisting scriptures in a vain attempt to justify sin in the presence of a Holy God.

Just as the sight of that burning bush attracted Moses to turn aside to see what it was all about, so also when our lives are on fire—not only *for* God but also *by* God—it will attract precious souls to come and see; and in coming, they can have an encounter with Him, not us. It is from this condition of being filled to overflowing with Him that He gave the commandment to go into all the world and preach the "good news" about it unto every creature.

> **Mark 16:15** "And he said unto them, Go ye into all the world, and **preach the gospel to every creature**."
>
> **Matt. 24:14** "And this **gospel of the kingdom** shall be preached in all the world **for a witness unto all nations**; and then shall the end come."
>
> **Luke 24:49** "And, behold, I send the promise of my Father upon you: but **tarry** ye in the city of Jerusalem, **until** ye be endued with **power from on high**."

The "gospel of the kingdom" is the good news that the King of Glory can be enthroned in the heart of man, and we can be his kingdom where His kingly dominion is made manifest by His consuming fire burning out of us everything that does not conform to His divine nature. The consuming fire of His testimony will burn out of our entire being all disobedience and will manifest the power of His life living within us and through us. It is a work that He does so completely that even the Outer Court manifests the power of His life in obedience, because it is filled (also) with the Shekinah (manifest glory of the presence of His Life).

The fourth item also shows the symbolical significance between gold being a symbol for the divine and brass being a symbol for judgment.

Please carefully note what the censers (incense carriers) were made out of and who they belonged to.

Num. 16:1	"Now Korah, the son of Izhar, the son of Kohath, the son of Levi, and Dathan and Abiram, the sons of Eliab, and On, the son of Peleth, sons of Reuben, **took men**."
Num. 16:2	"And they rose up before Moses, with certain of the children of Israel, **two hundred and fifty princes of the assembly**, famous in the congregation, men of renown."
Num. 16:3	"And they gathered themselves together against Moses and against Aaron, and said unto them, Ye take too much upon you, seeing all the congregation are holy, every one of them, and the LORD is among them: wherefore then lift ye up yourselves above the congregation of the LORD?"
Num. 16:4	"And when Moses heard it, he fell upon his face."
Num. 16:5	"And he spake unto Korah and unto all his company, saying, Even to morrow **the LORD will show who are his, and who is holy; and will cause him to come near unto him: even him whom he hath chosen will he cause to come near unto him**."

Num. 16:6	"This do; Take you **censers**, Korah, and all his company."
Num. 16:7	**"And put fire therein, and put incense in them before the LORD** to morrow: and it shall be that **the man whom the LORD doth choose, he shall be holy**: ye take too much upon you, ye sons of Levi."
Num. 16:8	"And Moses said unto Korah, Hear, I pray you, ye sons of Levi."
Num. 16:9	"Seemeth it but a small thing unto you, that the God of Israel hath separated you from the congregation of Israel, to bring you near to himself to do the service of the tabernacle of the LORD, and to stand before the congregation to minister unto them?"
Num. 16:10	"And he hath brought thee near to him, and all thy brethren the sons of Levi with thee: and seek ye the priesthood also?"
Num. 16:11	"For which cause both thou and all thy company are gathered together against the LORD: **and what is Aaron, that ye murmur against him?**"
Num. 16:12	"And Moses sent to call Dathan and Abiram, the sons of Eliab: which said, We will not come up."

Num. 16:13 "Is it a small thing that thou hast brought us up out of a land that floweth with milk and honey, to kill us in the wilderness, except thou make thyself altogether a prince over us?"

Num. 16:14 "Moreover thou hast not brought us into a land that floweth with milk and honey, or given us inheritance of fields and vineyards: wilt thou put out the eyes of these men? we will not come up."

Num. 16:15 "And Moses was very wroth, and said unto the LORD, Respect not thou their offering: I have not taken one ass from them, neither have I hurt one of them."

Num. 16:16 "And Moses said unto Korah, **Be thou and all thy company before the LORD, thou, and they, and Aaron**, to morrow."

Num. 16:17 "And take every man his **censer**, and put incense in them, and bring ye before the LORD every man his **censer, two hundred and fifty censers**; thou also, and Aaron, each of you his censer."

Num. 16:18 "And **they took every man his censer, and put fire in them, and laid incense thereon, and stood in the door of the tabernacle of the congregation with Moses and Aaron**."

Num. 16:19	"And Korah gathered all the congregation against them unto the door of the tabernacle of the congregation: and the glory of the LORD appeared unto all the congregation."
Num. 16:20	"And the LORD spake unto Moses and unto Aaron, saying."
Num. 16:21	"Separate yourselves from among this congregation, that I may consume them in a moment."
Num. 16:22	"And they fell upon their faces, and said, O God, the God of the spirits of all flesh, shall one man sin, and wilt thou be wroth with all the congregation?"
Num. 16:23	"And the LORD spake unto Moses, saying."
Num. 16:24	"Speak unto the congregation, saying, Get you up from about the tabernacle of Korah, Dathan, and Abiram."
Num. 16:25	"And Moses rose up and went unto Dathan and Abiram; and the elders of Israel followed him."
Num. 16:26	"And he spake unto the congregation, saying, Depart, I pray you, from the tents of these wicked men, and **touch nothing of theirs**, lest ye be consumed in all their sins."

Num. 16:27 "So they gat up from the tabernacle of Korah, Dathan, and Abiram, on every side: and Dathan and Abiram came out, and stood in the door of their tents, and their wives, and their sons, and their little children."

Num. 16:28 "And Moses said, Hereby ye shall know that the LORD hath sent me to do all these works; for I have not done them of mine own mind."

Num. 16:29 "If these men die the common death of all men, or if they be visited after the visitation of all men; then the LORD hath not sent me."

Num. 16:30 "But if the LORD make a new thing, and the earth open her mouth, and swallow them up, with all that appertain unto them, and they go down **quick** into the pit; then ye shall understand that these men have provoked the LORD."

Num. 16:31 "And it came to pass, as he had made an end of speaking all these words, that the ground clave asunder that was under them."

Num. 16:32 "And the earth opened her mouth, and swallowed them up, and their houses, and all the men that appertained unto Korah, and all their goods."

Num. 16:33   "They, and all that appertained to them, went down **alive** into the pit, and the earth closed upon them: and they perished from among the congregation."

Num. 16:34   "And all Israel that were round about them fled at the cry of them: for they said, Lest the earth swallow us up also."

Num. 16:35   **"And there came out a fire from the LORD, and consumed the two hundred and fifty men that offered incense."**

Num. 16:36   "And the LORD spake unto Moses, saying."

Num. 16:37   "Speak unto Eleazar the son of Aaron the priest, that he **take up the censers out of the burning, and scatter thou the fire yonder; for they are hallowed**."

Num. 16:38   "The **censers** of these sinners against their own souls, let them make them broad plates for a covering of the altar: for they offered them before the LORD, therefore they are hallowed: and they shall be a sign unto the children of Israel."

Num. 16:39   "And Eleazar the priest took the **brazen censers**, wherewith they that were burnt had offered; and they were made broad plates for a covering of the altar."

Num. 16:40 "To be a memorial unto the children of Israel, that no stranger, which is not of the seed of Aaron, come near to offer incense before the LORD; that he be not as Korah, and as his company: as the LORD said to him by the hand of Moses."

Num. 16:41 "But **on the morrow** all the congregation of the children of Israel murmured against Moses and against Aaron, saying, Ye have killed the people of the LORD."

Num. 16:42 "And it came to pass, when the congregation was gathered against Moses and against Aaron, that they looked toward the tabernacle of the congregation: and, behold, the cloud covered it, and the glory of the LORD appeared."

Num. 16:43 "And Moses and Aaron came before the tabernacle of the congregation."

Num. 16:44 "And the LORD spake unto Moses, saying."

Num. 16:45 "Get you up from among this congregation, that I may consume them as in a moment. And they fell upon their faces."

THE INCENSE AND THE GLORY

Num. 16:46   "And Moses said unto Aaron, Take a **censer**, and put fire therein from off the altar, and put on incense, and go quickly unto the congregation, and make an **atonement** for them: for there is wrath gone out from the LORD; the plague is begun."

Num. 16:47   "And Aaron took as Moses commanded, and ran into the midst of the congregation; and, behold, the plague was begun among the people: and he put on **incense**, and made an **atonement** for the people."

Num. 16:48   "And **he stood between the dead and the living; and the plague was stayed**."

Num. 16:49   "Now they that died in the plague were fourteen thousand and seven hundred, beside them that died about the matter of Korah."

Num. 16:50   "And Aaron returned unto Moses unto the door of the tabernacle of the congregation: **and the plague was stayed**."

Aaron's censer was made out of **gold** (**Heb. 9:4**; **Rev. 8:3**). Aaron was **divinely** appointed of God to serve in the office of the priesthood. Part of the service and responsibilities of the priesthood was to offer incense before God. It is in this passage that we can identify the symbolic application of both gold and brass.

The gold symbolizes deity or the divine and brass symbolizes judgment. The two hundred and fifty had censers that were made of

brass which symbolizes **judgment** (**Num. 16:39**). Without knowing it, they pronounced the outcome upon themselves by their attitudes and by their preparation of using brazen censers (judgment).

We can also see an interesting and very important detail:

> **Heb. 9:22** "And almost all things are by the law purged with blood; and **without shedding of blood is no remission**."

Without blood, there is no remission (removal, forgiveness, or atonement) of sins; and if there is no remission of sins, then neither is there any justification. How is it then that (**Num. 16:41–50**) something which was not blood (incense) could make an atonement for the sins of the people? We know that it worked, because the plague was stopped (**Num. 16:48,50**). Remember that *before* the fire and the incense were put on the golden altar for incense, it *first* had to be cleansed with the *same* blood of the yearly atonement (**Exo. 30:10**). Again, it is the blood of the atonement that gave meaning to the incense. The incense gave witness and testimony to the fact that the blood was on both the golden altar for incense and that it was upon the Mercy Seat. It is the **blood** that stopped the plague, but it worked **through** the incense!

Therefore, it is necessary to have the blood of the atonement upon the golden altar for incense, the correct fire (Holy Spirit), the correct incense, and the censer must be made out of gold symbolizing that it is a divine work (being done by God alone). All of these details instruct us in how to have the correct mental attitude when we approach the throne of God, because the golden altar for incense was in the Holy Place (mind).

The Correct Approach to the Throne and the Difference Between Perfect and Imperfect Sacrifices.

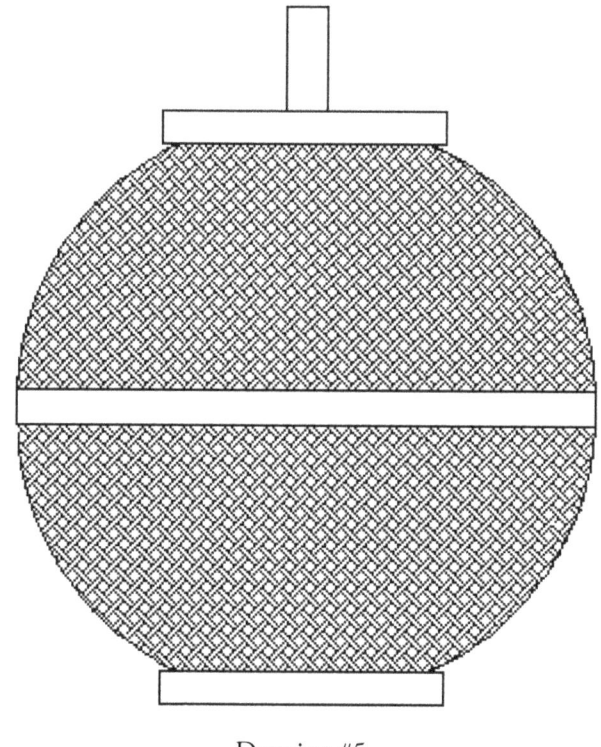

Drawing #5

CHAPTER 4

Approaching the Throne

Lev. 16:13 "And he shall put the incense upon the fire before the LORD, that the **cloud of the incense may cover the mercy seat** that is upon the testimony, **that he die not.**"

    This shows an intimate connection between the golden altar for incense and the Mercy Seat, where the Mercy Seat cannot even be approached until it is covered with the cloud of incense. The blood working **through** the witness and testimony of the incense, therefore, is the way to approach the Mercy Seat. There is no other acceptable approach to the Mercy Seat than through this way that God has provided. Any other approach will produce death. When we fully identify the symbolic meaning of the incense, we will understand why.

    Once the sacrifice had been slain on the altar for burnt offerings in the Outer Court (**Lev. 16:14–15**) and the blood was caught in a golden basin, the high priest then had to remove the garments that were to be used **only** in the Outer Court, wash his body with water (**Exo. 30:20**), clothe himself with the garments that were to **only** be used in the sanctuary (**Lev. 16:4; 23–24**), and anoint himself with the special perfumed oil that was only to be used in the sanctuary (**Exo. 30:31–38; 40:13**). The reverse of this procedure was used when the high priest was moving from the sanctuary to the Outer Court (**Eze. 44:19**).

After preparing the golden altar for incense by the blood of the atonement and putting the coals and incense into the golden censer, and when the high priest proceeded toward the Holy of Holies, he had to stop at the threshold of entering in and sprinkle of the blood seven times before the inner (or second) veil (**Lev. 4:6,17**), and then wait for the cloud of the incense to expand outward until it covered the Mercy Seat.

Only after the Mercy Seat was completely covered with the incense cloud of witness to the blood of the atonement could he enter into the Holy of Holies without fear of dying (**Lev. 16:13**).

Even then, we know that in the Jewish tradition, the high priest had a rope tied around one leg so that if his entrance was not accepted by God, the dead body could be removed without anyone going into the Holy of Holies to try to retrieve it.

Heb. 10:31 "It is a **fearful** thing to fall into the hands of the living God."

Php. 2:12 "Wherefore, my beloved, as ye have always obeyed, not as in my presence only, but now much more in my absence, work out your own salvation with **fear** and **trembling**."

Isa. 66:2 "For all those things hath mine hand made, and all those things have been, saith the LORD: **but to this man will I look**, even to him that is **poor** and of a **contrite spirit**, and **trembleth at my word**."

While the high priest was waiting with a golden vessel of the blood of the atonement in one hand and the golden censer of coals and incense in the other hand, he was not just idly standing there.

The high priest was moving or waving the golden censer so that the movement caused the air to fan the coals in the golden censer and thus caused the coals to burn hotter. As the coals burned hotter, it caused the smoke of the incense to billow out more quickly with more volume and with more density. Only after the Mercy Seat was **completely covered** with the cloud of the incense—and thereby the witness and testimony to the blood of the atonement that was upon the golden altar for incense—was the High Priest able to enter into the Holy of Holies without fear of dying.

> **Heb. 10:22** "Let us **draw near** with a true heart in full assurance of faith, having our hearts **sprinkled** from an evil conscience, and our bodies washed with pure water."

Once the high priest entered into the Holy of Holies, he sprinkled the blood of the atonement seven times before and upon the eastern side of the Mercy Seat, which was the side that was facing the veil and the golden altar for the incense. The sprinkling of the blood before the veil and before the Mercy Seat symbolizes the cleansing of our conscience in the presence of the God of holiness whose very life and presence produces obedience to the scriptural descriptions of how He behaves.

> **Lev. 16:11** "And Aaron shall bring **the bullock of the sin offering, which is for himself, and shall make an atonement for himself, and for his house**, and shall kill the bullock of the sin offering which is for himself."

> **Lev. 16:14** "And he shall take of the **blood** of the bullock, and **sprinkle it with his finger upon the mercy seat eastward**; and before the mercy seat shall he sprinkle of the blood with his finger **seven times**."

Lev. 16:15 "Then shall he kill **the goat of the sin offering, that is for the people**, and bring his blood within the veil, and do with that **blood** as he did with the **blood** of the bullock, and **sprinkle** it upon the **mercy seat, and before the mercy seat**."

There is some confusion that people have about the use of a bullock and of a goat. Please note that the bullock was for atonement, first for the high priest and for his household; and afterward, the goat was for atonement for the people. In the following chapters, we will see some important distinctions about the use of a lamb or ram and why some sacrifices were not perfect and a specific sacrifice was a perfect sacrifice.

Once the blood of the atonement for the people was applied to the Mercy Seat, the atonement was made, and the sins of the people were covered for another year. There is an important reference to something that the high priest had the privilege to do that is mentioned in the book of Revelations.

Rev. 2:17 "He that hath an ear, let him hear what the Spirit saith unto the churches; **To him that overcometh will I give to eat of the hidden manna**, and will give him a white stone, and in the stone a new name written, which no man knoweth saving he that receiveth it."

We know that the manna that was gathered each day in the journey through the desert could not be kept for the next day, because it perished (**Exo. 16:20**). Only on the sixth day was twice as much gathered and the remainder did not perish so that they could eat on the Sabbath day without having to go out to gather (**Exo. 16:22–25**).

Exo. 16:14	"And when the dew that lay was gone up, behold, upon the face of the wilderness there lay a small round thing, as small as the hoar frost on the ground."
Exo. 16:15	"And when the children of Israel saw it, they said one to another, It is manna: for they wist not what it was. And Moses said unto them, This is the bread which the LORD hath given you to eat."
Exo. 16:16	"This is the thing which the LORD hath commanded, Gather of it every man according to his eating, an omer for every man, according to the number of your persons; take ye every man for them which are in his tents."
Exo. 16:17	"And the children of Israel did so, and gathered, some more, some less."
Exo. 16:18	"And when they did mete it with an omer, he that gathered much had nothing over, and he that gathered little had no lack; they gathered every man according to his eating."
Exo. 16:19	**"And Moses said, Let no man leave of it till the morning."**
Exo. 16:20	"Notwithstanding they hearkened not unto Moses; **but some of them**

Exo. 16:21 "And they gathered it every morning, every man according to his eating: and **when the sun waxed hot, it melted.**"

Exo. 16:22 "And it came to pass, that **on the sixth day they gathered twice as much** bread, two omers for one man: and all the rulers of the congregation came and told Moses."

Exo. 16:23 "And he said unto them, This is that which the LORD hath said, To morrow is the rest of the holy sabbath unto the LORD: bake that which ye will bake to day, and seethe that ye will seethe; and **that which remaineth over lay up for you to be kept until the morning.**"

Exo. 16:24 "**And they laid it up till the morning, as Moses bade: and it did not stink, neither was there any worm therein.**"

Exo. 16:25 "**And Moses said, Eat that to day; for to day is a sabbath unto the LORD: to day ye shall not find it in the field.**"

Exo. 16:26	"Six days ye shall gather it; but on the seventh day, which is the sabbath, in it there shall be none."
Exo. 16:27	"And it came to pass, that there went out some of the people on the seventh day for to gather, and they found none."

The manna that did not perish by the next day was that portion that was gathered on the sixth day and which was supernaturally preserved for the "rest" of the Lord (the Sabbath). However, even *that* manna perished if there was any of it left until the first day of the week. It is because of this detail that everyone in Israel were participants in the miraculous preservation of the manna **every week**. God weekly performed a miracle of preservation and provision so they could eat on the Sabbath day without having to go out to gather. The *only* manna that *never* perished was that portion that was kept in the Holy of Holies and which was also supernaturally preserved by the glory of the presence of God—the Shekinah.

Exo. 16:31	"And the house of Israel called the name thereof Manna: and it was like coriander seed, white; and the taste of it was like wafers made with honey."
Exo. 16:32	"And Moses said, This is the thing which the LORD commandeth, **Fill an omer of it to be kept for your generations**; that they may see the bread wherewith I have fed you in the wilderness, when I brought you forth from the land of Egypt."

Exo. 16:33	"And Moses said unto Aaron, **Take a pot, and put an omer full of manna therein, and lay it up before the LORD, to be kept for your generations**."
Exo. 16:34	"As the LORD commanded Moses, so Aaron laid it up before the Testimony, to be kept."
Heb. 9:4	"Which had the golden censer, and the **ark of the covenant** overlaid round about with gold, **wherein was the golden pot that had manna**, and Aaron's rod that budded, and the tables of the covenant."
Heb. 9:5	"And over it the cherubims of glory shadowing the mercyseat; of which we cannot now speak particularly."

This is the "hidden" manna that is spoken about in **Rev. 2:17**. It is divinely provided sustenance that is provided to us daily, both for physical sustenance and also symbolizing spiritual sustenance or the spiritual food of divinely given revelation of the Word of God. It is given to those who overcome (by the blood working through the incense) to enter into the Holy of Holies into the presence of God (the Shekinah) and who make **that** presence their **constant** dwelling place and allow **that** presence to sanctify the entire tabernacle that they are.

Exo. 29:43	"And there I will meet with the children of Israel, **and the tabernacle shall be sanctified by my glory**."
Matt. 6:11	"Give us this day our **daily bread**."

John 6:48	"**I am** that **bread** of life."
John 6:51	"**I am** the **living bread which came down from heaven**: if any man eat of this bread, he shall live for ever: and the **bread** that I will give is my **flesh**, which I will give for the life of the world."
John 1:14	"And **the Word was made flesh**, and dwelt among us, (and we beheld his glory, the glory as of the only begotten of the Father,) full of grace and truth."

The incense has been clearly identified as the approach to the Mercy Seat. With the right approach, we can enter into the Holy of Holies and receive atonement, redemption, remission of sins, and **justification**.

Now to see the New Testament approach that the Lord Jesus told us about:

Luke 18:9	"And he spake this parable unto certain which **trusted in themselves** that they were righteous, and despised others."
Luke 18:10	"Two men went up into the temple to pray; the one a Pharisee, and the other a publican."
Luke 18:11	"The Pharisee stood and **prayed thus with himself**, God, I thank thee, that I am not as other men are, extortioners, unjust, adulterers, or even as this publican."

Luke 18:12	"I fast twice in the week, I give tithes of all that I possess."
Luke 18:13	"And the publican, standing afar off, would not lift up so much as his eyes unto heaven, but smote upon his breast, saying, God be merciful to me a sinner."
Luke 18:14	"I tell you, this man went down to his house **justified** rather than the other: for every one that exalteth himself shall be abased; and he that **humbleth** himself shall be exalted."

There are three important details in this parable that relate to our current Bible study. First, the Pharisee "prayed thus with himself, God," showing that because of his pride, his god was himself. Second, the publican (tax collector) went home **justified**; this means that he had the correct approach, the atonement was made, and his sins were covered. What was his approach? The third detail: humility. Humility is the New Testament approach to the throne of God that the Old Testament approach of the incense was symbolizing! It is based on the authority of the words Immanuel Himself.

Isa. 7:14	"Therefore the Lord himself shall give you a sign; Behold, a virgin shall conceive, and bear a son, and shall call his name **Immanuel**."
Matt. 1:23	"Behold, a virgin shall be with child, and shall bring forth a son, and they shall call his name **Emmanuel**, which being interpreted is, **God with us**."

There is a very commonly believed error that says that the incense is the prayers of the saints. This comes from a superficial reading of **Rev. 5:8**.

> **Rev. 5:8** "And when he had taken the book, the four beasts and four and twenty elders fell down before the Lamb, having every one of them harps, and golden **vials** full of **odours**, which are the **prayers** of saints."

Even though the King James Version of the Bible says "odours" and uses the plural tense, this is exactly the same word (thumiama) that is used in **Revelations 8 in both verses 3 and 4** that is translated as "incense" in the singular tense. Many other versions of the Bible translate it as "golden vials full of incense."

Therefore, the prayers (plural) relate to the vials (plural), and the incense (singular) is symbolic of humility and is not symbolic of the prayers (plural) of the saints. However, if the prayers that are being made are *not* **full** of humility before God, then the prayers are not identified as the kind of prayers that the saints offer to God. There is only one kind of true incense (or frankincense), and that is the incense that comes directly from Him (**Matt. 11:29**). Then in **Revelations 8,** even more humility is given that it should be offered together **with** the prayers of the saints (prayers full of humility).

> **Rev. 8:3** "And another angel came and stood at the altar, having a golden censer; and there was given unto him much **incense**, that he should offer it **with** the prayers of all saints upon the golden altar which was before the throne."
>
> **Rev. 8:4** "And the smoke of the **incense**, which came **with** the prayers of the

saints, ascended up before God out of the angel's hand."

Humility is the attitude that **will** come together with the prayers that the *saints* pray.

The reason why is because they are coming into the place of being priests before (in the presence of) God. When the high priest was waiting for the cloud of incense to expand into the Holy of Holies, he was standing in the midst of that very same cloud.

Therefore, not only did he have the golden censer in his hand, and not only was he waving it before the Shekinah, but his very body and clothing were covered with that cloud of incense, and it penetrated into every fiber of the clothing that he was wearing and every pore of his body.

Every time that we approach the Mercy Seat, it is to be **only** after our prayers are filled, our selves are covered with and penetrated by, and the throne is covered with the cloud of the incense of humility (**Lev. 16:12–13**). Note that the incense is to be finely ground up (beaten small, **Lev. 16:12**); in **Psa. 51:17**, the word *contrite* in Hebrew means "ground up" as wheat in a grinding mill.

It is important to notice also that in the temple, almost everything that was done had to be accompanied with incense. The Sabbath was to be observed with freewill offerings, including incense (**Exo. 35:2, 5, 8**). Every "willing hearted" offering such as tithes is to include incense (**2 Cor. 9:7; Exo. 35:5,8**).

Frankincense is literally "true incense" spoken about in **Exo. 30:9** as the opposite of a false incense or false humility.

Every offering of bread (breaking of bread symbolic of dividing the Word of truth—**2 Tim. 2:15**, i.e. preaching) is to be done with incense (**Lev. 2:1–2, 6:15, 24:7**).

First fruits offerings were to be offered with incense (**Lev. 2:15–16**).

Since we are kings and priests (**Rev. 1:6, 5:10**), the priestly ordinance of offering incense for sin offerings applies to us also (**Lev. 4:3,7,17**).

In **Num. 16:1–7, 16–22, 31–33,** God will not receive incense at the hand of the prideful and rebellious, and He slew them with fire.

Incense was used as an **atonement** (working together with the blood) to stop plagues among the people (natural: **Num. 16:46–48,** symbolic of the spiritual: **Joel 2:12–18**).

Incense was to be burned on every Sabbath and Rosh Chodesh (new moon, beginning of each month in the Hebrew calendar) for a **perpetual** ordinance (**2 Chr. 2:4**), even in eternity when there are new heavens and a new earth (**Isa. 66:22–23**).

Incense was to be offered every morning and evening when the lamps were trimmed for a perpetual ordinance (**Exo. 30:7–8**). Because of this, the altar of the incense and its connection with Yom Kippur (the Day of Atonement) shows that there is to be a **twice daily** (morning and evening) **humbling of ourselves to commemorate our atonement,** and it is a **yearlong observance** or memorial of Yom Kippur, the day of atonement!

Also, because it is done at lamp trimming time, it relates directly to the parable of the ten virgins who arose and trimmed their lamps (**Matt. 25:1–13**) and is one of the reasons how the wise virgins could have the extra vessel of oil together *with* their lamps and why the foolish virgins did not have it, because the wise virgins will be permanently humble before God to abide continually in His presence and to be living temples for the habitation of His glory.

The knowledge that we have access to the throne of mercy—**if** it is covered with a cloud of incense and that this is Gods provided approach, together with the certainty of the reality of our humility before God—gives us the ability to come boldly (**Heb. 4:16**).

Therefore, the key to the fullness of restoration and to being prepared for the Lord's return is the blood of the atonement *working through* the incense of humility! Through *this,* we have access for the entire tabernacle/temple that we are, to be filled with the Shekinah, and thereby sanctified by His glory in ways that God alone can do.

The Lifting, Tearing and Removal of the Veil

Raising the Veil

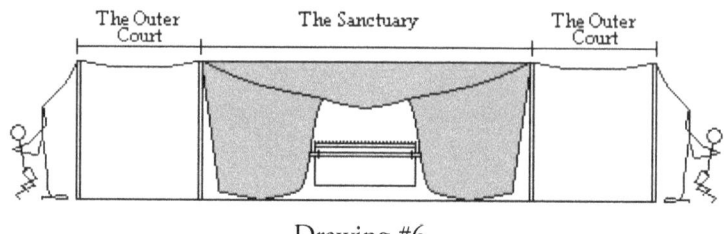

Drawing #6

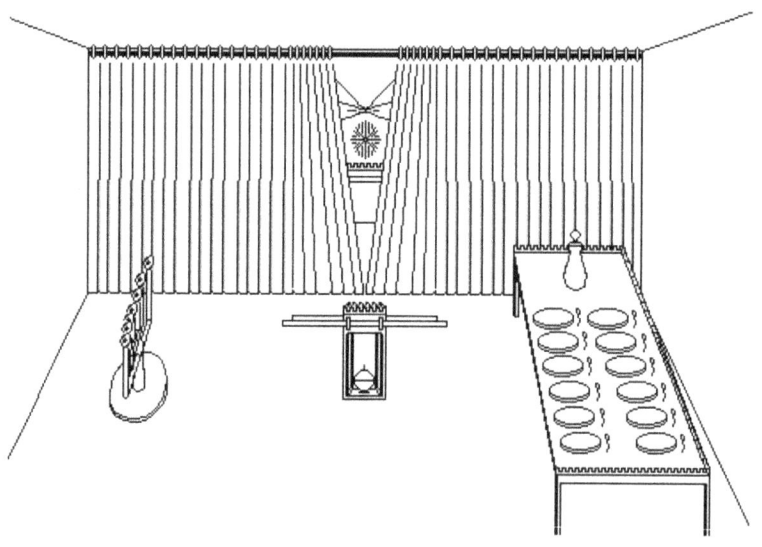

Drawing #7

CHAPTER 5

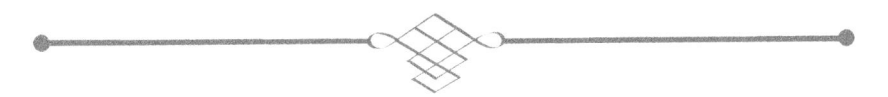

The Veil and the Covenant

The Lifting of the Veil

The veil was one piece.

The fact that the second veil was a single piece is shown by two interrelated details. First, there is no mention in the Word of God anywhere of a door or other opening that was used to pass from the Holy Place into the Holy of Holies. Second is when the veil was torn from the top to the bottom. There would not have been a need for the veil to be torn if there already was a way to go through it.

The Apostle Paul mentions that the way was opened and that we now have access into the Holy of Holies.

Heb. 6:17	"Wherein God, willing more abundantly to shew unto the heirs of promise the immutability of his counsel, confirmed it by an oath."
Heb. 6:18	"That by two immutable things, in which it was impossible for God to lie, we might have a strong consolation, who have fled for refuge to lay hold upon the hope set before us."

Heb. 6:19	"Which hope we have as an anchor of the soul, both sure and stedfast, **and which entereth into that within the veil**."
Heb. 6:20	"Whither the forerunner is for us entered, even Jesus, made an high priest for ever after the order of Melchisedec."

Because of the sacrifice of His sinless flesh and the power of the life that was in His blood, the way was consecrated for us to have access into the presence of a just and holy God and to make that place our **constant** habitation. We also can receive the benefit of the divine light of His presence illuminating our minds, to create in us all of His divine virtues and set His Word in order upon the Golden Table of Shewbread together with the incense of humility in a display of divine government (twelve loaves).

The veil went from wall-to-wall.

The high priest could not just walk around it, and the Apostle Paul made reference to it being **lifted** (**2 Cor. 3:14**; Revised Version).

2 Cor. 3:14	"but their minds were hardened: for until this very day at the reading of the old covenant the same veil remaineth **unlifted**; which veil is done away in Christ." (Revised Version)

The high priest was alone.

Lev. 16:17	"And there shall **be no man in the tabernacle of the congregation** when he goeth in to make an atone-

ment in the holy place, until he come out, and have made an atonement for himself, and for his household, and for all the congregation of Israel."

The high priest had his hands full.

The basin of blood in one hand and the golden censer in the other hand.
The curtain had to be opened for the incense cloud to expand into the Holy of Holies.
The Apostle Paul mentioned that the veil had to be lifted (2 Cor. 3:14, Revised Version).
Conclusion: There were helpers outside of the tabernacle.

The helpers are symbolic of the truth of the Old and New Testaments lifting (by the Holy Spirit) the veil of the darkness of error, ignorance, and prideful self-deceit that separates our minds and hearts.

> **2 Cor. 3:14** "but their minds were hardened: for until this very day at the reading of the old covenant the same veil remaineth **unlifted**; which veil is done away in Christ." (Revised Version)

The helpers waited until they heard a specific pattern of sounds from the bells that were in the border of the garment of the high priest (**Exo. 28:34, 39:26**). Once they heard the previously agreed upon pattern of sounds, they lifted the veil. The work of the helpers is now being done by the Holy Spirit that leads and guides us into all truth (as found in **both** the Old *and* the New Testaments) by the word of God, that not only lifts the veil, but actually *removes* it (all demonic influence upon our prideful minds and will, that keep us from a true understanding **of** and obedience **to** the Word of God).

The Torn Veil

In addition to everything else that was happening while the Lord Jesus was being crucified on the cross, there was a physical manifestation that happened in the temple when He died.

> **Mark 15:38** "And the veil of the temple was rent in twain from the top to the bottom."

The veil that separated between the Holy Place and the Holy of Holies was torn in two from the top to the bottom. There are several different opinions about the Veil. Some say that it was made out of between seven and eleven layers of different types of material. It was very heavy.

To tear through all of the layers of the veil would take a substantial amount of force. This is not only due to the multiple layers, but also due to the fact that the layers were made out of different types of material. Additionally, the fact that it was torn from the top-down and not from the bottom-up shows that it was a supernatural event.

If the veil had been torn from the bottom-up, then it could be argued that the tear was caused by the earthquakes that were happening at about the same time. However, if the earthquakes caused oscillations in the building that were great enough to tear the veil from the top-down, it would almost certainly have destroyed the building before it could have torn all of the layers of the veil for the entire distance from the top to the bottom.

This is due largely to two details. First, the veil was hung from a bar or beam of wood that spanned the width of the sanctuary. If the bar was broken, then the entire veil would have collapsed on the floor; this did not happen. Second, the veil was hung on hooks or loops and was not solidly fastened to the supporting bar. This means that there was some ability for a sliding movement of the hooks on the bar. When all of these details are considered, the only possible conclusion is that the veil was *supernaturally* torn.

It is important to recognize that it was a supernatural event because of what it symbolizes for us today.

> **John 6:44** "No man can come to me, except the Father which hath sent me draw him: and I will raise him up at the last day."
>
> **John 6:65** "And he said, Therefore said I unto you, that no man can come unto me, except it were given unto him of my Father."

If it were not for this supernatural tearing of the covering veil of our self-will, it would be impossible to even have a desire to know and draw near to God.

> **Gal. 5:17** "For the flesh lusteth against the Spirit, and the Spirit against the flesh: and these are contrary the one to the other: so that ye **cannot** do the things that ye would."

It is impossible to do by our own abilities (without God); thankfully, it does not depend upon *our* abilities.

> **Php. 2:13** "For **it is God** which worketh in you both to **will** and to **do** of his good pleasure."

Therefore, by the merciful working of His Holy Spirit, God starts the process of drawing us to Himself by first lifting the veil so that we can go in behind it into the presence of God in the Holy of Holies. If we persist in entering in behind the veil and staying in that blessed place of communion with God, then He tears down the veil of the idolatry of our stubborn pride that makes us set our own will above His will. By bringing our will into subjection to His will, the way is then open for His divine light to light up the holy place of our mind and for the holy fire of His presence to light the lamps in the lamp stand.

The Removal of the Veil

The removal of the veil allows for an entire series of events to happen that would not be possible otherwise.

1) It allows for two-way communication to happen between the mind and the heart (where God is seated) and between the body (where His works become visible to be a testimony) and the mind. The Golden Censer (divinely inspired **attitude** of prayer) with incense (humility) moving between the holy place and the Holy of Holies and the basket (supernaturally empowered **attitude** of willing subjection) moving between the Outer Court and the Holy Place.
2) It allows for the incense of humility to prepare the way for us to present supplications before the throne of God and in His presence, for those supplications to be accepted, and to receive a response.
3) It allows for the light of His presence to overflow into the mind (Holy Place) and the body (Outer Court).
4) It allows the presentation of wave offerings which come from the Outer Court to be presented in the Holy Place, in His presence (**Rom. 12:1–2**).

Circumcision was Given as a Sign of the
Covenant Between God and Man

Drawing #8

CHAPTER 6

The Covenant of Circumcision

The Context for the Covenant

In the Hebrew language, the very word *Hebrew* has the following meanings (collected from multiple sources):

1) "A region *across.*" "To *cross* over to the *opposite* side." Used very widely of any ***transition*** (literally or figuratively). "To go beyond." To bring, carry, come, conduct, convey, translate from one place over or beyond to another place, to deliver (as from bondage and/or into liberty), escape, make a partition or separation between, set apart, to cause anger to cease, be a peacemaker.
2) To ***cover*** (in copulation), specifically the consummation of marriage.

Note: those that do "walk by faith" and do have "spiritual vision" have their own unique language—Hebrew. Even if they speak other languages, their use of language carries "Hebrew (walk by faith) meaning."

Abraham was told by God to leave his native land and to walk by faith to a place that God through spiritual sight and prophetic vision would show him.

Gen. 12:1 "Now the LORD had said unto Abram, **Get thee out of thy coun-**

	try, and from thy kindred, and from thy father's house, **unto a land that I will shew thee**."
Gen. 12:2	"And I will make of thee a great nation, and I will bless thee, and make thy name great; and thou shalt be a blessing."
Gen. 12:3	"And I will bless them that bless thee, and curse him that curseth thee: **and in thee shall all families of the earth be blessed**."
Gen. 12:4	"So Abram departed, as the LORD had spoken unto him; and Lot went with him: and **Abram was seventy and five years old when he departed out of Haran**."
Gen. 12:5	"And Abram took Sarai his wife, and Lot his brother's son, and all their substance that they had gathered, and the souls that they had gotten in Haran; and they went forth to go into the land of Canaan; and into the land of Canaan they came."
Heb. 11:8	"**By faith Abraham**, when he was called to go out into a place which he should after receive for an inheritance, **obeyed**; and he went out, not knowing whither he went."
Heb. 11:9	"**By faith** he sojourned in the land of promise, as in a strange country,

dwelling in tabernacles with Isaac and Jacob, the heirs with him of **the same** promise."

Heb. 11:10 **"For he looked for a city which hath foundations, whose builder and maker is God."**

Heb. 11:11 **"Through faith** also Sara herself received strength to conceive seed, and was delivered of a child when she was past age, because she judged him faithful who had promised."

Heb. 11:12 "Therefore sprang there even of one, and him as good as dead, so many as the stars of the sky in multitude, and as the sand which is by the sea shore innumerable."

Heb. 11:13 **"These all died in faith, not having received the promises, but having seen them afar off**, and were persuaded of them, and embraced them, and confessed that they were strangers and pilgrims on the earth."

Heb. 11:14 **"For they that say such things declare plainly that they seek a country."**

Heb. 11:15 "And truly, if they had been mindful of that country from whence they came out, they might have had opportunity to have returned."

Heb. 11:16	"But now they desire a better country, that is, an heavenly: wherefore God is not ashamed to be called their God: **for he hath prepared for them a city.**"
Heb. 11:39	"**And these all, having obtained a good report through faith, received not the promise.**"
Heb. 11:40	"**God having provided some better thing for us, that they without us should not be made perfect.**"
Isa. 54:13	"**And all thy children shall be taught of the LORD**; and great shall be the peace of thy children."
Isa. 54:14	"**In righteousness shalt thou be established**: thou shalt be far from oppression; for thou shalt not fear: and from terror; for it shall not come near thee."
Isa. 54:15	"Behold, they shall surely gather together, but not by me: **whosoever shall gather together against thee shall fall for thy sake**."

When Abraham obeyed God, he became the first Hebrew of ALL those who walk by faith, by spiritual (prophetic) vision. Every time that Israel humbled themselves to be established in the righteousness of God, then God caused everyone that gathered themselves together to go against them to fall before them. The first place that the word Hebrew is used in the Bible is:

> **Gen. 14:13** "And there came one that had escaped, and told Abram the **Hebrew**; for he dwelt in the plain of Mamre the Amorite, brother of Eshcol, and brother of Aner: and these were confederate with Abram."

Even though Abram became a Hebrew when he left Ur of the Chaldees, it still took him some time to fulfill the further definition of the word *Hebrew* by separating himself "from thy kindred and from thy father's house." Please notice that in that second definition, "covering" and "obedience" come together in surrender and submission. When Abram left Ur of the Chaldees, he left with his father, Terah, and nephew, Lot.

> **Gen. 11:26** "And **Terah** lived seventy years, and begat **Abram**, Nahor, and **Haran**."

> **Gen. 11:27** "Now these are the generations of Terah: Terah begat **Abram**, Nahor, and **Haran**; and **Haran** begat **Lot**."

> **Gen. 11:28** "And **Haran** died before his father **Terah** in the land of his nativity, in **Ur of the Chaldees**."

> **Gen. 11:29** "And **Abram** and Nahor took them wives: the name of Abram's wife was Sarai; and the name of Nahor's wife, Milcah, the daughter of **Haran**, the father of Milcah, and the father of Iscah."

> **Gen. 11:30** "But Sarai was barren; she had no child."

Gen. 11:31 "And **Terah** took **Abram** his son, and **Lot** the son of **Haran** his son's son, and Sarai his daughter in law, his son **Abram's** wife; and they went forth with them from **Ur of the Chaldees**, to go into the land of Canaan; and they came unto **Haran**, and dwelt there."

Gen. 11:32 "And the days of **Terah** were two hundred and five years: and **Terah** died in **Haran**."

Notice that Haran was **both** the name of the father of Lot (verse 27 and 31) and **also** the name of a place (verses **31,32**).

The place that was named "Haran" is the same place that is mentioned in:

Gen. 12:4 "So Abram departed, as the LORD had spoken unto him; **and Lot went with him**: and Abram *was* seventy and five years old when he departed out of **Haran**."

Therefore, when Abram departed from Haran, he also separated himself from his father, because Terah was about 145 years old, and Abram was seventy-five when God spoke to Abram to separate himself from his father's house, and Terah lived for about another sixty years afterward (**Gen. 11:32**) to the age of 205. However, Abram still had a detail to fulfill before he became completely obedient to the commandment of God, because Lot was still with him.

Gen. 13:8 "And Abram said unto Lot, Let there be no strife, I pray thee, between me and thee, and between my herd-

	men and thy herdmen; for we be brethren."
Gen. 13:9	"Is not the whole land before thee? **separate thyself, I pray thee, from me**: if thou wilt take the left hand, then I will go to the right; or if thou depart to the right hand, then I will go to the left."
Gen. 13:10	"And Lot lifted up his eyes, and beheld all the plain of Jordan, that it was well watered every where, before the LORD destroyed Sodom and Gomorrah, even as the garden of the LORD, like the land of Egypt, as thou comest unto Zoar."
Gen. 13:11	"Then Lot chose him all the plain of Jordan; and Lot journeyed east: **and they separated themselves the one from the other**."
Gen. 13:12	"Abram dwelled in the land of Canaan, and Lot dwelled in the cities of the plain, and pitched his tent toward Sodom."

After Abram and Lot were separated, **then** God spoke to Abram again.

Gen. 13:14	"**And the LORD said unto Abram, after that Lot was separated from him**, Lift up now thine eyes, and look from the place where thou art

northward, and southward, and eastward, and westward."

Gen. 13:15 **"For all the land which thou seest, to thee will I give it, and to thy seed for ever."**

Gen. 13:16 "And I will make thy seed as the dust of the earth: so that if a man can number the dust of the earth, then shall thy seed also be numbered."

Gen. 13:17 **"Arise, walk through the land in the length of it and in the breadth of it; for I will give it unto thee."**

Gen. 13:18 "Then Abram removed his tent, and came and dwelt in the plain of Mamre, which is in Hebron, and built there an altar unto the LORD."

This shows us a vital concept, specifically that of obedience. This same concept is spoken about in another way:

1 John 1:7 "But if we **walk** in the light, as he is in the light, we have fellowship one with another, and the blood of Jesus Christ his Son cleanseth us from all sin."

All of this established the context for the covenant of circumcision that God made with Abram/Abraham, the Hebrew.

Gen. 15:1 "**After these things** the word of the LORD came unto Abram in a vision, saying, Fear not, Abram: I am

	thy shield, and thy exceeding great reward."
Gen. 15:2	"And Abram said, Lord GOD, what wilt thou give me, seeing I go childless, and the steward of my house is this Eliezer of Damascus?"
Gen. 15:3	"And Abram said, Behold, to me thou hast given no seed: and, lo, one born in my house is mine heir."
Gen. 15:4	"And, behold, the word of the LORD came unto him, saying, This shall not be thine heir; but **he that shall come forth out of thine own bowels shall be thine heir**."
Gen. 15:5	"And he brought him forth abroad, and said, Look now toward heaven, and tell the stars, if thou be able to number them: and he said unto him, So shall thy seed be."
Gen. 15:6	**"And he believed in the LORD; and He counted it to him for righteousness."**
Gen. 15:7	"And he said unto him, **I am the LORD that brought thee out of Ur of the Chaldees, to give thee this land to inherit it.**"
Gen. 15:8	**"And he said, Lord GOD, whereby shall I know that I shall inherit it?"**

God then, by the offering of sacrifices, gave to Abram a covenant and a sign of the covenant.

> **Gen. 15:9** "And he said unto him, Take me an heifer of three years old, and a she goat of three years old, and a ram of three years old, and a turtledove, and a young pigeon."
>
> **Gen. 15:10** "And he took unto him all these, and divided them in the midst, and laid each piece one against another: but the birds divided he not."
>
> **Gen. 15:11** "And when the fowls came down upon the carcasses, Abram drove them away."
>
> **Gen. 15:12** "And when the sun was going down, a deep sleep fell upon Abram; and, lo, an horror of great darkness fell upon him."

The sign of the covenant.

> **Gen. 15:13** "And he said unto Abram, Know of a surety that **thy seed shall be a stranger in a land that is not theirs, and shall serve them; and they shall afflict them four hundred years.**"
>
> **Gen. 15:14** "**And also that nation, whom they shall serve, will I judge: and afterward shall they come out with great substance.**"

Gen. 15:15	"And thou shalt go to thy fathers in peace; thou shalt be buried in a good old age."
Gen. 15:16	**"But in the fourth generation they shall come hither again**: for the iniquity of the Amorites is not yet full."
Gen. 15:17	"And it came to pass, that, when the sun went down, and it was dark, behold a smoking furnace, and a burning lamp that passed between those pieces."
Gen. 15:18	**"In the same day the LORD made a covenant with Abram, saying, Unto thy seed have I given this land, from the river of Egypt unto the great river, the river Euphrates**."
Gen. 15:19	"The Kenites, and the Kenizzites, and the Kadmonites."
Gen. 15:20	"And the Hittites, and the Perizzites, and the Rephaims."
Gen. 15:21	"And the Amorites, and the Canaanites, and the Girgashites, and the Jebusites."

Therefore, Israel dwelling in the land of Egypt for 400 years as slaves (they were there for thirty more years, but **not** as slaves) and then being delivered by the power of God was a sign given by God to Abraham that confirmed the covenant between the two of them.

Not only did God give the land to Abraham, but also everything that was on the land, including the people (**Gen. 15:19–21**). Sadly, in **Genesis chapter 16,** Sarai thought that God needed **her** interpretation (that denied the word of God that was spoken in **Gen. 2:23–24**) of His promise in order to fulfill His promise to Abram, but God showed the sacredness of the marriage vow by very graphically showing the same when He said:

> **Gen. 15:4** "And, behold, the word of the LORD came unto him, saying, This shall not be thine heir; but **he that shall come forth out of thine own bowels shall be thine heir.**"

God showed that Sarai was considered by Him to be part of Abram's own body, because she was his wife, and the promise could only be fulfilled in Abram/Sarai as one. The organs that surround the womb are the bowels (intestines), and the only womb that legitimately was part of Abraham was the womb of Sarah, his wife. The proof of this detail happened a number of years later by a statement that God Himself made.

> **Gen. 22:1** "And it came to pass after these things, that God did tempt Abraham, and said unto him, Abraham: and he said, Behold, here I am."

> **Gen. 22:2** "And he said, Take now thy son, **thine only son Isaac**, whom thou lovest, and get thee into the land of Moriah; and offer him there for a burnt offering upon one of the mountains which I will tell thee of."

By this, we can see that the ONLY offspring of Abraham that was considered as part of the fulfillment of the promise was Isaac, the product of **only** Abraham and Sarah (his legitimate wife by marriage), and that Ishmael (son of Hagar, the slave) was not part of the promise. This is exactly what the Apostle Paul said:

Gal. 4:22 "**For it is written, that Abraham had two sons**, the one by a bondmaid, the other by a freewoman."

Gal. 4:23 "But he who was of the bondwoman was born after the flesh; but he of the freewoman was by promise."

Gal. 4:24 "**Which things are an allegory**: for these are the two covenants; the one from the mount Sinai, which gendereth to bondage, which is Agar."

Gal. 4:25 "For this Agar is mount Sinai in Arabia, and answereth to Jerusalem which now is, and is in bondage with her children."

Gal. 4:26 "**But Jerusalem which is above is free, which is the mother of us all.**"

Therefore, even from the beginning, the fullness of the covenant and the promise was for a heavenly city (and citizens), a heavenly land, a walk of faith before God by faith in a prophetic vision that is to be done in **His** righteousness by a "Hebrew" people of faith that walk by prophetic vision.

That covenant was established by the offering (by God) of five sacrifices and also by signs of the covenant.

Sacrifices:

1) In the plain of Mamre, **Gen. 15:9–12.**

2) The offering of Isaac and God substituting a lamb/ram, **Gen. 22:1–19.**
3) The offering of the Lamb of God, in the gospels of **Matthew, Mark, Luke, and John.**
4) Taking up our cross to follow the Lamb, in the gospels of **Matthew, Mark, Luke, and John.**
5) Living sacrifices, **Rom. 12:1. Note:** it is God that offers this sacrifice to Himself. We are just the privileged and willing participants **with** Him in the offering.

Signs:

1) The prophecy and fulfillment of 400 years of bondage… then liberty, **Gen. 15:13–16.**
2) The sign of circumcision**, Gen. 17:1–27.**
3) The sign of the Prophet Jonah and of the resurrection, **Jonah 1:9–2:10, Matt. 12:38–41**, also shown symbolically in the **entire nation** in the fulfillment of **Gen. 15:13–16.**
4) The Spirit/Life of the sacrificed Lamb being poured out and removing the veil of separation, **Acts 2:2–4; 2 Cor. 3:14–16.**
5) The Lamb's circumcision producing a glorious church, and the *very* city and citizens that Abraham was seeking, **Col. 2:11; Eph. 5:27; Rev. 21:2,9–27.**

Just as Abraham walked by faith and was seeking a city, so also do **all** those that truly are Messianic Hebrews by the covenant of the circumcision of the heart seek a land and a city wherein dwelleth righteousness (because its citizens and King are righteous).

> **2 Pet. 3:13** "Nevertheless we, according to his promise, look for new heavens and a new earth, **wherein dwelleth righteousness.**"

Rom. 4:1	"What shall we say then that **Abraham our father**, as pertaining to the flesh, hath found?"
Rom. 4:2	"For if Abraham were justified by works, he hath whereof to glory; but not before God."
Rom. 4:3	"For what saith the scripture? Abraham believed God, and it was counted unto him for righteousness."
Rom. 4:4	"Now to him that worketh is the reward not reckoned of grace, but of debt."
Rom. 4:5	"But to him that worketh not, but believeth on him that justifieth the ungodly, his faith is counted for righteousness."
Rom. 4:6	"Even as David also describeth the blessedness of the man, unto whom God imputeth righteousness without works."
Rom. 4:7	"Saying, Blessed are they whose iniquities are forgiven, and whose sins are covered."
Rom. 4:8	"Blessed is the man to whom the Lord will not impute sin."
Rom. 4:9	"Cometh this blessedness then upon the circumcision only, or upon the uncircumcision also? for we say that

faith was reckoned to Abraham for righteousness."

Rom. 4:10 "How was it then reckoned? when he was in circumcision, or in uncircumcision? Not in circumcision, but in uncircumcision."

Rom. 4:11 "And **he received the sign of circumcision, a seal of the righteousness of the faith which he had yet being uncircumcised: that he might be the father of all them that believe, though they be not circumcised; that righteousness might be imputed unto them also.**"

Rom. 4:12 "**And the father of circumcision to them who are not of the circumcision only, but who also walk in the steps of that faith of our father Abraham, which he had being yet uncircumcised.**"

Rom. 4:13 "**For the promise, that he should be the heir of the world, was not to Abraham, or to his seed, through the law, but through the righteousness of faith.**"

Rom. 4:14 "For if they which are of the law be heirs, faith is made void, and the promise made of none effect."

Rom. 4:15 "Because the law worketh wrath: for where no law is, there is no transgression."

Rom. 4:16 "**Therefore it is of faith**, that it might be by grace; **to the end the promise might be sure to all the seed**; not to that **only** which is of the law, but to that **also** which is **of the faith of Abraham; who is the father of us all**."

Rom. 4:17 "(**As it is written, I have made thee a father of many nations**,) before him whom he believed, even God, who quickeneth the dead, and calleth those things which be not as though they were."

Rom. 4:18 "**Who against hope believed in hope, that he might become the father of many nations**, according to that which was spoken, **So shall thy seed be**."

Rom. 4:19 "And being not weak in faith, he considered not his own body now dead, when he was about an hundred years old, neither yet the deadness of Sara's womb."

Rom. 4:20 "**He staggered not at the promise of God through unbelief; but was strong in faith, giving glory to God**."

Rom. 4:21   "**And being fully persuaded that, what he had promised, he was able also to perform.**"

Rom. 4:22   "And therefore it was imputed to him for righteousness."

Rom. 4:23   "**Now it was not written for his sake alone**, that it was imputed to him."

Rom. 4:24   "**But for us also**, to whom it shall be imputed, if we believe on him that raised up Jesus our Lord from the dead."

Rom. 4:25   "Who was delivered for our offences, and was raised again for our justification."

The Covenant of Circumcision

From the above, we can safely conclude that even though Abraham received the sign of circumcision in his flesh, the sign in his flesh was neither the *only* circumcision that he had or even the most *important* circumcision.

Abraham was given circumcision as a sign of the covenant between God and him.

Gen. 17:10   "**This is my covenant**, which ye shall keep, between me and you **and thy seed after thee; Every man child among you shall be circumcised**."

Gen. 17:11   "And ye shall circumcise the flesh of your foreskin; and **it shall be a**

	token of the covenant betwixt me and you."
Gen. 17:12	"And he that is eight days old shall be circumcised among you, every man child in your generations, he that is born in the house, or bought with money of any stranger, which is not of thy seed."
Gen. 17:13	"He that is born in thy house, and he that is bought with thy money, must needs be circumcised: and **my covenant shall be in your flesh for an everlasting covenant.**"
Gen. 17:14	"**And the uncircumcised man child whose flesh of his foreskin is not circumcised, that soul shall be cut off from his people; he hath broken my covenant.**"

But there was another circumcision that Abraham had about which the Old Testament speaks of and of which many people are unaware, but which is **also** a sign to the "everlasting covenant." It is a sign of circumcision that **STILL** applies today.

Deut. 10:16	"**Circumcise** therefore the foreskin of your **heart**, and be no more stiffnecked."
Deut. 30:6	"And the LORD thy God will **circumcise thine heart**, and the **heart of thy seed**, to love the LORD thy God with all thine **heart**, and with all thy soul, that thou mayest **live**."

Jer. 4:4	"**Circumcise** yourselves to the LORD, and take away the foreskins of your **heart**, ye men of Judah and inhabitants of Jerusalem: lest my fury come forth like fire, and burn that none can quench it, because of the evil of your **doings**."
Rom. 2:26	"Therefore if the uncircumcision keep the righteousness of the law, shall not his uncircumcision be counted for circumcision?"
Rom. 2:27	"And shall not uncircumcision which is by nature, if it fulfil the law, judge thee, who by the letter and circumcision dost transgress the law?"
Rom. 2:28	"For he is not a Jew, which is one outwardly; **neither is that circumcision, which is outward in the flesh**."
Rom. 2:29	"**But he is a Jew, which is one inwardly; and circumcision is that of the heart, in the spirit, and not in the letter; whose praise is not of men, but of God**."
Rom. 15:8	"Now I say that **Jesus Christ was a minister of the circumcision for the truth of God, to confirm the promises** made unto the fathers."
Php. 3:3	"For **we** are the **circumcision**, which **worship** God in the **spirit**, and

rejoice in Christ Jesus, and have no confidence in the flesh."

Col. 2:11 "In whom also ye are **circumcised** with the **circumcision** made without hands, in putting off the body of the sins of the flesh by the **circumcision of Christ**."

How else was that circumcision of the heart spoken about in the Old Testament?

Eze. 11:19 "And I will give them one **heart**, and I will put a **new spirit** within you; and I will take the **stony heart** out of their flesh, and will give them an **heart of flesh**."

Eze. 36:26 "A **new heart** also will I give you, and a **new spirit** will I put within you: and I will take away the **stony heart** out of your flesh, and I will give you an **heart of flesh**."

2 Cor. 3:2 "Ye are our **epistle** written in our **hearts**, known and read of all men."

2 Cor. 3:3 "Forasmuch as ye are manifestly declared to **be the epistle of Christ** ministered by us, **written not with ink, but with the Spirit of the living God; not in tables of stone, but in fleshy tables of the heart**."

The removal of "hard heartedness" (stony) and rebellion of our flesh by the circumcision of the heart is directly related to the giving of the New Covenant.

Jer. 31:31	"Behold, the days come, saith the LORD, that I will make a **new covenant** with the house of Israel, and with the house of Judah."
Jer. 31:32	"Not according to the **covenant** that I made with their fathers in the day that I took them by the hand to bring them out of the land of Egypt; which my **covenant** they brake, **although I was an husband unto them**, saith the LORD."
Jer. 31:33	"But **this shall be the covenant** that I will make with the house of Israel; After those days, saith the LORD, **I will put my law in their inward parts, and write it in their hearts; and will be their God, and they shall be my people**."
Isa. 59:20	"And **the Redeemer shall come to Zion**, and unto them that turn from transgression in Jacob, saith the LORD."
Isa. 59:21	"As for me, **this is my covenant** with them, saith the LORD; **My spirit that is upon thee, and my words which I have put in thy mouth, shall not depart out of thy mouth, nor out of the mouth of thy seed,**

nor out of the mouth of thy seed's seed, saith the LORD, from henceforth and for ever."

Jer. 32:37 "Behold, I will gather them out of all countries, whither I have driven them in mine anger, and in my fury, and in great wrath; and I will bring them again unto this place, and I will cause them to dwell safely."

Jer. 32:38 **"And they shall be my people, and I will be their God."**

Jer. 32:39 "And **I will give them one heart, and one way**, that they may fear me for ever, for the good of them, and of their children after them."

Jer. 32:40 "And **I will make an everlasting covenant with them**, that I will not turn away from them, to do them good; but **I will put my fear in their hearts, that they shall not depart from me**."

Jer. 32:41 "Yea, I will rejoice over them to do them good, and I will plant them in this land assuredly with my whole heart and with my whole soul."

Jer. 50:4 "In those days, and in that time, saith the LORD, the children of Israel shall come, they and the children of Judah together, going and weeping: they shall go, and seek the LORD their God."

Jer. 50:5	"**They shall ask the way to Zion** with their faces thitherward, saying, **Come, and let us join ourselves to the LORD in a perpetual covenant that shall not be forgotten.**"
Jer. 50:6	"My people hath been lost sheep: their shepherds have caused them to go astray, they have turned them away on the mountains: they have gone from mountain to hill, they have forgotten their restingplace."
Eze. 16:8	"Now when I passed by thee, and looked upon thee, behold, thy time was the time of love; and **I spread my skirt over thee, and covered thy nakedness**: yea, **I sware unto thee, and entered into a covenant with thee, saith the Lord GOD, and thou becamest mine.**"

Therefore, the covenant of circumcision is symbolic of the promise of the Father to (by His Spirit, Ruach, breath, inspiration, revelation) give the New Covenant by removing the veil of covering that was between the heart and the mind. This makes possible the second definition of the word *Hebrew*. "I spread my skirt over thee and **covered** thy nakedness" is also related to the covenant.

Eze. 20:37	"And I will cause you to **pass under the rod**, and **I will bring you into the bond of the covenant.**"

The rod of discipline is also symbolized by the rod of Aaron and will cause the fruit of the righteousness of God to spring forth in our lives and cause His righteousness to clothe us (**Heb. 12:11; Isa. 6:1,4**).

> **Eze. 34:25** "And I will make with them a **covenant of peace**, and will cause the evil beasts to cease out of the land: and they shall dwell safely in the wilderness, and sleep in the woods."
>
> **Eze. 37:26** "Moreover I will make a **covenant of peace** with them; it shall be an **everlasting covenant** with them: and **I will place them**, and multiply them, **and will set my sanctuary in the midst of them for evermore**."

Thrones being placed (**Dan. 7:9,** God setting up His sanctuary), hearts being written upon (**Jer. 31:31–33**), people becoming temples of the Holy Spirit (**1 Cor. 3:16, 6:19**) through the circumcision of the heart (**Col. 2:11**), God writing His covenant (**2 Cor. 3:2–3**), THE Ancient of Days being seated (**Dan. 7:9,18,22,26–27**), the judge coming to His rightful throne, removing the veil *by* circumcising hearts (**2 Cor. 3:14–16**), making thrones to be pure and white by His presence.

> **2 Cor. 6:16** "And what agreement hath the temple of God with idols? for **ye are the temple of the living God; as God hath said, I will dwell in them, and walk in them; and I will be their God, and they shall be my people**."
>
> **2 Cor. 6:17** "Wherefore come out from among them, and be ye separate, saith the Lord, and touch not the unclean thing; and I will receive you."

2 Cor. 6:18 "And will be a Father unto you, and ye shall be my sons and daughters, saith the Lord Almighty."

The removal of the veil and the circumcision of the heart are the same thing. It can ONLY be done by the Holy Spirit, the glory of the presence of God, the Shekinah, and we can only get into that place by the blood of the Lamb working through the incense of humility.

Exchanging one covering for another.
Exchanging the veil for the Shekinah.

Joel 3:13 "Put ye in the sickle, for **the harvest is ripe**: come, get you down; for **the press is full**, the fats overflow; for their wickedness is great."

Joel 3:14 "Multitudes, multitudes in the **valley of decision**: for the day of the LORD is near in the valley of decision."

When the Law of God was first presented to Israel, it was not only presented as a sharp two-edged sword (blessing for obedience and cursing for disobedience), but also as a choice between life and death.

Deut. 30:11 "For this commandment which I command thee this day, it is not hidden from thee, neither is it far off."

Deut. 30:12 "It is not in heaven, that thou shouldest say, Who shall go up for us to heaven, and bring it unto us, that we may hear it, **and do it**?"

Deut. 30:13	"Neither is it beyond the sea, that thou shouldest say, Who shall go over the sea for us, and bring it unto us, that we may hear it, **and do it?**"
Deut. 30:14	"**But the word is very nigh unto thee**, in thy mouth, and **in thy heart**, that thou mayest do it."
Deut. 30:15	"See**, I have set before thee this day life and good, and death and evil**."
Deut. 30:16	"**In that I command thee this day to love the LORD thy God, to walk in his ways, and to keep his commandments and his statutes and his judgments, that thou mayest live and multiply: and the LORD thy God shall bless thee** in the land whither thou goest to possess it."
Deut. 30:17	"But if thine heart turn away, so that thou wilt not hear, but shalt be drawn away, and worship other gods, and serve them."
Deut. 30:18	"I denounce unto you this day, that ye shall surely perish, and that ye shall not prolong your days upon the land, whither thou passest over Jordan to go to possess it."
Deut. 30:19	"I call heaven and earth to record this day against you, that **I have set before you life and death, blessing and**

	cursing: therefore choose life, that both thou and thy seed may live."
Deut. 30:20	"That thou mayest love the LORD thy God, and that thou mayest obey his voice, and that thou mayest cleave unto him: for he is thy life, and the length of thy days: that thou mayest dwell in the land which the LORD sware unto thy fathers, to Abraham, to Isaac, and to Jacob, to give them."

It is a choice between the covering veil that keeps the mind in darkness and the covering of the Shekinah, the presence of THE King of Glory that He wants to entirely fill the temple of our entire bodies with. It is the choice between remaining in darkness and experiencing the second definition of the word *Hebrew* by allowing God to "cover" us with His glory and "transition" us from just being a Bride that is promised "unto" marriage (but that has not been married by taking the wedding vows *yet*) into being the Wife of the Lamb (**Rev. 19:7–9**). It is the choice between remaining in uncircumcision of heart or receiving the covering of the New (Marriage) Covenant (**Jer. 31:31–33**) and the sign of the covenant, which is the circumcision of the heart (**Col. 2:11**, the removal of the veil) that can only be done by the Lord Jesus Christ (**2 Cor. 3:14–16**).

PART 2
The Holy of Holies

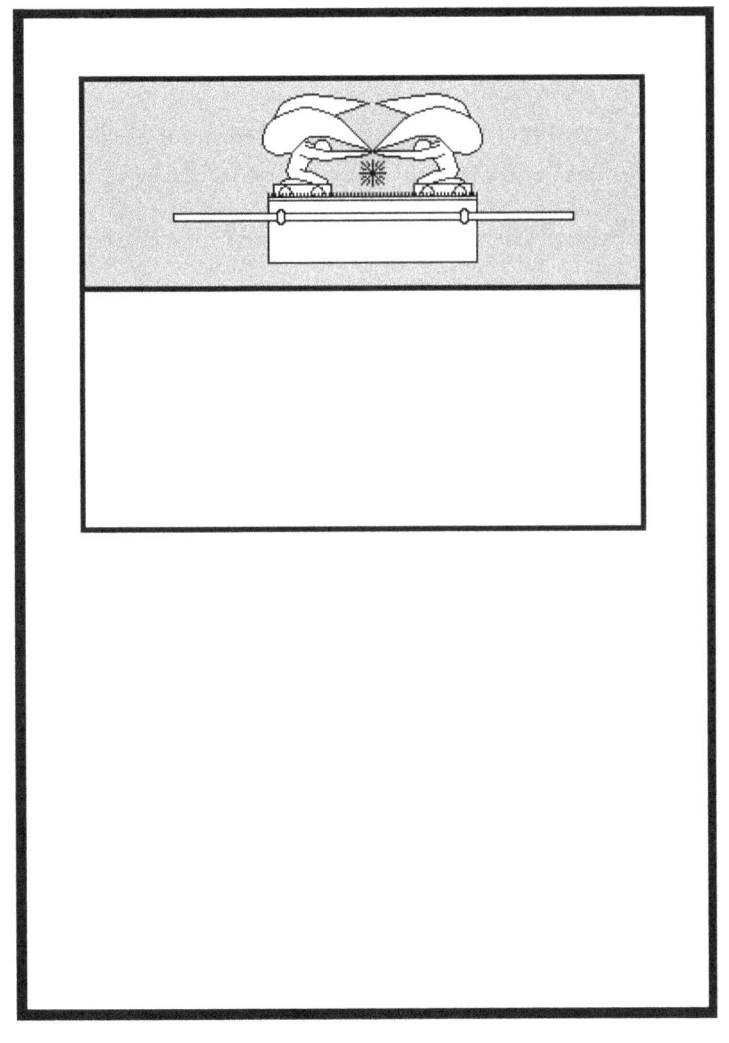

Drawing #9

The Difference Between the Offering of Bulls
and Goats and the Offering of the Lamb.

Holy of Holies

Drawing #10

CHAPTER 7

The Atonement Sacrifices

In the Temple, there were two animals that were used for the yearly atonement—a bullock for the sins of the high priest, his family, and tribe, and a goat for the sins of the people.

Lev. 16:11	"And Aaron shall bring **the bullock of the sin offering, which is for himself, and shall make an atonement for himself, and for his house**, and shall kill the bullock of the sin offering **which is for himself**."
Lev. 16:14	"And he shall take of the blood of the bullock, and sprinkle it with his finger upon the mercy seat eastward; and before the mercy seat shall he sprinkle of the blood with his finger seven times."
Lev. 16:15	"Then shall he **kill the goat of the sin offering, that is for the people**, and bring his blood within the veil, and do with that blood as he did with the blood of the bullock, and sprinkle it upon the mercy seat, and before the mercy seat."

However, the scriptures clearly speak about the Lord Jesus as the Lamb of God and that He is the atonement for the sins of the world. Please note that propitiation is paying the required price for atonement and reconciliation or for being reconciled to relationship and fellowship with God, which is the result of the atonement.

John 1:29 "The next day, John seeth Jesus coming unto him, and saith, Behold the **Lamb** of God, which taketh away the sin of the world."

Rom. 5:11 "And not only so, but we also joy in **God through our Lord Jesus Christ, by whom we have now received the atonement**."

1 John 2:2 "And he is the **propitiation** for our sins: and not for ours only, but also **for the sins of the whole world**."

2 Cor. 5:18 "And all things are of **God, who hath reconciled us to himself by Jesus Christ**, and hath given to us the ministry of reconciliation."

2 Cor. 5:19 "To wit, that **God was in Christ, reconciling the world unto himself**, not imputing their trespasses unto them; and hath committed unto us the word of reconciliation."

Col. 1:20 "And, **having made peace through the blood of his cross, by him to reconcile all things unto himself**; by him, I say, **whether they**

> **be things in earth, or things in heaven.**"

While it has been surmised, and rightfully so, that the following scriptures relate to the Lord Jesus Christ, it would be better if we could see a more direct connection between the atonement and the Lamb.

> **Gen. 3:21** "Unto Adam also and to his wife did **the LORD God make coats of skins, and clothed them.**"
>
> **Rom. 13:14** "But **put ye on the Lord Jesus Christ**, and make not provision for the flesh, to fulfil the lusts thereof."
>
> **Gal. 3:27** "For as many of you as have been baptized into Christ have **put on Christ.**"

The term "have **put on** Christ" literally means "been **clothed with** Christ."

> **Gen. 22:8** "And Abraham said, My son, God will provide himself a **lamb** for a burnt offering: so they went both of them together."
>
> **Gen. 22:13** "And Abraham lifted up his eyes, and looked, and behold behind him a ram caught in a thicket by his horns: and Abraham went and took the **ram**, and offered him up for a burnt offering in the stead of his son."

When the priests were being consecrated for the service of the priesthood to serve God in the temple, there was a seven-day process that they had to go through.

Exo. 29:1		"And this is the thing that thou shalt do unto them to **hallow** them, to minister unto me in the priest's office: Take one young **bullock**, and **two rams** without blemish."
Exo. 29:2		"And unleavened bread, and cakes unleavened tempered with oil, and wafers unleavened anointed with oil: of wheaten flour shalt thou make them."
Exo. 29:3		"And thou shalt put them into one basket, and bring them in the basket, with the **bullock** and the **two rams**."
Exo. 29:4		"And Aaron and his sons thou shalt bring unto the door of the tabernacle of the congregation, and shalt wash them with water."
Exo. 29:5		"And thou shalt take the garments, and put upon Aaron the coat, and the robe of the ephod, and the ephod, and the breastplate, and gird him with the curious girdle of the ephod."
Exo. 29:6		"And thou shalt put the mitre upon his head, and put the holy crown upon the mitre."

Exo. 29:7	"Then shalt thou take the **anointing** oil, and pour it upon his head, and anoint him."
Exo. 29:8	"And thou shalt bring his sons, and put coats upon them."
Exo. 29:9	"And thou shalt gird them with girdles, Aaron and his sons, and put the bonnets on them: and the priest's office shall be theirs for a perpetual statute: and thou shalt **consecrate** Aaron and his sons."
Exo. 29:10	"And thou shalt cause a **bullock** to be brought before the tabernacle of the congregation: and Aaron and his sons shall put their hands upon the head of the **bullock**."
Exo. 29:11	"And thou shalt kill the **bullock** before the LORD, by the door of the tabernacle of the congregation."
Exo. 29:12	"And thou shalt take of the blood of the **bullock**, and put it upon the horns of the altar with thy finger, and pour all the blood beside the bottom of the altar."
Exo. 29:13	"And thou shalt take all the fat that covereth the inwards, and the caul that is above the liver, and the two kidneys, and the fat that is upon them, and burn them upon the altar."

Exo. 29:14 "But the flesh of the **bullock**, and his skin, and his dung, shalt thou burn with fire without the camp: it is a sin **offering**."

Exo. 29:15 "Thou shalt also take one **ram**; and Aaron and his sons shall put their hands upon the head of the **ram**."

Exo. 29:16 "And thou shalt slay the **ram**, and thou shalt take his blood, and sprinkle it round about upon the altar."

Exo. 29:17 "And thou shalt cut the **ram** in pieces, and wash the inwards of him, and his legs, and put them unto his pieces, and unto his head."

Exo. 29:18 "And thou shalt burn the whole **ram** upon the altar: it is a **burnt offering** unto the LORD: it is a **sweet savour**, an offering made by fire unto the LORD."

Please refer to:

Gen. 22:8 "And Abraham said, My son, God will provide himself a **lamb** for a **burnt offering**."

Abraham, being a prophet, was not only speaking to the fulfillment that happened a few moments later, but also spoke to the details of the atonement for the consecration of the priesthood and to the ultimate fulfillment in the Messiah (consecrating kings and priests, **Rev. 1:6, 5:10**). Also, we can see that "lamb" in **Gen. 22:8** is used interchangeably with "ram" in **Gen. 22:13**.

Exo. 29:19	"And thou shalt take the other **ram**; and Aaron and his sons shall put their hands upon the head of the **ram**."
Exo. 29:20	"Then shalt thou kill the **ram**, and take of his blood, and put it upon the tip of the right ear of Aaron, and upon the tip of the right ear of his sons, and upon the thumb of their right hand, and upon the great toe of their right foot, and sprinkle the blood upon the altar round about."
Exo. 29:21	"And thou shalt take of the blood that is upon the altar, and of the **anointing** oil, and sprinkle it upon Aaron, and upon his garments, and upon his sons, and upon the garments of his sons with him: and he shall be **hallowed**, and his garments, and his sons, and his sons' garments with him."
Exo. 29:22	"Also thou shalt take of the **ram** the fat and the rump, and the fat that covereth the inwards, and the caul above the liver, and the two kidneys, and the fat that is upon them, and the right shoulder; for it is a **ram** of **consecration**."
Exo. 29:23	"And one loaf of bread, and one cake of oiled bread, and one wafer out of the basket of the unleavened bread that is before the LORD."

Exo. 29:24	"And thou shalt put all in the hands of Aaron, and in the hands of his sons; and shalt wave them for a wave **offering** before the LORD."
Exo. 29:25	"And thou shalt receive them of their hands, and burn them upon the altar for a burnt **offering**, for a **sweet savour** before the LORD: it is an **offering** made by fire unto the LORD."
Exo. 29:26	"And thou shalt take the breast of the **ram** of Aaron's **consecration**, and wave it for a wave **offering** before the LORD: and it shall be thy part."
Exo. 29:27	"And thou shalt sanctify the breast of the wave **offering**, and the shoulder of the heave **offering**, which is waved, and which is heaved up, of the **ram** of the **consecration**, even of that which is for Aaron, and of that which is for his sons."
Exo. 29:28	"And it shall be Aaron's and his sons' by a statute for ever from the children of Israel: for it is an heave **offering**: and it shall be an heave **offering** from the children of Israel of the sacrifice of their peace **offerings**, even their heave **offering** unto the LORD."
Exo. 29:29	"And the holy garments of Aaron shall be his sons' after him, to be

	anointed therein, and to be **consecrated** in them."
Exo. 29:30	"And that son that is priest in his stead shall put them on **seven days**, when he cometh into the tabernacle of the congregation to minister in the holy place."
Exo. 29:31	"And thou shalt take the **ram of the consecration**, and seethe his flesh in the holy place."
Exo. 29:32	"And Aaron and his sons shall eat the flesh of the **ram**, and the bread that is in the basket, by the door of the tabernacle of the congregation."
Exo. 29:33	"And they shall eat those things wherewith the **atonement** was made, to **consecrate** and to **sanctify** them: but a stranger shall not eat thereof, because they are holy."
Exo. 29:34	"And if ought of the flesh of the **consecrations**, or of the bread, remain unto the morning, then thou shalt burn the remainder with fire: it shall not be eaten, because it is holy."
Exo. 29:35	"And thus shalt thou do unto Aaron, and to his sons, according to all things which I have commanded thee: **seven days shalt thou consecrate them**."

Exo. 29:36 "And thou shalt offer **every day a bullock for a sin offering for atonement**: and **thou shalt cleanse the altar, when thou hast made an atonement for it, and thou shalt anoint it, to sanctify it.**"

Exo. 29:37 "**Seven days thou shalt make an atonement for the altar, and sanctify it; and it shall be an altar most holy: whatsoever toucheth the altar shall be holy.**"

Exo. 29:38 "Now this is that which thou shalt **offer** upon the altar; **two lambs** of the first year day by day continually."

Exo. 29:39 "**The one lamb thou shalt offer in the morning; and the other lamb thou shalt offer at even.**"

Exo. 29:40 "And with the one **lamb** a tenth deal of flour mingled with the fourth part of an hin of beaten oil; and the fourth part of an hin of wine for a drink offering."

Exo. 29:41 "And **the other lamb thou shalt offer at even**, and shalt do thereto according to the meat **offering** of the morning, and according to the drink **offering** thereof, for a **sweet savour**, an **offering** made by fire unto the LORD."

Exo. 29:42	"This shall be a continual burnt offering throughout your generations at the door of the tabernacle of the congregation before the LORD: where I will meet you, to speak there unto thee."
Exo. 29:43	"And there I will meet with the children of Israel, and the tabernacle shall be sanctified by my glory."
Exo. 29:44	"And I will sanctify the tabernacle of the congregation, and the altar: I will sanctify also both Aaron and his sons, to minister to me in the priest's office."
Exo. 29:45	"And I will dwell among the children of Israel, and will be their God."
Exo. 29:46	"**And they shall know that I am the LORD their God**, that brought them forth out of the land of Egypt, **that I may dwell among them**: I am the LORD their God."

Please note that there was a ram offered every morning and another one offered every evening for seven days to consecrate the priests for the service of the priesthood. The explanation about the seven days will require another entire book to explain properly, but in brief, it relates to **Rev. 1:12–16**. However, the *first* lamb that was offered in the morning and the *last* lamb that was offered in the evening are extremely important. But first, we will take a brief look at the will of God for His people.

Exo. 19:5   "Now therefore, if ye will obey my voice indeed, and keep my covenant, then ye shall be a peculiar treasure unto me above all people: for all the earth is mine."

Exo. 19:6   "And ye shall be unto me a **kingdom of priests**, and an **holy nation**. These are the words which thou shalt speak unto the children of Israel."

It was the desire of God that **all** the people be priests for His service. Because of their fear and sin, they were unable to fulfill that desire. However, the desire of God **will** be fulfilled, and that fulfillment is spoken about in:

Rev. 5:9   "And they sung a new song, saying, Thou art worthy to take the book, and to open the seals thereof: for thou wast slain, and hast **redeemed** us to God by thy blood out of **every** kindred, and tongue, and people, and nation;

Rev. 5:10   "And hast **made us unto our God kings and priests**: and we shall reign on the earth."

How does this relate to the use of a lamb for atonement?

Exo. 29:33   "And they shall eat those things wherewith the **atonement** was made, to **consecrate** and to **sanctify** them: but a stranger shall not eat thereof, because they are holy."

Exo. 29:37	**"Seven days thou shalt make an atonement for the altar, and sanctify it; and it shall be an altar most holy: whatsoever toucheth the altar shall be holy."**
Exo. 29:38	"Now this is that which thou shalt offer upon the altar; **two lambs** of the first year day by day continually."
Exo. 29:39	**"The one lamb thou shalt offer in the morning; and the other lamb thou shalt offer at even."**

Now we will see the extreme importance of the *first* **lamb** that was offered in the morning and the *last* **lamb** that was offered in the evening—the *first* and the *last*.

In the book of **Revelations**, the Lord Jesus used three terms to describe Himself. These three terms were the first and the last, the beginning and the end, and the Alpha and Omega (in Hebrew, Alef and Tav).

Rev. 1:11	"Saying, I am **Alpha** and **Omega**, the **first** and the **last**: and, What thou seest, write in a book, and send it unto the seven churches which are in Asia; unto Ephesus, and unto Smyrna, and unto Pergamos, and unto Thyatira, and unto Sardis, and unto Philadelphia, and unto Laodicea."
Rev. 1:17	"And when I saw him, I fell at his feet as dead. And he laid his right hand upon me, saying unto me, Fear not; I am the **first** and the **last**."

Rev. 2:8 "And unto the angel of the church in Smyrna write; These things saith the **first** and the **last**, which was dead, and is alive."

Rev. 21:6 "And he said unto me, **It is done**. I am **Alpha** and **Omega**, the **beginning** and the **end**. I will give unto him that is athirst of the fountain of the water of life freely."

Rev. 22:13 "I am **Alpha** and **Omega**, the **beginning** and the **end**, the **first** and the **last**."

The same thing was said in the Old Testament.

Isa. 41:4 "Who hath wrought and done it, calling the generations from the **beginning**? I the LORD, the **first**, and with the **last**; I am he."

Isa. 44:6 "Thus saith **the LORD the King of Israel**, and his **redeemer** the **LORD of hosts**; I am the **first**, and I am the **last**; and beside me there is no God."

Isa. 48:12 "Hearken unto me, O Jacob and Israel, my called; I am he; I am the **first**, I also am the **last**."

In this, we can see that the Lamb as atonement **only** makes sense in the context of the consecration of **priests**. Seeing that it was the desire of God in the beginning for all of His people to be priests and that **this** is what He **will** achieve in the end, we can now see that the declaration of John the Baptist (**John 1:29**) was not just a declaration. It was also a prophecy and a speaking forth of divinely given insight or revelation into the word of God and a pronouncement into the earth of the purpose of God. We can also see that He (Jesus, Yeshua) is the **first** ram for the burnt offering of atonement and the **last** ram for consecration—**the first and the last**.

> **John 1:29** "The next day John seeth Jesus coming unto him, and saith, Behold the **Lamb** of God, which taketh away the **sin of the world**."

The fulfillment of this prophetic proclamation is in:

> **Rev. 5:9** "…and hast **redeemed** us to God by thy blood out of **every** kindred, and tongue, and people, and nation."

We can also see that the desire of God is never thwarted, but He will surely achieve all of His desire as is stated in the following scripture.

> **Isa. 46:9** "Remember the former things of old: for **I am God, and there is none else; I am God, and there is none like me**."

> **Isa. 46:10** "Declaring the **end** from the **beginning**, and from ancient times the things that are not yet done, saying, **My counsel shall stand, and I will do all my pleasure**."

> **Isa. 55:11** "**So shall my word be that goeth forth out of my mouth: it shall not return unto me void, but it shall accomplish that which I please,**

and it shall prosper in the thing whereto I sent it."

John 1:1 "In the beginning was the **Word**, and the **Word** was with God, and **the Word was God**."

John 1:14 "And the **Word** was made flesh, and dwelt among us, (and we beheld his glory, the glory as of the only begotten of the Father,) full of grace and truth."

Jesus Christ (Yeshua HaMesiach), who is the Word of God and who is also the Lamb of God and who also is Immanuel/Emmanuel (**Isa. 7:14**, **8:8**; **Matt. 1:23**), absolutely succeeded in the purpose that He came to do, for He has **redeemed** us out of **every** kindred and tongue and people and nation **to be** kings and **priests** before Him in all manner of holiness and righteousness so that His glory may be known and made manifest; because we are the temple of the Holy Spirit, and the train of His righteousness fills the whole temple.

1 Cor. 3:16 "Know ye not that **ye are the temple of God**, and that the Spirit of God dwelleth in you?"

Isa. 6:1 "In the year that king Uzziah died I saw also the Lord sitting upon a throne, high and lifted up, and **his train filled the temple**."

In **Matthew chapter 5,** we can see the application of this same concept:

Matt. 5:6 "Blessed are they which do hunger and thirst after righteousness: for they shall be **filled**."

The train of His garments, of His righteousness, **shall** fill all of those temples that are hungering and thirsting for **that** filling.

>**Matt. 5:17** "Think not that I am come to destroy the law, or the prophets: I am not come to destroy, but to fulfil."
>
>**Matt. 5:18** "For verily I say unto you, Till heaven and earth pass, one jot or one tittle shall in no wise pass from the law, till all be fulfilled."
>
>**Matt. 5:19** "Whosoever therefore shall break one of these least commandments, and shall teach men so, he shall be called the least in the kingdom of heaven: but whosoever shall do and teach them, the same shall be called great in the kingdom of heaven."

Verse **19** literally is an explanation of verses **17** & **18,** and the application is to "whosoever." The Lord Jesus fulfilled (as the second Adam) the work of Redeemer for us as the church, and He is "him that was to come" in **Rom. 5:14**.

>**Rom. 5:14** "Nevertheless death reigned from Adam to Moses, even over them that had not sinned after the similitude of Adam's transgression, who is the **figure** of **him that was to come**."

According to **1 Tim. 2:14,** the first Adam (the man) did not directly incur the transgression, but it was Adam (the woman, **Gen. 5:1–2** "…called **their** name Adam") that incurred the transgression.

1 Tim. 2:14 "And Adam was **not deceived**, but the woman **being deceived** was in the transgression."

Gen. 5:1 "This is the book of the generations of Adam. In the day that God created man, in the likeness of God made he him."

Gen. 5:2 "Male and female created he them; and blessed them, and called **their name** Adam, in the day when they were created."

Adam (the man) as "the figure of Him that was to come" did not incur the transgression directly, just as it was not the Lord Jesus (the second Adam) that had sin; it was us, and He redeemed us to God (**Rev. 5:9**). This is what the first man (Adam) did for the first woman (Adam), and in doing so, he became the *figure* for the second Adam—the Lord Jesus Christ.

What this also shows is that according to **Matt. 5:17**, as the Lamb was the morning sacrifice, the Lord Jesus fulfilled the offering in flesh that was born without sin, and it is STILL Him, the Lamb of the evening sacrifice, fulfilling the offering in the end of time (for the church, the congregation of the redeemed); but NOW He is doing it in flesh that was born **in** sin **but** that has been redeemed.

Therefore, He is the **First** Lamb and He is the **Last** Lamb fulfilling the consecration of the priesthood, and He has brought His people (all that believe in Him) into **that** fulfillment with Him; and through that evening time fulfillment, He has made us to be kings and **priests**.

Isa. 41:4 "Who hath wrought and done it, calling the generations from the beginning? I the LORD, the **first**, and with the **last**; **I am** he."

Isa. 44:6	"Thus saith the LORD the King of Israel, and his **redeemer** the LORD of hosts; **I am** the **first**, and **I am** the **last**; and **beside me there is no God**."
Isa. 47:4	**"As for our redeemer, the LORD of hosts is his name, the Holy One of Israel."**
Isa. 48:12	"Hearken unto me, O Jacob and Israel, my called; **I am** he; **I am** the **first**, I also **am** the **last**."
Isa. 48:17	"Thus saith the LORD, thy Redeemer, the Holy One of Israel; **I am** the **LORD thy God** which teacheth thee to profit, **which leadeth thee by the way that thou shouldest go**."
Isa. 49:7	"Thus saith the **LORD**, the **Redeemer of Israel**, and his Holy One, to him whom man despiseth, to him whom the nation abhorreth, to a servant of rulers, Kings shall see and arise, princes also shall worship, because of **the LORD that is faithful**, and the Holy One of Israel, and **he shall choose thee**."
Isa. 54:5	"For **thy Maker is thine husband; the LORD of hosts is his name**; and thy **Redeemer** the Holy One of Israel; **The God of the whole earth shall he be called**."

Isa. 63:16	"Doubtless thou art our father, though Abraham be ignorant of us, and Israel acknowledge us not: **thou, O LORD**, art our father, our **redeemer**; **thy name is from everlasting**."
Rev. 1:8	"I am **Alpha** and **Omega**, the **beginning** and the **ending**, saith the Lord, which is, and which was, and which is to come, the Almighty."
Rev. 2:8	"And unto the angel of the church in Smyrna write; These things saith the **first** and the **last**, which was dead, and is alive."
Rev. 5:9	"And they sung a new song, saying, Thou art worthy to take the book, and to open the seals thereof: for thou wast slain, and hast **redeemed** us to God by thy blood out of every kindred, and tongue, and people, and nation."
Rev. 5:10	"And hast made us unto our God **kings** and **priests**: and we shall reign on the earth."
Rev. 22:12	"And, behold, I come quickly; and my reward is with me, to give every man according as his work shall be."
Rev. 22:13	"**I am Alpha** and **Omega**, the **beginning** and the **end**, the **first** and the **last**."

Who is He? Yeshua the Redeemer, the King of Israel.

> **Matt. 1:21** "And she shall bring forth a son, and thou shalt call his name JESUS: for **he shall save his people from their sins.**"
>
> **Matt. 1:22** "Now all this was done, that it might be fulfilled which was spoken of the Lord by the prophet, saying."
>
> **Matt. 1:23** "Behold, a virgin shall be with child, and shall bring forth a son, and they shall call his name **Emmanuel**, which being interpreted is, **God with us**."

And the king of saints.

> **Rev. 15:3** "And they sing the song of Moses the servant of God, and the song of the Lamb, saying, Great and marvellous are thy works, Lord God Almighty; just and true are thy ways, **thou King of saints**."
>
> **Rev. 15:4** "Who shall not fear thee, O Lord, and glorify thy name? for thou only art holy: for all nations shall come and worship before thee; for thy judgments are made manifest."

Why Some Sacrifices are Imperfect, Even Though They do not Have Any Physical Blemish, and Why a Specific Sacrifice Was a Perfect Sacrifice

Drawing #11

CHAPTER 8

Perfect and Imperfect Sacrifices

There are two types of imperfect sacrifices—those that have a physical blemish and those that cannot do a *complete* work of atonement. In the Temple, almost all sacrifices either had to be animals without a blemish or (in the case of a first fruit that had a blemish) redeemed by an animal without blemish. However, we will be focusing on the second type of imperfection, that which cannot do a **complete** work of atonement.

Even though most of the animals that were offered in the temple were without a *physical* blemish, *all* of those sacrifices were imperfect, because they were not able to do a **complete** work of atonement.

Remember that the work of atonement is to do the following—propitiation, redemption, justification, remission, reconciliation, and restoration.

Propitiation is paying the required price for atonement.

Redemption, what the atonement does, redeems us back to God.

Justification—the condition, position, and relationship that the atonement brings the worshipper into, in which their sins do not come into remembrance before God, and He considers them as though they **never** had sin.

Remission—what happens to the sins because of the blood being on the Mercy Seat.

Reconciliation—being reconciled to relationship and fellowship with God as the result of atonement.

The fullness of restoration will only be complete when our bodies are changed from mortal to immortal, from corruption to incorruption, and death is swallowed up in victory.

1 Cor. 15:49 "And as we have borne the image of the earthy, **we shall also bear the image of the heavenly**."

1 Cor. 15:50 "Now this I say, brethren, that flesh and blood cannot inherit the kingdom of God; neither doth corruption inherit incorruption."

1 Cor. 15:51 "Behold, I shew you a mystery; We shall not all sleep, but **we shall all be changed**."

1 Cor. 15:52 "In a moment, in the twinkling of an eye, at the last trump: for the trumpet shall sound, and the dead shall be raised incorruptible, and we shall be changed."

1 Cor. 15:53 "For this **corruptible** must put on **incorruption**, and this **mortal** must put on **immortality**."

1 Cor. 15:54 "So when this **corruptible** shall have put on **incorruption**, and this **mortal** shall have put on **immortality**, then shall be brought to pass the saying that is written, **Death is swallowed up in victory**."

All of these details are part of the work that the atonement does for us. Even though the animals that were sacrificed had no conscience of sin and were without a physical blemish, **no** animal can be a perfect sacrifice or atonement. Why is this so? It is for some very simple and basic reasons. The first is:

Gen. 1:26 "And God said, Let **us** make man in **our** image, after **our** likeness: and let **them** have dominion over the fish of the sea, and over the fowl of the air, and over the cattle, and over all the earth, and over every creeping thing that creepeth upon the earth."

Gen. 1:27 "So **God created man in his own image**, in the image of God created he him; **male and female created he them**."

Gen. 5:1 "This is the book of the generations of Adam. **In the day** that God created man, **in the likeness of God made he him**."

Gen. 5:2 "Male and female created he **them**; and blessed **them**, and called **their** name Adam, in the day when **they** were created."

Please note that in **Gen. 5 verse 2,** the Hebrew word *shem* (name) does appear in the original text. Therefore, the Hebrew word *aw-dam* is positively identified as a proper name instead of being a general title of "mankind" as some versions of the Bible present it to be. To translate the Hebrew word *aw-dam* in **verse 2** as the word mankind constitutes an arbitrary removal of the Hebrew word *shem* and can only serve to obscure the deeper meaning in the verse; it also is a disobedience of the following Scriptures:

Deut. 4:2	"Ye shall not add unto the word which I command you, neither shall ye diminish ought from it, that ye may keep the commandments of the LORD your God which I command you."
Deut. 12:32	"What thing soever I command you, observe to do it: thou shalt not add thereto, nor diminish from it."
Prov. 30:5	"Every word of God is pure: he is a shield unto them that put their trust in him."
Prov. 30:6	"Add thou not unto his words, lest he reprove thee, and thou be found a liar."

Also, God did not create the animals in His image and likeness; neither did He create them in the image and likeness of man, and neither was man created in the image and likeness of animals. God created man in His own image and likeness. It is for this reason that there is a basic incompatibility between the spirit of life that is in man and the spirit of life that is in animals (**Ecc. 3:21**). Also, note that the **only** name that was applied to the woman until *after* the fall was Adam: "…called **their name** Adam, in the day when **they** were created" (**Gen. 5:2**).

There is a difference between the spirit of life that's in man that is separate and distinct (incompatible) from the spirit of life that is in animals.

Ecc. 3:21	"Who knoweth the **spirit of man** that goeth **upward**, and the **spirit of the beast** that goeth **downward** to the earth?"

Also, remember the scriptures that say that the life is in the blood?

Lev. 17:11 "For the **life of the flesh is in the blood**: and I have given it to you upon the altar to make an atonement for your souls: for it is the **blood** that maketh an **atonement** for the soul."

Lev. 17:14 "For it is the **life** of all flesh; the **blood** of it is for the **life** thereof: therefore I said unto the children of Israel, Ye shall eat the **blood** of no manner of flesh: for the **life** of all flesh is the **blood** thereof: whosoever eateth it shall be cut off."

Deut. 12:23 "Only be sure that thou eat not the **blood**: for the **blood** is the **life**; and thou mayest not eat the **life** with the flesh."

Even in the New Testament, there was a prohibition against eating blood.

Acts 15:20 "But that we write unto them, that they **abstain** from pollutions of idols, and from fornication, and from things strangled, and from **blood**."

Acts 15:29 "That ye **abstain** from meats offered to idols, and from **blood**, and from things strangled, and from fornication: from which if ye keep yourselves, ye shall do well. Fare ye well."

It is for this reason that the innocence of sin that was in the animals that were used for atonement cannot come back upon the worshipper to impart to the worshipper the same innocence of sin that was in the animal. There is only one place in the scriptures where anything similar happened and it is found in **Daniel 4:4-37**.

> **Dan. 4:16** "Let his heart be changed from man's, and let a beast's heart be given unto him: and let seven times pass over him."

This was hardly a blessing, but rather a curse, and not the kind of thing that God would give as a response to accepting the atoning blood. Therefore, the blood of those animals could **only** cover the sins of the people until a truly perfect sacrifice could come. A sacrifice that was both innocent of sin and which had a spirit of life in it that was compatible with man. **That** sacrifice could be offered up by none other than Immanuel (God with us), the Messiah and Redeemer of Israel. He is the **only** one that was entirely innocent of sin **and** who had a spirit of life within him that was compatible with man (**Rev. 5:3-6**).

This was made manifest when Immanuel came down to earth.

> **Matt. 1:20** "But while he thought on these things, behold, the angel of the Lord appeared unto him in a dream, saying, Joseph, thou son of David, fear not to take unto thee Mary thy wife: for that which is conceived in her is of the Holy Ghost."
>
> **Matt. 1:21** "And she shall bring forth a son, and **thou shalt call his name JESUS: for he shall save his people from their sins.**"

Matt. 1:22	"Now all this was done, that it might be fulfilled which was spoken of the Lord by the prophet, saying."
Matt. 1:23	"Behold, a virgin shall be with child, and shall bring forth a son, and they shall call his name **Emmanuel**, which being interpreted is, God with us."
Isa. 7:14	"Therefore the Lord himself shall give you a sign; Behold, a virgin shall conceive, and bear a son, and shall call his name **Immanuel**."

Also, the very name of Jesus comes from the Hebrew word *Yeshua*, which means "savior" and is the word that is used in the following verses.

Psa. 106:21	"They forgat God their **saviour**, which had done great things in Egypt."
Isa. 19:20	"And it shall be for a sign and for a witness unto the LORD of hosts in the land of Egypt: for they shall cry unto the LORD because of the oppressors, and he shall send them a **saviour**, and a great one, and he shall deliver them."
Isa. 25:9	"And it shall be said in that day, Lo, this is our God; we have waited for him, and he will save us: this is the LORD; we have waited for him,

we will be glad and rejoice in his **salvation**."

Isa. 43:3 "For I am the LORD thy God, the Holy One of Israel, thy **Saviour**: I gave Egypt for thy ransom, Ethiopia and Seba for thee."

Isa. 43:11 "I, even I, am the LORD; and beside me there is no **saviour**."

Isa. 45:15 "Verily thou art a God that hidest thyself, O God of Israel, the **Saviour**."

Isa. 45:21 "Tell ye, and bring them near; yea, let them take counsel together: who hath declared this from ancient time? who hath told it from that time? have not I the LORD? and there is no God else beside me; a just God and a **Saviour**; there is none beside me."

Isa. 63:8 "For he said, Surely they are my people, children that will not lie: so he was their **Saviour**."

Hos. 13:4 "Yet I am the LORD thy God from the land of Egypt, and thou shalt know no god but me: for there is no **saviour** beside me."

The following two verses also show that the Savior (Yeshua) is also the Redeemer, the one who will be the true atonement, He who is innocent of sin and in whose blood dwells the Spirit of Life that is compatible with man and who alone can impart to man His own innocence of sin.

> **Isa. 49:26** "And I will feed them that oppress thee with their own flesh; and they shall be drunken with their own blood, as with sweet wine: and all flesh shall know that I the LORD am thy **Saviour** and thy **Redeemer**, the mighty One of Jacob."

> **Isa. 60:16** "Thou shalt also suck the milk of the Gentiles, and shalt suck the breast of kings: and thou shalt know that I the LORD am thy **Saviour** and thy **Redeemer**, the mighty One of Jacob."

He also said about Himself that he was the bread of life (**John 6:31–58**). This can only be correctly understood on the basis of the following two verses.

> **John 1:1** "In the beginning was the **Word**, and the **Word** was with God, and **the Word was God**."

> **John 1:14** "And the **Word** was made **flesh**, and dwelt among us, (and we beheld his glory, the glory as of the only begotten of the Father,) full of grace and truth."

Please note also that the word *eat* also means "partake of," and this is true even in **Genesis chapters 2 and 3**; in this way, we can **partake** of trees that produce shade, we can **partake** of the beautiful flowers of trees that produce flowers, and we can **partake** of trees that produce a sweet smelling aroma, even if those types of trees do not produce an edible fruit.

> **John 6:27** "Labour not for the meat which perisheth, **but for that meat which endureth unto everlasting life**, which the Son of man shall give unto you: for him hath God the Father sealed."
>
> **John 6:28** "Then said they unto him, What shall we do, that we might work the works of God?"
>
> **John 6:29** "Jesus answered and said unto them, This is the work of God, that ye **believe on him whom he hath sent**."

Also refer to **Matt. 26:26, Mar 14:22, Luke 22:19, 1 Cor. 10:16**, **1 Cor. 11:23–28, Matt. 6:11,** and **Luke 11:3**. Believing on him whom God has sent is a reference to the following scripture.

> **Deut. 18:15** "The LORD thy **God will raise up unto thee a Prophet** from the midst of thee, of thy brethren, **like unto me**; unto him ye shall hearken."
>
> **Deut. 18:16** "According to all that thou desiredst of the LORD thy God in Horeb in the day of the assembly, saying, Let me not hear again the voice of the LORD my God, neither let me see this great fire any more, that I die not."

Deut. 18:17	"And the LORD said unto me, They have well spoken that which they have spoken."
Deut. 18:18	"**I will raise them up a Prophet** from among their brethren, **like unto thee**, and will put my words in his mouth; and he shall speak unto them all that I shall command him."
Deut. 18:19	"And it shall come to pass, that **whosoever will not hearken unto my words which he shall speak in my name, I will require it of him**."

Therefore, believing on him whom God has sent also means to believe the faithful witness of all of the prophetic messengers (**Amos 3:7** and **Eph. 4:11–13**) that are ordained and sent by God. The Hebrew word *aw-men* is translated into two English words in the Old Testament: *believe* and *faith*. Because of this, the ability to correctly identify, believe, and have faith (or *aw-men*), the witness of God in His ordained or sent messengers is one of the primary works that God does.

The manna that Israel ate (partook of) in the desert for forty years is called the "bread from heaven," and the Lord Jesus tells us the deeper meaning that the manna symbolized.

John 6:30	"They said therefore unto him, What sign showest thou then, that we may see, and believe thee? what dost thou work?"
John 6:31	"Our fathers did eat manna in the desert; as it is written, He gave them **bread from heaven** to eat."

John 6:32	"Then Jesus said unto them, Verily, verily, I say unto you, Moses gave you not **that** bread from heaven; but my Father giveth you the **true bread** from heaven."

By this, He showed that the manna was *symbolic* of something that was a greater fulfilment. What "**true bread**" was He talking about?

John 6:27	"Labour not for the meat which perisheth, **but for that meat which endureth unto everlasting life**, which the Son of man shall give unto you: for him hath God the Father sealed."
John 6:33	"For the **bread** of God is **he which cometh down from heaven**, and giveth life unto the world."
John 6:34	"Then said they unto him, Lord, evermore give us this **bread**."
John 6:35	"And Jesus said unto them, **I am** the **bread** of life: he that **cometh** to me shall never hunger; and he that **believeth** on me shall never thirst."
John 6:36	"But I said unto you, That ye also have seen me, and believe not."
John 6:37	"All that the Father giveth me shall come to me; and him that cometh to me I will in no wise cast out."

John 6:38	"For **I came down from heaven**, not to do mine own will, but the will of him that sent me."
John 6:39	"And this is the Father's will which hath sent me, that of all which he hath given me I should lose nothing, but should raise it up again at the last day."
John 6:40	"And this is the will of him that sent me, that every one which seeth the Son, and **believeth** on him, may have everlasting life: and I will raise him up at the last day."
John 6:41	"The Jews then murmured at him, because he said, **I am the bread** which came down from heaven."
John 6:42	"And they said, Is not this Jesus, the son of Joseph, whose father and mother we know? how is it then that he saith, I came down from heaven?"
John 6:43	"Jesus therefore answered and said unto them, Murmur not among yourselves."
John 6:44	"No man can come to me, except the Father which hath sent me draw him: and I will raise him up at the last day."
John 6:45	"It is written in the prophets, And they shall be all taught of God. Every man therefore that hath heard, **and**

hath learned of the Father, cometh unto me."

John 6:46 "Not that any man hath seen the Father, save he which is of God, he hath seen the Father."

John 6:47 "Verily, verily, I say unto you, He that **believeth** on me hath everlasting life."

John 6:48 "I am that **bread** of life."

John 6:49 "Your fathers did eat manna in the wilderness, and are dead."

John 6:50 "This is the **bread** which cometh down from heaven, that a man may eat thereof, and not die."

John 6:51 "I am the **living bread** which came down from heaven: if any man eat of this **bread**, he shall live for ever: and the **bread** that I will give is my flesh, which I will give for the life of the world."

John 6:52 "The Jews therefore strove among themselves, saying, How can this man give us his flesh to eat?"

John 6:53 "Then Jesus said unto them, Verily, verily, I say unto you, Except ye eat the flesh of the Son of man, and drink his blood, ye have no life in you."

John 6:54	"Whoso eateth my flesh, and drinketh my blood, hath eternal life; and I will raise him up at the last day."
John 6:55	"For my flesh is meat indeed, and my blood is drink indeed."
John 6:56	"He that eateth my flesh, and drinketh my blood, dwelleth in me, and I in him."
John 6:57	"As the living Father hath sent me, and I live by the Father: so he that eateth me, even he shall live by me."
John 6:58	"This is that **bread** which came down from heaven: not as your fathers did eat manna, and are dead: he that eateth of this **bread** shall live for ever."

What is the "bread of life?" It is the living Word of God made flesh, Emmanuel, Yeshua the Redeemer, and the atonement for the sins of the world! He is the perfect sacrifice, the bread from heaven, the Word made flesh and the atonement! According to **verse 53** above, if we do not partake of the Word of God in a way that makes it to live in and through us, then we have no life in us. Why is this so? Because the ONLY life that can make the Word of God to live in us is HIS Life, and ONLY HIS Life is eternal Life.

Through all of this, we can see that the pouring out of the Holy Spirit on the day of the Feast of Weeks (Pentecost) was not a separate event from the death, burial, and resurrection, but rather, it was the very purpose that it all had to happen for. It was there (in the upper room) that the innocent Spirit of Life (the Ruach Ha Kodesh—Spirit of Holiness) that was in Him and in His blood began to impart to the believers the same innocence of sin (Holiness) that was in Him.

Acts 2:1 "And when the day of Pentecost was fully come, they were all with one accord in one place."

Acts 2:2 "And suddenly there came a sound from heaven as of a rushing mighty wind, and it filled all the house where they were sitting."

Acts 2:3 "And there appeared unto them cloven tongues like as of fire, and **it sat upon each of them**."

Acts 2:4 "And they were all **filled with the Holy Ghost**, and began to speak with other tongues, as the Spirit gave them utterance."

Acts 2:5 "And there were dwelling at Jerusalem Jews, devout men, out of every nation under heaven."

Acts 2:6 "Now when this was noised abroad, the multitude came together, and were confounded, because that every man heard them speak in his own language."

Acts 2:7 "And they were all amazed and marvelled, saying one to another, Behold, are not all these which speak Galilaeans?"

Acts 2:8	"And how hear we every man in our own tongue, wherein we were born?"
Acts 2:9	"Parthians, and Medes, and Elamites, and the dwellers in Mesopotamia, and in Judaea, and Cappadocia, in Pontus, and Asia."
Acts 2:10	"Phrygia, and Pamphylia, in Egypt, and in the parts of Libya about Cyrene, and strangers of Rome, Jews and proselytes."
Acts 2:11	"Cretes and Arabians, we do hear them speak in our tongues the wonderful works of God."
Acts 2:12	"And they were all amazed, and were in doubt, saying one to another, What meaneth this?"

It means that the way to absolute innocence of sin, as Adam was in the beginning before the fall, has been opened by a perfect atonement! It is by salvation that redeems, Yeshua the Redeemer, the Messiah, the Lord Jesus Christ, our atonement, the perfect sacrifice, and the life that was in His blood **is** that Spirit (Holy Spirit, Ruach Ha Kodesh) which comes upon the worshipper to impart His own innocence of sin (holiness, kodesh). It is the Word made flesh and that is **still** being made flesh, but now **in** us! ONLY *that* life is eternal life. This is the way that the will of God as it is in heaven is to be done in earth, in the earth of our flesh, but by the supernatural working of the Spirit of His life that was in the blood of our atonement.

The Contents of the Ark Symbolize the Word of God and Produce Supernaturally Empowered Joyful Obedience.

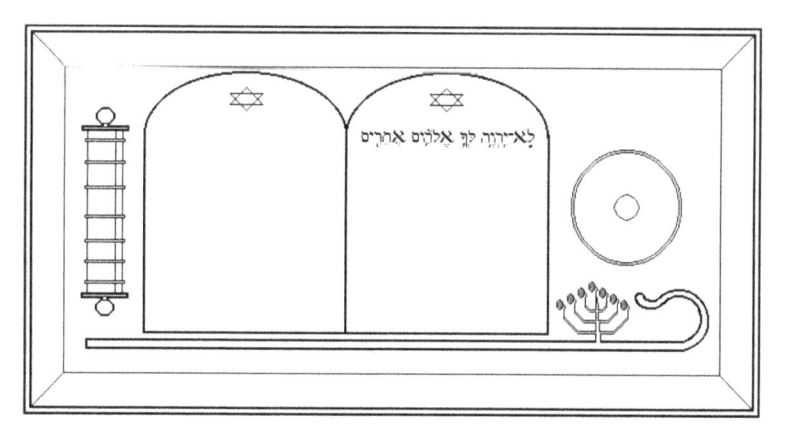

Drawing #12

CHAPTER 9

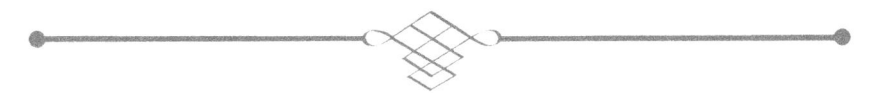

The Contents of the Ark

The Ark of the Covenant contained several items. The exact number of items and what they were is sometimes the subject of heated debate. In order to understand just what was inside the Ark of the Covenant, it is necessary to understand how a common phrase was used. The phrase was to put something "before" the Lord.

Sometimes, this meant that an object was placed in the Tabernacle in such a way that as one proceeds from outside of the Tabernacle toward the Mercy Seat, these objects were encountered "before" arriving at the Mercy Seat. Because the Mercy Seat was also known as the place where the Lord dwelt (**1 Sam. 4:4**; **2 Sam. 6:2**; **1 Chr. 13:6**), it was synonymous to say "before the Mercy Seat" and to say "before the Lord." The following are examples of the use of this phrase, "before the Lord," that show that it also could mean "inside" of the Ark of the Covenant. They are also scriptures that show that there were actually five things that were *inside* the Ark of the Covenant.

The General Commandment

Exo. 25:16 "And thou shalt put **into the ark** the **testimony** which I shall give thee."

Exo. 25:21 "And thou shalt put the mercy seat above upon the ark; and **in the ark** thou shalt put the **testimony** that I shall give thee."

The Pot of Manna

Exo. 16:33 "And Moses said unto Aaron, Take a **pot**, and put an omer full of **manna** therein, and lay it up **before the LORD**, to be kept for your generations."

Exo. 16:34 "As the **LORD commanded** Moses, so Aaron laid it up **before the Testimony**, to be kept."

Heb. 9:2 "For there was a tabernacle made; the first, wherein was the candlestick, and the table, and the shewbread; which is called the sanctuary."

Heb. 9:3 "And after the second veil, the tabernacle which is called the **Holiest of all**."

Heb. 9:4 "Which had the golden censer, and **the ark of the covenant** overlaid round about with gold, **wherein was the golden pot that had manna**, and Aaron's rod that budded, and the tables of the covenant."

The Rod of Aaron

Num. 17:7 "And Moses **laid up the rods before the LORD** in the tabernacle of witness."

Num. 17:8	"And it came to pass, that on the morrow Moses went into the tabernacle of witness; and, behold, the **rod** of Aaron for the house of Levi was budded, and brought forth buds, and bloomed blossoms, and yielded **almonds**."
Num. 17:9	"And Moses brought out all **the rods from before the LORD** unto all the children of Israel: and they looked, and took every man his rod."
Num. 17:10	"And the LORD said unto Moses, Bring Aaron's **rod again before the testimony**, to be kept for a token against the rebels; and thou shalt quite take away their murmurings from me, that they die not."
Num. 17:11	"And Moses did so: as the **LORD commanded** him, so did he."

We see that in **Num. 17:10,** the words *again* and *before* have the following meanings: The rod was placed "again" in the same place where it was earlier, and that place was "before" the LORD. When we examine this use of the word *before* (**Exo. 16:34**) and compare it with the following verse, we can prove that "before" meant *inside* of the ark.

Heb. 9:4	"Which had the golden censer, and the ark of the covenant overlaid round about with gold, **wherein** was the golden pot that had manna, and **Aaron's rod that budded**, and the tables of the covenant."

The Stone Tablets

Exo. 31:18 "And he gave unto Moses, when he had made an end of communing with him upon mount Sinai, **two tables of testimony, tables of stone**, written with the finger of God."

Exo. 32:15 "And Moses turned, and went down from the mount, and the **two tables of the testimony** were in his hand: the tables were written on both their sides; on the one side and on the other were they written."

Exo. 34:29 "And it came to pass, when Moses came down from mount Sinai with the **two tables of testimony** in Moses' hand, when he came down from the mount, that Moses wist not that the skin of his face shone while he talked with him."

Exo. 40:20 "And he took and put **the testimony into the ark**, and set the staves on the ark, and put the mercy seat above upon the ark."

Deut. 9:9 "When I was gone up into the mount to receive the **tables of stone**, even the **tables of the covenant** which the LORD made with you, then I abode in the mount forty days and forty nights, I neither did eat bread nor drink water."

Deut. 9:11	"And it came to pass at the end of forty days and forty nights, that the LORD gave me the **two tables of stone**, even **the tables of the covenant**."
Deut. 9:15	"So I turned and came down from the mount, and the mount burned with fire: and the **two tables of the covenant** were in my two hands."
Deut. 10:5	"And I turned myself and came down from the mount, and **put the tables in the ark** which I had made; and there they be, as the **LORD commanded me**."
1 Kings 8:6	"And the priests brought in the **ark of the covenant** of the LORD unto his place, into the oracle of the house, to the most holy place, even under the wings of the cherubims."
1 Kings 8:21	"And I have set there a place for the ark, **wherein is the covenant** of the LORD, which he made with our fathers, when he brought them out of the land of Egypt."
2 Chr. 6:11	"And in it have I put **the ark, wherein is the covenant** of the LORD, that he made with the children of Israel."

It is interesting to note that the stone tablets of the Ten Commandments were referred to with six different terms: the testimony, the tables of stone, the tables of testimony, the tables of the covenant, the tables, and the covenant.

The Book of the Law

Deut. 31:24 "And it came to pass, when Moses had made an end of **writing the words of this law in a book**, until they were finished."

Deut. 31:25 "That Moses commanded the Levites, which bare the ark of the covenant of the LORD, saying."

Deut. 31:26 "**Take this book of the law, and put it in the side of the ark of the covenant of the LORD your God**, that it may be there for a witness against thee."

Some of the Items Listed

Heb. 9:4 "Which had the golden censer, and the **ark of the covenant** overlaid round about with gold, **wherein** was the golden pot that had **manna**, and Aaron's **rod** that **budded**, and the **tables** of the covenant."

Almonds

Num. 17:8 "And it came to pass, that on the morrow Moses went into the tabernacle of witness; and, behold, the

	rod of Aaron for the house of Levi was budded, and brought forth **buds**, and bloomed blossoms, and yielded **almonds**."
Num. 17:10	"And the LORD said unto Moses, Bring Aaron's **rod again before the testimony**, to be kept for a token against the rebels; and thou shalt quite take away their murmurings from me, that they die not."

Even though the term *testimony* (**Exo. 25:16,21**) originally referred to the pillar of fire, all of the items that were placed into the ark were put there as a witness and testimony of the covenant between God and man. Four of the five types of objects that were inside of the Ark of the Covenant were put there by the hand of man (**Eph. 4:11**) as they were commanded by God. The fifth item was put there supernaturally by God Himself, the **almonds**.

Also note that the very reason for the rod to be put inside of the ark again is because of the almonds and how they give witness to the supernatural power and work of God. The contents all symbolize the Word of God in some way and all relate to the promise of the New Covenant to living epistles and to **Matt. 10:16**.

Jer. 31:31	"Behold, the days come, saith the LORD, that I will make a **new covenant** with the house of Israel, and with the house of Judah."
Jer. 31:32	"**Not according to the covenant that I made with their fathers** in the day that I took them by the hand to bring them out of the land of Egypt; which my covenant they

	brake, although I was an husband unto them, saith the LORD."
Jer. 31:33	"But **this shall be the covenant** that I will make with the house of Israel; After those days, saith the LORD, **I will put my law in their inward parts, and write it in their hearts**; and will be their God, and they shall be my people."

As we have already seen, the Holy of Holies is the heart and the Ark of the Covenant was in the Holy of Holies. Therefore, to recognize that each of the items in the Ark of the Covenant symbolize the word of God is to recognize that we are talking about the New Covenant being written in our hearts, and this was all symbolized from the time that the Tabernacle was first made. This is further referred to in the following scriptures.

Prov. 3:3	"Let not mercy and truth forsake thee: bind them about thy neck; write them upon the **table of thine heart**."

From this verse and **Jer. 31:31–33,** we can see that the Law of God is referred to as **"mercy"** and "truth."

Prov. 7:3	"Bind them upon thy fingers, write them upon the **table of thine heart**."
2 Cor. 3:3	"Forasmuch as ye are manifestly declared to be the epistle of Christ ministered by us, written not with ink, but with the Spirit of the living God; not in tables of stone, but in fleshly **tables of the heart**."

Heb. 8:6	"But now hath he obtained a more excellent ministry, by how much also he is the mediator of a better **covenant**, which was established upon better promises."
Heb. 8:7	"For if that **first covenant** had been faultless, then should no place have been sought for the **second**."
Heb. 8:8	"For finding fault with them, he saith, Behold, the days come, saith the Lord, when I will make a **new covenant** with the house of Israel and with the house of Judah."
Heb. 8:9	"Not according to the **covenant** that I made with their fathers in the day when I took them by the hand to lead them out of the land of Egypt; because they continued not in my **covenant**, and I regarded them not, saith the Lord."
Heb. 8:10	"For this is the **covenant** that I will make with the house of Israel after those days, saith the Lord; **I will put my laws into their mind, and write them in their hearts**: and I will be to them a God, and they shall be to me a people."
Heb. 8:13	"In that he saith, A new **covenant**, he hath made the first old. Now that which decayeth and waxeth old is ready to vanish away."

Heb. 9:1 "Then verily the first **covenant** had also ordinances of divine service, and a worldly sanctuary."

Heb. 9:4 "Which had the golden censer, and the ark of the **covenant** overlaid round about with gold, wherein was the golden pot that had manna, and Aaron's rod that budded, and the tables of the **covenant**."

Heb. 10:16 "This is the **covenant** that I will make with them after those days, saith the Lord, **I will put my laws into their hearts, and in their minds will I write them**."

Heb. 10:29 "Of how much sorer punishment, suppose ye, shall he be thought worthy, who hath trodden under foot the Son of God, and hath counted the **blood** of the **covenant**, wherewith he was sanctified, an unholy thing, and hath done despite unto the **Spirit** of grace?"

Heb. 12:24 "And to Jesus the mediator of the **new covenant**, and to the blood of sprinkling, that speaketh better things than that of Abel."

Heb. 13:20 "Now the God of peace, that brought again from the dead our Lord Jesus, that great shepherd of the sheep, through the blood of the **everlasting covenant**."

Notice in **Heb. 10:29,** the reference to the "blood" and the "Spirit," and refer to the previous chapter about perfect and imperfect sacrifices.

Now we will consider how each of these items relate to ourselves. First, the stone tablets of the Ten Commandments.

Something that is "written in stone" is something that is unchangeable; however, even though God will write His laws upon our hearts as unchangeable as though it were written in stone, He has promised:

Eze. 11:19	"And I will give them **one heart**, and I will put a new spirit within you; and I will take the **stony heart** out of their flesh, and will give them an **heart of flesh**."
Eze. 36:26	"A **new heart** also will I give you, and a new spirit will I put within you: and I will take away the **stony heart** out of your flesh, and I will give you an **heart of flesh**."
Jer. 31:31	"Behold, the days come, saith the LORD, that I will make a **new covenant** with the house of Israel, and with the house of Judah."
Jer. 31:32	"**Not according to the covenant that I made with their fathers** in the day that I took them by the hand to bring them out of the land of Egypt; which my covenant they brake, although I was an husband unto them, saith the LORD."

Jer. 31:33 "But **this shall be the covenant** that I will make with the house of Israel; After those days, saith the LORD, **I will put my law in their inward parts, and write it in their hearts**; and will be their God, and they shall be my people."

This is a way of saying that the law will be unchangeable within our hearts while at the same time as being tenderhearted.

The book (scrolls) of the law was written on parchment (animal skins, usually sheepskin), but now it is written on a different kind of flesh and by the Spirit of the Lamb of God as sheep of His sheepfold.

1 Cor. 3:3 "Forasmuch as ye are manifestly declared to be the epistle of Christ ministered by us, written not with ink, but with the **Spirit of the living God**; not in tables of stone, but in **fleshly tables of the heart**."

Heb. 10:16 "This is the **covenant** that I will make with them after those days, saith the Lord, **I will put my laws into their hearts, and in their minds will I write them**."

Heb. 10:17 "And their sins and iniquities will I remember no more."

Manna is symbolic of a daily portion that is given fresh and new every day. Remember that there was a portion that was hidden away inside of the Ark of the Covenant and which was kept fresh and new continually by the Shekinah (the glory of the presence of God).

Rev. 2:17	"He that hath an ear, let him hear what the Spirit saith unto the churches; **To him that overcometh** will I give to **eat** of the **hidden manna**, and will give him a white stone, and in the stone a new name written, which no man knoweth saving he that receiveth it."

God will give to those who overcome to eat or partake of the hidden manna. This also refers to the portion of the Lord's prayer, which He taught to the Apostles (**Luke 6:11**).

Matt. 6:10	"**Thy kingdom come**. Thy will be done in earth, as it is in heaven."
Matt. 6:11	"**Give us this day our daily bread.**"

But what is the overcoming that is being spoken about? The key to overcoming is in the phrase "Thy **kingdom** come." Remember that God said:

Zech. 4:6	"Then he answered and spake unto me, saying, This is the word of the LORD unto Zerubbabel, saying, **Not by might, nor by power, but by my spirit**, saith the LORD of hosts."

How do we reconcile that we overcome "by the Spirit of God" together with overcoming by the "blood of the Lamb?"

Rev. 12:10	"And I heard a loud voice saying in heaven, Now is come salvation, and strength, and the kingdom of our God, and the power of his Christ:

for the accuser of our brethren is cast down, which accused them before our God day and night."

Rev. 12:11 "And they **overcame** him by the **blood of the Lamb**, and by the word of their testimony; and they loved not their lives unto the death."

It is because the Spirit of God is the life that is in the blood of the Lamb of God.

Acts 20:28 "Take heed therefore unto yourselves, and to all the flock, over the which the Holy Ghost hath made you overseers, to feed the church of **God**, which **he** hath purchased with **his own blood**."

When we get the correct approach to the throne of God by offering the incense of humility before Him and stay there long enough for "He who is the overcomer" to be seated on His rightful throne in our hearts, He will establish His throne and kingdom in all of our being and make us to be overcomers also together with Him.

Therefore, it is not by our power and might. As He *also* said:

Zech. 4:6 "Then he answered and spake unto me, saying, This is the word of the LORD unto Zerubbabel, saying, **Not by might, nor by power, but by my spirit**, saith the LORD of hosts."

John 15:5 "I am the vine, ye are the branches: He that abideth in me, and I in him, the same bringeth forth much fruit: for **without me ye can do nothing**."

Matt. 19:26 "But Jesus beheld them, and said unto them, With men this is impossible; **but with God all things are possible**."

Mark 10:27 "And Jesus looking upon them saith, With men it is impossible, but not with God: for **with God all things are possible**."

Therefore, by coming into a place of intimacy with Him by humility and remaining there, we have access to partake of a daily portion of divinely given revelation of the true bread of life that came down from heaven. That revelation is not something that is only given *to* us, but when it has been correctly received, it will manifest the reality of its living power *through* us. This is given so that He can put His majesty and glory on display.

Isa. 43:7 "Even every one that is called by my name: for I have created him for my glory, I have formed him; yea, I have made him."

That display that is the supernatural working of God's own obedience in and through us is the only way that the promise to Abraham can be fulfilled.

Gen. 22:18 "And **in thy seed shall all the nations of the earth be blessed**; because thou hast **obeyed** my voice."

Gen. 26:4 "And I will make thy seed to multiply as the stars of heaven, and will give unto thy seed all these countries; and **in thy seed shall all the nations of the earth be blessed.**"

Gen. 28:14 "And thy seed shall be as the dust of the earth, and thou shalt spread abroad to the west, and to the east, and to the north, and to the south: and in thee and **in thy seed shall all the families of the earth be blessed.**"

Psa. 112:2 "His seed shall be mighty upon earth: **the generation of the upright shall be blessed.**"

Isa. 61:9 "And their seed shall be known among the Gentiles, and their offspring among the people: all that see them shall acknowledge them, that **they are the seed which the LORD hath blessed.**"

Isa. 65:23 "They shall not labour in vain, nor bring forth for trouble; for **they are the seed of the blessed of the LORD**, and their offspring with them."

Acts 3:25 "Ye are the children of the prophets, and of the covenant which God made with our fathers, saying unto Abraham, And **in thy seed shall all the kindreds of the earth be blessed.**"

How are we "the children of the prophets and of the covenant?" Just as Abraham was in the beginning because of obeying (through submission and the incense of humility) the voice (prophets) of the Lord as it is written:

> **2 Chr. 20:20** "And they rose early in the morning, and went forth into the wilderness of Tekoa: and as they went forth, Jehoshaphat stood and said, Hear me, O Judah, and ye inhabitants of Jerusalem; **Believe in the LORD your God, so shall ye be established; believe his prophets, so shall ye prosper.**"

In this, we recognize that *being* a blessing is greater than receiving a blessing, because *being* a blessing includes receiving, and it is through *being* a blessing that we are established as a house that is built upon a solid rock and prosper to the blessing of nations through His supernaturally manifested obedience working in and through us.

A rod is symbolic of discipline. The rod of Aaron was not a stick that was over two meters long like many people imagine. Remember that it had to be short enough to be placed inside of the Ark of the Covenant which was two and one half cubits long, a distance of about one and a third meters measured on the outside.

The rod of Aaron was made out of the wood from an almond tree. The Hebrew word for almond is *shaw-kad* and means "alert" or "watchful," and it was the earliest of all of the fruit trees to bloom or that which **hastened** to bloom first. This rod of **discipline** that **hastened** to bring forth **fruit** in just one night in the presence of the Shekinah is a symbolic reference to the first part of **Hebrews chapter 12**:

> **Heb. 12:11** "Now no **chastening** for the present seemeth to be joyous, but grievous: nevertheless afterward it yieldeth

the peaceable **fruit of righteousness** unto them which are exercised thereby."

It is also the item and the context of being inside of the ark that was being referred to in the following verses.

Jer. 1:11 "Moreover the word of the LORD came unto me, saying, Jeremiah, what seest thou? And I said, I see a **rod of an almond tree**."

Jer. 1:12 "Then said the LORD unto me, Thou hast well seen: for I will **hasten** my word to **perform** it."

Please note that the rod of correction must be administered in the correct context in order for it to produce fruit. The rod of Aaron remained just a dead dry stick until it came into the presence of the Shekinah. If discipline is administered in any other context, then it will fulfill the scripture that says:

2 Cor. 3:6 "Who also hath made us able ministers of the new testament; not of the letter, but of the spirit: for **the letter killeth, but the spirit giveth life**."

When that same rod is brought into the Shekinah, then the letter that killeth will spring forth into life and produce fruit, and according to the book of Hebrews, it is the fruit of righteousness.

We know that our own righteousnesses are as filthy rags (**Isaiah 46:6**); therefore, the righteousness that is being spoken about must be the righteousness of God or the train of His robes that fill the temple which we are.

> **Isa. 6:1** "In the year that king Uzziah died I saw also the Lord sitting upon a throne, high and lifted up, and **his train filled the temple**."

It is also the skins that we must be covered with so that the shame of our nakedness will not appear.

> **Rev. 3:18** "I counsel thee to **buy of me** gold tried in the fire, that thou mayest be rich; and **white raiment**, that thou mayest **be clothed**, and that the **shame of thy nakedness do not appear**; and anoint thine eyes with eyesalve, that thou mayest see."

The price that we pay is to humble ourselves to God and allow Him to produce His character and nature in us until we have been disciplined and discipled enough for His righteousness to be as natural and automatic as the skin that we are clothed with. If we respond to the discipline with a humble heart, then it will hasten to produce the fruit of the righteousness of God in us, just as He said in **Jer. 1:11–12**.

> **Jer. 1:11** "Moreover the word of the LORD came unto me, saying, Jeremiah, what seest thou? And I said, I see a rod of an **almond** tree."

> **Jer. 1:12** "Then said the LORD unto me, Thou hast well seen: for I will **hasten** my **word** to perform it."

Note that **He** is the one who *hastens* it to perform it, but **we** are the ones that He will fulfill it in and through. The word *hasten* in **Jer. 1:12** is also a reference to **Rom. 9:28**.

>**Rom. 9:28** "For he will finish the work, and cut it short in righteousness: because a short work will the Lord make upon the earth."

He brings this to our attention in a very specific way in these two verses (**Jer. 1:11–12**). As we have seen, the Hebrew word for almond is *shaw-kad*, and the word for hasten is *shaw-ked*. In Hebrew, the only difference between the two words is the location of a single "jot" or "tittle" which signifies either the vowel "a" or "e" depending upon the placement. Therefore, at the same time that He is telling us that the obedience is His obedience that He will perform in and through us, He is also showing us the importance of every "jot" and "tittle" of His word.

>**Matt. 5:18** "For verily I say unto you, **Till heaven and earth pass, one jot or one tittle shall in no wise pass from the law, till all be fulfilled**."

He is the one that by His Spirit will **hasten** the fulfillment of His word in us. For those who want to take the attitude that the only fulfillment that is necessary is that which He has already done, you only need to look at the very next verse to see that this is not true.

>**Matt. 5:19** "**Whosoever** therefore shall break one of these least commandments, and shall teach men so, he shall be called the **least** in the kingdom of heaven: but **whosoever** shall do and teach them, the same shall be called **great** in the kingdom of heaven."

But how do we do them? By humbling ourselves before God so profoundly that **He** is the one who performs it in and through us. It is because of this that the following can be said:

Obedience depends upon surrender, not on effort. If we need a greater obedience, this only shows us that we need to surrender more to God. If we want to put forth an effort in order to become more obedient, then that effort should be directed into surrendering more. How do we know that we are surrendering enough? When the obedience that is being manifested in and through us is supernaturally empowered because of it being **Him** in us producing it. This is how we overcome by His Spirit, might, and power, and this is how we obtain the victory. Many people have commented about how difficult this is; the response is, how much do you love him?

John 14:15	"If ye **love** me, **keep** my commandments."
John 14:23	"Jesus answered and said unto him, If a man **love** me, he will **keep** my words: and my Father will love him, and we will come unto him, and make our abode with him."
John 15:10	"If ye **keep** my commandments, ye shall abide in my **love**; even as I have kept my Father's commandments, and abide in his love."
1 John 5:2	"By this we know that we **love** the children of God, when we **love** God, and **keep** his commandments."
1 John 5:3	"For this is the **love** of God, that we **keep** his commandments: and his commandments are **not grievous**."
Jude 1:21	"Keep yourselves in the **love** of God, looking for the mercy of our Lord Jesus Christ unto eternal life."

As our love for Him becomes more profound and passionate, then the obedience will become easier and will come more quickly (hasten). This happens as we offer the incense of humility before His throne in our hearts as a continual ordinance.

The Same Thing that Was the "Mercy Seat" with the Blood of the Atonement Upon It Became a Judgment seat When the Blood was not Current and How the Atonement was not Only for Israel, but for All Nations

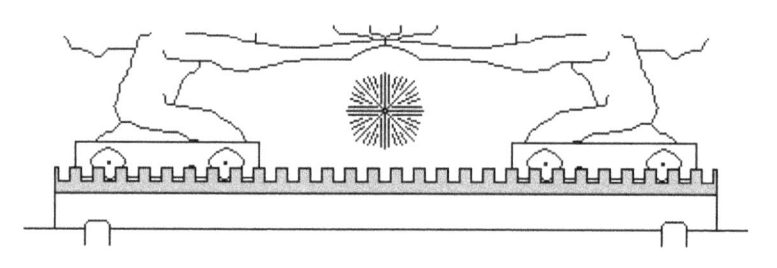

Drawing #13

CHAPTER 10

The Throne of Mercy and Judgment

Many people think that when the atonement was offered in the temple that it was only for the sins of the nation of Israel. However, there is scriptural evidence to show that this was not the case. In fact, when the atonement was made, it covered the sins of the whole world, whether they knew about it or not. At the same time, we will see that the Mercy Seat was only a mercy seat while the blood of the atonement was less than one year old upon it. After the blood of the atonement was on the Mercy Seat for more than one year, then the Mercy Seat became a judgment seat. It is for this reason that the incense that gave witness to the blood of the new atonement was necessary and had to precede the high priest when he went into the Holy of Holies.

1 Sam. 4:1 "And the word of Samuel came to all Israel. Now Israel went out against the Philistines to battle, and pitched beside Ebenezer: and the Philistines pitched in Aphek."

1 Sam. 4:2 "And the Philistines put themselves in array against Israel: and when they joined battle, Israel was smitten before the Philistines: and they slew of the army in the field about four thousand men."

1 Sam. 4:3	"And when the people were come into the camp, the elders of Israel said, Wherefore hath the LORD smitten us to day before the Philistines? Let us fetch the **ark of the covenant** of the LORD out of Shiloh unto us, that, when it cometh among us, it may save us out of the hand of our enemies."
1 Sam. 4:4	"So the people sent to Shiloh, that they might bring from thence **the ark of the covenant** of the LORD of hosts, which dwelleth between the cherubims: and the two sons of Eli, Hophni and Phinehas, were there with the **ark of the covenant** of God."
1 Sam. 4:5	"And when the **ark of the covenant** of the LORD came into the camp, all Israel shouted with a great shout, so that the earth rang again."
1 Sam. 4:6	"And when the Philistines heard the noise of the shout, they said, What meaneth the noise of this great shout in the camp of the Hebrews? And they understood that the **ark of the LORD** was come into the camp."
1 Sam. 4:7	"And the Philistines were afraid, for they said, God is come into the camp. And they said, Woe unto us! for there hath not been such a thing heretofore."

1 Sam. 4:8	"Woe unto us! who shall deliver us out of the hand of these mighty Gods? these are the Gods that smote the Egyptians with all the plagues in the wilderness."
1 Sam. 4:9	"Be strong, and quit yourselves like men, O ye Philistines, that ye be not servants unto the Hebrews, as they have been to you: quit yourselves like men, and fight."
1 Sam. 4:10	"And the Philistines fought, and Israel was smitten, and they fled every man into his tent: and there was a very great slaughter; for there fell of Israel thirty thousand footmen."
1 Sam. 4:11	"And the **ark of God** was taken; and the two sons of Eli, Hophni and Phinehas, were slain."

Note that the Philistines touched the Ark to carry it away and that they did not die the instant that they touched it.

1 Sam. 4:12	"And there ran a man of Benjamin out of the army, and came to Shiloh the same day with his clothes rent, and with earth upon his head."
1 Sam. 4:13	"And when he came, lo, Eli sat upon a seat by the wayside watching: for his heart trembled for the ark of God. And when the man came into the city, and told it, all the city cried out."

1 Sam. 4:14	"And when Eli heard the noise of the crying, he said, What meaneth the noise of this tumult? And the man came in hastily, and told Eli."
1 Sam. 4:15	"Now Eli was ninety and eight years old; and his eyes were dim, that he could not see."
1 Sam. 4:16	"And the man said unto Eli, I am he that came out of the army, and I fled to day out of the army. And he said, What is there done, my son?"
1 Sam. 4:17	"And the messenger answered and said, Israel is fled before the Philistines, and there hath been also a great slaughter among the people, and thy two sons also, Hophni and Phinehas, are dead, and the **ark of God** is taken."
1 Sam. 4:18	"And it came to pass, when he made mention of the **ark of God**, that he fell from off the seat backward by the side of the gate, and his neck brake, and he died: for he was an old man, and heavy. And he had judged Israel forty years."
1 Sam. 4:19	"And his daughter in law, Phinehas' wife, was with child, near to be delivered: and when she heard the tidings that the **ark of God** was taken, and that her father in law and her husband were dead, she bowed herself

and travailed; for her pains came upon her."

1 Sam. 4:20 "And about the time of her death the women that stood by her said unto her, Fear not; for thou hast borne a son. But she answered not, neither did she regard it."

1 Sam. 4:21 "And she named the child Ichabod, saying, The glory is departed from Israel: because the **ark of God** was taken, and because of her father in law and her husband."

1 Sam. 4:22 "And she said, The glory is departed from Israel: for the **ark of God** is taken."

First Samuel chapter 5 describes the plagues that happened to the Philistines, but in **1 Sam. 6:2–12,** they recognized that the Ark was not in its rightful place. By the context, we can see that even the Philistines recognized that the plagues that were falling upon them were falling, because the Ark was not in its place. Also, we can see in **verse one** that it was among the Philistines for only seven months, a time that was short enough for the blood to still be current upon the Mercy Seat.

1 Sam. 6:1 "And the **ark of the LORD** was in the country of the Philistines **seven months**."

1 Sam. 6:2 "And the Philistines called for the priests and the diviners, saying, What shall we do to the **ark of the**

1 Sam. 6:3 LORD? tell us wherewith we shall send it **to his place**."

1 Sam. 6:3 "And they said, If ye send away the **ark of the God of Israel**, send it not empty; but in any wise return him a trespass offering: then ye shall be healed, and it shall be known to you why his hand is not removed from you."

1 Sam. 6:4 "Then said they, What shall be the trespass offering which we shall return to him? They answered, Five golden emerods, and five golden mice, according to the number of the lords of the Philistines: for one plague was on you all, and on your lords."

1 Sam. 6:5 "Wherefore ye shall make images of your emerods, and images of your mice that mar the land; and ye shall give glory unto the God of Israel: peradventure he will lighten his hand from off you, and from off your gods, and from off your land."

1 Sam. 6:6 "Wherefore then do ye harden your hearts, as the Egyptians and Pharaoh hardened their hearts? when he had wrought wonderfully among them, did they not let the people go, and they departed?"

1 Sam. 6:7   "Now therefore make a new cart, and take two milch kine, on which there hath come no yoke, and tie the kine to the cart, and bring their calves home from them."

1 Sam. 6:8   "And take the **ark of the LORD**, and lay it upon the cart; and put the jewels of gold, which ye return him for a trespass offering, in a coffer by the side thereof; and send it away, that it may go."

1 Sam. 6:9   "And see, if it goeth up by the way of his own coast to Bethshemesh, then he hath done us this great evil: but if not, then we shall know that it is not his hand that smote us: it was a chance that happened to us."

1 Sam. 6:10   "And the men did so; and took two milch kine, and tied them to the cart, and shut up their calves at home."

1 Sam. 6:11   "And they laid the **ark of the LORD** upon the cart, and the coffer with the mice of gold and the images of their emerods."

1 Sam. 6:12   "And the kine took the straight way to the way of Bethshemesh, and went along the highway, lowing as they went, and turned not aside to the right hand or to the left; and the lords of the Philistines

went after them unto the border of Bethshemesh."

1 Sam. 6:13 "And they of Bethshemesh were reaping their wheat harvest in the valley: and they lifted up their eyes, and saw the **ark**, and rejoiced to see it."

1 Sam. 6:14 "And the cart came into the field of Joshua, a Bethshemite, and stood there, where there was a great stone: and they clave the wood of the cart, and offered the kine a burnt offering unto the LORD."

1 Sam. 6:15 "And the Levites took down the **ark of the LORD**, and the coffer that was with it, wherein the jewels of gold were, and put them on the great stone: and the men of Bethshemesh offered burnt offerings and sacrificed sacrifices the same day unto the LORD."

They did not die the instant that they touched the Ark. In **verse 19,** the plague that came upon Bethshemesh was because "**they had looked into the ark of the LORD**;" Again, it was not because they touched it, but because they did not treat it with the reverence and respect that it deserved.

1 Sam. 6:16 "And when the five lords of the Philistines had seen it, they returned to Ekron the same day."

1 Sam. 6:17 "And these are the golden emerods which the Philistines returned for a trespass offering unto the LORD; for Ashdod one, for Gaza one, for Askelon one, for Gath one, for Ekron one."

1 Sam. 6:18 "And the golden mice, according to the number of all the cities of the Philistines belonging to the five lords, both of fenced cities, and of country villages, even unto the great stone of Abel, whereon they set down the **ark of the LORD**: which stone remaineth unto this day in the field of Joshua, the Bethshemite."

1 Sam. 6:19 "And he smote the men of Bethshemesh, **because they had looked into the ark of the LORD**, even he smote of the people fifty thousand and threescore and ten men: and the people lamented, because the LORD had smitten many of the people with a great slaughter."

1 Sam. 6:20 "And the men of Bethshemesh said, Who is able to stand before this holy LORD God? and to whom shall he go up from us?"

1 Sam. 6:21 "And they sent messengers to the inhabitants of Kirjathjearim, saying, The Philistines have brought

	again the **ark of the LORD**; come ye down, and fetch it up to you."
1 Sam. 7:1	"And the men of Kirjathjearim came, and fetched up the **ark of the LORD**, and brought it into the house of Abinadab in the hill, and sanctified Eleazar his son to keep the ark of the LORD."
1 Sam. 7:2	"And it came to pass, while the **ark** abode in Kirjathjearim, that **the time was long**; for it was **twenty years**: and all the house of Israel **lamented after the LORD**.

The men of Kirjathjearim did not die because of touching it either. Afterward, it remained outside of the Tabernacle for twenty years, and because of this, the atonement could not be done because the Ark had to be in the Tabernacle and inside of the Holy of Holies in order for all of the process of the offering of the atonement to be done. It is because of this that "**all the house of Israel lamented after the LORD,**" because their sins were not being covered.

Twenty years later, something happened.

2 Sam. 6:2	"And David arose, and went with all the people that were with him from Baale of Judah, to bring up from thence the **ark of God**, whose name is called by the name of the LORD of hosts that dwelleth between the cherubims."
2 Sam. 6:3	"And they set the **ark of God** upon a new cart, and brought it out of the house of Abinadab that was in Gibeah: and Uzzah and Ahio, the

	sons of Abinadab, drave the new cart."
2 Sam. 6:4	"And they brought it out of the house of Abinadab which was at Gibeah, accompanying the **ark of God**: and Ahio went before the ark."
2 Sam. 6:5	"And David and all the house of Israel played before the LORD on all manner of instruments made of fir wood, even on harps, and on psalteries, and on timbrels, and on cornets, and on cymbals."
2 Sam. 6:6	"And when they came to Nachon's threshingfloor, Uzzah put forth his hand to the **ark of God**, and took hold of it; for the oxen shook it."
2 Sam. 6:7	"And the anger of the LORD was kindled against Uzzah; and God smote him there for his error; and there he died by the **ark of God**."

Without there being a current atonement upon the Mercy Seat, it was no longer a mercy seat, but rather, a judgment seat. Therefore, when Uzzah touched it, he died.

From this, we can see that if the Philistines did not die the instant that they touched it, then some aspect of the atonement had to be covering them also, and if their sins were covered, then also the sins of the whole world were covered. Even they recognized that the plagues that fell upon them were not because of touching the Ark of the Covenant, but because they had carried it away out of its place. This is further evidenced by the fact that when they sent it back to Israel, the plagues stopped.

The Statement that "All Judgment is Given Unto the Son" Can be True at the Same Time as the One that Says "The Saints Shall Judge the Earth."

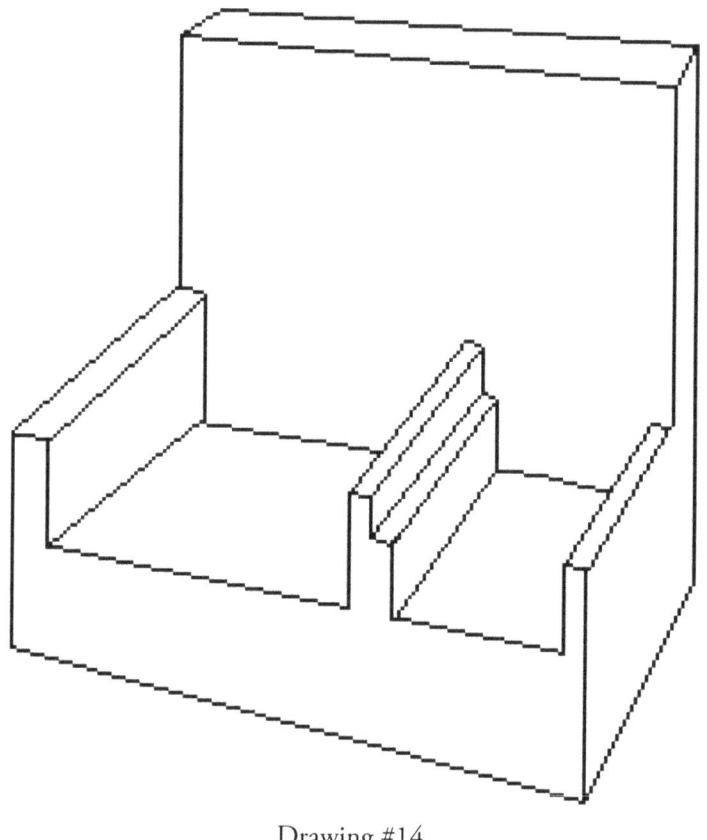

Drawing #14

CHAPTER 11

The Beginning of Judgment

This chapter deals with the very difficult and often misunderstood topic of judgment. It is necessary that it be understood in order for the church to walk in true holiness before God at the same time as not being legalistic, judgmental, or condemning toward those precious souls that God wants to bring into blessed fellowship with Him. All of this needs to happen at the same time as not compromising on the standards of holiness that God has established in His word.

Judgment happens on several different levels, the most important of which is personal.

> **1 Cor. 11:31** "For if we would **judge ourselves**, we should not be judged."
>
> **1 Cor. 11:32** "But when we are judged, we are **chastened of the Lord, that we should not be condemned** with the world."

Therefore, there is a judgment that is for holiness and salvation and not for condemnation. It is upon this basis that we will begin.

For many years, a well-known phrase has been used: "Judgment begins at the house of the Lord." This statement comes from the scripture.

> **Eze. 9:6** "Slay utterly old and young, both maids, and little children, and

women: but come not near any man upon whom is the mark; and begin at my sanctuary. **Then they began at the ancient men which were before the house.**"

Eze. 9:7 "And he said unto them, Defile the **house**, and fill the **courts** with the slain: go ye forth. And they went forth, and slew in the **city**."

While these verses do use the words of *house* and *courts*, they also use the word *city*. How can it be proven that the "city" is the church? We must first look at the context that the scriptures establish for **Ezekiel chapter 9**. This context is found in **chapter 8**. Here, we can see multiple references to the Temple.

Eze. 8:1 "And it came to pass in the sixth year, in the sixth month, in the fifth day of the month, as I sat in mine house, and the elders of Judah sat before me, that the hand of the Lord GOD fell there upon me."

Eze. 8:2 "Then I beheld, and lo a likeness as the appearance of fire: from the appearance of his loins even downward, fire; and from his loins even upward, as the appearance of brightness, as the colour of amber."

Eze. 8:3 "And he put forth the form of an hand, and took me by a lock of mine head; and the spirit lifted me up between the earth and the heaven, and brought me in the visions of God

	to Jerusalem, to the **door of the inner gate that looketh toward the north**; where was the seat of the image of jealousy, which provoketh to jealousy."
Eze. 8:4	"And, behold, the glory of the God of Israel was there, according to the vision that I saw in the plain."
Eze. 8:5	"Then said he unto me, Son of man, lift up thine eyes now the way toward the **north**. So I lifted up mine eyes the way toward the north, and behold **northward at the gate of the altar** this image of jealousy in the entry."
Eze. 8:6	"He said furthermore unto me, Son of man, seest thou what they do? even the great abominations that the house of Israel committeth here, that I should go far off from my **sanctuary**? but turn thee yet again, and thou shalt see greater abominations."
Eze. 8:7	"And he brought me to the **door of the court**; and when I looked, behold a hole in the wall."
Eze. 8:8	"Then said he unto me, Son of man, dig now in the wall: and when I had digged in the wall, behold a door."
Eze. 8:9	"And he said unto me, Go in, and behold the wicked abominations that they do here."

Eze. 8:10 "So I went in and saw; and behold every form of creeping things, and abominable beasts, and all the idols of the house of Israel, portrayed upon the wall round about."

Eze. 8:11 "And there stood before them seventy men of the ancients of the house of Israel, and in the midst of them stood Jaazaniah the son of Shaphan, with every man his **censer** in his hand; and **a thick cloud of incense** went up."

Eze. 8:12 "Then said he unto me, Son of man, hast thou seen what the ancients of the house of Israel do in the dark, every man in the chambers of his **imagery**? for they say, The LORD seeth us not; the LORD hath forsaken the earth."

But it was a false and an unacceptable offering of incense (false humility), because it did not produce obedience.

Eze. 8:13 "He said also unto me, Turn thee yet again, and thou shalt see greater abominations that they do."

Eze. 8:14 "Then he brought me to **the door of the gate of the LORD'S house which was toward the north**; and, behold, there sat women weeping for Tammuz."

Eze. 8:15	"Then said he unto me, Hast thou seen this, O son of man? turn thee yet again, and thou shalt see greater abominations than these."
Eze. 8:16	"And he brought me into the **inner court of the LORD'S house**, and, behold, at the **door of the temple of the LORD, between the porch and the altar**, were about five and twenty men, with their backs toward the **temple** of the LORD, and their faces toward the east; and they worshipped the sun toward the east."
Eze. 8:17	"Then he said unto me, Hast thou seen this, O son of man? Is it a light thing to the house of Judah that they commit the abominations which they commit here? for they have filled the land with violence, and have returned to provoke me to anger: and, lo, they put the branch to their nose."
Eze. 8:18	"Therefore will I also deal in fury: mine eye shall not spare, neither will I have pity: and though they cry in mine ears with a loud voice, yet will I not hear them."

The context therefore is that of the Temple, the house of the Lord. Therefore, when chapter 9 begins by mentioning "city," the context has already been established that the Temple is being referred to. How is the house of God related to a city? First of all, a city is a grouping of houses that have been constructed in close proximity to each other for some mutual benefit. Many times, the mutual benefit is for protection, economic benefit, or political association. The scriptures refer to each of us as "temples."

> **1 Cor. 3:16** "Know ye not that ye are the **temple** of God, and that the Spirit of God dwelleth in you?"

The Hebrew word for *temple* is the word *beth*. It is also the word for "house." In the following verse is the reference in the New Testament to the scripture in **Ezekiel chapter 9** which at the same time refers to us as the "house of God."

> **1 Pet. 4:17** "For the time is come that **judgment must begin at the house of God**: and **if it first begin at us**, what shall the end be of them that obey not the gospel of God?"

There are other scriptures that further reinforce this concept by speaking about us in either a natural or spiritual way as a house.

> **2 Cor. 5:1** "For we know that if our earthly **house** of this **tabernacle** were dissolved, we have a **building** of God, an **house** not made with hands, eternal in the heavens."

> **Matt. 7:24** "Therefore whosoever heareth these sayings of mine, and doeth them, I will liken him unto a wise man, which built his **house** upon a rock."

> **Matt. 7:26** "And every one that heareth these sayings of mine, and doeth them not, shall be likened unto a foolish

	man, which built his **house** upon the sand."
Luke 6:48	"He is like a man which built an **house**, and digged deep, and laid the foundation on a rock: and when the flood arose, the stream beat vehemently upon that **house**, and could not shake it: for it was founded upon a rock."
Luke 6:49	"But he that heareth, and doeth not, is like a man that without a foundation built an **house** upon the earth; against which the stream did beat vehemently, and immediately it fell; and the ruin of that **house** was great."
Eph. 2:20	"And are built upon the **foundation** of the apostles and prophets, Jesus Christ himself being the **chief corner stone**."
Col. 2:7	"Rooted and **built** up in him, and stablished in the faith, as ye have been taught, abounding therein with thanksgiving."
1 Pet. 2:5	"Ye also, as **lively stones**, are **built** up a **spiritual house**, an holy priesthood, to offer up spiritual sacrifices, acceptable to God by Jesus Christ.

If we each are houses, then when we congregate together in the church, the church is a grouping of houses for mutual benefit and therefore constitutes a city. It is for this reason that when **chapter 9** begins by talking about the "city," it is speaking about the church. When it says that judgment begins at the house of God, we can see that there are requirements that must be met in order to be spared.

Eze. 9:4	"And the LORD said unto him, Go through the midst of the **city**, through the midst of **Jerusalem**, and set a mark upon the foreheads of the men **that sigh and that cry for all the abominations that be done in the midst thereof**."
Eze. 9:5	"And to the others he said in mine hearing, Go ye after him through the **city**, and smite: let not your eye spare, neither have ye pity."
Eze. 9:6	"Slay utterly old and young, both maids, and little children, and women: but **come not near any man upon whom is the mark**; and **begin at my sanctuary**. Then **they began at the ancient men which were before the house**."
Eze. 9:9	"Then said he unto me, The **iniquity of the house** of Israel and Judah is exceeding great, and the land is full of blood, and the **city full of perverseness**: for they say, The LORD hath forsaken the earth, and the LORD seeth not."

Those that sigh and cry because of the abominations that are done even inside of the church are the same ones that know how to enter into His presence, offering the incense of humility. They are not praying for judgment for condemnation, but rather that the lives of people would be changed and transformed to conform to God's precepts, and thereby, for them to enter into the blessings that He pours out upon the obedient and by obedience to escape the penalty that comes upon the disobedient. The Lord Jesus spoke about those abominations in another way.

    Matt. 5:13   "Ye are the **salt** of the earth: but **if the salt have lost his savour**, wherewith shall it be **salted**? it is thenceforth good for nothing, but to be cast out, and to be trodden under foot of men."

The church loses its savour when it leaves off true holiness and begins to allow abominations to remain in it. Abominations are those things that God hates such as pride, vanity, rebellion, willful disobedience against the precepts of God, and all of the fruits that those things produce. When the Apostle Paul was speaking about taking the Lord's Supper, he said:

    1 Cor. 11:26   "For as often as ye eat this bread, and drink this cup, ye do show the Lord's death till he come."

    1 Cor. 11:27   "Wherefore whosoever shall eat this bread, and drink this cup of the Lord, unworthily, shall be guilty of the body and blood of the Lord."

    1 Cor. 11:28   "But **let a man examine himself**, and so let him eat of that bread, and drink of that cup."

1 Cor. 11:29	"For he that eateth and drinketh unworthily, eateth and drinketh damnation to himself, not discerning the Lord's body."
1 Cor. 11:30	"For this cause many are weak and sickly among you, and many sleep."
1 Cor. 11:31	"For if we would **judge ourselves**, we should not be judged."
1 Cor. 11:32	"But **when we are judged**, we are chastened of the Lord, **that we should not be condemned with the world**."

If we would enter into a self-examination by the word of God, then our sins can be identified as sin and can be repented of. When we repent of our sins, they are sent on before to the judgment and condemned before we ourselves arrive. In this way, when we arrive at the judgment, there is nothing left against us for us to be condemned by. This is far better than for us to arrive at the judgment and then for our sins that we have not repented of to arrive to witness against us.

1 Tim. 5:24	"**Some men's sins are** open beforehand, **going before to judgment; and some** men **they follow after**."
1 Tim. 5:25	"Likewise also the good works of some are manifest beforehand; and they that are otherwise cannot be hid."

Therefore, if there is a judgment of self-examination that is for blessing and salvation and this is what we want for ourselves, then when the following scripture is applied…

Luke 6:31	"**And as ye would that men should do to you, do ye also to them likewise.**"
Matt. 5:44	"But I say unto you, **Love your enemies**, **bless them** that curse you, **do good** to them that hate you, and **pray for** them which despitefully use you, and persecute you."
Matt. 5:45	"**That ye may be the children of your Father which is in heaven**: for he maketh his sun to rise on the evil and on the good, and sendeth rain on the just and on the unjust."

...this judgment for the sake of mercy and salvation that we want for ourselves is what we will extend to others. If this is what we do, then we will not have a problem with the following verse:

Matt. 7:2	"For with what judgment ye judge, ye shall be judged: and with what measure ye mete, it shall be measured to you again."

Therefore, if our judgment is for mercy and salvation, then mercy and salvation is what we will receive. If we judge for condemnation, then condemnation is what we will receive. The power of mercy and salvation to rescue from the penalty of the law (that comes upon the disobedient) is the power to produce a genuine obedience in and through us. The penalty of disobedience does not come upon the obedient; therefore, God is just in His judgment.

Matt. 16:27	"For the Son of man shall come in the glory of his Father with his

angels; and then he shall **reward every man according to his works**."

2 Cor. 11:15 "Therefore it is no great thing if his ministers also be transformed as the ministers of righteousness; **whose end shall be according to their works**."

2 Tim. 1:9 "Who hath saved us, and called us with an holy calling, not according to **our works**, **but according to his own purpose and grace**, which was given us in Christ Jesus before the world began."

Rev. 2:23 "And I will kill her children with death; and all the churches shall know that I am he which searcheth the reins and hearts: and **I will give unto every one of you according to your works**."

Rev. 20:12 "And I saw the dead, small and great, stand before God; and the books were opened: and another book was opened, which is the book of life: and the dead were judged out of those things which were written in the books, **according to their works**."

Rev. 20:13 "And the sea gave up the dead which were in it; and death and hell delivered up the dead which were in

> them: and they were judged every man **according to their works**."

When the obedience that is in us is that of God Himself working through our surrender and humility, then it will not be condemned. Rather than being condemned, it will be the working of His righteousness and salvation and will manifest the reality of the work of His grace not only to us but also in our own selves and for many others that come to believe in Him through the testimony of His witness (glory of His righteousness and obedience) that shines forth in and through us.

What Makes the Difference Between Just and Unjust Judgment

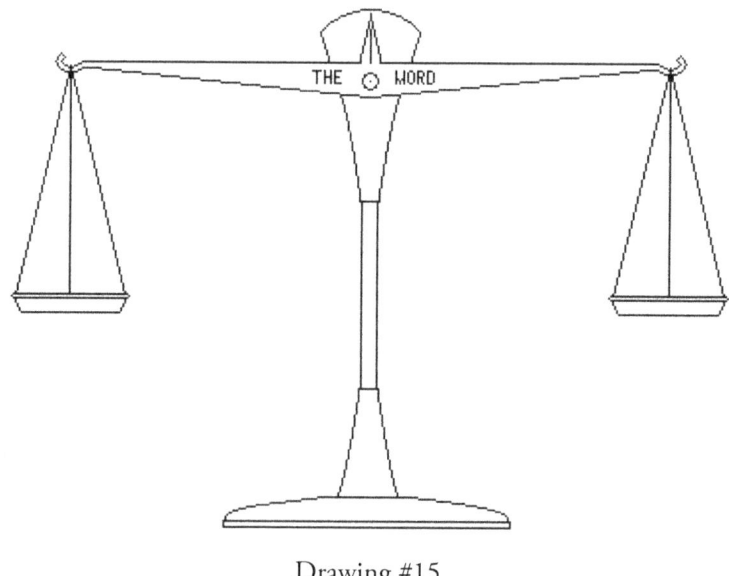

Drawing #15

CHAPTER 12

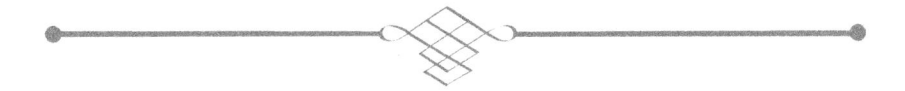

Righteous Judgment

Many people have heard the following verse quoted many times:

Matt. 7:1 "**Judge not, that ye be not judged**."

But they have heard it preached in a context that incorrectly leads them to think that they should not judge anything at all.

However, if it is read in the context of the verses that follow it, we can see that it is not saying that we should not judge anything at all, but rather that we should be sure (self-examination) that we are not guilty of the very thing that we are trying to correct our fellow servant of God about (note **verse 5**).

Matt. 7:1 "**Judge not**, that ye be not judged."

Matt. 7:2 "For with what judgment ye judge, ye shall be judged: and with what measure ye mete, it shall be measured to you again."

Matt. 7:3 "And why beholdest thou the mote that is in thy brother's eye, but considerest not the beam that is in thine own eye?"

Matt. 7:4 "Or how wilt thou say to thy brother, Let me pull out the mote out of thine eye; and, behold, a beam is in thine own eye?"

Matt. 7:5   "Thou hypocrite, first cast out the beam out of thine own eye; and **then shalt thou see clearly** to cast out the mote out of thy brother's eye."

At the same time that the scripture says in **Matthew 7:1,** "Judge not," the scripture also says:

John 7:24   "Judge not according to the appearance, **but judge righteous judgment.**"

There is not a contradiction, but rather, these scriptures complement each other to make us look for a fuller and more complete meaning. From this, we can see that righteous judgment does not judge **only** based upon appearances. Righteous judgment must go much deeper.

John 8:15   "Ye judge **after the flesh; I judge no man.**"

John 8:16   "And yet if I judge, my judgment is true: for I am not alone, but I and the Father that sent me."

There is implicit in the verses above that the way that the Lord Jesus judges is not "after the flesh." If it is not after the flesh, then it must be after the Spirit.

John 5:22   "For the Father judgeth no man, but hath committed **all** judgment unto the Son."

All judgment is committed unto the Son, but not as unto a carnal man. The reality of the very life that He lived and that He is still living in and through His people is that which the world will judge themselves by. Whether they accept or reject that living reality is the largest part of what judgment is all about, again, self-judgment.

John 12:47	"And if any man hear my words, and believe not, I judge him not: for **I came not to judge the world, but to save the world**."
John 12:48	"He that rejecteth me, and receiveth not my words, hath one that judgeth him: **the word that I have spoken, the same shall judge him in the last day**."
Acts 17:31	"Because he hath **appointed a day**, in the which he will judge the **world in righteousness** by that man whom he hath ordained; whereof he hath given assurance unto all men, in that he hath raised him from the dead."
Rom. 14:13	"Let us **not therefore judge one another any more**: but **judge this rather, that no man put a stumblingblock or an occasion to fall in his brother's way**."

The Apostle Paul caught this same concept and expressed it in the verse above; to not judge to condemn, but rather for salvation by not setting an example that could be used to cause a fellow servant to fall away from the precepts of the word of God. It requires the kind of judgment that is self-examining to not be a stumbling block by our example, but rather, an encouragement through divinely empowered obedience.

1 Cor. 4:5	"Therefore judge nothing **before the time**, until the Lord come, who both will bring to light the hidden things of darkness, and will make manifest the counsels of the hearts: and then shall every man have praise of God."
Matt. 16:27	"For the Son of man shall come in the glory of his Father with his angels; and then he shall reward every man **according to his works**."
2 Cor. 11:15	"Therefore it is no great thing if his ministers also be transformed as the ministers of righteousness; whose end shall be **according to their works**."
Rev. 2:23	"And I will kill her children with death; and all the churches shall know that I am he which searcheth the reins and hearts: and I will give unto every one of you **according to your works**."
Rev. 18:6	"Reward her even as she rewarded you, and double unto her double **according to her works**: in the cup which she hath filled fill to her double."

Rev. 20:12 "And I saw the dead, small and great, stand before God; and the books were opened: and another book was opened, which is the book of life: and the dead were judged out of those things which were written in the books, **according to their works**."

Rev. 20:13 "And the sea gave up the dead which were in it; and death and hell delivered up the dead which were in them: and they were judged every man **according to their works**."

God has an appointed time for the judgment in which everyone will receive according to their own works, whether it is for praise or for shame. There are several important items in the following passage of scripture.

1 Cor. 6:2 "Do ye not know **that the saints shall judge the world**? and **if the world shall be judged by you, are ye unworthy to judge the smallest matters?**"

1 Cor. 6:3 "**Know ye not that we shall judge angels?** how much more things that pertain to this life?"

1 Cor. 6:4 "If then ye have judgments of things pertaining to this life, **set them to judge who are least esteemed in the church**."

1 Cor. 6:5   "I speak to your shame. Is it so, that there is not a wise man among you? no, not one that shall be able to judge between his brethren?"

First of all is the question that arises that if God has "committed **all** judgment unto the Son," then how is it that "the **saints** shall judge the world?" We will see the answer to this question in the next chapter.

The second point is that the saints will even judge angels. We know that the angels that did not fall have always served God and the heirs of salvation (**Hebrews 1:14**), but those angels that did not "keep their first estate (**Jude 1:6**)" are also known as demons and have afflicted the saints. Therefore, it is the saints that will judge and condemn the demons (fallen angels) to "everlasting chains under darkness."

The third point is very important also. Many translations of the Bible make **1 Corinthians 6:4** to be a question, because they do not understand how that it could be a statement or a commandment.

Please consider this: it is pride that caused Satan to fall in the beginning and it is pride that he tries to use to cause the fall of every person. Every case of conflict between brethren happens because Satan has sown a seed of pride in one or the other of those that have the conflict. In the majority of the circumstances, the seed of pride is in both of them. If those who are having the conflict have to submit in humility to having their conflict resolved by the one that is considered to be the least among them, then the very root (pride) of the problem is being attacked.

Also, many times, those who are humble are also the best equipped by God to judge problems amongst brethren and they are the very ones that the prideful will esteem to be the least. In all cases, if all roots and seeds of pride are constantly being purged out by divinely given humility, then Satan will not be able to work to cause division and strife in the body of Christ.

2 Tim. 4:1 "I Charge thee therefore before God, and the Lord Jesus Christ, who shall judge the quick and the dead at his appearing and his **kingdom**."

If we are the kingdom of God and He is seated in the throne of our hearts, then we are being prepared for His coming and are able to judge righteous judgment.

Jam. 2:12 "So speak ye, and so do, as they that shall be judged by the **law of liberty**."

Jam. 2:13 "For he shall have judgment without mercy, that hath showed no mercy; and **mercy rejoiceth against judgment**."

The law of liberty is merciful, a law we use to judge, and it rejoices against the judgment that is for condemnation, because the law of liberty is for the purpose of salvation.

1 Pet. 1:17 "And if ye call on the Father, who without respect of persons judgeth according to every man's work, **pass the time of your sojourning here in fear**."

1 Pet. 2:23 "Who, when he was reviled, reviled not again; when he suffered, he threatened not; but **committed himself to him that judgeth righteously**."

But if the law of liberty (which is for mercy) is rejected, then the only thing that remains is condemnation. During our journey through life, we should walk in that reverential fear and commit ourselves to our heavenly Father who judges righteously according to the law of liberty for the purpose of mercy and salvation.

> **Deut. 16:18** "Judges and officers shalt thou make thee in all thy gates, which the LORD thy God giveth thee, throughout thy tribes: and they shall judge the people with **just judgment**."
>
> **Deut. 16:19** "Thou shalt **not wrest judgment**; thou shalt not respect persons, neither take a gift: for a gift doth blind the eyes of the wise, and pervert the words of the righteous."
>
> **Deut. 16:20** "That which is **altogether just** shalt thou follow, **that thou mayest live, and inherit the land which the LORD thy God giveth thee**."

In this, we can see even in the symbolic that if we do this righteous and just judgment, then it is part of the requirements for inheriting the land of promises and even life.

> **John 5:30** "I can of mine own self do nothing: as I hear, I judge: and **my judgment is just; because I seek not mine own will, but the will of the Father which hath sent me**."

The just or righteous judgment that the Lord Jesus used (and that He wants for us) was that which conformed to the will of His heavenly Father. What was/is the will of our heavenly Father?

2 Pet. 3:9   "The Lord is not slack concerning his promise, as some men count slackness; but is longsuffering to us-ward, **not willing that any should perish, but that all should come to repentance**."

His will is that none should perish but that all should come to repentance and thereby receive of His blessings instead of condemnation, and praise instead of shame. What is it that we repent of? We repent of disobedience and rebellion against God's precepts.

How do we come into the place of receiving the praise of God? By a humility and subjection being so profound that the obedience that is expressed through us is supernaturally, joyfully, and divinely empowered, setting an example for others and bringing into earthly manifestation the blessings of heaven.

What the Great White Throne Judgment Is and How to be Seated on the Right Side

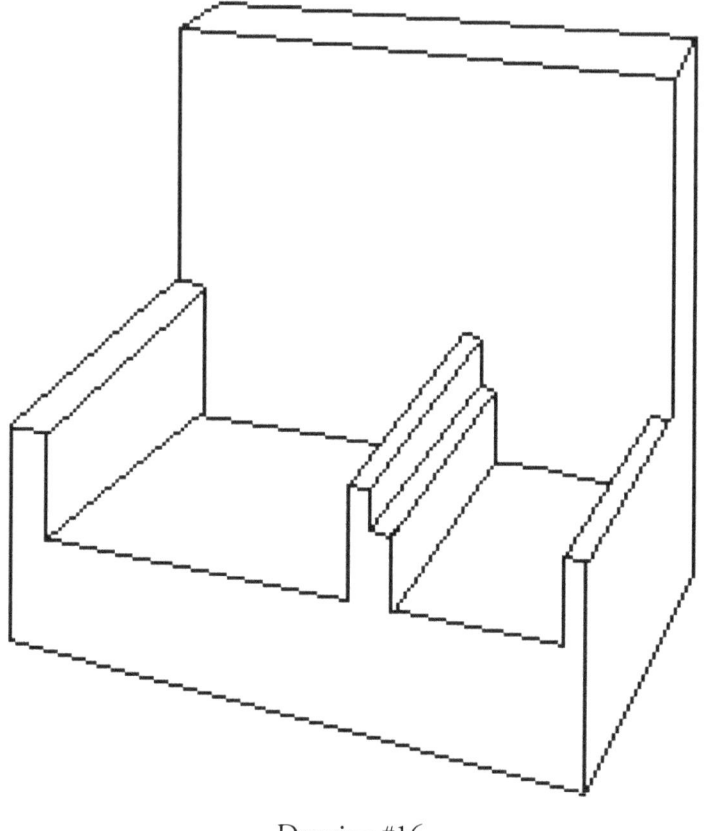

Drawing #16

CHAPTER 13

When Judgment Is Set

The promise of the New Covenant was given in the Old Testament, but it was spoken in terms of writing His **law** in our hearts and minds. This is even stated in the New Testament in the same way of writing His **law** in our hearts and minds, and even making us to be living books that He writes for the purpose of being known and read of all men.

Jer. 31:31 "Behold, the days come, saith the LORD, that I will make a **new covenant** with the house of Israel, and with the house of Judah."

Jer. 31:32 "**Not according to the covenant that I made with their fathers** in the day that I took them by the hand to bring them out of the land of Egypt; which my covenant they brake, although I was an husband unto them, saith the LORD."

Jer. 31:33 "**But this shall be the covenant** that I will make with the house of Israel; After those days, saith the LORD, **I will put my law in their inward parts, and write it in their hearts**;

	and will be their God, and they shall be my people."
Heb. 8:8	"For finding fault with them, he saith, Behold, the days come, saith the Lord, when I will make a **new covenant** with the house of Israel and with the house of Judah."
Heb. 8:9	"**Not according to the covenant that I made with their fathers** in the day when I took them by the hand to lead them out of the land of Egypt; because they continued not in my covenant, and I regarded them not, saith the Lord."

The phrase "**Not according to the covenant that I made with their fathers**" (**Heb. 8:9**) also relates to the statement "**written not with ink, but with the Spirit of the living God; not in tables of stone, but in fleshly tables of the heart**" (**2 Cor. 3:3**).

Heb. 8:10	"For **this is the covenant** that I will make with the house of Israel after those days, saith the Lord; **I will put my laws into their mind, and write them in their hearts**: and I will be to them a God, and they shall be to me a people."
2 Cor. 3:2	"Ye are our epistle **written in our hearts, known and read of all men**."
2 Cor. 3:3	"Forasmuch as ye are manifestly declared to be the epistle of Christ ministered by us, **written not with**

>   ink, but with the Spirit of the living God; not in tables of stone, but in fleshly tables of the heart."

2 Cor. 3:4   "And such trust have we through Christ to God-ward."

2 Cor. 3:5   "Not that we are sufficient of ourselves to think any thing as of ourselves; but **our sufficiency is of God**."

2 Cor. 3:6   "Who also hath made us able **ministers of the new testament; not of the letter, but of the spirit: for the letter killeth, but the spirit giveth life**."

But it is still referred to as **law**. Sadly, many people have heard the law of God being spoken about as though it were the law of sin and death. The question is, when did the law of sin and death come into effect in the world? Was it at the fall in sin or when God gave His law to Moses to be written? If it only came into being when Moses wrote the law, then why did everyone before Moses (except for Enoch) die instead of still being alive?

It is not because of the flood, because many died even before the flood. We need a better understanding about the law in order to understand about the New Covenant, because if the law was entirely done away with, then just exactly what is it that will be written in our hearts and minds? It is stated in both the Old and the New Testaments that the New Covenant is God writing His **law** in our hearts and minds. If the law is entirely done away with, then there is nothing left to be written!

Many times, the law is spoken and preached about as though there was nothing good in it at all or that it was only given so that God could have a reason to bludgeon mankind when he failed to fulfill it. Additionally, the law of God does not **only** contain curses and condemnation. It **also** contains promises, blessings, and the seeds of salvation. If the entirety of the law of God is done away with, then so also are the promises and blessings done away. We need to seriously ask ourselves the question, "Do we believe that God **is** love or don't we?" John was very clear about it when he wrote.

> **1 John 4:7** "Beloved, let us **love** one another: for **love is of God**; and **every one that loveth is born of God, and knoweth God**."
>
> **1 John 4:8** "He that **loveth** not knoweth not God; **for God is love**."
>
> **1 John 4:9** "In this was manifested the **love** of God toward us, because that God sent his only begotten Son into the world, that we might live through him."
>
> **1 John 4:10** "Herein is **love**, **not that we loved God, but that he loved us**, and sent his Son to be the propitiation for our sins."
>
> **1 John 4:11** "Beloved, if God so **loved** us, we ought also to **love** one another."
>
> **1 John 4:12** "No man hath seen God at any time. **If we love one another, God dwelleth in us, and his love is perfected in us**."

1 John 4:13 "**Hereby know we that we dwell in him, and he in us**, because he hath given us of his Spirit."

1 John 4:14 "And we have seen and do testify that the Father sent the Son to be the Saviour of the world."

1 John 4:15 "Whosoever shall confess that Jesus is the Son of God, God dwelleth in him, and he in God."

1 John 4:16 "And we have known and believed the **love** that God hath to us. **God is love; and he that dwelleth in love dwelleth in God, and God in him**."

1 John 4:17 "**Herein is our love made perfect**, that we may have boldness in the day of judgment: **because as he is, so are we in this world**."

1 John 4:18 "There is no fear in **love**; but perfect **love** casteth out fear: because fear hath torment. He that feareth is not made perfect in **love**."

1 John 4:19 "We **love** him, because **he first loved us**."

1 John 4:20 "If a man say, I love God, and hateth his brother, he is a liar: for he that loveth not his brother whom he hath seen, how can he love God whom he hath not seen?"

1 John 4:21	"And this **commandment** have we from him, That **he who loveth God love his brother also**."
1 John 5:1	"Whosoever believeth that Jesus is the Christ is born of God: and **every one that loveth him that begat loveth him also that is begotten of him**."
1 John 5:2	"**By this** we know that we **love** the children of God, **when we love God, and keep his commandments**."
1 John 5:3	"**For this is the love of God, that we keep his commandments: and his commandments are not grievous**."

A God of love would have a loving motive in giving us His statutes, precepts, commandments, and laws. A better explanation is that they were given as descriptions and examples of how His character and nature behaves itself in different circumstances. He is so loving that He did not leave it up to our whim (while still in a fallen condition) to try to imitate something that we have absolutely no guidelines to describe what it is. However, which is better: to have **descriptions** of the character of God? Or to have the **living reality** of that character dwelling within us? This is the same thing that the Apostle Paul was speaking about in the following scriptures.

Col. 2:16	"Let no man therefore judge you in meat, or in drink, or in respect of an holyday, or of the new moon, or of the sabbath days."
Col. 2:17	"Which are a **shadow of things to come**; but the body is of Christ."

Heb. 8:1	"Now of the things which we have spoken this is the sum: We have such an high priest, who is set on the right hand of the throne of the Majesty in the heavens."
Heb. 8:2	"A minister of the sanctuary, and of the true tabernacle, which the Lord pitched, and not man."
Heb. 8:3	"For every high priest is ordained to offer gifts and sacrifices: wherefore it is of necessity that this man have somewhat also to offer."
Heb. 8:4	"For if he were on earth, he should not be a priest, seeing that there are priests that offer gifts according to the law."
Heb. 8:5	"**Who serve unto the example and shadow of heavenly things**, as Moses was admonished of God when he was about to make the tabernacle: for, See, saith he, that thou make all things according to the **pattern showed to thee in the mount**."
Heb. 8:6	"But now hath he obtained a **more excellent ministry**, by how much also he is the mediator of a **better covenant**, which was **established upon better promises**."

Heb. 8:7	"**For if that first covenant had been faultless, then should no place have been sought for the second.**"
Heb. 8:8	"For finding fault with them, he saith, Behold, the days come, saith the Lord, when I will make a **new covenant** with the house of Israel and with the house of Judah."
Heb. 8:9	"**Not according to the covenant that I made with their fathers** in the day when I took them by the hand to lead them out of the land of Egypt; because they continued not in my covenant, and I regarded them not, saith the Lord."
Heb. 8:10	"For **this is the covenant** that I will make with the house of Israel after those days, saith the Lord; **I will put my laws into their mind, and write them in their hearts**: and I will be to them a God, and they shall be to me a people."
Heb. 9:8	"**The Holy Ghost this signifying, that the way into the holiest of all was not yet made manifest**, while as the first tabernacle was yet standing."
Heb. 9:9	"**Which was a figure for the time then present**, in which were offered both gifts and sacrifices, that **could not make him that did the ser-**

vice perfect, as pertaining to the conscience."

Heb. 9:10 "Which stood only in meats and drinks, and divers washings, and carnal ordinances, imposed on them until the time of reformation."

Heb. 9:11 "But Christ being come an high priest of **good things to come**, by a greater and more perfect tabernacle, not made with hands, that is to say, not of this building."

Heb. 9:12 "Neither by the blood of goats and calves, but by his own blood he entered in once into the holy place, having obtained eternal redemption for us."

Heb. 9:13 "For if the blood of bulls and of goats, and the ashes of an heifer sprinkling the unclean, sanctifieth to the purifying of the flesh."

Heb. 9:14 "How much more shall the blood of Christ, who through the eternal Spirit offered himself without spot to God, purge your conscience from dead works to serve the living God?"

Heb. 9:15 "And **for this cause he is the mediator of the new testament**, that by means of death, for the redemption of the transgressions that were under the first testament, **they which are** called might receive the promise of eternal inheritance."

Heb. 10:1 "For the law having a **shadow of good things to come**, and **not the very image of the things**, can **never with those sacrifices** which they offered year by year continually **make the comers thereunto perfect**."

Heb. 10:2 "For then **would they not have ceased to be offered**? because that the **worshippers once purged should have had no more conscience of sins**."

Heb. 10:3 "But in those sacrifices there is a remembrance again made of sins every year."

Heb. 10:4 "For **it is not possible that the blood of bulls and of goats should take away sins**."

The blood of bulls and goats could not take away sin, but the blood of Immanuel, the Lamb of God, can take away sin and has power (His life that was in His blood) to take away sin and manifest His obedience in us and through us. In this, we can see that when the work of atonement is complete, "the worshippers once **purged** should have had no more conscience of sins." We can also conclude that they do not have any more conscience of sin, because sin no longer exists in them, and not because it still exists, but they are unaware of it. This is the power of the transforming work of the Holy Spirit. Once the transformation has happened, the sin no longer exists in us, and in its place is holiness. Sin is the transgression or disobedience of the law (**1 John 3:4**), or in other words, sin is everything that is contrary to the image and likeness or the character of God.

Holiness, therefore, is everything that manifests the living reality of His image, likeness, and character. This is only possible if He is seated on the throne of our hearts and the train of the robes of His righteousness fills the entire temple that we are, just as the Shekinah filled that Temple and drove out every shadow. He promised that this would be when he said:

Hag. 2:7	"And I will shake all nations, and the desire of all nations shall come: and **I will fill this house with glory**, saith the LORD of hosts."
Hag. 2:8	"The silver is mine, and the gold is mine, saith the LORD of hosts."
Hag. 2:9	"**The glory of this latter house shall be greater than of the former**, saith the LORD of hosts: and in this place will I give peace, saith the LORD of hosts."

When the King is Seated on the Throne

When the King is seated on the throne of our hearts, what will happen? Note, when **Daniel 7:9** says "till the **thrones** were cast down," this means "humbled," not destroyed. In other translations, it says "till the thrones were established." In this, we can see that when our hearts have been humbled, they are established so that the King, the Ancient of Days, can take His rightful throne of being seated in our hearts.

Dan. 7:9	"I beheld till the **thrones** were cast down, and **the Ancient of days did sit**, whose garment was white as

snow, and the hair of his head like the pure wool: **his throne was like the fiery flame**, and **his wheels as burning fire**."

When this happens, our hearts burn with a passionate love for Him, and that fire consumes and destroys everything that cannot abide in His presence. The wheels show that these thrones are mobile, and everywhere that they go, the fire of His anointing and presence is there.

Dan. 7:10 "**A fiery stream issued and came forth from before him**: thousand thousands ministered unto him, and ten thousand times ten thousand stood before him: **the judgment was set, and the books were opened**."

From the abundance of the heart speaketh the tongue (**Matt. 12:34; Luke 6:45**); therefore, the words that come from our mouths will be anointed with the fire of God. When He completes His writing in these living books, He will put them on display (open them) to be known and read of all man.

Jam. 3:2 "For in many things we offend all. **If any man offend not in word, the same is a perfect man, and able also to bridle the whole body**."

When this happens, "the judgment was set, and the books were opened," what books? The living epistles that we are, when He has written every last jot and tittle in living reality within us, then he will put the books on display (**2 Cor. 3:2–3**) and proclaim, "Here is the living proof that it **is** possible to walk perfect before me." What will it do? It will slay the beast (**Dan. 7:11**). We will not have to worry about the mark of the beast; we already have the mark of God upon us and will be the ones that slay the beast.

>Dan. 7:11   "I beheld then because of the voice of the great words which the horn spake: I beheld **even till the beast was slain**, and his body destroyed, and given to the burning flame."

>Dan. 7:12   "As concerning the rest of the beasts, **they had their dominion taken away**: yet their lives were prolonged for a season and time."

>Dan. 7:13   "I saw in the night visions, and, behold, one like the Son of man came with the clouds of heaven, and came to the **Ancient of days**, and they brought him near before him."

>Dan. 7:14   "And there was **given him dominion, and glory, and a kingdom, that all people, nations, and languages, should serve him: his dominion is an everlasting dominion, which shall not pass away, and his kingdom that which shall not be destroyed**."

>Dan. 7:15   "I Daniel was grieved in my spirit in the midst of my body, and the visions of my head troubled me."

>Dan. 7:16   "Came near unto one of them that stood by, and asked him the truth of all this. So he told me, and made

	me know the interpretation of the things."
Dan. 7:17	"These great beasts, which are four, are four kings, which shall arise out of the earth."
Dan. 7:18	**"But the saints of the most High shall take the kingdom, and possess the kingdom for ever, even for ever and ever."**
Dan. 7:19	"Then I would know the truth of the fourth beast, which was diverse from all the others, exceeding dreadful, whose teeth were of iron, and his nails of brass; which devoured, brake in pieces, and stamped the residue with his feet."
Dan. 7:20	"And of the ten horns that were in his head, and of the other which came up, and before whom three fell; even of that horn that had eyes, and a mouth that spake very great things, whose look was more stout than his fellows."
Dan. 7:21	"I beheld, and **the same horn made war with the saints, and prevailed against them.**"
Dan. 7:22	"**Until the Ancient of days came**, and **judgment was given to the saints of the most High; and the time came that the saints possessed the kingdom.**"

Dan. 7:23	"Thus he said, The fourth beast shall be the fourth kingdom upon earth, which shall be diverse from all kingdoms, and shall devour the whole earth, and shall tread it down, and break it in pieces."
Dan. 7:24	"And the ten horns out of this kingdom are ten kings that shall arise: and another shall rise after them; and he shall be diverse from the first, and he shall subdue three kings."
Dan. 7:25	"And he shall **speak great words against the most High, and shall wear out the saints of the most High, and think to change times and laws: and they shall be given into his hand until a time and times and the dividing of time.**"
Dan. 7:26	"But **the judgment shall sit, and they shall take away his dominion, to consume and to destroy it unto the end.**"
Dan. 7:27	"And **the kingdom and dominion, and the greatness of the kingdom under the whole heaven, shall be given to the people of the saints of the most High, whose kingdom is an everlasting kingdom, and all dominions shall serve and obey him.**"

All dominions shall serve and obey Him! Every principality and power, all might and glory, praise, honor, and majesty belong to the Lamb that is seated on the throne.

The Great White Throne

The following scriptures proclaim that Jesus Christ will judge the living and the dead.

John 5:22	"For the Father judgeth no man, but hath **committed all judgment unto the Son**."
Rom. 2:16	"In the day when **God shall judge the secrets of men by Jesus Christ** according to my gospel."
2 Tim. 4:1	"I Charge thee therefore before God, and **the Lord Jesus Christ, who shall judge the quick and the dead at his appearing and his kingdom**."

And the next scriptures declare that the saints shall judge the world and even angels.

1 Cor. 6:2	"Do ye not know **that the saints shall judge the world**? and if **the world shall be judged by you**, are ye unworthy to judge the smallest matters?"
1 Cor. 6:3	"**Know ye not that we shall judge angels**? how much more things that pertain to this life?"

It is not a contradiction. The Lord Jesus Christ is the Lamb of God which shall be seated upon the thrones of our hearts. When He is seated upon those thrones, the glory of the presence of His holiness will cleanse every one of those thrones. Those thrones were not clean and white before He was seated, but He makes them as white and pure as snow.

When all of the dead in Christ are raised up in the first resurrection and gathered together with those who are alive and remain until His coming, they will constitute the entire body of Christ all together in one place and at one time. Then, when they are gathered together with He who is the head of the body, all of the thrones that were made white will make up THE Great White Throne.

> **Rev. 20:4** "And I saw **thrones**, and **they** sat upon them, and **judgment was given unto them**: and I saw the souls of them that were beheaded for the witness of Jesus, and for the word of God, and which had not worshipped the beast, neither his image, neither had received his mark upon their foreheads, or in their hands; and they lived and reigned with Christ a thousand years."

> **Rev. 20:11** "And **I saw a great white throne**, and him that sat on it, from whose face the earth and the heaven fled away; and there was found no place for them."

It is then that the judgment is set and there is no contradiction to it being Him who judges the earth, but He does it from within His throne in the hearts of His people, the ones that He has cleansed and sanctified by His blood and made to be saints. The thrones can only be established and prepared for this position by the incense of humility working together with and by the power of the life that is in the blood of our atonement.

PART 3
The Holy Place

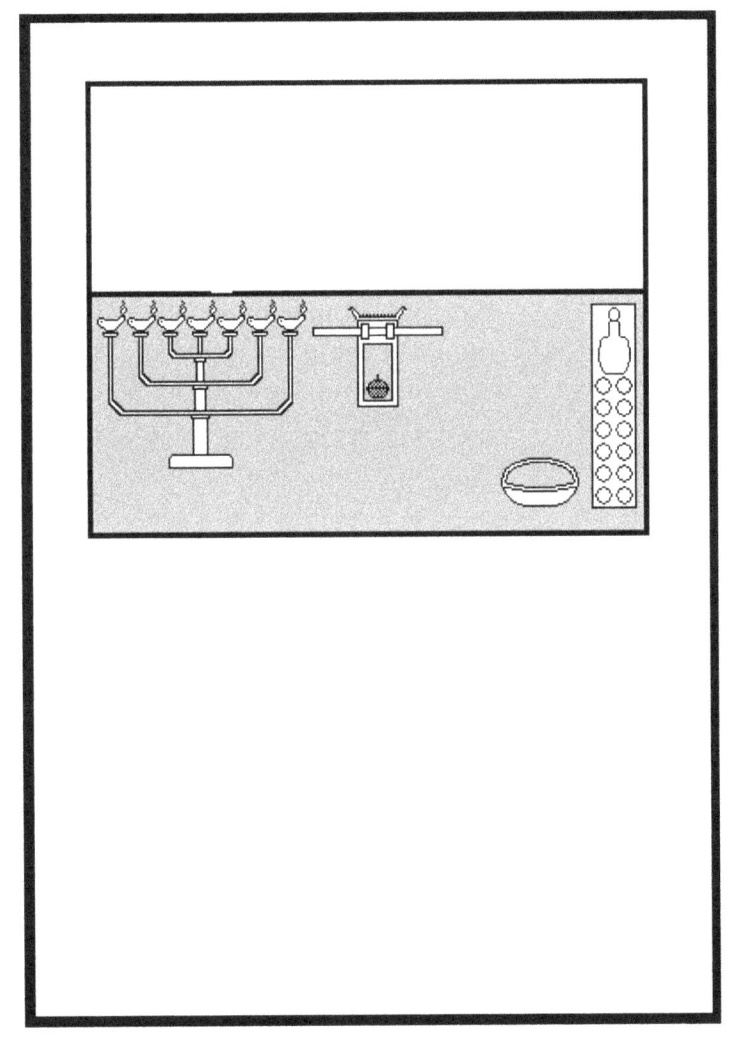

Drawing #17

The Connection Between the Holy of Holies and the
Holy Place is Made Through the Golden Lampstand,
and the Names of Each of the Lamps are Shown

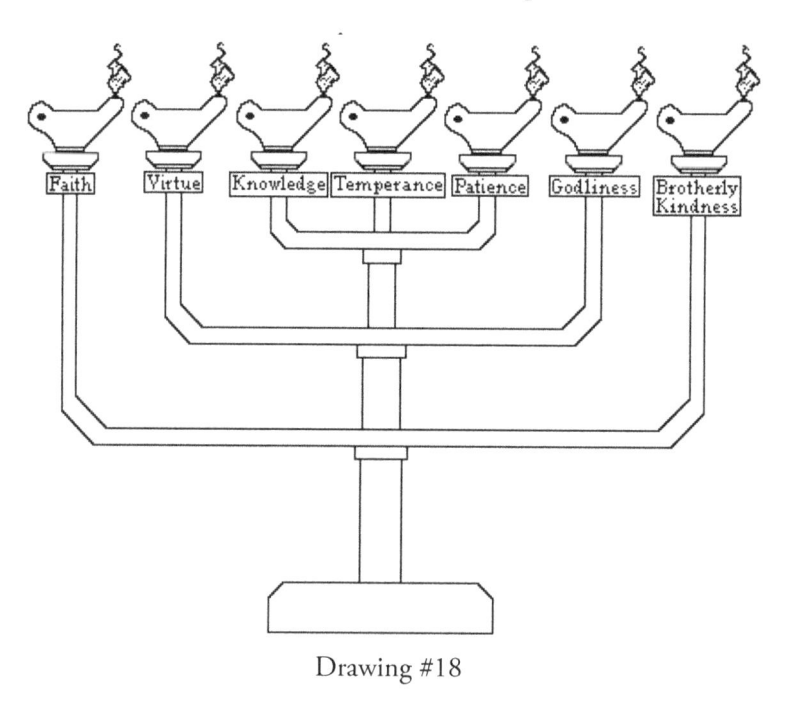

Drawing #18

CHAPTER 14

Reflections from the Holy of Holies

God commanded for a lampstand and lamps to be made out of pure beaten gold and for it to be placed in the Holy Place. The entire lampstand with its six branches, the seven lamps with their bowls, knops, and flowers together with the tongs and snuff dishes were all to be made out of one talent of pure gold. Considering the density of gold, even if the lampstand and its branches were hollow, it could not have been very large and certainly not some four meters high as some claim.

Exo. 25:31 "And thou shalt make a **candlestick** of **pure gold**: of beaten work shall the **candlestick** be made: his shaft, and his branches, his bowls, his knops, and his flowers, shall be of the same."

Exo. 25:32 "And six branches shall come out of the sides of it; three branches of the **candlestick** out of the one side, and three branches of the **candlestick** out of the other side."

Exo. 25:33 "Three bowls made like unto **almonds**, with a knop and a flower in one branch; and three bowls made like **almonds** in the other branch, with a knop and a flower: so in the six branches that come out of the candlestick."

Exo. 25:34 "And in the **candlestick** shall be four bowls made like unto **almonds**, with their knops and their flowers."

Exo. 25:35 "And **there shall be a knop under two branches of the same, and a knop under two branches of the same, and a knop under two branches of the same, according to the six branches** that proceed out of the **candlestick**."

Exo. 25:36 "Their knops and their branches shall be of the same: **all it shall be one beaten work of pure gold**."

Exo. 25:37 "And thou shalt make the **seven lamps** thereof: and they shall light the lamps thereof, that they may give light over against it."

Exo. 25:38 "And the tongs thereof, and the snuffdishes thereof, shall be of **pure gold**."

Exo. 25:39 "Of **a talent of pure gold shall he make it, with all these vessels**."

Exo. 25:40 "And look that thou **make them after their pattern, which was showed thee in the mount**."

Because of the shape and use that was given to the lampstand and to the lamps, we can see that it had an intimate connection with several other items in the Tabernacle. The shape of the lamps were like almonds and are described as having "a knop and a flower" in each branch. It is understood that the "knop" of the lamps was in the shape of the almond nut, and as such, the knops that that were under each of the branches were also in the shape of almonds. This shape of almonds shows an intimate connection between the lampstand and the rod of Aaron that was placed inside the Ark of the Covenant and produced the fruit of almond nuts in just one night (hastened, **Jer. 1:12**) in the presence of the Shekinah (**Exo. 37:19–20; Num. 17:8; Jer. 1:11–12**).

While some may want to argue that no such connection can be made because the lampstand was made before the rod was placed into the Ark, we only need to look at the following scripture.

Isa. 46:9	"Remember the former things of old: for I am God, and there is none else; **I am God, and there is none like me**."
Isa. 46:10	"**Declaring the end from the beginning, and from ancient times the things that are not yet done**, saying, My counsel shall stand, and I will do all my pleasure."

Therefore, it was not something unexpected for God that the witness of the almond rod happened. He knew from before the beginning that it would be that way and made the design of the lampstand to have all of the symbolic connections that He wanted so that He could later use them as examples.

Part of the importance that the lampstand has by the lamps being made in the shape of almonds is so that we could make a connection between the Holy Place and the Holy of Holies. Even though the scriptures do not specify how many almonds grew on the rod of

Aaron, because of the lampstand, it is thought that there were at least seven almonds. Also, we can see that the real almonds that grew in the Holy of Holies were far more real than the lamps in the Holy Place (**Exo. 37:19–20; Num. 17:8; Jer. 1:11–12**).

If the almonds were planted in the ground and watered, they would have produced an almond tree and would have produced fruit after their own kind. This is not so with the lamps. If they were planted in the ground, all that would happen is that there would be some buried gold. This is not said to be disrespectful, but rather, to prove an important point. There are several magnitudes of difference between the reality of the almonds in the Holy of Holies and the lamps in the shape of almonds that were in the Holy Place.

In the same way, the fire that was upon the lamps was vastly inferior to that great fire which appeared above the Mercy Seat between the cherubim. It is safe to say that the very materials that the Tabernacle, all of its furnishings, and even the very world and universe that the Tabernacle was in, were all created by and from **that** fire that was in the Holy of Holies. It may be asked, "How could that fire on the lamps be inferior to the Shekinah if they were originally lit by the fire that proceeded out of the Holy of Holies?"

Very simple. The fire that was on the lamps could be moved from lamp to lamp, it could be extinguished or could go out if the wick burned out or the oil was consumed. All of this is not true about the fire that was in the Holy of Holies. That fire is "self-existing" and not dependent on anything to sustain it, and neither can it be manipulated in any way by the hand of man. Just the opposite is true; if man is in the correct place with God, it is the hands of man that will be moved by that fire, just as his mind is inspired by it, and his heart burns with a passionate love for it. That fire is the very fire that was in the burning bush (**Exodus 3:2–6**) that fell upon the altar on Mount Carmel with Elijah (**1 Kings 18:18–40**), that burned in the heart of Jeremiah (**Jeremiah 20:9**), that filled the one hundred and twenty (**Acts 2:3–4**) in the upper room on Moed Shavuot (the Feast of Weeks, the day of Pentecost), and that appeared to Saul of Tarsus on the road to Damascus (**Acts 9:3–5**) and told Saul, "I am Jesus whom thou persecutest."

From this, we can see that with the seven lamps in the Holy Place that were pointing to and giving testimony of the Shekinah and that in the sanctuary (which includes both the Holy Place and the Holy of Holies), there were eight (not just seven) open flames. If the lampstand, therefore, was for seven of those flames, then the entire Tabernacle is the lamp for that eighth flame. This is further evidenced by the times that the Shekinah filled the entire temple.

Exo. 40:34	"Then a cloud covered the tent of the congregation, and **the glory of the LORD filled the tabernacle**."
Exo. 40:35	"And Moses was not able to enter into the tent of the congregation, because the cloud abode thereon, and **the glory of the LORD filled the tabernacle**."
1 Kings 8:11	"So that the priests could not stand to minister because of the cloud: for **the glory of the LORD had filled the house of the LORD**."
2 Chr. 5:14	"So that the priests could not stand to minister by reason of the cloud: for **the glory of the LORD had filled the house of God**."
2 Chr. 7:1	"Now when Solomon had made an end of praying, the fire came down from heaven, and consumed the burnt offering and the sacrifices; and **the glory of the LORD filled the house**."

2 Chr. 7:2	"And the priests could not enter into the house of the LORD, because **the glory of the LORD had filled the LORD'S house**."
Eze. 10:4	"Then **the glory of the LORD** went up from the cherub, and stood over the threshold of the house; and **the house was filled with the cloud, and the court was full of the brightness of the LORD'S glory**."
Eze. 43:5	"So the spirit took me up, and brought me into the inner court; and, behold, the **glory of the LORD filled the house**."
Eze. 44:4	"Then brought he me the way of the north gate before the house: and I looked, and, behold, **the glory of the LORD filled the house of the LORD**: and I fell upon my face."
Rev. 15:8	"And **the temple was filled with smoke from the glory of God**, and from his power; and no man was able to enter into the temple, till the seven plagues of the seven angels were fulfilled."

It is also evidenced by the references to the Sanctuary as the Tabernacle of witness.

Num. 17:7	"And Moses laid up the rods before the LORD in the **tabernacle of witness**."

Num. 17:8	"And it came to pass, that on the morrow Moses went into the **tabernacle of witness**; and, behold, the rod of Aaron for the house of Levi was budded, and brought forth buds, and bloomed blossoms, and yielded almonds."
Num. 18:2	"And thy brethren also of the tribe of Levi, the tribe of thy father, bring thou with thee, and they may be joined unto thee, and minister unto thee: but thou and thy sons with thee shall minister before the **tabernacle of witness**."
2 Chr. 24:6	"And the king called for Jehoiada the chief, and said unto him, Why hast thou not required of the Levites to bring in out of Judah and out of Jerusalem the collection, according to the commandment of Moses the servant of the LORD, and of the congregation of Israel, for the **tabernacle of witness**?"
Acts 7:44	"Our fathers had the **tabernacle of witness** in the wilderness, as he had appointed, speaking unto Moses, that he should make it according to the fashion that he had seen."

That which is known as simply the "Tabernacle" and is referred to as the "Tabernacle of Witness" in the scriptures above is also known as the "Tabernacle of Testimony (**Exo. 38:21; Num. 1:50,53, 9:15, 10:11; Rev. 15:5**)." We know that the original "witness" was the pillar of fire and that the articles of witness were the five things that were in the ark and are the things that made the ark to be made known as the "Ark of the Testimony (**Exo. 25:22,26, 26:33–34, 30:6,26, 31:7, 39:35, 40:3,5,21; Num. 4:5, 7:89; Josh 4:16**)."

See Chapter 2: The Throne of God and the section on The Testimony.

It is important that we understand the connection between two words in the Hebrew language: *ayd* (Strong's reference #**5707**) and *aydooth* (Strong's reference #**5715**). The word *ayd* means "witness," and it is the root word for *aydooth* which means "testimony." Therefore, every reference to the "ark of the testimony" is also referring to the ark where the "witness" resides.

From this, we can also see again that every reference to the "Tabernacle of Witness" is also a reference to the "Tabernacle of Testimony." Also, the "witness" is the pillar of fire, which is the Holy Spirit, and included in that "witness" are all of the evidences that are provided as a "testimony." We also know that all of those evidences were symbolic of the Word of God, not as a dead letter, but rather, as the living Word that in the presence of the Shekinah (the glory of the presence of God) will absolutely spring forth to produce life.

This is exactly what the Apostle Paul was talking about when he said that our bodies are the temple of the Holy Spirit (**1 Cor. 3:16**). It is in this way that God gives witness and testimony that He has made us to be His habitation (**Eph. 2:22**) and is further shown by the scripture that says that we are living epistles (letters or books, **2 Cor. 3:1–2**) that are written of God by the Holy Spirit (**Jer. 31:31–33; Heb. 8:8–10, 12:22–29**) for a purpose, to be known and read of all men as a witness to the glory of God. Therefore, we are the very earthen vessels (**Jer. 32:14; Lam. 4:2; 2 Cor. 4:7**) that God wants to use to fill all the earth with His glory (**Num. 14:21; Isa. 6:3; Hab. 2:14; Psa. 72:19, 102:15, 108:5, 148:13; Isa. 60:2; Eze. 43:2; Hag. 2:4-9; 1 Sam. 2:8; 2 Chr. 29:11; Jer. 9:24; Eze. 26:20**).

There is only one place in the scriptures which perfectly matches this pattern of seven flames and one flame, and this is found in **2 Peter 1:5–8.**

2 Pet. 1:5	"And beside this, giving all diligence, add to your **faith virtue**; and to **virtue knowledge**."
2 Pet. 1:6	"And to **knowledge temperance**; and to **temperance patience**; and to **patience godliness**."
2 Pet. 1:7	"And to **godliness brotherly kindness**; and to **brotherly kindness charity**."
2 Pet. 1:8	"For if these things be in you, and abound, they make you that ye shall neither be barren nor unfruitful in the knowledge of our Lord Jesus Christ."

The word *charity* that is used in this passage of scripture is the Greek word *agape* or divine love. We can see that the "agape" would relate to the Shekinah and says exactly the same thing as the following scriptures.

1 John 4:8	"He that loveth not knoweth not God; for **God is love**."
1 John 4:16	"And we have known and believed the **love** that God hath to us. **God is love**; and he that dwelleth in **love** dwelleth in God, and God in him."

Each instance of the word *love* in the verses above are the Greek word *agape*. In **Jude 1:12**, it is also translated into the word *feast*. As such, when the virtues are sealed with divine love, that sealing is literally the invitation that is spoken about in **Rev. 19:9** (**see also Epilogue**).

It is from this that we can determine that the titles for each of the lamps in the lampstand are faith, virtue, knowledge, temperance, patience, godliness, and brotherly kindness, and the name that applies to the fire in the Holy of Holies is agape or divine love.

Not only does the lampstand relate to the rod of Aaron (by the symbol of the almonds) and the Shekinah (by the flames), but we can also see another relationship which is to the golden altar for incense in the following scripture.

Exo. 30:7 "And Aaron shall burn thereon sweet incense **every morning: when he dresseth the lamps**, he shall burn incense upon it."

Exo. 30:8 "And **when Aaron lighteth the lamps at even**, he shall burn incense upon it, a perpetual incense before the LORD throughout your generations."

Therefore, when we are offering our year-long atonement memorial offering by our twice daily (morning and evening) offering of the incense of humility before the Lord, we should also be asking Him to help us to keep the lamps trimmed and full of oil so that they can burn brightly. This is also related, therefore, to the parable of the ten virgins who rose up and trimmed their lamps. But first we will consider the oil that went into the lamps.

Identifies that the Olive Oil in the Lampstand is Inspired Teaching of the Word that is Both Given by and Received into Vessels that are Humble Before God

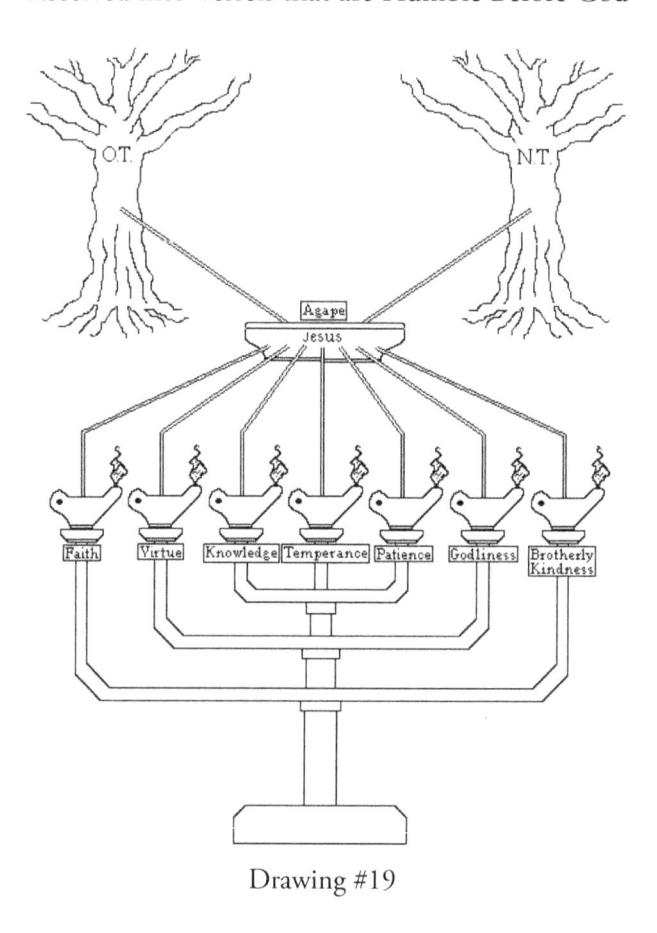

Drawing #19

CHAPTER 15

The Olive Oil for the Lamps

There are two symbolic meanings for the olive oil depending on the usage. The first is what the people provide for the Levites, and the second is what the Levites provide to the people.

Exo. 27:20	"And thou shalt **command the children of Israel, that they bring thee pure oil olive beaten for the light**, to cause the lamp to burn always."
Lev. 24:2	"**Command the children of Israel, that they bring unto thee pure oil olive beaten for the light**, to cause the lamps to burn **continually**."
Lev. 24:3	"Without the veil of the testimony, in the tabernacle of the congregation, **shall Aaron order it** from the evening unto the morning **before the LORD continually**: it shall be **a statute for ever** in your generations."
Lev. 24:4	"**He shall order the lamps upon the pure candlestick before the LORD continually**."

The children of Israel were commanded to provide so that the priests could serve continually and that the lamps should be set in order to burn continually. In this respect, the first symbolic meaning is that the olive oil is the same as the following verse.

> **Mal. 3:10** "Bring ye all the **tithes** into the storehouse, **that there may be meat in mine house**, and prove me now herewith, saith the LORD of hosts, if I will not open you the windows of heaven, and pour you out a blessing, that there shall not be room enough to receive it."

What is the purpose of providing for the priesthood? That there should be light in the Holy Place (minds) continually before the Lord. It is to burn continually for the purpose of setting in order the lamps of faith, virtue, knowledge, temperance, patience, godliness, and brotherly kindness in the Holy Place (mind) and so that the agape (divine love) in the Holy of Holies (heart) can burn brightly.

Who are the priesthood today?

> **Eph. 4:11** "And he gave some, **apostles; and some, prophets; and some, evangelists; and some, pastors and teachers**."

> **Eph. 4:12** "For the perfecting of the saints, **for the work of the ministry**, for the edifying of the body of Christ."

> **Eph. 4:13** "**Till we all come** in the unity of the faith, and of the knowledge of the Son of God, unto a perfect man, **unto the measure of the stature of the fullness of Christ**."

2 Cor. 3:5 "Not that we are sufficient of ourselves to think anything as of ourselves; but **our sufficiency is of God.**"

2 Cor. 3:6 "Who also hath **made us able ministers of the new testament**; not of the letter, but **of the spirit**: for the letter killeth, but **the spirit giveth life.**"

The New Covenant is not written with pen and ink but by the Holy Spirit in the tables of the heart.

2 Cor. 3:3 "Forasmuch as ye are manifestly declared to be the epistle of Christ ministered by us, **written not with ink, but with the Spirit of the living God**; not in tables of stone, **but in fleshly tables of the heart.**"

Just as God promised to give it in the heart and in the mind.

Jer. 31:31 "Behold, the days come, saith the LORD, that I will make a **new covenant** with the house of Israel, and with the house of Judah."

Jer. 31:32 "Not according to the covenant that I made with their fathers in the day that I took them by the hand to bring them out of the land of Egypt; which my covenant they brake, although I was an husband unto them, saith the LORD."

> **Jer. 31:33** "But **this shall be the covenant** that I will make with the house of Israel; After those days, saith the LORD, **I will put my law in their inward parts, and write it in their hearts**; and will be their God, and they shall be my people."

Therefore, just as the testimony was placed inside of the ark by the hands of the priests (at the commandment of God) so that it became the Ark of the Testimony, so also today the work of the ministry has a commandment given by God to take the word of God and sow it into people's hearts and minds.

However, even if the ministry speaks the word of God clearly and under the inspiration of the Holy Spirit; if it is not received and heard by the same inspiration being upon the hearers, then it will not be written, because it is the Spirit that does the writing (**Matt. 13:4–7**). But if it is written by the Spirit, then it will produce fruits (works) in living reality. It is for this reason that He said:

> **Mal. 3:8** "Will a man rob God? Yet ye have robbed me. But ye say, Wherein have we robbed thee? In tithes **and offerings**."

A tithe is a set amount (10 percent), but an offering is an amount that the Spirit places upon the heart, and many times, He even gives a specific reason and timing for the giving. There is a prerequisite for the giving of an offering that our hearts be tender enough before God and the turbulent storms of our thoughts calmed enough that when His "still small voice" speaks, we can both hear it and be obedient.

> **1 Kings 19:12** "And after the earthquake a fire; but the LORD was not in the fire: and after the fire a **still small voice**."

> **1 Kings 19:13** "And it was so, when Elijah heard it that he wrapped his face in his mantle, and went out, and stood in the entering in of the cave. And, behold, **there came a voice unto him**, and said, What doest thou here, Elijah?"

Which robbery is greatest? Not giving an offering to God when He speaks to us? Or withholding from Him a heart that is tender and humble before Him? But if our hearts truly are tender before Him, then we will both hear **and** be obedient (the Hebrew word *shamah* in **Deut. 6:4**). Therefore, it is only the fire of God, His presence, and anointing that gives us the ability to truly hear **and** be obedient. Now that we have covered the children of Israel bringing the olive oil to the priests, we can consider about the priests consecrating the oil for the lamps.

Remember that the priests use the oil to set in order the lamps of faith, virtue, knowledge, temperance, patience, godliness, and brotherly kindness in the Holy Place (mind) and that these open flames are not alone in the sanctuary, but there also was the agape in the Holy of Holies (heart). However, there is something that is to be done at the same time on the golden altar for incense.

> **Exo. 30:7** "And Aaron shall **burn thereon sweet incense** every morning: **when he dresseth the lamps**, he shall burn incense upon it."
>
> **Exo. 30:8** "And when Aaron **lighteth the lamps** at even, he shall **burn incense** upon it, a **perpetual incense** before the LORD throughout your generations."

Seeing that the incense is humility, the ministry must preach in an attitude of humility before God with the understanding that only a supernatural and divine work of the Holy Spirit can write the word of God in the hearts and minds of the hearers. The preaching of the word in humility and the people receiving it with humble hearts will set the conditions for the Holy Spirit to cause the discipline (rod) to produce obedience (almonds).

Jer. 1:11 "Moreover the word of the LORD came unto me, saying, Jeremiah, what seest thou? And I said, I see **a rod of an almond tree**."

Jer. 1:12 "Then said the LORD unto me, Thou hast well seen: for **I will hasten my word to perform it**."

A rod is symbolic of discipline.

Heb. 12:11 "Now no **chastening** for the present seemeth to be joyous, but grievous: nevertheless afterward it **yieldeth the peaceable fruit of righteousness** unto them which are exercised thereby."

Heb. 12:12 "**Wherefore lift up the hands which hang down, and the feeble knees**."

Heb. 12:13 "And **make straight paths for your feet**, lest that which is lame be turned out of the way; **but let it rather be healed**."

Only when the word is obeyed from the heart can it bring the fullness of the blessing and strengthening that it was sent to bring. It is then that the "fruit can remain," because it is Him doing it (the obedience) in us.

John 15:16 "Ye have not chosen me, but **I have chosen** you, **and ordained you, that ye should go and bring forth fruit**, and that **your fruit should remain**: that whatsoever ye shall ask of the Father in my name, he may give it you."

Before we enter into the last aspect about the olive oil for the lamp, we must ask ourselves the question, is the Word of God—**both** the Old Testament **and** the New—anointed?" It must be, because if it is not, then it will not be able to fulfill the following scripture.

Isa. 55:11 "So shall **my word** be that goeth forth out of my mouth: it **shall not return unto me void**, but it **shall accomplish** that which I please, and it **shall prosper** in the thing whereto I sent it."

The Two Olive Trees

In order to avoid a huge theological dilemma, we need to correctly identify the biblical use of the symbol of the two olive trees.

Zech. 4:2 "And said unto me, What seest thou? And I said, I have looked, and behold a candlestick all of gold, with a **bowl** upon the top of it, and his seven lamps thereon, and seven pipes to the seven lamps, which are upon the top thereof."

Zech. 4:3 "And **two olive trees** by it, one upon the right side of the bowl, and the other upon the left side thereof."

Zech. 4:11	"Then answered I, and said unto him, What are these **two olive trees** upon the right side of the candlestick and upon the left side thereof?"
Zech. 4:12	"And I answered again, and said unto him, What be these **two olive branches** which **through the two golden pipes empty the golden oil out of themselves**?"
Zech. 4:13	"And he answered me and said, Knowest thou not what these be? And I said, No, my lord."
Zech. 4:14	"Then said he, **These are the two anointed ones, that stand by the Lord of the whole earth**."

The key to correctly apply the symbols of the "two olive trees" or "two olive branches" is in verse **12**—"two olive branches which through the two golden pipes empty the golden oil out of themselves"—and in understanding where they empty into. The two golden pipes (from the olive trees) empty the olive oil into the bowl (symbolizing Christ), and then from the bowl, the olive oil is emptied into the seven lamps through seven pipes which symbolize either the virtues of **2 Pet. 1:5–7** (personal application) or the seven churches in **Revelations Chapters 2** and **3** (congregational and historical application).

There are two apparently opposing viewpoints on the meaning of the two olive trees. The first is the viewpoint that the two trees symbolize the Old and New Testaments. The second viewpoint is based on the following verses and concludes that the two trees are the two witnesses.

Rev. 11:3	"And I will give power unto my two witnesses, and they shall prophesy a thousand two hundred and threescore days, clothed in sackcloth."
Rev. 11:4	"These are the **two olive trees**, and the two candlesticks **standing before the God of the earth**."

We know that the fullness of the truth is that which makes *all* of the word of God to be true. The theological dilemma is that the two witnesses are obviously anointed men with the prophetic ministry (identified by their works as Moses and Elijah). As such, how could it be that two men pour out the anointing that is in them into Christ?

It is important to understand that *both* viewpoints have merit and a portion of the truth, but it is equally important to understand that even though in some aspects, one thing can be used to symbolize another, this does not mean that it *is* the other.

An example of this is in the Tabernacle. Even though the Tabernacle symbolized and was made after the pattern of the heavenly temple, this does not mean that the earthly tabernacle *was* the heavenly temple. This same detail is mentioned by the Apostle Paul in:

Heb. 8:1	"Now of the things which we have spoken this is the sum: We have such an high priest, who is set on the right hand of the throne of the Majesty **in the heavens**."
Heb. 8:2	**"A minister of the sanctuary, and of the true tabernacle, which the Lord pitched, and not man."**
Heb. 8:3	"For every high priest is ordained to offer gifts and sacrifices: wherefore

	it is of necessity that this man have somewhat also to offer."
Heb. 8:4	"For **if he were on earth**, he should not be a priest, seeing that there are priests that offer gifts according to the law."
Heb. 8:5	"Who serve unto the **example and shadow of heavenly things**, as Moses was admonished of God when he was about to make the tabernacle: for, See, saith he, that thou **make all things according to the pattern shewed to thee in the mount**."
Heb. 9:23	"It was therefore necessary that the **patterns of things in the heavens** should be purified with these; but the **heavenly things themselves** with better sacrifices than these."
Heb. 9:24	"For Christ is not entered into the holy places **made with hands**, which are the **figures of the true**; but into **heaven itself**, now to appear in the presence of God for us."

Therefore, even though the two witnesses *symbolize* the Old and New Testaments, they are not the books of the Testaments themselves. They are anointed servants of God that have the prophetic ministry and are faithful and obedient (stand) before the "the God of the earth;" and as with almost every other prophet, they or the lives they live have symbolic meaning. From this, we can also see a very important point in the prophet that symbolizes the New Testament. Elijah went up in a chariot of fire (**2 Kings 2:11**) and symbolized a New Testament group that will also meet the Lord in the air (**1 Thess. 4:17**). A testament is something that gives witness and testimony to something else. We can see this witness and testimony in the following verse.

> **Rev. 19:10** "And I fell at his feet to worship him. And he said unto me, See thou do it not: I am thy fellowservant, and of thy brethren that have the testimony of Jesus: worship God: for **the testimony of Jesus is the spirit of prophecy**."

In all of this, we can now see how, without contradiction, that the Old and the New Testaments are the anointed word of God:

> **Zech. 4:14** "Then said he, **These are the two anointed ones**, that stand by the Lord of the whole earth."

Which was poured into the Lord Jesus who is the Word made flesh.

> **John 1:14** "And **the Word was made flesh**, and dwelt among us, (and we beheld his glory, the glory as of the only begotten of the Father,) full of grace and truth."

It is only in this way that the following verses can make sense.

> **Zech. 4:2** "And said unto me, What seest thou? And I said, I have looked, and behold a candlestick all of gold, with a **bowl** upon the top of it, and his seven lamps thereon, and seven

	pipes to the seven lamps, which are upon the top thereof."
Zech. 4:3	"And **two olive trees** by it, one upon the right side of the **bowl**, and the other upon the left side thereof."
Zech. 4:11	"Then answered I, and said unto him, What are these **two olive trees** upon the right side of the candlestick and upon the left side thereof?"
Zech. 4:12	"And I answered again, and said unto him, What be these **two olive branches which through the two golden pipes empty the golden oil out of themselves**?"

Only in the context of the Lord Jesus being the bowl that all of the Word of God was poured into—and then from Him (by the inspiration of the Holy Spirit), the Word was poured out into the lampstand (of **2 Pet. 1:5–8** and **Rev. 1:4,11–16,20**) and that it was Him **hastening His word to perform it** (in us)—can the entirety of **Zechariah chapter 4** make sense. We can also see that the parallel of **Revelations Chapters 2** and **3** have an application that is at a higher level of kingdom manifestation than the personal (specifically, the church).

Jer. 1:11	"Moreover the word of the LORD came unto me, saying, Jeremiah, what seest thou? And I said, I see **a rod of an almond tree**."
Jer. 1:12	"Then said the LORD unto me, Thou hast well seen: for **I will hasten my word to perform it**."

Zech. 4:1	"And the angel that talked with me came again, and waked me, as a man that is wakened out of his sleep."
Zech. 4:2	"And said unto me, What seest thou? And I said, I have looked, and behold a **candlestick** all of gold, with a **bowl** upon the top of it, and his **seven lamps** thereon, and **seven pipes** to the **seven lamps**, which are upon the top thereof."
Zech. 4:3	"And **two olive trees** by it, one upon the right side of the bowl, and the other upon the left side thereof."
Zech. 4:4	"So I answered and spake to the angel that talked with me, saying, What are these, my lord?"
Zech. 4:5	"Then the angel that talked with me answered and said unto me, Knowest thou not what these be? And I said, No, my lord."
Zech. 4:6	"Then he answered and spake unto me, saying, This is the word of the LORD unto Zerubbabel, saying, Not by might, nor by power, but by my spirit, saith the LORD of hosts."
Zech. 4:7	"Who art thou, O great mountain? before Zerubbabel thou shalt become a plain: and he shall bring forth the headstone thereof with

shoutings, crying, Grace, grace unto it."

Zech. 4:8 "Moreover the word of the LORD came unto me, saying."

Zech. 4:9 "The hands of Zerubbabel have laid the foundation of this house; his hands shall also finish it; and thou shalt know that the LORD of hosts hath sent me unto you."

Zech. 4:10 "For who hath despised the day of small things? for they shall rejoice, and shall see the plummet in the hand of Zerubbabel with those seven; they are the eyes of the LORD, which run to and fro through the whole earth."

Zech. 4:11 "Then answered I, and said unto him, What are these **two olive trees** upon the right side of the **candlestick** and upon the left side thereof?"

Zech. 4:12 "And I answered again, and said unto him, What be these **two olive branches** which through the **two golden pipes** empty the **golden oil** out of themselves?"

Zech. 4:13 "And he answered me and said, Knowest thou not what these be? And I said, No, my lord."

Zech. 4:14   "Then said he, These are the **two anointed ones**, that stand by the Lord of the whole earth."

Therefore, the entire Word of God, Old Testament and New, were poured into Christ (**Zechariah 4:12**), and He pours Himself (**Zechariah 4:2**) into the virtues of **2 Peter 1:5–8** by **Ephesians 4:11** into the hearts and minds of His children and anoints it by the Holy Spirit to discipline and disciple (**Hebrews 12:11**) us to bring forth the fruits of His righteousness, producing in us the fullness of the perfect man Christ Jesus (**Ephesians 4:13**). This is so that the light of His glory (**Haggai 2:9**) can shine forth in living temples (**1 Corinthians 3:16**) in the fulfillment of His promise to give the New Covenant (**Jeremiah 31:31–33**), setting on display living books (**2 Corinthians 3:2**) that are written by His hand (Spirit) to be known and read of all men; and all of it happening at every step and level by the incense of His divine humility that makes us to be willing and yielded vessels.

Therefore, the olive oil symbolizes inspired teaching from both the Old and New Testaments that God gives through the preaching of the gospel to illuminate our minds and keep us aware of what is happening both within us and in the world around us from the perspective of God. This will only happen in a temple where the incense of humility is offered up every time the lamps in the lampstand are trimmed and lit (**Exo. 30:7–8**).

How Divine Understanding and Revelation Flow
from Throne of God to Illuminate Our Minds.

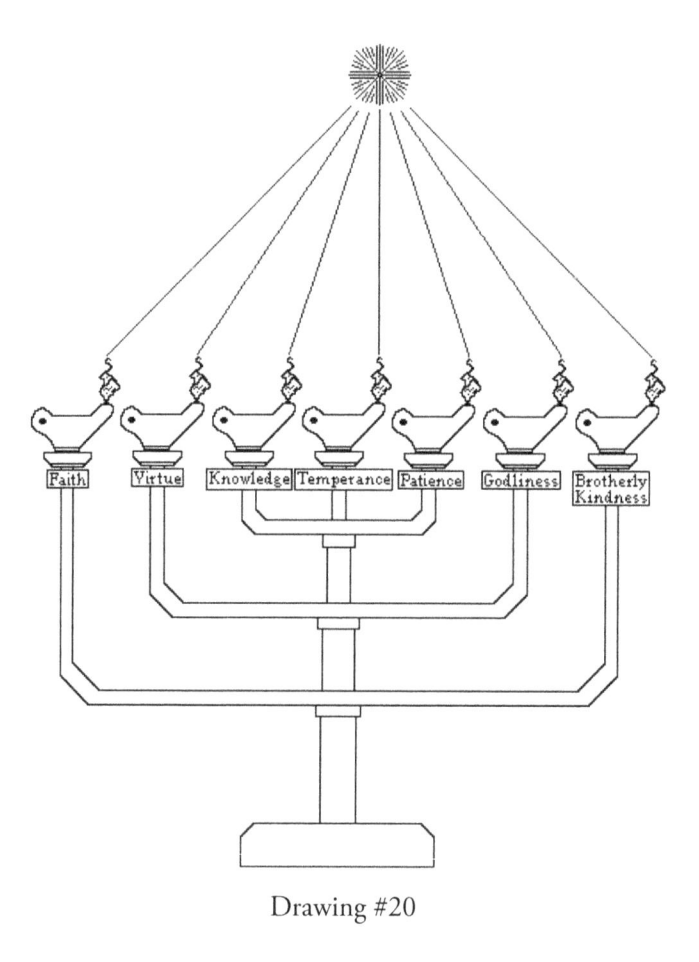

Drawing #20

CHAPTER 16

Lighting the Holy Place

We have seen how the Holy of Holies is the heart, the Holy Place is the mind, and that there is a veil of a self-will that is contrary to the will of God which separates between the two. That veil is not removed until the heart turns to the Lord, then He removes it in the circumcision of the heart.

When this happens, then the divine light of His presence will come into our hearts and overflow from our hearts into our minds.

2 Cor. 3:14 "But their **minds** were blinded: for until this day remaineth the same **vail** untaken away in the reading of the old testament; **which vail is done away in Christ**."

2 Cor. 3:15 "But even unto this day, when Moses is read, **the vail is upon their heart**."

2 Cor. 3:16 "Nevertheless **when it shall turn to the Lord, the vail shall be taken away**."

The phrase "when it shall turn to the Lord" is speaking about the heart. When the heart turns to the Lord, then "the veil shall be taken away." When the veil is taken away, the mind can be illuminated by the divine light of His presence (**John 1:4**). This is impossible to fully happen before the heart is converted/circumcised. Therefore, turning to the Lord with all of our hearts is the same as having our hearts converted to the Lord. It is in **this** that the promise of the New Covenant begins to be fulfilled.

Jer. 31:31 "Behold, the days come, saith the LORD, that I will make a **new covenant** with the house of Israel, and with the house of Judah."

Jer. 31:32 "Not according to the covenant that I made with their fathers in the day that I took them by the hand to bring them out of the land of Egypt; which my covenant they brake, although I was an husband unto them, saith the LORD."

Jer. 31:33 "But **this shall be the covenant** that I will make with the house of Israel; After those days, saith the LORD, **I will put my law** in their inward parts, **and write it in their hearts**; and will be their God, and they shall be my people."

With this, we can see that the New Covenant is a supernatural work that begins when we humble ourselves enough for God to come into our hearts when He is then seated in His throne and He begins to rule and reign over every aspect of our lives as King. Just as a king is given the title of "king," there is also a title that is given to the people that joyfully and willingly allow themselves to be ruled by their king; that title is "subjects."

Subjects are people that are in subjection to their king. If we are in subjection to our King, then, by our subjection, we are proclaiming that He is our King. If we are not in subjection to Him as is due for Him as King, then by our lack of subjection, we are proclaiming that we do not fully recognize Him as our King, even though we may say so with our words. When He comes in, He begins to write His Law (descriptions of how His character behaves) in our hearts. Sadly, many people have believed a lie about the law of God, and because of that lie, they have rejected the very thing that the New Covenant is—the law of God written within our hearts. How can this be? Because of a very subtle lie about the most basic characteristic of the nature of God—that God is love.

Everything that God does is done as an expression of His love toward us. If we think any other way about what God does, then we are misunderstanding Him. Sadly, some people say that they believe that God is a God of love and then think about His laws as though He is **only** a God of vengeance and condemnation. Some people think that when the Apostle Paul was speaking about the "law of sin and death" that he was speaking about the Law of Moses (the Law of God that was given through Moses). To understand that this is not the case, we only have to consider that when the **law** of sin and death entered into the world, it is the very moment that sin and death **also** entered into the world, and that was at the fall in sin. The law of sin and death was at work in the world many years before Moses was even born! Paul spoke about various laws, the law of sin and death, the law of the Spirit and of grace, and the law of God among others.

Because of a lack of discerning between the laws that Paul spoke about (and how they interact with each other), there is a horrible confusion that causes people to unknowingly reject the very thing that the New Covenant consists of. A God of love and who is described that He **is** love would not give a law **just so** that He could bludgeon mankind when they failed to be obedient. Just the opposite, He lovingly gave the law as descriptions of His character and nature and as examples of how He behaves Himself in different situations. He gave those examples so that we could have definite guidelines that we could use to identify the work that is happening in us, instead of depending upon our own whim and that of a fallen nature. It is for this that King David, a man after God's own heart, said:

Psa. 19:7	"The law of the LORD is perfect, converting the soul: the testimony of the LORD is sure, making wise the simple."
Psa. 19:8	"The statutes of the LORD are right, rejoicing the **heart**: the commandment of the LORD is pure, enlightening the eyes."
Psa. 19:9	"The fear of the LORD is clean, enduring for ever: the judgments of the LORD are true and righteous altogether."
Psa. 19:10	"More to be desired are they than gold, yea, than much fine gold: sweeter also than honey and the honeycomb."
Psa. 19:11	"Moreover by them is thy servant warned: and in keeping of them there is great reward."
Psa. 119:103	"How sweet are thy words unto my taste! yea, sweeter than honey to my mouth!"
Psa. 119:104	"Through thy precepts I get **understanding**: therefore I hate every false way."
Psa. 119:105	"NUN. Thy word is a lamp unto my feet, and a light unto my path."

From all of this, we can see with deeper appreciation of just what was happening after the resurrection when the scriptures say:

Luke 24:45 "Then opened he their **understanding**, that they might **understand** the **scriptures**."

He (who is the Word made flesh) was already beginning to impart to them (as the perfect sacrifice) His innocence of sin. He started in their minds by the blood being applied to the altar of incense (humility) and by giving them of His supernatural humility (incense, **Exo. 30:7–8**) so that they could understand (have the lamps burning in the Holy Place/mind) the scriptures. Then on the day of the Feast of Weeks (the day of Pentecost), He came into their hearts and began removing the veil of rebellious self-will, and then:

Eph. 1:18 "The eyes of your **understanding** being enlightened; that ye may know what is the hope of his calling, and what the riches of the glory of his inheritance in the saints."

Eph. 5:17 "Wherefore be ye not unwise, but **understanding** what the will of the Lord is."

Col. 1:9 "For this cause we also, since the day we heard it, do not cease to pray for you, and to desire that ye might be filled with the **knowledge** of his will in all **wisdom** and spiritual **understanding**."

Col. 2:2 "That their **hearts** might be comforted, being knit together in love, and unto all riches of the full assurance of **understanding**, to the acknowledgment of the mystery of God, and of the Father, and of Christ."

1 John 5:20   "And we know that **the Son of God is come**, and hath **given us** an **understanding**, that we may know him that is true, and we are in him that is true, even in his Son Jesus Christ. This is the true God, and eternal life."

True understanding is spiritual and not carnal. In the following scriptures, we see that true understanding flows from the heart and that when it does not, then there cannot be true spiritual understanding. All of this is because of hardness (or not being converted or circumcised) of the heart.

Rom. 10:9   "That if thou shalt confess with thy mouth the Lord Jesus, and shalt **believe in thine heart** that God hath raised him from the dead, thou shalt be saved."

Rom. 10:10   "For with the **heart** man **believeth** unto righteousness; and with the mouth confession is made unto salvation."

1 Cor. 1:19   "For it is written, I will destroy the **wisdom** of the **wise**, and will bring to nothing the **understanding** of the **prudent**."

1 Cor. 14:20   "Brethren, be not children in **understanding**: howbeit in malice be ye children, but in **understanding** be men."

Matt. 13:13   "Therefore speak I to them in parables: because they seeing see not; and hearing they hear not, neither do they **understand**."

Matt. 13:14   "And in them is fulfilled the prophecy of Esaias, which saith, By hearing ye shall hear, and shall not **understand**; and seeing ye shall see, and shall not perceive."

Matt. 13:15   "For this people's **heart** is waxed gross, and their ears are dull of hearing, and their eyes they have closed; lest at any time they should see with their eyes and hear with their ears, and should **understand** with their **heart**, and should be **converted**, and I should heal them."

Matt. 13:19   "When any one heareth the word of the kingdom, and **understandeth** it not, then cometh the wicked one, and catcheth away that which was sown in his **heart**. This is he which received seed by the way side."

Matt. 13:23   "But he that received seed into the good ground is he that heareth the word, and **understandeth** it; which **also** beareth fruit, and bringeth

	forth, some an hundredfold, some sixty, some thirty."
Mark 8:17	"And when Jesus knew it, he saith unto them, Why reason ye, because ye have no bread? perceive ye not yet, neither **understand**? have ye your **heart** yet hardened?"
Mark 12:33	"And to love him with all the **heart**, and with all the **understanding**, and with all the soul, and with all the strength, and to love his neighbour as himself, is more than all whole burnt offerings and sacrifices."
John 12:36	"While ye have light, believe in the light, that ye may be the children of light. These things spake Jesus, and departed, and did hide himself from them."
John 12:37	"But though he had done so many miracles before them, yet they believed not on him."
John 12:38	"That the saying of Esaias the prophet might be fulfilled, which he spake, Lord, who hath believed our report? and to whom hath the arm of the Lord been revealed?"
John 12:39	"Therefore they could not believe, because that Esaias said again."

John 12:40	"He hath blinded their eyes, and **hardened their heart**; that they should not see with their eyes, nor **understand with their heart**, and be **converted**, and I should heal them."
John 12:41	"These things said Esaias, when he saw his glory, and spake of him."
John 12:42	"Nevertheless among the chief rulers also many believed on him; but because of the Pharisees they did not confess him, lest they should be put out of the synagogue."
John 12:43	"For they loved the praise of men more than the praise of God."
John 12:44	"Jesus cried and said, He that believeth on me, believeth not on me, but on him that sent me."
John 12:45	"And he that seeth me seeth him that sent me."
John 12:46	"I am come a light into the world, that whosoever believeth on me should not abide in darkness."
John 12:47	"And if any man hear my **words**, and believe not, I judge him not: for I came not to judge the world, but to save the world."

John 12:48	"He that rejecteth me, and receiveth not my **words**, hath one that judgeth him: the **word** that I have spoken, the same shall judge him in the last day."
John 12:49	"For I have not spoken of myself; but the Father which sent me, he gave me a commandment, what I should say, and what I should speak."
John 12:50	"And I know that **his commandment is life everlasting**: whatsoever I speak therefore, even as the Father said unto me, so I speak."
Acts 28:26	"Saying, Go unto this people, and say, Hearing ye shall hear, and shall not **understand**; and seeing ye shall see, and not perceive."
Acts 28:27	"For the **heart** of this people is waxed gross, and their ears are dull of hearing, and their eyes have they closed; lest they should see with their eyes, and hear with their ears, and **understand** with their **hear**t, and should be **converted**, and I should heal them."
Rom. 1:20	"For the invisible things of him from the creation of the world are clearly seen, being **understood** by the things that are made, even his eternal power and Godhead; so that they are without excuse."

Php. 4:7   "And the peace of God, which passeth all **understanding**, shall keep your **hearts** and **minds** through Christ Jesus."

Col. 1:9   "For this cause we also, since the day we heard it, do not cease to pray for you, and to desire that ye might be filled with the **knowledge** of his will in all **wisdom** and **spiritual understanding**."

Heb. 11:3   "Through **faith** we **understand** that the worlds were framed by the **word** of God, so that things which are seen were not made of things which do appear."

2 Pet. 2:12   "But these, as natural brute beasts, made to be taken and destroyed, speak evil of the things that they **understand** not; and shall utterly perish in their own corruption."

2 Pet. 3:16   "As also in all his epistles, speaking in them of these things; in which are some things hard to be **understood**, which they that are unlearned and unstable wrest, as they do also the other scriptures, unto their own destruction."

Therefore, as we remain humble in the presence of God, He will give us all the understanding that we need. We are to study the word of God.

2 Tim. 2:15 "**Study** to show thyself approved unto God, a workman that needeth not to be ashamed, rightly dividing the word of truth."

But not to try to figure it out by our own intellectual abilities devoid of the divine inspiration of God; rather, to believe it with all of our hearts until we come to the understanding (by the work of the Spirit) that all of the Word of God is true, that there are no contradictions, and that His ways are **always** the best ways.

Prov. 3:5 "Trust in the LORD with all thine **heart**; and lean not unto thine own **understanding**."

Prov. 3:6 "In all thy ways acknowledge him, and he shall direct thy paths."

Prov. 3:7 "Be not **wise** in thine own eyes: fear the LORD, and depart from evil."

Prov. 3:8 "It shall be health to thy navel, and marrow to thy bones."

Because "rightly dividing the word of truth" will make every jot and tittle of the word of God to be true 100 percent of the time, and it will be true, not only **to** us, but **in** us, **through** us, and supernaturally displayed **around** us as divinely appointed earthen vessels to put His glory on display and to fill the earth with it.

The Connection Between the Temple Lampstand and the Lamps that are Spoken About in the Parable of the Ten Virgins and that the Original Oil that They Had was the Olive Oil of Divinely Inspired Teaching

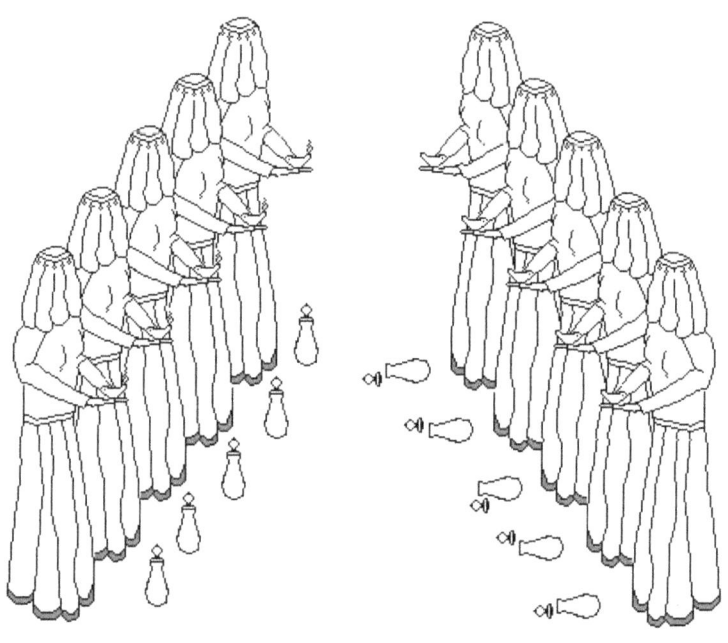

Drawing #21

CHAPTER 17

The Lamps and the Ten Virgins

We have seen a connection between the lamps being trimmed and lighted and the golden altar for incense. We have seen that the incense of humility must be offered up every morning and every evening as a continual ordinance. We have also seen that the olive oil is inspired teaching from both the Old and New Testaments.

The lamps that were in the Holy Place (mind) were supposed to be continually burning. Our understanding is supposed to be continually inspired by the anointing (fire) of the Lord so that it may continually give off light. The same light will manifest itself or be openly displayed through our flesh. We will see more on that when we come to the Outer Court.

In the parable of the ten virgins, we can see that they all started out with oil in their lamps, because all of their lamps were burning. But the five foolish virgins did not have the extra portion of oil with them that the wise virgins had.

Matt. 25:1	"Then shall the kingdom of heaven be likened unto **ten virgins**, which took their **lamps**, and went forth to meet the bridegroom."
Matt. 25:2	"And five of them were wise, and five were foolish."
Matt. 25:3	"They that were foolish took their **lamps**, and took no oil **with** them."

Matt. 25:4   "But the wise took oil in their **vessels with** their **lamps**."

Matt. 25:5   "While the bridegroom tarried, they all slumbered and slept."

Matt. 25:6   "And at midnight there was a cry made, Behold, the bridegroom cometh; go ye out to meet him."

Matt. 25:7   "Then **all those virgins arose, and trimmed their lamps**."

Matt. 25:8   "And the foolish said unto the wise, Give us of your oil; for **our lamps are gone out**."

Matt. 25:9   "But the wise answered, saying, Not so; lest there be not enough for us and you: but go ye rather to them that sell, and buy for yourselves."

Matt. 25:10   "And while they went to buy, the bridegroom came; and they that were ready went in with him to the marriage: and the door was shut."

Matt. 25:11   "Afterward came also the other virgins, saying, Lord, Lord, open to us."

Matt. 25:12   "But he answered and said, Verily I say unto you, I know you not."

> **Matt. 25:13** "Watch therefore, for ye know neither the day nor the hour wherein the Son of man cometh."

Notice, a lamp cannot go out if it was never lit. Therefore, they all started out with oil (olive oil, divinely inspired teaching) in their lamps; but when **Matthew 25:3** says about the foolish virgins that they "took no oil **with** them," it is in the context of **Matthew 25:4** that says about the wise virgins that they "took oil in their **vessels with** their lamps." It may even be that the foolish virgins had the extra vessels, just that the vessels were empty. Also note that the parable never explicitly says that the foolish virgins **ever** obtained the extra portion of oil.

It is easy to understand that everything that we need in order to be prepared for the coming of the Lord can **only** be obtained by entering into the Holy of Holies and remaining in the presence of the King in an attitude of humility and subjection **until** the work is complete. How do we know that the work is complete? There are two supernatural evidences that God gives that witness to the completeness of the work in us.

The first is that He removes the veil of separation between our hearts and minds in the circumcision of the heart. When the veil is removed, there will be a conforming of our thoughts to the will of God as He has expressed it in His Word together with the resultant obedience.

The second is when our mortal bodies are transformed to immortal and from corruptible to incorruptible in the twinkling of an eye so that we can go with Him to the Great Feast of Tabernacles—the Wedding Supper of the Lamb.

> **Luke 24:49** "And, behold, I send the promise of my Father upon you: but tarry ye in the city of Jerusalem, **until** ye be endued with power from on high."

We know that this supernatural provision began after various (ten) days and nights of nonstop waiting on God for the promise, and we see the testimony of it in:

> **Acts 2:2** "And suddenly there came a sound from heaven as of a rushing mighty wind, and it filled all the house where they were sitting."
>
> **Acts 2:3** "And there appeared unto them cloven tongues like as of fire, and it sat upon each of them."
>
> **Acts 2:4** "**And they were all filled with the Holy Ghost**, and began to speak with other tongues, as the Spirit gave them utterance."

The one hundred and twenty that were in the upper room were filled with the Holy Ghost, the Spirit of Holiness. The term "Holy Ghost" or "Holy Spirit" in Hebrew is "Ruach Ha Kodesh" or literally the "Spirit of Holiness." Holiness is divinely produced obedience to the law of God which proceeds from the heart where God is seated as King. We have already seen that the law was given as descriptions of how the character and nature of God behaves itself. Therefore, what happened in the upper room is that there was a divine impartation of the Spirit that produced the living reality of the character and nature of God in the lives of the believers.

Because of this, we can see that what happened in the upper room was "the promise of my Father" being made manifest. That promise was given in:

> **Jer. 31:31** "Behold, the days come, saith the LORD, that **I will make a new covenant** with the house of Israel, and with the house of Judah."

Jer. 31:32	"Not according to the covenant that I made with their fathers in the day that I took them by the hand to bring them out of the land of Egypt; which my covenant they brake, although I was an husband unto them, saith the LORD."
Jer. 31:33	"But this shall be the **covenant** that I will make with the house of Israel; After those days, saith the LORD, **I will put my law in their inward parts, and write it in their hearts**; and will be their God, and they shall be my people."

Therefore, the promise of the Father is that He would give the New Covenant of writing His character and nature (law) by His Spirit in the hearts and minds (the Sanctuary: Holy of Holies and the Holy Place) of His people, and that in doing so, they would be "endued with power from on high" to manifest the reality of who He is to a lost and dying world (in the Outer Court of the flesh).

The supernatural power of God manifesting Himself through His children is a power that no other principality or power in the universe can resist. It is the power of divine (agape) love physically manifesting itself as Holiness or divinely expressed obedience (**Jer. 1:12**) in which the children of God will move, live, and have their being (**Acts 17:28**).

How is the giving of the Holy Spirit connected to God writing His law in our hearts and minds? Consider the following scripture:

Eze. 36:26	"A **new heart** also will I give you, and a **new spirit** will I put within you: and I will take away the stony heart out of your flesh, and I will give you an heart of flesh."

Eze. 36:27	"And I will put **my spirit** within you, **and cause you to walk in my statutes, and ye shall keep my judgments, and do them.**"
Psa. 37:31	"The law of his God is in his heart; **none** of his steps shall slide."
2 Pet. 1:10	"Wherefore the rather, brethren, give diligence to make your calling and election sure: for **if ye do these things**, ye shall **never** fall."

If we do **what** things?

2 Pet. 1:2	"Grace and peace be multiplied unto you through the knowledge of God, and of Jesus our Lord."
2 Pet. 1:3	"According as his divine power hath given unto us all things that pertain unto life and godliness, through the knowledge of him that hath called us to glory and virtue."
2 Pet. 1:4	"Whereby are given unto us exceeding great and precious promises: that by these ye might be partakers of the divine nature, having escaped the corruption that is in the world through lust."
2 Pet. 1:5	"And beside this, giving all diligence, **add to your faith virtue; and to virtue knowledge.**"

2 Pet. 1:6	"And to knowledge temperance; and to temperance patience; and to patience godliness."
2 Pet. 1:7	"And to godliness brotherly kindness; and to brotherly kindness charity."
2 Pet. 1:8	"For **if these things be in you, and abound**, they make you that ye shall neither be barren nor unfruitful in the knowledge of our Lord Jesus Christ."
2 Pet. 1:9	"But he that lacketh these things is blind, and cannot see afar off, and hath forgotten that he was purged from his old sins."
2 Pet. 1:10	"Wherefore the rather, brethren, give diligence to make your calling and election sure: for if ye **do** these things, ye shall **never** fall."
2 Pet. 1:11	"For so an entrance shall be ministered unto you abundantly into the everlasting kingdom of our Lord and Saviour Jesus Christ."
2 Pet. 1:12	"Wherefore I will not be negligent to put you always in remembrance of these things, though ye know them, and be established in the present truth."

In this, we see yet again a connection between the lampstand (and the names of each lamp) and the ten virgins. We can also see that the law of God or the expressions of His character and nature are manifested and move through faith, virtue, knowledge, temperance, patience, godliness, brotherly kindness, and charity (agape love). When these virtues come to their fullest maturity in the life of the believer, it will fulfill every jot and tittle of the law; all of His character and nature will be put on display. In other words, the New Covenant producing a church without spot or wrinkle, living books written for the purpose of being known and read of all man.

We need to ask ourselves, do we want for God to call us **great** (rulers and kings) in His kingdom? Or do we want for God to call us **least** (insignificant) in His kingdom?

Matt. 5:18	"For verily I say unto you, **Till heaven and earth pass, one jot or one tittle shall in no wise pass from the law, till all be fulfilled.**"
Matt. 5:19	"**Whosoever therefore shall break one of these least commandments, and shall teach men so**, he shall be called the **least** in the kingdom of heaven: but **whosoever shall do and teach them**, the same shall be called **great** in the kingdom of heaven."
Psa. 40:8	"I delight to do thy **will**, O my God: yea, thy **law** is within my **heart**."
Psa. 119:34	"Give me **understanding**, and I shall keep thy **law**; yea, I shall **observe** it with my whole **heart**."

If everything that we need in order to be prepared for the coming of the Lord can only be obtained by entering into the Holy of

Holies and remaining in the presence of the King, until then, we can conclude that the wise virgins entered into His presence and remained there until they obtained the extra vessel full of oil.

Conversely, the foolish virgins did not remain there. They may have loved to enter into His presence but fulfilled the following scripture:

> **Jam. 4:3** "Ye ask, and receive not, because ye ask amiss, that ye may **consume** it upon your **lusts**."

There are those who throw away all of the benefits (oil) of entering into the Holy of Holies by consuming those blessings upon their lusts. They do this by continuing to live their lives according to the rebellion of the fallen nature (by not being subjects) and not letting God truly be King over their lives. Because of this, their own will is not broken or torn (as was the inner veil) to be subject to the will of God, and therefore, **they remove themselves** from participating in the will of God being done on (and in) earth as it is in heaven. The first piece of earth that the will of God must be done in is that piece of clay that our bodies are made out of.

> **John 12:43** "For they loved the praise of men **more** than the praise of God."

However, those who **do** live their lives continually in the blessed presence of God **will** experience not only His blessings, but also:

> **2 Tim. 3:12** "Yea, and **all** that will live godly in Christ Jesus **shall** suffer persecution."

Because it will be misunderstood by those who do not continually live in that place of the divine presence of God. But He has given us specific instructions.

Isa. 51:7 "Hearken unto me, ye that know righteousness, the people in whose **heart** is my **law; fear ye not the reproach of men, neither be ye afraid of their revilings**."

But rather:

Matt. 5:10 "Blessed are they which are persecuted for righteousness' sake: for theirs is the kingdom of heaven."

Matt. 5:11 "Blessed are ye, when men shall revile you, and persecute you, and shall say all manner of evil against you falsely, for my sake."

Matt. 5:12 "**Rejoice**, and be **exceeding glad**: for **great** is your reward in heaven: for so persecuted they the prophets which were before you."

Now we can see that the detail which makes the difference between the foolish virgins and the wise virgins is that the wise virgins love the presence of God more than to live their lives their own way. The difference is expressed in the parable in the terms of having the extra vessel of oil. Therefore, how do we make the connection between constantly abiding in the presence of God and the extra vessel of oil?

Remember that four out of the five items that were in the Ark of the Covenant were put there by the hand of man as they were commanded by God to do. We have also seen that all of the items that were inside of the Ark of the Covenant symbolize the word of God in some way. This process of putting the word of God into the heart comes through **Ephesians 4:11–13**.

> **Eph. 4:11** "And he gave some, **apostles**; and some, **prophets**; and some, **evangelists**; and some, **pastors** and **teachers**."
>
> **Eph. 4:12** "For the perfecting of the saints, for the work of the ministry, for the edifying of the body of Christ."
>
> **Eph. 4:13** "**Till we all come** in the unity of the faith, and of the knowledge of the Son of God, unto a perfect man, **unto the measure of the stature of the fulness of Christ**."

In other words, it is olive oil, inspired teaching that comes from both the Old and the New Testaments (the two olive trees, **Zech. 4:14**) through the Word that was made flesh (**John 1:14**; **Zech. 4:2–3,12**) and poured out from **that** bowl through **Eph. 4:11** and into the virtues of His character in individuals and the church throughout history.

However, just as the preaching of the gospel did not profit those who did not receive it with faith:

> **Heb. 4:2** "For **unto us was the gospel preached**, as well as unto them: **but the word preached did not profit them**, **not being mixed with faith** in them that heard it."

And faith without works or faith that does not come with heart-felt obedience is dead.

> **Jam. 2:14** "What doth it profit, my brethren, though a man say he hath **faith**,

and have not **works**? can **faith** save him?"

Jam. 2:17 "Even so **faith**, if it hath not **works**, is **dead**, being alone."

Jam. 2:20 "But wilt thou know, O vain man, that **faith without works is dead**?"

Jam. 2:21 "Was not Abraham our father justified by works, when he had offered Isaac his son upon the altar?"

Jam. 2:22 "Seest thou how **faith wrought with his works**, and **by works was faith made perfect**?"

Jam. 2:23 "And the scripture was fulfilled which saith, Abraham believed God, and it was imputed unto him for righteousness: and he was called the Friend of God."

Jam. 2:24 "Ye see then how that by works a man is justified, and not by faith **only**."

Jam. 2:26 "For as the body without the spirit is dead, so **faith without works is dead** also.

Therefore, works without faith cannot save, but if our faith is real enough to save, then it is real enough to produce works. The works that we do, we do **because** we **are** saved, not in order to **be** saved. What are the works? They are **not** the product of our carnal abilities. They are the product of the divine power of the very life of God working within us by the Word and the Spirit of God.

Jer. 1:11 "Moreover the word of the LORD came unto me, saying, Jeremiah, what seest thou? And I said, I see a **rod** of an **almond** tree."

Jer. 1:12 "Then said the LORD unto me, Thou hast well seen: for **I** will **hasten** my word to **perform** it."

Heb. 12:11 "Now no **chastening** for the present seemeth to be joyous, but grievous: nevertheless afterward it yieldeth the peaceable **fruit** of righteousness unto them which are exercised thereby."

Heb. 12:12 "Wherefore lift up the hands which hang down, and the feeble knees."

Heb. 12:13 "And **make straight paths for your feet**, lest that which is lame be turned out of the way; **but let it rather be healed**."

Rom. 9:28 "For he will finish the work, and cut it short in **righteousness**: because a **short** work will the **Lord make** upon the earth."

We can see that the rod (symbolic of discipline) in the presence of God will quickly produce works of righteousness. But they are produced by God and by His power working within us. **This** is the righteousness (His) with which the Bride of Christ is clothed (wedding garments), those who become kings and priests in His presence.

Psa. 132:9	"Let thy **priests** be **clothed** with **righteousness**; and let thy **saints** shout for joy."
Rev. 1:5	"And from Jesus Christ, who is the faithful witness, and the first begotten of the dead, and the prince of the kings of the earth. Unto him that loved us, and washed us from our sins in his own blood."
Rev. 1:6	"And hath made us **kings** and **priests** unto God and his Father; to him be glory and dominion for ever and ever. Amen."
Rev. 5:10	"And hast made us unto our God **kings** and **priests**: and we shall reign on the earth."
Rev. 19:8	"And to her was granted that she should be arrayed in **fine linen, clean and white**: for **the fine linen is the righteousness of saints**."
Isa. 64:6	"But we are all as an unclean thing, and **all our righteousnesses are as filthy rags**; and we all do fade as a leaf; and our iniquities, like the wind, have taken us away."

Therefore, the righteousness is the righteousness of God and it is the manifestation of the power of His life. It is the righteousness with which the saints are clothed. It is a supernatural and divine provision that is only produced from constantly abiding in the Holy of Holies and gaining access through the incense of humility.

2 Pet. 1:3 "According as **his divine power** hath given unto us **all things that pertain unto life and godliness,** through the knowledge of him that hath **called us to glory and virtue.**"

The only one of the five items inside of the Ark of the Covenant that was not put there by the hand of man was the almonds. The only substance that is supernaturally produced in the Holy of Holies is the almonds, which symbolize the divine works of His righteous obedience that is made manifest in us and that only the wise virgins stayed long enough to get. But the symbol is oil; how do we connect the almonds to the oil?

An almond nut has a hard shell around it; however, the word says:

Luke 17:10 "So likewise ye, when ye shall have done **all** those things which are commanded you, **say**, We are unprofitable servants: we have done that which was our duty to do."

Therefore, we are to break off any hard shell of pride that we might have about our obedience (His in us) and discard it, because it can only serve to block the free flow of the oil that is the exclusive product of divine provision.

The light in the Holy Place (mind) was to be burning always. But the lamps of the foolish virgins were going out, their minds or their understanding were being darkened. Even though they had divinely inspired teaching, they were:

2 Tim. 3:7 "Ever learning, and **never** able to come to the **knowledge** of the truth."

Luke 8:18   "Take heed therefore **how** ye hear: for whosoever hath, to him shall be given; and whosoever hath not, from him shall be taken even that which he **seemeth** to have."

Why? Because they didn't come into the presence of the Shekinah or they wanted it as only an occasional anointing so that:

Jam. 4:3   "Ye ask, and receive not, because ye ask amiss, that ye may **consume** it upon your lusts."

But they didn't want a continual abiding in the Shekinah so that it could give the necessary strength to bear the fruit of obedience (almonds). They didn't want to "pay the price" of "taking up their cross" every day to follow Him. This oil does not cost money.

Isa. 55:1   "Ho, every one that thirsteth, come ye to the waters, and he that hath no money; come ye, **buy**, and eat; yea, come, **buy** wine and milk **without money and without price**."

The wine of divine inspiration and the milk of a sincere heart that is humble before God, it is obtained without money, but there **is** a price to pay.

1 Chr. 21:24   "And king David said to Ornan, Nay; but I will verily **buy** it for the full price: for I will not take that which is thine for the LORD, nor offer burnt offerings without **cost**."

Job 22:27	"Thou shalt make thy prayer unto him, and he shall hear thee, and thou shalt **pay** thy vows."
Psa. 22:25	"My praise shall be of thee in the great congregation: I will **pay** my vows before them that fear him."
Psa. 50:14	"Offer unto God thanksgiving; and **pay** thy vows unto the most High."
Psa. 66:13	"I will go into thy house with burnt offerings: I will **pay** thee my vows."
Psa. 116:14	"I will **pay** my vows unto the LORD now in the presence of all his people."
Psa. 116:18	"I will **pay** my vows unto the LORD now in the presence of all his people."
Ecc. 5:4	"When thou vowest a vow unto God, defer not to **pay** it; for he hath no pleasure in fools: **pay** that which thou hast vowed."
Ecc. 5:5	"Better is it that thou shouldest not vow, than that thou shouldest vow and not **pay**."
Jonah 2:9	"But I will sacrifice unto thee with the voice of thanksgiving; I will **pay** that that I have vowed. Salvation is of the LORD."

Many can say that "Jesus paid the price," and He did for salvation and access to the promises and the blessings. Without the price that He paid, nothing else that we might do would be of any worth, but because of the price that He paid, we can identify ourselves with our sacrifice by laying our hands upon our sacrifice by dying out to ourselves (the old man of sin), and **that** identification has value. Please consider the following scriptures:

Lev. 3:2 "And he shall **lay his hand** upon the head of his offering, and kill it at the door of the tabernacle of the congregation: and Aaron's sons the priests shall sprinkle the blood upon the altar round about."

Lev. 3:8 "And he shall **lay his hand** upon the head of his offering, and kill it before the tabernacle of the congregation: and Aaron's sons shall sprinkle the blood thereof round about upon the altar."

Lev. 3:13 "And he shall **lay his hand** upon the head of it, and kill it before the tabernacle of the congregation: and the sons of Aaron shall sprinkle the blood thereof upon the altar round about."

Lev. 4:4 "And he shall bring the bullock unto the door of the tabernacle of the congregation before the LORD; and shall **lay his hand** upon the bullock's head, and kill the bullock before the LORD."

Lev. 4:15 "And the elders of the congregation shall **lay their hands** upon the head of the bullock before the LORD: and the bullock shall be killed before the LORD."

Lev. 4:24 "And he shall **lay his hand** upon the head of the goat, and kill it in the place where they kill the burnt offering before the LORD: it is a sin offering."

Lev. 4:29 "And he shall **lay his hand** upon the head of the sin offering, and slay the sin offering in the place of the burnt offering."

Lev. 4:33 "And he shall **lay his hand** upon the head of the sin offering, and slay it for a sin offering in the place where they kill the burnt offering."

Lev. 16:21 "And Aaron shall **lay both his hands** upon the head of the live goat, and confess over him all the iniquities of the children of Israel, and all their transgressions in all their sins, **putting them upon** the head of the goat, and shall send him away by the hand of a fit man into the wilderness."

Num. 8:12 "And the Levites shall **lay their hands** upon the heads of the bullocks: and thou shalt offer the one for a sin offering, and the other for a burnt offering, unto the LORD, to make an atonement for the Levites."

It was by laying their hands upon their sacrifice that they identified themselves with the death of the sacrifice. In doing so, two things were happening: first, their sins were transferred to the sacrifice; and second, they were proclaiming that the sacrifice was dying in their place. When we "take up our cross" to follow Him, we are fulfilling the reality that "laying their hands" was symbolizing. As we die out to the old man of sin, there is a two-way transference that happens. Our sins (that even yet we commit) are transferred to Him, and His life is transferred to us, thereby making it possible to walk in the reality of His life.

> **Heb. 7:25** "Wherefore he is able also to save them to the uttermost that come unto God by him, seeing **he ever liveth to make intercession for them**."

But the question remains—how do the almonds become oil?

The Kind of Oil that was in the Extra Vessel that the Wise Virgins Had and How to Obtain It.

Almond oil

Drawing #22

CHAPTER 18

The Oil in the Extra Vessel

The difference between the foolish and the wise virgins is that the foolish virgins did not make the presence of the Shekinah (the manifest Glory of the Presence of God) their constant dwelling place. Only the Shekinah can bring forth the almonds. Because of this, the almonds of divinely produced obedience could not be obtained by the foolish virgins. Remaining in the presence of God is how we purchase the almonds from which the oil for the extra vessel comes and also how the veil of self-will that is demonically influenced to rebel is removed in the circumcision of the heart. Therefore, the wise virgins had almonds and the veil removed, and the foolish virgins did not have either the almonds or the veil removed. But how do you get from almonds to an extra vessel of oil? Even though the almonds (obedience) are produced supernaturally, it is still possible for us to become prideful about our obedience as though it was the product of our own ability.

This pride is like the shell of hardness that surrounds the almond nut. But it is for this reason that the Lord Jesus said:

Luke 17:10 "So likewise ye, when ye shall have done **all** those things which are commanded you, say, We are unprofitable servants: we have done that which was our duty to do."

We have to break that hard shell of pride off of our obedience and discard it, because it is unprofitable and only fit for the fire. After the shell of pride has been removed from around our obedience, then the almond must be put through the grinding of trials to prove that it is real or perfect and that it is the obedience that comes from above as the result of the power of His Life.

    Heb. 5:8   "Though he were a Son, yet learned he obedience by the things which he **suffered**."

    Heb. 5:9   "And being made perfect, he became the author of eternal salvation unto all them that obey."

Not as though He wasn't already perfect, but His obedience had to be proven to be perfect so that He could become "the author of eternal salvation unto all them that **obey** Him."

    1 Pet. 5:10   "But the God of all grace, who hath called us unto his eternal glory by Christ Jesus, after that ye have **suffered** a while, make you perfect, stablish, strengthen, settle you."

And if His obedience had to be put to the test to prove that it was real, then our (His in us) obedience will also have to be proven to be real.

    Deut. 8:2   "And thou shalt remember all the way which the LORD thy God led thee these forty years in the wilderness, to **humble** thee, and to **prove** thee, to know what was in thine **heart**, whether thou wouldest **keep** his commandments, or no."

Deut. 8:3 "And he **humbled** thee, and suffered thee to hunger, and fed thee with manna, which thou knewest not, neither did thy fathers know; that he might **make thee know** that man doth not live by bread only, but by **every word** that proceedeth out of the mouth of the LORD doth man live."

Now that we know that the incense is humility, we can see that He desired for them to offer up the incense (of humility) in their hearts to come into His presence and receive His supernatural provision of power to live by "**every word** that proceedeth out of the mouth of the LORD." Those words (law) were and are the descriptions of His character. In other words, He wanted them to be so surrendered to Him (as subjects to their King) so that He could supernaturally empower them to manifest, in the fullness of living reality, His divine nature and to show that He **does** have the power for this to be possible, even while we are still in flesh and while we are still in the earth, because with God, **all** things are possible. After the grinding, the almonds (of obedience) are put under pressure to see if it will fail or turn aside from following after Him.

Heb. 5:7 "Who in the days of his flesh, when he had offered up prayers and supplications with **strong crying and tears** unto him that was able to save him from death, and was heard in that he feared;"

Luke 22:42 "Saying, Father, if thou be willing, remove this cup from me: nevertheless **not my will, but thine, be done**."

Luke 22:44 "And **being in an agony he prayed more earnestly**: and his sweat was as it were great drops of blood falling down to the ground.

He agonized over His obedience, but what do you get when the almond nuts have been both ground up and pressed out? Oil! Therefore, the oil that is in the extra vessel of oil that the wise virgins had is almond oil, not olive oil. It is a special (divinely imparted) instruction that the wise virgins receive directly from God without man's intervention and which is received because of constantly abiding in the Shekinah until the veil of demonically inspired rebellious self-will is removed.

The Cycle of Increase

Therefore, the Shekinah brings forth the almonds of obedience. As long as we remain in His presence, then there will be a constant provision of the almonds of divinely imparted obedience together with its related circumcision of heart.

The extra vessel of oil comes from the almonds and is constantly being poured into the lamps so that:

2 Pet. 1:8 "For if these things be in you, and abound, they make you that ye shall neither be barren nor unfruitful in the knowledge of our Lord Jesus Christ."

And "to cause the lamp to burn always," but this time with the divinely produced almond oil of a supernatural obedience instead of the olive oil of teaching (though divinely inspired) that comes through man. This is so in order for us to be:

Jam. 1:22	"But be ye **doers of the word**, and not hearers only, deceiving your own selves."
Jam. 1:23	"For if any be a hearer of the word, and not a **doer**, he is like unto a man beholding his natural face in a glass."
Jam. 1:24	"For he beholdeth himself, and goeth his way, and straightway forgetteth what manner of man he was."
Jam. 1:25	"But whoso looketh into the perfect law of liberty, and **continueth** therein, he being not a forgetful hearer, but a **doer** of the work, this man shall be blessed in his deed."
Rom. 2:13	"For not the hearers of the law are just before God, but the **doers** of the law shall be justified."

Those who actually are obedient (subject) to put on display the works that manifest the character and nature of God. The lamps are perpetually lit because of the extra vessel of oil. The light of our understanding does not go out because of the supernatural provision that enables us to:

1 John 1:7	"But if we **walk in the light**, as he is in the light, we have fellowship one with another, and the blood of Jesus Christ his Son cleanseth us from **all** sin."
1 John 1:4	"And these things write we unto you, that your joy may be full."

1 John 1:5	"This then is the message which we have heard of him, and declare unto you, that God is light, and in him is no darkness at all."
1 John 1:6	"If we say that we have fellowship with him, and **walk** in darkness, we lie, and **do** not the truth."
1 John 2:3	"And hereby we do know that we know him, if we **keep** his commandments."
1 John 2:4	"He that saith, I know him, and keepeth not his commandments, is a liar, and the truth is not in him."
1 John 2:5	"But whoso **keepeth** his word, in him verily is the love of God **perfected**: hereby know we that we are in him."
1 John 2:6	"He that saith he abideth in him ought himself also so to **walk**, even as he walked."

The light in the lampstand burns brighter, reflecting the divine light in the Holy of Holies. The divine light (Shekinah) in the Holy of Holies gets brighter, brings forth more almonds, more oil, more light in the lampstand reflecting more Shekinah. The cycle continues until the entire tabernacle is filled with light, until the entire temple becomes a burning lamp filled with the glory of the light of His life, until it becomes so intense that this mortal must put on immortality, and this corruption must put on incorruption. Until this world can no longer contain it and fulfills **Dan. 7:27** to then go into the wedding supper with the bridegroom. It is for this reason that the Spirit of Holiness commands **us,** just as He commanded the disciples to abide in the Holy of Holies with Him…**until**.

But **our** "until" is not just to be filled with power from on high in a superficial way, but to abide in the presence of the Shekinah **until** we go into the wedding supper of the Lamb. The objective is not to just have manifestations of power, but to be fully clothed upon with His image and likeness again (His perfect righteousness, linen garments, wedding garments, character, and nature) until He brings us forth from our closet of preparation, just as it says in:

Joel 2:12 "Therefore also now, saith the LORD, turn ye even to me with all your **heart**, and with fasting, and with weeping, and with mourning."

Joel 2:13 "And rend your **heart**, and not your garments, and **turn** unto the LORD your God: for he is gracious and merciful, slow to anger, and of great kindness, and repenteth him of the evil."

Joel 2:14 "Who knoweth if he will return and repent, and leave a blessing behind him; even a meat offering and a drink offering unto the LORD your God?"

Joel 2:15 "Blow the trumpet in Zion, sanctify a fast, call a solemn assembly."

Joel 2:16 "Gather the people, sanctify the congregation, assemble the elders, gather the children, and those that suck the breasts: **let the bridegroom**

go forth of his chamber**, and the bride out of her closet.**"

Joel 2:17 "**Let the priests, the ministers of the LORD**, weep between the porch and the altar, and let them say, Spare thy people, O LORD, and give not thine heritage to reproach, that the heathen should rule over them: wherefore should they say among the people, Where is their God?"

Joel 2:18 "Then will the LORD be jealous for his land, and pity his people."

Joel 2:19 "Yea, the LORD will answer and say unto his people, Behold, I will send you corn, and wine, and oil, and ye shall be satisfied therewith: and I will no more make you a reproach among the heathen."

Why does the bride come forth out of her closet? Because the time has come for the bride to make the transition from just being a bride that is "promised unto" marriage into being the wife that has taken the wedding vows and entered into the New (wedding) Covenant with the Bridegroom, the Lord Jesus Christ (**Jer. 31:31–33**). Just as a man and a woman become one flesh when they are married.

Gen. 2:24 "Therefore shall a man leave his father and his mother, and shall cleave unto his wife: and **they shall be one flesh.**"

Matt. 19:5	"And said, For this cause shall a man leave father and mother, and shall cleave to his wife: and **they twain shall be one flesh**?"
Matt. 19:6	"Wherefore **they are no more twain, but one flesh**. What therefore God hath joined together, let not man put asunder."
Mark 10:8	"And **they twain shall be one flesh**: so then **they are no more twain, but one flesh**."
Eph. 5:31	"For this cause shall a man leave his father and mother, and shall be joined unto his wife, and **they two shall be one flesh**."

When the bride becomes the wife, she becomes one flesh with the bridegroom, and he is:

John 1:14	"And **the Word was made flesh, and dwelt among us**, (and we beheld his glory, the glory as of the only begotten of the Father,) full of grace and truth."

When the bride becomes the wife, she also becomes the Word of God that is made flesh and fulfills exactly the portion of the parable of the ten virgins that speaks about the wise virgins.

Matt. 25:10	"And while they went to buy, the bridegroom came; and **they that were ready** went in with him to the **marriage**: and the **door** was shut."

Luke 13:25	"When once the master of the house is risen up, and hath shut to the **door**, and ye begin to stand without, and to knock at the **door,** saying, Lord, Lord, open unto us; and he shall answer and say unto you, I know you not whence ye are."
Rev. 3:7	"And to the angel of the church in Philadelphia write; These things saith he that is holy, he that is true, he that hath the key of David, **he that openeth, and no man shutteth; and shutteth, and no man openeth**."
Rev. 3:8	"I know thy works: behold, I have set before thee an **open door**, and no man can shut it: for thou hast a little strength, and hast kept my word, and hast not denied my name."
John 10:7	"Then said Jesus unto them again, Verily, verily, I say unto you, **I am the door** of the sheep."
John 10:9	"**I am the door**: by me if any man enter in, he shall be saved, and shall go in and out, and find pasture."

The pasture that we find is the same hidden manna that is hidden away in the golden vessel in the Holy of Holies, inside of the Ark of the Covenant. It is only found in His presence, in the Shekinah Glory. It is the Husband fulfilling His duty as Husband to provide that true bread from heaven to sustain His wife.

Here are the keys to the door and the specific instructions on how to be ready for His coming. **These** are the details that He has so lovingly and plainly laid out from the beginning for our **instruction** so that those who **hunger and thirst** after it will not miss the **mark** of the prize of the high calling of God in Christ Jesus.

Rom. 15:4	"For whatsoever things were written aforetime were written for our **learning**, that we through patience and comfort of the scriptures might have hope."
Gal. 3:24	"Wherefore the law was our **schoolmaster** to bring us unto Christ, that we might be justified by faith."
Heb. 12:10	"For they verily for a few days chastened us after their own pleasure; but he for our **profit**, that we might be **partakers** of his holiness."
Matt. 5:6	"Blessed are they which do **hunger and thirst** after righteousness: for they shall be **filled**."
Php. 3:13	"Brethren, I count not myself to have apprehended: but this one thing I do, forgetting those things which are behind, and reaching forth unto those things which are before."
Php. 3:14	"I press toward the **mark** for the prize of the high calling of God in Christ Jesus."
Php. 3:15	"Let us therefore, as many as be **perfect**, be thus minded: and if in any

thing ye be otherwise minded, God shall reveal even this unto you."

Php. 3:16 "Nevertheless, whereto we have already attained, let us **walk** by the same rule, let us **mind** the same thing."

It is obtained by the blood of the Lamb working **through** the incense of humility to provide access into His presence so that His presence can produce the fruits of His living reality (the reality of His Life) in us and for those fruits to be known and read of all men (**2 Cor. 3:2**).

Connects the Table for the Shewbread to the Lampstand and the Golden Altar for the Incense and Shows the Importance of the Wheat Being Ground into Fine Flour

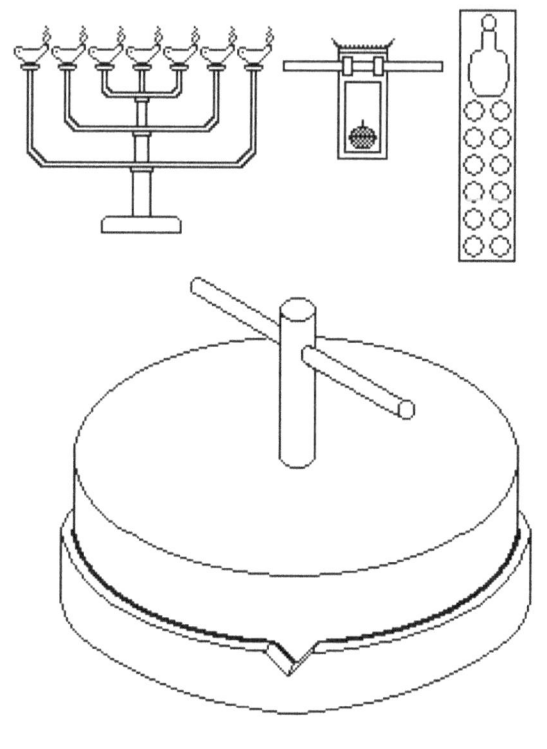

Drawing #23

CHAPTER 19

The Table and the Feasts

In order to understand the use and purpose of the golden table for the shewbread, it is necessary to understand the patterns that are part of the function of the other furnishings in the Holy Place.

Mal. 3:6 "For I am the LORD, **I change not**; therefore ye sons of Jacob are not consumed."

Normally, at least once per year, the glory of the presence of God (the Shekinah) came down and filled the Tabernacle with divine light. It was the response that God did as a sign that He accepted the blood of the atonement. This happened each year on Yom Kippur (the day of atonement) after the high priest finished the work of offering the blood of the atonement on the Mercy Seat.

As a memorial of that light (of His Life) filling the Tabernacle, the lamps in the lampstand were to be burning continually throughout every day of the year.

Lev. 24:2 "Command the children of Israel, that they bring unto thee pure oil olive beaten for the light, to cause the lamps to **burn continually**."

In the same way, just as the incense working together with the blood of the atonement opened the way so that the high priest could enter into the Holy of Holies, there was a twice daily **memorial** of the atonement that was made **throughout** the year.

That memorial was for the incense to be burnt upon the golden altar for incense **every morning and evening**, **every day** of the year.

> **Exo. 30:7** "And Aaron shall **burn thereon sweet incense every morning**: when he dresseth the lamps, he shall burn incense upon it."
>
> **Exo. 30:8** "And when Aaron lighteth the lamps **at even**, he shall **burn incense** upon it, a perpetual incense before the LORD **throughout your generations**."

Now that we see the pattern of memorial observance that was in the lampstand and the golden altar for incense, we are ready to understand the golden table for the shewbread.

Once per year, there was an offering of loaves of bread that were a wave offering before the Lord.

> **Lev. 23:15** "And ye shall count unto you from the morrow after the sabbath, from the day that ye brought **the sheaf of the wave offering**; seven sabbaths shall be complete."
>
> **Lev. 23:16** "Even unto the morrow after the seventh sabbath shall ye number fifty days; and ye shall offer a **new meat offering** unto the LORD."
>
> **Lev. 23:17** "Ye shall bring out of your habitations **two wave loaves** of two tenth deals: they shall be **of fine flour**;

	they shall be baken with leaven; they are the firstfruits unto the LORD."
Lev. 23:18	"And ye shall offer with the **bread** seven lambs without blemish of the first year, and one young bullock, and two rams: they shall be for a burnt offering unto the LORD, with their **meat** offering, and their drink offerings, even an offering made by fire, of sweet savour unto the LORD."
Lev. 23:19	"Then ye shall sacrifice one kid of the goats for a sin offering, and two lambs of the first year for a sacrifice of peace offerings."
Lev. 23:20	"And the priest shall **wave them with the bread of the firstfruits for a wave offering** before the LORD with the two lambs: they shall be holy to the LORD for the priest."
Lev. 23:21	"And ye shall proclaim on the selfsame day, that it may be an holy convocation unto you: ye shall do no servile work therein: it shall be a statute for ever in all your dwellings throughout your generations."

Lev. 23:22 "And when ye reap the harvest of your land, thou shalt not make clean riddance of the corners of thy field when thou reapest, neither shalt thou gather any gleaning of thy harvest: thou shalt leave them unto the poor, and to the stranger: I am the LORD your God."

Notice that in **Lev. 23:18,** the "meat" offering is the "bread." In the Bible, the word *meat* refers to bread and not to the flesh of the animal sacrifices. There was also a memorial of that offering that was upon the table throughout the entire year. The wave offering that was memorialized in the shewbread was the offering of the fruits of the ingathering. In this, we can see the connection between the feast of ingathering and the golden table for the shewbread.

Lev. 24:1 "And the LORD spake unto Moses, saying."

Lev. 24:2 "Command the children of Israel, that they bring unto thee pure oil olive beaten for the light, to cause the lamps to burn continually."

Lev. 24:3 "Without the veil of the testimony, in the tabernacle of the congregation, shall Aaron order it from the evening unto the morning before the LORD continually: it shall be a statute for ever in your generations."

Lev. 24:4 "He shall order the lamps upon the pure candlestick before the LORD continually."

Lev. 24:5	"And thou shalt take **fine flour**, and bake **twelve cakes** thereof: two tenth deals shall be in one cake."
Lev. 24:6	"And thou shalt set them in two rows, six on a row, upon the pure table before the LORD."
Lev. 24:7	"And thou shalt **put pure frankincense upon each row**, that it may be on the bread for a **memorial**, even an offering made by fire unto the LORD."
Lev. 24:8	"**Every sabbath he shall set it in order** before the LORD continually, being taken from the children of Israel by an **everlasting covenant**."
Lev. 24:9	"And it shall be Aaron's and his sons'; and they shall eat it in the holy place: for it is most holy unto him of the offerings of the LORD made by fire by a **perpetual statute**."

In addition to the incense being the connection between the golden table of the shewbread and the Golden altar for the incense (**Lev. 24:7**), we can also see that there is a connection between the firstfruits (beginning) of the harvest and the ingathering (end) or the "fullness" of the harvest. This is one of the applications of the "beginning and end" that the Lord Jesus used to refer to Himself with, since He is not only the Lamb that makes the harvest possible, but He is also the one who, by His power and grace, brings forth the firstfruits **and** the fullness of the harvest.

The sheaf of the firstfruits waved before God proclaimed in His presence that by these firstfruits, there is a promise of more to come.

The apostles and prophets that have come before were the firstfruits of the work of salvation and were the promise of God that more fruit of His atoning work were coming to maturity. In the same way, the loaves of the ingathering that were waved before the Lord also proclaim that He who promised by bringing to maturity the firstfruits is also faithful to bring forth the fullness of the harvest. This is the scriptural meaning behind every mention of "end time harvest."

Apart from quantity, a major difference between the firstfruits and the ingathering is that in the ingathering, the grain had to be ground into fine flour in order to make loaves. When the grinding was complete, the individual distinctness of the wheat or barley grains was lost in the mingling of the grinding. This same symbolic meaning was shown in the New Covenant in the following verses.

Acts 2:44 "And all that believed were **together**, and had **all things common**."

Acts 4:32 "And the **multitude of them that believed were of one heart and of one soul**: neither said any of them that ought of the things which he possessed was his own; but they had **all things common**."

It is important to notice that this happened during a time of persecution or crisis—grinding. Even the detail of placing the golden table for the shewbread on the north side of the Holy Place has a prophetic meaning.

Exo. 26:35 "And thou shalt set the table without the veil, and the candlestick over against the table on the side of the tabernacle toward the south: and thou shalt put the **table** on the **north** side.

In every Bible prophecy where the word *north* is used, it is in the context of being symbolic of the "end of time." If those prophecies are read with **that** understanding, they become much easier to understand. Therefore, it is very appropriate that the golden table for the fruits of the ingathering at the end (or fullness) of the harvest was to be placed on the north side of the Holy Place, symbolizing that the fullness of the harvest will happen in the end of time. The following are a few examples of the use of the word *north* meaning "the end of time."

Psa. 48:2 "Beautiful for situation, the joy of the whole earth, is mount Zion, on the sides of the **north**, the city of the great King."

Isa. 41:25 "I have raised up one from the **north**, and he shall come: from the rising of the sun shall he call upon my name: and he shall come upon princes as upon mortar, and as the potter treadeth clay."

Jer. 1:15 "For, lo, I will call all the families of the kingdoms of the **north**, saith the LORD; and they shall come, and they shall set every one his throne at the entering of the gates of Jerusalem, and against all the walls thereof round about, and against all the cities of Judah."

Jer. 3:12 "Go and proclaim these words toward the **north**, and say, Return, thou backsliding Israel, saith the LORD; and I will not cause mine anger to fall upon you: for I am merciful, saith the LORD, and I will not keep anger for ever."

Jer. 3:18 "In those days the house of Judah shall walk with the house of Israel, and they shall come together out of the land of the **north** to the land that I have given for an inheritance unto your fathers."

Jer. 13:20 "Lift up your eyes, and behold them that come from the **north**: where is the flock that was given thee, thy beautiful flock?"

Jer. 16:15 "But, The LORD liveth, that brought up the children of Israel from the land of the **north**, and from all the lands whither he had driven them: and I will bring them again into their land that I gave unto their fathers."

Jer. 23:8 "But, The LORD liveth, which brought up and which led the seed of the house of Israel out of the **north** country, and from all countries whither I had driven them; and they shall dwell in their own land."

Jer. 25:9 "Behold, I will send and take all the families of the **north**, saith the LORD, and Nebuchadrezzar the king of Babylon, my servant, and will bring them against this land, and against the inhabitants thereof, and against all these nations round about, and will utterly destroy them, and make them an astonishment, and an hissing, and perpetual desolations."

Jer. 31:8 "Behold, I will bring them from the **north** country, and gather them from the coasts of the earth, and with them the blind and the lame, the woman with child and her that travaileth with child together: a great company shall return thither."

Eze. 38:15 "And thou shalt come from thy place out of the **north** parts, thou, and many people with thee, all of them riding upon horses, a great company, and a mighty army."

Eze. 39:2 "And I will turn thee back, and leave but the sixth part of thee, and will cause thee to come up from the **north** parts, and will bring thee upon the mountains of Israel."

Eze. 44:4 "Then brought he me the way of the **north** gate before the house: and I looked, and, behold, the glory of the LORD filled the house of the LORD: and I fell upon my face."

Zech. 2:6 "**Ho, ho, come forth, and flee from the land of the north**, saith the LORD: for I have spread you abroad as the four winds of the heaven, saith the LORD."

Most of these examples show that at the end of time (north), God will gather all of the families of Israel back to the land that was sworn to their fathers. The golden table relates to several different items in the temple worship. The feast of firstfruits and the feast of the ingathering of the harvest, the example that was given of the prophets, the glorious church without spot or wrinkle, the caring and unity in the body of Christ, and specific instructions for the establishment of divine government. The scriptures clearly show the parallel between us and wheat or barley.

The following verses relate to the church being taken into the wedding supper of the Lamb and to judgment falling on the unrighteous:

Matt. 3:12   "Whose fan is in his hand, and he will thoroughly purge his floor, and gather his **wheat** into the garner; but he will burn up the **chaff** with unquenchable fire."

Luke 3:17   "Whose fan is in his hand, and he will thoroughly purge his floor, and will gather the **wheat** into his garner; but the **chaff** he will burn with fire unquenchable."

Wheat is symbolic of the righteous and chaff is symbolic of the unrighteous. The following verses show another symbolic parallel of the unrighteous being symbolized as tares and that the unrighteous can even be in the churches right beside the righteous.

Matt. 13:24   "Another parable put he forth unto them, saying, The kingdom of

	heaven is likened unto a man which sowed good seed in his field."
Matt. 13:25	"But while men slept, his enemy came and sowed **tares** among the **wheat**, and went his way."
Matt. 13:26	"But when the blade was sprung up, and brought forth fruit, then appeared the **tares** also."
Matt. 13:27	"So the servants of the householder came and said unto him, Sir, didst not thou sow good seed in thy field? from whence then hath it **tares**?"
Matt. 13:28	"He said unto them, An enemy hath done this. The servants said unto him, Wilt thou then that we go and gather them up?"
Matt. 13:29	"But he said, Nay; lest while ye gather up the **tares**, ye root up also the **wheat** with them."
Matt. 13:30	"Let both grow together until the harvest: and in the time of harvest I will say to the reapers, Gather ye together first the **tares**, and bind them in bundles to burn them: but gather the **wheat** into my barn."

Tares look identical to wheat **until** the time of the harvest. It is for this reason that they were not to be separated until that time. But when the fruit of the harvest begins to appear, the tares do not produce a seed that has weight (glory also means weight), and the wheat produces a seed that is much larger and heavier. Because of this difference, the fruit bearing head of the tares always stand straight up (pride, rebellion, refusal to be subject), but the wheat head bows (humility/incense, subjection) under the weight (glory) of the wheat seed.

When this happens, a clear distinction can be seen between the wheat and the tares, and they can safely be separated without the risk of uprooting the wheat. According to the parable, God will have servants in the time of the final harvest that He has given the wisdom to in order to **discern** between the prideful and the humble, between those who are subject and obedient to display the character and nature of God and those who do not. This should not be a surprise. We find something similar in the book of Malachi.

Mal. 3:16 "Then they that feared the LORD spake often one to another: and the LORD hearkened, and heard it, and a book of remembrance was written before him for them that feared the LORD, and that thought upon his name."

Mal. 3:17 "And they shall be mine, saith the LORD of hosts, in that day when I make up my jewels; and I will spare them, as a man spareth his own son that serveth him."

Mal. 3:18 "Then shall ye return, and **discern** between the righteous and the wicked, between him that serveth God and him that serveth him not."

These servants, in the end of time:

> **Eze. 44:23** "And they shall teach my people the difference between the holy and profane, and cause them to **discern** between the unclean and the clean."
>
> **Eze. 44:24** "And in controversy they shall stand in judgment; and they shall judge it according to my judgments: and they shall keep my laws and my statutes **in all mine assemblies**; and they shall hallow my sabbaths."

They will discern between the righteous (wheat) that serve God and the wicked (tares) that do not serve God. One of the primary evidences of the humility/maturity of the wheat is that they will become obedient to the word of God. Another scripture that shows this symbolic parallel of wheat is:

> **John 12:23** "And Jesus answered them, saying, The hour is come, that the Son of man should be glorified."
>
> **John 12:24** "Verily, verily, I say unto you, Except a corn of **wheat** fall into the ground and **die**, it abideth alone: **but if it die, it bringeth forth much fruit**."
>
> **John 12:25** "**He that loveth his life shall lose it; and he that hateth his life in this world shall keep it unto life eternal**."
>
> **John 12:26** "If any man serve me, let him follow me; and where I am, there shall also

> my servant be: if any man serve me, him will my Father honour."

In this, we can see that one of the ways that the symbol of wheat "falling into the ground" applies to us is in the context of "taking up our cross to follow Him" (**Matt. 16:24; Mark 8:34, 10:21; Luke 9:23**) and also as the Apostle Paul said about "I die daily" (**1 Cor. 15:31**). It is obvious that God brought forth an abundant harvest through the Apostle Paul's willingness to be a grain of wheat that fell into the ground and died (daily).

Exo. 23:16 "And **the feast of harvest, the firstfruits** of thy labours, which thou hast sown in the field: and the **feast of ingathering, which is in the end of the year**, when thou hast gathered in thy labours out of the field."

Exo. 34:22 "And thou shalt observe the **feast of weeks**, of the **firstfruits** of wheat harvest, and **the feast of ingathering at the year's end**."

The feast of the ingathering in the end of the year is the feast of Tabernacles.

Lev. 23:39 "Also in the fifteenth day of the seventh month, when ye have **gathered** in the fruit of the land, ye shall keep a feast unto the LORD seven days: on the first day shall be a sabbath, and on the eighth day shall be a sabbath."

Lev. 23:40 "And ye shall take you on the first day the boughs of goodly trees,

	branches of palm trees, and the boughs of thick trees, and willows of the brook; and ye shall rejoice before the LORD your God seven days."
Lev. 23:41	"And ye shall keep it a feast unto the LORD seven days in the year. It shall be a statute for ever in your generations: ye shall celebrate it in the seventh month."
Lev. 23:42	"Ye shall dwell in booths seven days; all that are Israelites born shall dwell in booths."
Lev. 23:43	"That your generations may know that I made the children of Israel to dwell in booths, when I brought them out of the land of Egypt: I am the LORD your God."

Therefore, to be the true wheat that is gathered in the time of the ingathering (north), "in the end of the year/time," we will have to take up our cross to follow him (be ground up) so that He can make us (by grinding) into a loaf of wave offering to be waved before Him in His presence (Shekinah). This is exactly what is spoken about symbolically when the twelve loaves are put upon the table together with the incense (humility).

Lev. 24:5	"And thou shalt take fine flour, and bake **twelve cakes** thereof: two tenth deals shall be in one cake."
Lev. 24:6	"And thou shalt set them in two rows, six on a row, upon the pure table before the LORD."

Lev. 24:7 "And thou shalt **put pure frankincense upon each row**, that it may be on **the bread for a memorial**, even an offering made by fire unto the LORD."

Lev. 24:8 "Every sabbath he shall set it in order before the LORD continually, being taken from the children of Israel by an **everlasting covenant**."

Lev. 24:9 "And it shall be Aaron's and his sons'; and they shall eat it in the holy place: for it is most holy unto him of the offerings of the LORD made by fire by a **perpetual statute**."

In this, we can see that every time we gather together to hear the preaching of the word (breaking of bread), we are to approach in humility (as ground up wheat with frankincense) and for a purpose of maturing to become obedient to the word of God. All of this happens in a time when the fruit of the land will be gathered and the tabernacles of our bodies as temples of the Holy Spirit are gathered together to the Great Feast of Tabernacles. Tabernacles gathered together around the very origin of the plan for the Tabernacle that Moses looked into heaven and saw while he was on the mount. The Great Feast of Tabernacles that will be celebrated in heaven is also known by the term of "the marriage supper of the Lamb."

Rev. 19:5 "And a voice came out of the throne, saying, Praise our God, all ye his servants, and ye that fear him, both small and great."

Rev. 19:6 "And I heard as it were the voice of a great multitude, and as the voice

	of many waters, and as the voice of mighty thunderings, saying, Alleluia: for the Lord God omnipotent reigneth."
Rev. 19:7	"Let us be glad and rejoice, and give honour to him: for the **marriage** of the Lamb is come, and his **wife** hath made herself ready."
Rev. 19:8	"And to her was granted that she should be arrayed in fine linen, clean and white: for the **fine linen is the righteousness of saints**."
Rev. 19:9	"And he saith unto me, Write, Blessed are they which are called unto the **marriage supper of the Lamb**. And he saith unto me, These are the true sayings of God."

The marriage supper of the Lamb is for those who were willing to continually offer the incense of humility to be ground into fine flour (**Psa. 51:17; Isa. 57:15**) as wheat that has come to full maturity, who loved not their lives unto death (**Rev. 12:11**), who gained their lives by losing it (**Matt. 16:25**) for His sake, and who humbled themselves to become obedient (**Phil. 2:8**), even unto death.

The question is, how passionate are we about our love for God? Are we passionate enough to enter into the realms of supernaturally empowered obedience (**John 14:15; 1 John 5:2–3; Jer. 1:11-12**)? Are we passionate enough to allow His Spirit of holiness to change and transform our minds until our thoughts conform to His thoughts to proclaim that EVERY word of God is true and entirely without contradiction, and therefore, worthy of obedience?

Shows that the Lord Jesus and the Apostles Were the Foundation, Setting the Example for the Church and They were Also the Firstfruits of the Harvest when the Fullness Comes In

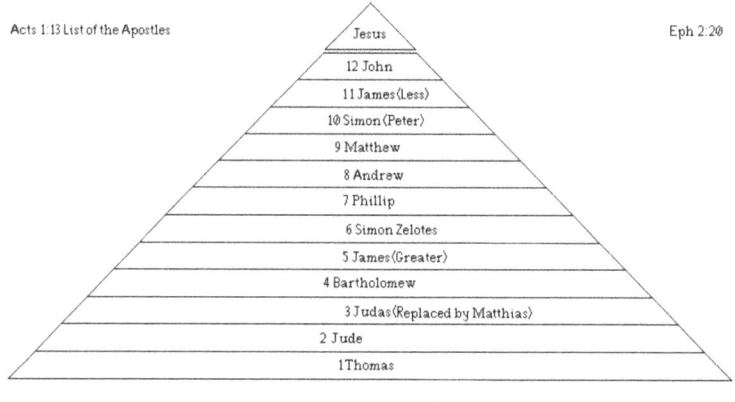

Acts 1:13 List of the Apostles

Jesus
12 John
11 James (Less)
10 Simon (Peter)
9 Matthew
8 Andrew
7 Phillip
6 Simon Zelotes
5 James (Greater)
4 Bartholomew
3 Judas (Replaced by Matthias)
2 Jude
1 Thomas

Eph 2:20

Drawing #24

CHAPTER 20

Righteous Seed and the Promise of Harvest

In the previous chapter, we saw the parallels between the firstfruits and the ingathering, the first and the last of the harvest, the wave sheaf and the wave loaf, and the memorial (with incense) of the twelve loaves on the golden table of the shewbread.

Now we will examine in closer detail about the wave sheaf and the wave loaf. A sheaf was a cluster of ripe grain that had their stalks cut off close to the ground and which were then tied to bind them together. The wave sheaf was a sheaf of the first ripe grain in the harvest. In the following verses, we see that the Lord Jesus is called the firstfruits. In this, a pattern is established for interpreting the wave sheaf and the wave loaf.

> **1 Cor. 15:20** "But now is Christ risen from the dead, and become the **firstfruits** of them that slept."
>
> **1 Cor. 15:23** "But every man in his own order: Christ the **firstfruits**; afterward they that are Christ's at his coming."

We can see in the following verses that included in this sheaf of first ripe grain is also the apostles and prophets and that the symbol is extended (**1 Cor. 15:23** "But every man in his own order") to include the entire body of believers (as part of the fullness of the harvest); and the symbol of our bodies being the temple of the Holy Spirit is also expanded upon to a new level (to see more on how this expansion is extended, refer to "The Introduction to the Incense and the Glory: The Seven Levels of Kingdom Power").

First, the apostles and prophets are part of that foundation and are also symbolic of first ripe grain. Just as Christ is the firstfruits and the chief cornerstone for the foundation and, as part of the foundation being firstfruits, also applies to the apostles and prophets.

Eph. 2:18 "For through him we both have access by one Spirit unto the Father."

Eph. 2:19 "Now therefore ye are no more strangers and foreigners, but fellowcitizens with the saints, and of the household of God."

Eph. 2:20 "And are built upon the **foundation** of the **apostles** and **prophets**, Jesus Christ himself being the chief corner stone."

Eph. 2:21 "In whom all the building fitly framed together groweth unto an holy temple in the Lord."

Eph. 2:22 "In whom ye also are builded together for an habitation of God through the Spirit."

Then, Jesus Christ is the foundation. Also, the temple as it applies to our bodies is extended to another level—the entire body of believers.

> **1 Cor. 3:11** "For other **foundation** can no man lay than that is laid, which is Jesus Christ."
>
> **1 Cor. 15:23** "But **every man** in his own order: Christ the firstfruits; afterward they that are Christ's at his coming."

From this, we can conclude that the lives that the apostles and prophets lived were actually the very life of Jesus Christ being expressed and manifested in them. The very attributes of those lives as first ripe grain were a divine promise of a full harvest that was yet to come. That promise extends to "every one that nameth the name of Christ."

> **2 Tim. 2:19** "Nevertheless the **foundation** of God standeth sure, having this seal, The Lord knoweth them that are his. And, Let **every one that nameth the name of Christ** depart from iniquity."

What is iniquity? Knowing to do good (the law of descriptions of how the character of God behaves) and doing it not (**Jas. 4:17**). It will come to a harvest that will be so great as to include people from every nation.

> **Joel 2:28** "And it shall come to pass afterward, that I will pour out my spirit upon **all flesh**; and your sons and your daughters shall prophesy, your old men shall dream dreams, your young men shall see visions."

Joel 2:29 "And also upon the servants and upon the handmaids in those days will I pour out my spirit."

Because of His Spirit being poured out, it will have specific results. Notice that "cast down" in the following verse means "humbled," and in some translations of the Bible, it is translated as "established." We have already seen that the throne of God is in the heart; when hearts are humbled, they are also being established to be His dwelling place or throne for God "to be seated."

Dan. 7:9 "I beheld till the **thrones** were **cast down**, and the Ancient of days did sit, whose garment was white as snow, and the hair of his head like the pure wool: his throne was like the fiery flame, and his wheels as burning fire."

Dan. 7:10 "A fiery stream issued and came forth from before him: thousand thousands ministered unto him, and ten thousand times ten thousand stood before him: **the judgment was set**, and the books were opened."

When the Bride finally realizes that the key to having their hearts prepared and established to be the throne of God is humility (incense), she will move into a covenantal relationship with Him of matrimony to cease being only a Bride that is promised **unto** marriage (but has not yet taken the wedding vows) and take her place as His Wife.

Dan. 7:26 "But **the judgment shall sit**, and they shall take away his dominion,

Dan. 7:27 "And the kingdom and dominion, and the greatness of the kingdom under the **whole** heaven, shall be given to the people of the saints of the most High, whose kingdom is an everlasting kingdom, and **all** dominions shall serve and obey him."

Then will be fulfilled the promise of filling **all** of the earth with His glory.

Num. 14:20 "And the LORD said, I have pardoned according to thy word."

Num. 14:21 "But as truly as I live, **all** the earth shall be filled with the glory of the LORD."

It is of great importance for us to realize that we have a role to play in His glory being revealed. Even though we understand that the following verses are speaking about the Lord Jesus, the only way that "all flesh" will see "the glory of the LORD" is if that glory is put on display in His Wife. This is true, because when the Lord Jesus came the first time, it was not fulfilled that **all** flesh saw it.

We also know that the following verses are speaking about His first coming, because of John the Baptist's proclamation (**Matt. 3:1–3; Mark 1:2–4; Luke 3:1–6; John 1:19–23**).

Isa. 40:3 "The voice of him that crieth in the wilderness, Prepare ye the way of the LORD, make straight in the desert a highway for our God."

Isa. 40:4 "Every valley shall be exalted, and every mountain and hill shall be made low: and the crooked shall be made straight, and the rough places plain."

But the fullness of the following verse can only be fulfilled in the end of time (north) when the glorious church without spot or wrinkle or any such thing stands up to be the Wife of the Lamb.

Isa. 40:5 "And the glory of the LORD shall be revealed, and **all** flesh shall see it together: for the mouth of the LORD hath spoken it."

Also, the following verses specifically say that His glory will be revealed **in** us.

Rom. 8:18 "For I reckon that the sufferings of this present time are not worthy to be compared with the **glory** which shall **be revealed in us**."

1 Pet. 4:13 "But rejoice, inasmuch as ye are partakers of Christ's sufferings; that, when his **glory shall be revealed**, ye may be glad also with exceeding joy."

1 Pet. 5:1 "The elders which are among you I exhort, who am also an elder, and a witness of the sufferings of Christ, and also a partaker of the **glory that shall be revealed**."

The glory that is to be revealed is the glory of God. Some may try to use the following verse to say that that it cannot be.

Isa. 42:8	"I am the LORD: that is my name: and **my glory will I not give to another**, neither my praise to graven images."
Isa. 48:9	"For my name's sake will I defer mine anger, and for my praise will I refrain for thee, that I cut thee not off."
Isa. 48:10	"Behold, I have refined thee, but not with silver; I have chosen thee in the furnace of affliction."
Isa. 48:11	"For mine own sake, even for mine own sake, will I do it: for how should my name be polluted? and **I will not give my glory unto another**."
Isa. 48:12	"Hearken unto me, O Jacob and Israel, my called; I am he; **I am the first, I also am the last**."

We can see in **verse 12** that He immediately makes the connection between Him being the first and the last with His glory (see the First in **Gen. 1:26** speaking together **with** His Bride and the Last in **Rev. 22:17** speaking together **with** His Wife) and therefore bringing His Wife into **that** identity with Him as part of the First and the Last. Therefore, it is not a contradiction to the above verses to say that the glory of the "glorious church" is the glory of God, because that church is His Wife and part of Him because of the marriage covenant (**Jer. 31:32; John 1:14; Gen. 2:23–24; Matt. 19:4–6; Rev. 19:7, 21:9**)

Eph. 5:27	"That he might present it to himself a **glorious** church, not having spot,

or wrinkle, or any such thing; but that it should be holy and without blemish."

A further proof is also found in the connection between the word *affliction* in **Isa. 48:10** and the Hebrew root word for valley of *Achor* in the following scripture passage, which also means affliction.

Hos. 2:14	"Therefore, behold, I will allure her, and bring her into the wilderness, and speak comfortably unto her."
Hos. 2:15	"And I will give her her vineyards from thence, and the valley of **Achor** for a door of hope: and she shall sing there, as in the days of her youth, and as in the day when she came up out of the land of Egypt."
Hos. 2:16	"And it shall be at that day, saith the LORD, that thou shalt call me **Ishi**; and shalt call me no more **Baali**."
Hos. 2:17	"For I will take away the names of **Baalim** out of her mouth, and they shall no more be remembered by their name."
Hos. 2:18	"And in that day will I make a **covenant** for them with the beasts of the field, and with the fowls of heaven, and with the creeping things of the ground: and I will break the bow and the sword and the battle out of the earth, and will make them to lie down safely."

Hos. 2:19	"And I will **betroth** thee unto me for ever; yea, I will **betroth** thee unto me in righteousness, and in judgment, and in lovingkindness, and in mercies."
Hos. 2:20	"I will even **betroth** thee unto me in faithfulness: and thou shalt know the LORD."

The word *ishi* means "my husband," and the word *baali* means "my master who rules with rigor," and the "covenant" in verse **18** is identified to be a "marriage" covenant in verses **19** and **20**.

The Timing of the Harvest in Relation to the Feasts

In the following verses, we see some of the timing of the harvest. Part of the grain came to maturity fifty days before the harvest was fully gathered in, and a **sheaf** of it was waved before the Lord. Then fifty days later, a **loaf** of the same grain was also waved before the Lord. The only time period between feasts that exactly had a fifty-day time lapse was the time period between the feast of Passover and the Feast of Weeks or Pentecost. From this, we can conclude that the beginning of the harvest that is being spoken about is happening in the early spring at the feast of Passover.

When we consider that the grain plants had to have had time to sprout and grow and come to maturity in early spring, then the grain that is being spoken about is a winter grain. Since wheat is a summer grain, we can conclude that the grain being referred to in the following verses was Barley, a winter grain.

First the wave offering of the sheaf.

Lev. 23:10	"Speak unto the children of Israel, and say unto them, When ye be come into the land which I give unto you, and shall reap the harvest

thereof, then ye shall bring a **sheaf of the firstfruits** of your harvest unto the priest."

Lev. 23:11 "And he shall **wave the sheaf** before the LORD, to be accepted for you: on the morrow after the sabbath the priest shall **wave** it."

Lev. 23:12 "And ye shall offer that day when ye **wave the sheaf** an he lamb without blemish of the first year for a burnt offering unto the LORD."

Then the wave offering of the loaf made from finely ground flour.

Lev. 23:15 "And ye shall count unto you from the morrow after the sabbath, from the day that ye brought the **sheaf** of the **wave** offering; **seven sabbaths** shall be complete."

Lev. 23:16 "Even unto the morrow after the seventh sabbath shall ye number **fifty days**; and ye shall offer a new meat offering unto the LORD."

Lev. 23:17 "Ye shall bring out of your habitations two **wave loaves** of two tenth deals: they shall be of fine flour; they shall be baken with leaven; they are the firstfruits unto the LORD."

Lev. 23:18 "And ye shall offer with the bread seven lambs without blemish of the first year, and one young bullock, and two rams: they shall be for a burnt offering unto the LORD, with their meat offering, and their drink offerings, even an offering made by fire, of sweet savour unto the LORD."

Lev. 23:19 "Then ye shall sacrifice one kid of the goats for a sin offering, and two lambs of the first year for a sacrifice of peace offerings."

Lev. 23:20 "And the priest shall **wave them with the bread** of the firstfruits for a **wave** offering before the LORD, with the two lambs: they shall be holy to the LORD for the priest."

Lev. 23:21 "And ye shall proclaim on the selfsame day, that it may be an holy convocation unto you: ye shall do no servile work therein: it shall be a statute for ever in all your dwellings throughout your generations."

The word *wave* in **Lev. 23:20** is the Hebrew word *nuph*" It is also translated into the following words: *wave, shake, lift, offer, move, sift, strike, quiver, vibrate* (up and down), *rock* (to and fro), *send*, and *perfume*. In one word, we see that those who offer themselves to the Lord in humility (incense) are presenting a sweet smelling savor (perfume) of a **wave** offering in His presence. They are proclaiming to God that they are available to be **moved** (nuph) by His Spirit. It is to be offered as a loaf made of finely ground flour (**Joel 2:15; Psa. 51:17; Isa. 57:17, 66:1–2**) before the Mercy Seat of the Atonement (**Rom. 12:1–2**) holy and acceptable unto Him.

A perpetual memorial is to be constantly upon the golden table in the Holy Place (mind) throughout the year. The same loaves of bread (accompanied with the incense that was on the table) were to be together with the offering of other sacrifices.

> **Exo. 29:22** "Also thou shalt take of the ram the fat and the rump, and the fat that covereth the inwards, and the caul above the liver, and the two kidneys, and the fat that is upon them, and the right shoulder; for it is a ram of consecration."
>
> **Exo. 29:23** "And one loaf of bread, and one cake of oiled bread, and one wafer out of the basket of the unleavened bread that is before the LORD."
>
> **Exo. 29:24** "And thou shalt put all in the hands of Aaron, and in the hands of his sons; and shalt **wave them for a wave offering** before the LORD."
>
> **Exo. 29:25** "And thou shalt receive them of their hands, and burn them upon the altar for a burnt offering, for a sweet savour before the LORD: it is an offering made by fire unto the LORD."
>
> **Exo. 29:26** "And thou shalt take the breast of the ram of Aaron's consecration, and wave it for a **wave offering** before the LORD: and it shall be thy part."

Exo. 29:27 "And thou shalt sanctify the breast of the **wave offering**, and the shoulder of the **heave offering, which is waved**, and which is **heaved** up, of the ram of the consecration, even of that which is for Aaron, and of that which is for his sons."

Therefore, the example of meekness, humility, and brokenness that has been set for us by the apostles, prophets, and by the Lord Jesus Himself as first ripe fruits was God establishing the foundation.

1 Cor. 3:9 "For we are labourers together with God: ye are God's husbandry, ye are God's building."

1 Cor. 3:10 "According to the grace of God which is given unto me, as a wise masterbuilder, I have laid the foundation, and another buildeth thereon. But let every man take heed how he buildeth thereupon."

1 Cor. 3:11 "For **other foundation can no man lay** than that is laid, which is Jesus Christ."

1 Cor. 3:12 "Now if any man build upon this foundation gold, silver, precious stones, wood, hay, stubble."

1 Cor. 3:13 "Every man's work shall be made manifest: for the day shall declare it, because it shall be revealed by fire; and the fire shall try every man's work of what sort it is."

1 Cor. 3:14	"If any man's work abide which he hath built thereupon, he shall receive a reward."
1 Cor. 3:15	"If any man's work shall be burned, he shall suffer loss: but he himself shall be saved; yet so as by fire."

If we build upon **that** foundation, we will have eternal life, but if we try to establish any **other** foundation, then in effect, we have made for ourselves another gospel and the following scriptures may apply.

Gal. 1:8	"But though we, or an angel from heaven, preach **any other gospel** unto you than that which we have preached unto you, let him be accursed."
Gal. 1:9	"As we said before, so say I now again, If any man preach any other gospel unto you than that ye have received, **let him be accursed**."
Luke 6:47	"Whosoever cometh to me, and heareth my sayings**, and doeth them**, I will shew you to whom he is like."
Luke 6:48	"He is like a man which built an house, and digged deep, and **laid the foundation on a rock**: and when the flood arose, the stream beat vehemently upon that house, and **could not shake it**: for it was founded upon a rock."

Luke 6:49 "But he that heareth, and **doeth not**, is like a man that **without a foundation** built an house upon the earth; against which the stream did beat vehemently, and immediately it fell; and the ruin of that house was great."

Because even though we are not saved by works, yet:

Jam. 2:26 "For as the body without the spirit is dead, so **faith without works is dead** also."

Therefore, understanding that a faith that is dead cannot save, we must recognize that a faith that is alive enough to save is also real and alive enough to produce the works of His obedience. Otherwise, we would have to conclude that God (who does not lie) spoke a lie when He said:

Isa. 55:11 "So shall **my word be that goeth forth out of my mouth: it shall not return unto me void**, but it **shall** accomplish that which I please, and it shall **prosper** in the thing whereto I sent it."

Isa. 55:12 "For ye shall go out with joy, and be led forth with peace: the mountains and the hills shall break forth before you into singing, and all the trees of the field shall clap their hands."

Isa. 55:13 "Instead of the thorn shall come up the fir tree, and instead of the brier shall come up the myrtle tree: **and it shall be to the LORD for a name,**

for an everlasting sign that shall not be cut off."

And a part of **that** everlasting sign is that He will fulfill His word not only **in** us, but **through** us, and even by filling the Outer Court with His glory, by our bodies being subject to Him, by coming into His supernaturally empowered obedience.

1 Pet. 1:18 "Forasmuch as ye know that **ye were not redeemed with corruptible things**, as silver and gold, from your vain conversation received by tradition from your fathers."

1 Pet. 1:19 "**But with the precious blood of Christ**, as of a lamb without blemish and without spot."

1 Pet. 1:20 "Who verily was foreordained before the foundation of the world, but was **manifest** in these last times for you."

1 Pet. 1:21 "Who by him do believe in God, that raised him up from the dead, and gave him glory; that your faith and hope might be in God."

1 Pet. 1:22 "Seeing **ye have purified your souls in obeying the truth through the Spirit unto unfeigned love** of the brethren, see that ye love one another with a pure heart fervently."

1 Pet. 1:23 "**Being born again**, not of corruptible seed, but **of incorruptible, by**

the word of God, which liveth and abideth for ever."

In this is made manifest the righteous seed that is born of the Word of God and identifies just what the promised harvest will look like and how the gospel must be preached to bring about **that** harvest. We can also see what the key details (humility/incense) are that will separate the wheat from the tares in the final harvest.

The Basket of Sacrifices Moved Back and Forth Between
the Holy Place and the Outer Court, Connecting and
Showing the Communication Between the Two

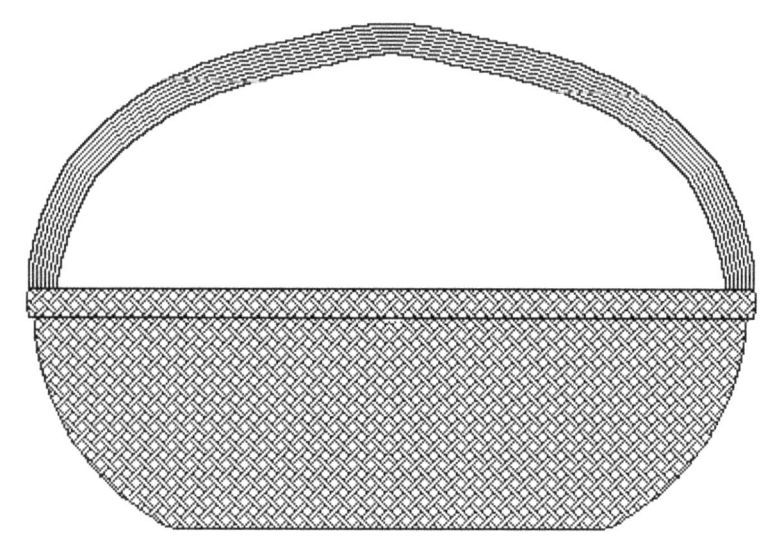

Drawing #25

CHAPTER 21

The Basket of Sacrifices

In previous chapters, it was shown how the golden censer of incense moves back and forth between the Holy Place (mind) and the Holy of Holies (heart) at ordained times (Yom Kippur—The Day of Atonement) and during other offerings for sin. By understanding that the golden censer of incense was **only** inside of the Holy of Holies **while** the atonement was being offered, we can understand a more profound meaning behind what the Apostle Paul was speaking in the following verses.

Heb. 9:1	"Then verily the first covenant had also ordinances of divine service, and a worldly sanctuary."
Heb. 9:2	"For there was a tabernacle made; the first, wherein was the candlestick, and the table, and the shewbread; which is called the sanctuary."
Heb. 9:3	"And after the second veil, the tabernacle which is called the **Holiest of all**."
Heb. 9:4	"**Which had the golden censer**, and the ark of the covenant overlaid round about with gold, wherein was the golden pot that had manna, and

	Aaron's rod that budded, and the tables of the covenant."
Heb. 9:5	"And over it the cherubims of glory shadowing the mercyseat; of which we cannot now speak particularly."

Therefore, the context of the atonement being offered is set for the remaining verses in the chapter, and if they are read with that understanding, the entire chapter takes on a **much** more profound meaning.

We have also seen that the way to have access to the Holy of Holies is by the blood of the atoning sacrifice working **through** the incense of humility. This access can set the conditions (the Mercy Seat and the Ark of the Covenant being covered by the incense of humility) for the throne of God to be located in its required position that is necessary for Him to then be seated in our hearts.

The scripture says that God is light (**1 John 1:5** and **John 1:4**) and in Him is no darkness at all. If He is seated (enthroned) in our hearts, then our hearts will be filled with His glorious light, and because the veil of rebellious self-will is removed, that light can fill our minds also.

A similar pattern of movement as what happens with the golden censer of incense also happens between the Holy Place and the Outer Court through the basket of the sacrifices. Notice verses **3, 23,** and **32** in the following passage and what items were placed into the basket.

Exo. 29:1	"And this is the thing that thou shalt do unto them to hallow them, to minister unto me in the priest's office: Take one young bullock, and two rams without blemish."

To hallow or consecrate who? All of those who will minister before Him as priests (**Rev. 1:6, 5:10, 20:6**).

Exo. 29:2   "And unleavened bread, and cakes unleavened tempered with oil, and wafers unleavened anointed with oil: of wheaten flour shalt thou make them."

Exo. 29:3   "And thou shalt put them into one **basket**, and bring them in the basket, **with** the bullock and the two rams."

Therefore, the basket was not just to take the bread and the incense out to the Outer Court to be burnt upon the altar for burnt offerings. It was **also** used to bring the parts of the bullock and rams into the Holy Placed to be waved (**Exo. 29:24,26,27**) before the Lord, boiled (**v. 31**), and eaten (**v. 32**) by the priests before the Lord.

Exo. 29:4   "And Aaron and his sons thou shalt bring unto the door of the tabernacle of the congregation, and shalt wash them with water."

Exo. 29:5   "And thou shalt take the garments, and put upon Aaron the coat, and the robe of the ephod, and the ephod, and the breastplate, and gird him with the curious girdle of the ephod."

Exo. 29:6   "And thou shalt put the mitre upon his head, and put the holy crown upon the mitre."

Exo. 29:7   "Then shalt thou take the anointing oil, and pour it upon his head, and anoint him."

Exo. 29:8	"And thou shalt bring his sons, and put coats upon them."
Exo. 29:9	"And thou shalt gird them with girdles, Aaron and his sons, and put the bonnets on them: and the priest's office shall be theirs for a **perpetual statute**: and thou shalt consecrate Aaron and his sons."
Exo. 29:10	"And thou shalt cause a bullock to be brought before the tabernacle of the congregation: and Aaron and his sons shall put their hands upon the head of the bullock."
Exo. 29:11	"And thou shalt kill the bullock before the LORD, by the door of the tabernacle of the congregation."
Exo. 29:12	"And thou shalt take of the blood of the bullock, and put it upon the horns of the altar with thy finger, and pour all the blood beside the bottom of the altar."
Exo. 29:13	"And thou shalt take all the fat that covereth the inwards, and the caul that is above the liver, and the two kidneys, and the fat that is upon them, and burn them upon the altar."
Exo. 29:14	"But the flesh of the bullock, and his skin, and his dung, shalt thou burn

with fire without the camp: it is a sin offering."

Exo. 29:15 "Thou shalt also take one ram; and Aaron and his sons shall put their hands upon the head of the ram."

Exo. 29:16 "And thou shalt slay the ram, and thou shalt take his blood, and sprinkle it round about upon the altar."

Exo. 29:17 "And thou shalt cut the ram in pieces, and **wash the inwards of him**, and his legs, and put them unto his pieces, and unto his head."

Exo. 29:18 "And thou shalt burn the whole ram upon the altar: it is a burnt offering unto the LORD: it is a sweet savour, an offering made by fire unto the LORD."

Exo. 29:19 "And thou shalt take the other ram; and Aaron and his sons shall put their hands upon the head of the ram."

Exo. 29:20 "Then shalt thou kill the ram, and take of his blood, and put it upon the tip of the right ear of Aaron, and upon the tip of the right ear of his sons, and upon the thumb of their right hand, and upon the great toe of their right foot, and sprinkle the blood upon the altar round about."

Exo. 29:21 "And thou shalt take of the blood that is upon the altar, and of the anointing oil, and sprinkle it upon Aaron, and upon his garments, and upon his sons, and upon the garments of his sons with him: and he shall be hallowed, and his garments, and his sons, and his sons' garments with him."

Exo. 29:22 "Also thou shalt take of the ram the fat and the rump, and the fat that covereth the inwards, and the caul above the liver, and the two kidneys, and the fat that is upon them, and the right shoulder; for it is a **ram of consecration**."

Exo. 29:23 "And one loaf of bread, and one cake of oiled bread, and one wafer out of the **basket** of the unleavened bread that is before the LORD."

Exo. 29:24 "And thou shalt put all in the hands of Aaron, and in the hands of his sons; and shalt wave them for a wave offering before the LORD."

Exo. 29:25 "And thou shalt receive them of their hands, and burn them upon the altar for a burnt offering, for a sweet savour before the LORD: it is an offering made by fire unto the LORD."

Exo. 29:26 "And thou shalt take the breast of the ram of Aaron's consecration, and wave it for a wave offering before the LORD: and it shall be thy part."

Exo. 29:27 "And thou shalt sanctify the breast of the wave offering, and the shoulder of the heave offering, which is waved, and which is heaved up, of the ram of the consecration, even of that which is for Aaron, and of that which is for his sons."

Exo. 29:28 "And it shall be Aaron's and his sons' **by a statute for ever** from the children of Israel: for it is an heave offering: and it shall be an heave offering from the children of Israel of the sacrifice of their peace offerings, even their heave offering unto the LORD."

Exo. 29:29 "And the holy garments of Aaron shall be his sons' after him, to be anointed therein, and to be consecrated in them."

Exo. 29:30 "And that son that is priest in his stead shall put them on seven days, when he cometh into the tabernacle of the congregation to minister in the holy place."

Exo. 29:31 "And thou shalt take the ram of the consecration, and **seethe** his flesh in the holy place."

Exo. 29:32 "And Aaron and his sons shall **eat** the flesh of the ram, and the bread that is in the **basket**, by the door of the tabernacle of the congregation."

Exo. 29:33 "And they shall eat those things wherewith the atonement was made, to consecrate and to sanctify them: but a stranger shall not eat thereof, because they are holy."

Exo. 29:34 "And if ought of the flesh of the consecrations, or of the bread, remain unto the morning, then thou shalt burn the remainder with fire: it shall not be eaten, because it is holy."

Exo. 29:35 "And thus shalt thou do unto Aaron, and to his sons, according to all things which I have commanded thee: seven days shalt thou consecrate them."

Exo. 29:36 "And thou shalt offer every day a bullock for a sin offering for atonement: and thou shalt cleanse the altar, when thou hast made an atonement for it, and thou shalt anoint it, to sanctify it."

Exo. 29:37 "Seven days thou shalt make an atonement for the altar, and sanctify it; and it shall be an altar most holy: whatsoever toucheth the altar shall be holy."

Exo. 29:38 "Now this is that which thou shalt offer upon the altar; two lambs of the first year day by day continually."

Exo. 29:39 "The one lamb thou shalt offer in the morning; and the other lamb thou shalt offer at even."

Exo. 29:40 "And with the one lamb a tenth deal of flour mingled with the fourth part of an hin of beaten oil; and the fourth part of an hin of wine for a drink offering."

Exo. 29:41 "And the other lamb thou shalt offer at even, and shalt do thereto according to the meat offering of the morning, and according to the drink offering thereof, for a sweet savour, an offering made by fire unto the LORD."

Exo. 29:42 "This shall be a continual burnt offering **throughout your generations** at the door of the tabernacle of the congregation before the LORD: **where I will meet you, to speak there unto thee.**"

Exo. 29:43 **"And there I will meet with the children of Israel, and the tabernacle shall be sanctified by my glory."**

Exo. 29:44 "And I will sanctify the tabernacle of the congregation, and the altar: I will sanctify also both Aaron and his

	sons, to minister to me in the priest's office."
Exo. 29:45	"And I will dwell among the children of Israel, and will be their God."
Exo. 29:46	"And they shall know that I am the LORD their God, that brought them forth out of the land of Egypt, that I may dwell among them: I am the LORD their God."

The following are additional scriptures that show the basket in relation to the consecration of the priests for service (**Lev. 8:1–36; Num. 6:1–27).**

We know that the bullock, goats, and ram sacrifices were only done on the altar that was in the outer court because they were not done upon the only altar (for incense) that was in the Holy Place.

We know this, because when the instructions were being given about the golden altar for incense, the following was said:

Exo. 30:9	"Ye shall offer no strange incense thereon, **nor burnt sacrifice, nor meat offering; neither shall ye pour drink offering thereon.**"

Therefore, **all** burnt offerings and slaying of sacrifices were done in the Outer Court on the altar for burnt offerings. The blood that was to be put upon the golden altar for incense and upon the mercy seat was caught in a vessel in which it was transported into the Holy Place. The only cooking of flesh that was ever done in the Holy Place (**Exo. 29:31**) was for some portions to be seethed or boiled but not slain or burnt.

The only container that was not made of gold that entered into the Holy Place was the basket. Nothing that was made of brass ever entered into the Holy Place. However, when the bread was taken into the Outer Court to be burnt upon the altar for burnt sacrifices, the incense that was put upon the bread upon the golden table also went with the bread.

> **Lev. 24:7** "And thou shalt put pure **frankincense** upon each row, that it may be on the **bread** for a memorial, even **an offering made by fire** unto the LORD."

Because the golden altar for the incense in the Holy Place could not be used for anything other than incense, when the bread with the incense (frankincense simply means the true or "frank" incense) was offered by fire, it was only offered in the Outer Court on the brazen altar for burnt sacrifices and, therefore, was transported to the Outer Court together with the bread in the basket.

These details are important to know, because the first time that the Tabernacle was set up, the heads of each tribe brought a special offering unto the Lord.

> **Exo. 25:29** "And thou shalt make the dishes thereof, and **spoons** thereof, and covers thereof, and bowls thereof, to cover withal: of **pure gold** shalt thou make them."

> **Exo. 37:16** "And he made the vessels which were upon the table, his dishes, and his **spoons**, and his bowls, and his covers to cover withal, of **pure gold**."

> **Num. 4:7** "And upon the table of shewbread they shall spread a cloth of blue, and put thereon the dishes, and the **spoons**, and the bowls, and covers

to cover withal: and the continual bread shall be thereon."

Num. 7:14   "One **spoon** of ten shekels of **gold, full of incense**."

Num. 7:20   "One **spoon** of **gold** of ten shekels, **full of incense**."

Num. 7:26   "One **golden spoon** of ten shekels, **full of incense**."

Num. 7:32   "One **golden spoon** of ten shekels, **full of incense**."

Num. 7:38   "One **golden spoon** of ten shekels, full of **incense**."

Num. 7:44   "One **golden spoon** of ten shekels, full of **incense**."

Num. 7:50   "One **golden spoon** of ten shekels, full of **incense**."

Num. 7:56   "One **golden spoon** of ten shekels, full of **incense**."

Num. 7:62   "One **golden spoon** of ten shekels, full of **incense**."

Num. 7:68   "One **golden spoon** of ten shekels, full of **incense**."

Num. 7:74   "One **golden spoon** of ten shekels, full of **incense**."

Num. 7:80	"One **golden spoon** of ten shekels, full of **incense**."
Num. 7:84	"This was the dedication of the altar, in the day when it was anointed, by the princes of Israel: twelve chargers of silver, twelve silver bowls, **twelve spoons of gold**."
Num. 7:86	"The **golden spoons were twelve, full of incense**, weighing ten shekels apiece, after the shekel of the sanctuary: all the **gold** of the **spoons** was an hundred and twenty shekels."

    The incense that was in the spoons had to also be burnt upon the altar in the Outer Court together with the bread and the animal sacrifice. Therefore, the golden spoons were also put into the basket and were taken into the Outer Court, and (besides the golden vessel for the blood) they were the only items that were made of gold which were taken from the sanctuary (Holy Place and the Holy of Holies) into the Outer Court.

    This symbolizes that there is always an element of the divine (gold) that comes from within the sanctuary and which **must** accompany (with the incense of humility) **every** offering of obedience that is offered to God in the Outer Court of our flesh.

    We also know that there was a process that the priests had to go through in order to pass back and forth between the Outer Court and the Holy Place.

Exo. 29:4	"And Aaron and his sons thou shalt bring unto the door of the tabernacle of the congregation, and shalt wash them with water."

Exo. 29:5	"And thou shalt take the garments, and put upon Aaron the coat, and the robe of the ephod, and the ephod, and the breastplate, and gird him with the curious girdle of the ephod."
Exo. 29:6	"And thou shalt put the mitre upon his head, and put the holy crown upon the mitre."
Exo. 29:7	"Then shalt thou take the anointing oil, and pour it upon his head, and anoint him."
Exo. 29:8	"And thou shalt bring his sons, and put coats upon them."
Exo. 29:9	"And thou shalt gird them with girdles, Aaron and his sons, and put the bonnets on them: and the priest's office shall be theirs for a **perpetual statute**: and thou shalt consecrate Aaron and his sons."

Their bodies had to be washed and they had to put on all of the clothing that was to be used exclusively for the sanctuary (the Holy Place and the Holy of Holies) in order to pass from the Outer Court into the sanctuary. Also, when they passed from the sanctuary to the Outer Court, they had to put off those garments and had to put on the garments that were to be used in the Outer Court.

It is because of this that the basket was necessary, first to take the bread and incense that was in the Holy Place out to the Outer Court to be burnt upon the altar for burnt offerings, and second, to bring the wave offerings of the offerings of flesh into the Holy Place to be waved before the Lord. Since those items could not be contaminated by allowing them to touch the ground—and since they could not hold them in their hands at the same time they were washing, putting on the clothing and anointing with the holy oil—God provided the basket. Any offering that was done upon the altar for burnt offerings in the Outer Court without the presence of the divine (golden spoons) and the incense (of humility) could not offer up to the Lord a sweet savor (smell).

Every time that an offering was made to the Lord that is described as having a sweet savor, it should be automatically understood that it was **only** a sweet savor because of the presence of the gold and the burning of the incense that accompanied the bread and the flesh of the sacrificial animals.

Lev. 6:8	"And the LORD spake unto Moses, saying."
Lev. 6:9	"Command Aaron and his sons, saying, This is the law of the burnt offering: It is the burnt offering, because of the burning upon the altar all night unto the morning, and the fire of the altar shall be burning in it."
Lev. 6:10	"And the priest shall put on his linen garment, and his linen breeches shall he put upon his flesh, and take up the ashes which the fire hath consumed with the burnt offering on the altar, and he shall put them beside the altar."
Lev. 6:11	"And he shall put off his garments, and put on other garments, and carry forth the ashes without the camp unto a clean place."

Lev. 6:12	"And the fire upon the altar shall be burning in it; it shall not be put out: and the priest shall burn wood on it every morning, and lay the burnt offering in order upon it; and he shall burn thereon the fat of the peace offerings."
Lev. 6:13	"The fire shall **ever** be burning upon the altar; it shall **never** go out."

Because the fire and sacrifices were to **never** cease upon the altar for burnt offerings in the Outer Court, we can now see that our lives are to be offered as a continual sacrifice unto the Lord.

Rom. 12:1	"I beseech you therefore, brethren, by the mercies of God, that ye present your **bodies** a **living sacrifice**, holy, acceptable unto God, which is your reasonable service."
Rom. 12:2	"And be not conformed to this world: but be ye transformed by the renewing of your mind, that ye may prove what is that good, and acceptable, and perfect, will of God."
Lev. 16:23	"And Aaron shall come into the tabernacle of the congregation, and shall put off the linen garments, which he put on when he went into the holy place, and shall leave them there."
Lev. 16:24	"And he shall wash his flesh with water in the holy place, and put on his garments, and come forth, and

offer his burnt offering, and the burnt offering of the people, and make an atonement for himself, and for the people."

Lev. 16:25 "And the fat of the sin offering shall he burn upon the altar."

Lev. 16:26 "And he that let go the goat for the scapegoat shall wash his clothes, and bathe his flesh in water, and afterward come into the camp."

Lev. 16:27 "And the bullock for the sin offering, and the goat for the sin offering, whose blood was brought in to make atonement in the holy place, shall one carry forth without the camp; and they shall burn in the fire their skins, and their flesh, and their dung."

Lev. 16:28 "And he that burneth them shall wash his clothes, and bathe his flesh in water, and afterward he shall come into the camp."

An important note is that the only three items that moved between all three courts were blood, incense, and fire.

Lev. 4:7 "And the priest shall put some of the **blood** upon the horns of the **altar of sweet incense** before the LORD, which is in the tabernacle of the congregation; and shall pour all the **blood** of the bullock at the bottom of the **altar of the burnt offering**, which is at the door of the tabernacle of the congregation."

Grain, bread, wave, and heave offerings—all of them together with the incense—were placed inside the basket and moved back and forth between the Holy Place and the Outer Court.

There is also an excellent example of how the same symbol can have a slightly different meaning depending upon the level of kingdom power and manifestation that we are examining.

When examined on a personal level, the grain is the word of God that is sown into our lives (**Matt. 13:3–23; Mark 4:2–20; Luke 8:4–20**) either through preaching or through personal Bible study.

There the grains of the word of God that are received in an attitude of brokenness (grinding) and mixed with inspired teaching or divinely imparted revelation (olive oil, **Luke 24:45**), baked with the fire of Holy Spirit anointing (**Matt. 3:11; Luke 3:16**), becomes the bread of life (as a staple food or basic sustenance (**John 6:28–58**). Then together with the incense of humility that was upon the bread on the table (**Lev. 2:1–2, 6:15, 24:7**), it is put into the basket and moves back and forth between the Holy Place and the Outer Court.

It moves between the mind where knowledge of God's word becomes understanding and the Outer Court of our bodies where **the understanding is demonstrated** by the lives that we live, and there it is proved to either be wisdom (by obedience) or just an intellectual exercise (by knowing to do good but not actually *doing* it, **James 4:17**). The bread is the inspired word of God with the incense of humility that moves into the Outer Court of our bodies for the specific purpose of producing the **visible** manifestation (**2 Cor. 3:2–3**) of the Lordship of Christ over us and the evidence (**Rom. 12:2**) that shows the world that we are His dwelling place.

2 Cor. 3:2	"Ye are our epistle written in our hearts, **known and read of all men**."

2 Cor. 3:3   "Forasmuch as ye are **manifestly declared** to be the epistle of Christ ministered by us, written not with ink, but with the Spirit of the living God; not in tables of stone, but in fleshy tables of the heart."

Rom. 12:2   "And be not conformed to this world: but be ye transformed by the renewing of your mind, **that ye may prove** what is that good, and acceptable, and perfect, will of God."

Lev. 2:1   "And when any will offer a meat offering unto the LORD, his offering shall be of fine flour; and he shall pour oil upon it, and put **frankincense** thereon."

Lev. 2:2   "And he shall bring it to Aaron's sons the priests: and he shall take thereout his handful of the flour thereof, and of the oil thereof, with all the **frankincense** thereof; and the priest shall **burn** the memorial of it **upon the altar**, to be **an offering made by fire**, of a sweet savour unto the LORD."

Lev. 2:15   "And thou shalt put oil upon it, and lay **frankincense** thereon: it is a meat offering."

Lev. 2:16   "And the priest shall burn the memorial of it, part of the beaten corn thereof, and part of the oil thereof,

Lev. 6:15   with all the **frankincense** thereof: it is an **offering made by fire** unto the LORD."

"And he shall take of it his handful, of the flour of the meat offering, and of the oil thereof, and all the **frankincense** which is upon the meat offering, and **shall burn it upon the altar** for a **sweet savour**, even the memorial of it, unto the LORD."

Therefore, obedience is not what **we** do to try to be saved; it is a willing and joyful memorial that He supernaturally empowers of the saving work that He has already done **for** us and **in** us that then is done (by Him) **through** us (**1 Cor. 3:9; Obadiah 1:23**).

It is in the same way, that the word of God, through family devotions, comes into our family lives (**Deut. 4:9, 6:4–9**) where (if it is received in the correct attitude, the incense of humility) it becomes in us, not only an intellectual knowledge, but also a divinely revealed understanding and (through supernaturally empowered obedience) the wisdom of God on display. When the wisdom of God is made manifest in our lives by supernaturally anointed obedience with joyous humility and submission, then the power of God is set in motion to bring all kinds of blessing and family unity and to possess the promises of God. Also, it removes every claim that the enemy has to try to keep us from inheriting everything that God has for us.

In a like manner, when the word of God is received in the church with the right attitude (brokenness, humility, and subjection), it will bind the church together in unity as one body (grain becoming bread) and give the church a vision to impact the community in a way that releases unity and purpose for the blessings of God to flow. It flows in the community by inspired ideas and invention, blessings, and increase which can begin to flow and divinely given prosperity (shalom) can be experienced by all. It also cuts off every work and design of the enemy to separate and destroy.

The enemy, by subtly removing the necessary attitudes of brokenness, humility, subjection, and obedience to God and by removing personal and familial devotions by diverse pressures of life has usurped the flow of blessing and prosperity that God wants to bless us with and has replaced it with financial disaster, strife, and turmoil at every level (all seven).

If **every** individual began to realize just what their own **personal** responsibilities are before God, and then carried those results over into their families, churches, and communities, to continually abide all together in the right attitude (incense, humility) and the obedience of manifested wisdom which comes from those personal and familial devotions of the sowing of the word of God into their lives. If we also realize that this responsibility is a divinely appointed charge to impact the world with the will of God (as it is in heaven) and become faithful to that purpose, then practically overnight, every disaster and strife brought on by the enemy would be swept away by the manifest glory of God!

The glory of God is His **manifest presence**. When His glory fills His temples so much that there is no room for any shadow, it will be displayed even in the Outer Court of our bodies. That display brings His will as it is done to perfection in heaven into manifestation in earthen vessels. It openly shows that His power is so great that even in the lowliest vessels, His word is effective to cast down to the uttermost every expression of the fallen condition.

When His glory fills His temples so much that there is an overflowing that touches everything that is around them, it becomes the *manifest* glory of God. It comes into vessels that are willing for the sweet aroma of the incense of heaven (humility) to fill the temple of their being day and night. It is an irresistible invitation for the Lord of Glory to come into His temple and be seated as King. It proclaims to Him that "we are your subjects, Oh King of saints, come and make your dominion to be of renown in us."

He wants to send a tsunami or avalanche of His **manifest glory** onto the earth. That is what will be the result when the **golden censer** filled with much incense (humility) is cast into the earth (**Rev. 8:3–5**). It will produce the **thundering** of the God of heaven, speaking from within His throne in yielded hearts, and brilliant flashes of lightning of the effective results of divine obedience to drive back the darkness, and the **whole earth** will tremble under the impact of it. However, this time, it will not **only** be the earth that trembles under the impact of it.

Hag. 2:5 "According to the word that I covenanted with you when ye came out of Egypt, so my spirit remaineth among you: fear ye not."

Hag. 2:6 "For thus saith the LORD of hosts; Yet once, it is a little while, and **I will shake the heavens, and the earth**, and the sea, and the dry land."

Hag. 2:7 "And I will shake all nations, and the desire of all nations shall come: **and I will fill this house with glory**, saith the LORD of hosts."

Hag. 2:8 "The silver is mine, and the gold is mine, saith the LORD of hosts."

Hag. 2:9 **"The glory of this latter house shall be greater than of the former, saith the LORD of hosts: and in this place will I give peace, saith the LORD of hosts."**

Hag. 2:18 "Consider now from this day and upward, from the four and twentieth day of the ninth month, even from the day that the foundation of the LORD'S temple was laid, consider it."

Hag. 2:19	"Is the seed yet in the barn? yea, as yet the vine, and the fig tree, and the pomegranate, and the olive tree, hath not brought forth: from this day will I bless you."
Hag. 2:20	"And again the word of the LORD came unto Haggai in the four and twentieth day of the month, saying."
Hag. 2:21	"Speak to Zerubbabel, governor of Judah, saying, **I will shake the heavens and the earth**."
Hag. 2:22	"And I will overthrow the throne of kingdoms, and I will destroy the strength of the kingdoms of the heathen; and I will overthrow the chariots, and those that ride in them; and the horses and their riders shall come down, every one by the sword of his brother."
Hag. 2:23	"In that day, saith the LORD of hosts, will I take thee, O Zerubbabel, my servant, the son of Shealtiel, saith the LORD, and will make thee as a signet: for I have chosen thee, saith the LORD of hosts."
Joel 2:1	"**Blow ye the trumpet in Zion, and sound an alarm in my holy mountain**: let all the inhabitants of the land **tremble**: for the day of the LORD cometh, for it is nigh at hand."

Joel 2:2	"A day of darkness and of gloominess, a day of clouds and of thick darkness, as the morning spread upon the mountains: a great people and a strong; there hath not been ever the like, neither shall be any more after it, even to the years of many generations."
Joel 2:3	"A fire devoureth before them; and behind them a flame burneth: the land is as the garden of Eden before them, and behind them a desolate wilderness; yea, and nothing shall escape them."
Joel 2:4	"The appearance of them is as the appearance of horses; and as horsemen, so shall they run."
Joel 2:5	"Like the noise of chariots on the tops of mountains shall they leap, like the noise of a flame of fire that devoureth the stubble, as a strong people set in battle array."
Joel 2:6	"Before their face the people shall be much pained: all faces shall gather blackness."
Joel 2:7	"They shall run like mighty men; they shall climb the wall like men of war; and they shall march every one on his ways, and they shall not break their ranks."

Joel 2:8	"Neither shall one thrust another; they shall walk every one in his path: and when they fall upon the sword, they shall not be wounded."
Joel 2:9	"They shall run to and fro in the city; they shall run upon the wall, they shall climb up upon the houses; they shall enter in at the windows like a thief."
Joel 2:10	"The **earth shall quake before them**; the **heavens shall tremble**: the sun and the moon shall be dark, and the stars shall withdraw their shining."
Joel 2:11	"And the LORD shall utter his voice before his army: for his camp is very great: for he is strong that executeth his word: for the day of the LORD is great and very terrible; and who can abide it?"
Joel 2:12	"**Therefore also now, saith the LORD, turn ye even to me with all your heart, and with fasting, and with weeping, and with mourning.**"
Joel 2:13	"**And rend your heart, and not your garments, and turn unto the LORD your God: for he is gracious and merciful, slow to anger, and of great kindness, and repenteth him of the evil.**"

Joel 2:14 "Who knoweth if he will return and repent, and leave a blessing behind him; even a meat offering and a drink offering unto the LORD your God?"

Joel 2:15 **"Blow the trumpet in Zion, sanctify a fast, call a solemn assembly."**

Joel 2:16 **"Gather the people, sanctify the congregation, assemble the elders, gather the children, and those that suck the breasts: let the bridegroom go forth of his chamber, and the bride out of her closet."**

Joel 2:17 **"Let the priests, the ministers of the LORD, weep between the porch and the altar, and let them say, Spare thy people, O LORD, and give not thine heritage to reproach, that the heathen should rule over them: wherefore should they say among the people, Where is their God?"**

Joel 2:18 "Then will the LORD be jealous for his land, and pity his people."

Joel 2:19 "Yea, the LORD will answer and say unto his people, Behold, I will send you corn, and wine, and oil, and ye shall be satisfied therewith: and I will no more make you a reproach among the heathen."

Joel 2:20	"But **I will remove far off from you the northern army**, and will drive him into a land barren and desolate, with his face toward the east sea, and his hinder part toward the utmost sea, and his stink shall come up, and his ill savour shall come up, because he hath done great things."
Joel 2:21	"Fear not, O land; be glad and rejoice: for **the LORD will do great things**."
Joel 3:13	"**Put ye in the sickle, for the harvest is ripe**: come, get you down; for the press is full, the fats overflow; for their wickedness is great."
Joel 3:14	"**Multitudes, multitudes in the valley of decision: for the day of the LORD is near in the valley of decision**."
Joel 3:15	"The sun and the moon shall be darkened, and the stars shall withdraw their shining."
Joel 3:16	"The LORD also shall roar out of Zion, and utter his voice from Jerusalem; and **the heavens and the earth shall shake**: but **the LORD will be the hope of his people, and the strength of the children of Israel**."

Joel 3:17 **"So shall ye know that I am the LORD your God dwelling in Zion, my holy mountain: then shall Jerusalem be holy**, and there shall no strangers pass through her any more."

Joel 3:18 "And it shall come to pass in that day, that the mountains shall drop down new wine, and the hills shall flow with milk, and all the rivers of Judah shall flow with waters, and a fountain shall come forth of the house of the LORD, and shall water the valley of Shittim."

How is it that the heavens will tremble also? When Satan came among the sons of God (**Job 1:6 and 2:1**), it is not because he was one of them, but because he is the accuser of the brethren.

Rev. 12:10 "And I heard a loud voice saying in heaven, Now is come salvation, and strength, and the kingdom of our God, and the power of his Christ: **for the accuser of our brethren is cast down, which accused them before our God day and night**."

When the last enemy is put under the feet of the saints of God:

1 Cor. 15:26 "The **last enemy** that shall be destroyed is death."

By the transforming of our mortal bodies, the Outer Court being sanctified (put in order):

Exo. 29:43 "And there I will meet with the children of Israel, and **the tabernacle shall be sanctified by my glory**."

1 Cor. 15:51 "Behold, I shew you a mystery; We shall not all sleep, but **we shall all be changed**."

1 Cor. 15:52 "**In a moment, in the twinkling of an eye**, at the last trump: for the trumpet shall sound, and the dead shall be raised incorruptible, and **we shall be changed**."

1 Cor. 15:53 "**For this corruptible must put on incorruption, and this mortal must put on immortality**."

1 Cor. 15:54 "**So when this corruptible shall have put on incorruption, and this mortal shall have put on immortality, then shall be brought to pass the saying that is written, Death is swallowed up in victory**."

Then Satan is cast out of heaven and will no longer be allowed to accuse them before God, because when that transformation happens, the last result of the fall into the original sin will be removed.

This all happens as the result of (**Dan. 7:25–27**) **THE Ancient of Days** being seated in hearts that are positionally placed (**Dan. 7:9**) by the incense of humility to be **His** throne.

Dan. 7:25 "And he shall speak great words against the most High, and shall wear out the saints of the most High, and think to change times and laws: and they shall be given into his hand until a time and times and the dividing of time."

Dan. 7:26 "But the judgment shall sit, and **they shall take away his dominion**, to consume and to destroy it unto the end."

Dan. 7:27 "**And the kingdom and dominion, and the greatness of the kingdom under the whole heaven, shall be given to the people of the saints of the most High, whose kingdom is an everlasting kingdom, and all dominions shall serve and obey him.**" The Master Plan for the Temple in the Beginning is the Same in the End

Drawing #26

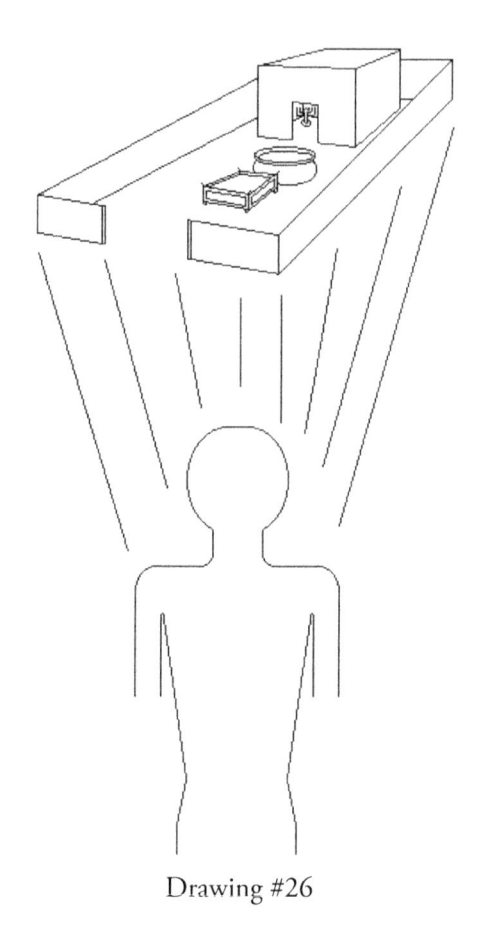

CHAPTER 22

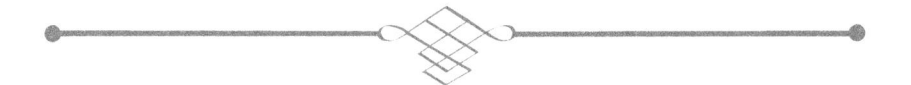

The Architect's Master Plan

The plans for the tabernacle were given to Moses.

> **Exo. 25:8** "And let them make me a sanctuary; that I may dwell among them."
>
> **Exo. 25:9** "**According to all that I shew thee, after the pattern of the tabernacle, and the pattern of all the instruments** thereof, even so shall ye make it."

Moses was in the mountain when God showed him the design of the tabernacle.

> **Exo. 25:40** "And look that thou make them after their pattern, **which was shewed thee in the mount.**"

The earthly tabernacle was an example and shadow of the tabernacle in heaven.

> **Heb. 8:4** "For if he were on earth, he should not be a priest, seeing that there are priests that offer gifts according to the."

Heb. 8:5 "Who serve unto the **example and shadow of heavenly things,** as Moses was admonished of God when he was about to make the tabernacle: for, See, saith He, that thou make all things **according to the pattern shewed to thee in the mount.**"

But the earthly tabernacle was NOT the very image of the heavenly tabernacle.

Heb. 10:1 "For the law **having a shadow of good things to come, and not the very image of the things,** can never with those sacrifices which they offered year by year continually make the comers thereunto perfect."

Heb. 10:2 "For then would they not have ceased to be offered because that the worshippers once purged should have had no more conscience of sins."

Heb. 10:3 "But in those sacrifices there is a remembrance again made of sins every year."

Heb. 10:4 "For it is not possible that the blood of bulls and of goats should take away sins."

Heb. 10:5 "Wherefore when he cometh into the world, he saith, Sacrifice and offering thou wouldest not, **but a body hast thou prepared.**"

However, the "very image" relates to a body and not to a building that is made by the hands of man.

Acts 7:48	"Howbeit **the most High dwelleth not in temples made with hands;** as saith the."
Acts 7:49	"Heaven is my throne, and earth is my footstool: what house will ye build me? saith the Lord: or what is the place of my rest?"

That New Testament scripture came directly from one in the Old Testament.

Isa. 66:1	"Thus saith the LORD, The heaven is my throne, and the earth is my footstool: **where is the house that ye build unto me?** and where is the place of my rest?"
Isa. 66:2	"For all those things hath mine hand made, and all those things have been, saith the LORD: **but to this man will I look, even to him that is poor and of a contrite spirit, and trembleth at my word.**"

The Old Testament scripture also contains specific instructions that show us the correct attitude that is necessary for us to be built up to be His temple and resting place (habitation). In **Heb. 10:5,** the heavenly tabernacle was a body because:

Heb. 9:11	"But the Messiah being come an high priest of good things to come, by **a greater and more perfect tab-**

ernacle, not made with hands,** that is to say, not of this."

But there was a **body** prepared.

Heb. 9:23 "It was therefore necessary that the **patterns** of things in the heavens should be purified with these; but the **heavenly things themselves with better sacrifices than these.**"

Heb. 9:24 "For the Messiah is not entered into the holy places made with hands, **which are the figures of the true; but into heaven itself,** now to appear in the presence of God for us."

Notice that (**Heb. 9:23**) the "**patterns** of things in the heavens" is plural. Therefore, there was not just only one pattern, but several. Also, something about the "pattern" needed to be purified.

Many people believe that the "pattern" singular that Moses saw on the mountain was a symbolism for the Lord Jesus Christ. But the Lord Jesus Christ never had the veil of separation between His heart and His mind like we do. It is for this reason that we can conclude that the pattern that Moses saw in the mountain was symbolic of man in his current condition and that God was using **that** pattern to demonstrate His plan for restoring man back to the original condition and position that Adam had in the beginning before the fall. It is for this reason that when the perfect sacrifice of the Lamb of God was made, the second or inner veil of separation was torn supernaturally from the top to the bottom. It is in this way that the demonic influence of the fifth cherubim, the dragon, was removed in accordance to **2 Cor. 3:14–16**. Also in this way, the temple that symbolized the condition of man was restored back to the original image and likeness of God as it was in **Gen. 1:26–27**.

The only things that remained were for the divine light of the life of God to illuminate the Holy Place of the mind and for the glory of the presence of God to fill all three porches of the temple. Only then could the "pattern" singular, be restored back to the image and likeness of the original pattern—the Lord Jesus Christ—without a veil of separation between the heart and mind and with the entirety of the three porches of our being filled with the glory of the presence of God, the Shekinah. Therefore, Emmanuel, the Lord Jesus Christ, the fullness of the Godhead bodily (**Col. 2:9**), was the original pattern for the then corrupted pattern that Moses saw, and through His sacrifice, the patterns of things in the heavens were purified.

> **Heb. 8:1** "Now of the things which we have spoken this is the sum: We have such an high priest, who is set on the right hand of the throne of the Majesty in the heavens;"

> **Heb. 8:2** "A minister of the **sanctuary**, and of the **true tabernacle, which the Lord pitched, and not man.**"

The Lord pitched that tabernacle two times, once in **Gen. 1:26–27** and **2:7,** and the second time in the birth of the Lord Jesus Christ and the tabernacles that God pitched, and not man, are called **sons**.

Therefore, Moses was also shown the pattern to the pattern in the heavenly:

> **Exo. 33:18** "And he said, I beseech thee, shew me thy glory."

> **Exo. 33:19** "And he said, I will make all my goodness pass before thee, and I will proclaim the name of the LORD before thee; and will be gracious to

	whom I will be gracious, and will shew mercy on whom I will shew mercy."
Exo. 33:20	"And he said, Thou canst not see my face: for there shall no man see me, and live."
Exo. 33:21	"And the LORD said, Behold, there is a place by me, and thou shalt stand upon a rock:"
Exo. 33:22	"And it shall come to pass, while my glory passeth by, that I will put thee in a cleft of the rock, and will cover thee with my hand while I pass by."
Exo. 33:23	"And I will take away mine hand, and **thou shalt see my back parts:** but my face shall not be seen."

Notice the pattern that Moses saw was only the back parts of that heavenly pattern to the pattern and not the face of it. For a man to see the face of it before the perfect sacrifice was offered would have been more than the earthly part of the man (in his fallen condition) could have resisted and he would have died. But that even more perfect pattern in heaven that Moses saw the backside of, was the pattern to the pattern of the temple, about which we will see even more scriptural evidence for in this chapter. Jesus (Yeshua) Himself testified to this when He said:

John 2:19	"**Jesus** answered and said unto them, **Destroy this temple, and in three days I will raise it up**."

John 2:20	"Then said the Jews, Forty and six years was this temple in building, and wilt thou rear it up in three days?"
John 2:21	**"But he spake of the temple of his body."**

The chief priests and Pharisees understood Him perfectly, even though they tried to deny it, but they did that denial in order to accuse Him. They showed that they understood perfectly by the words of their own mouths **after** the crucifixion.

Matt. 27:62	"Now the next day, that followed the day of the preparation, the chief priests and Pharisees came together unto Pilate,"
Matt. 27:63	"Saying, Sir, we remember that that deceiver said, while he was yet alive, **After three days I will rise again**."

Therefore, when we refer to…

1 Cor. 3:16	"Know ye not that **ye are the temple of God,** and that the Spirit of God dwelleth in you?"

…we are not only recognizing the symbolism of the natural temple typing the spiritual temple (that we are and that was made in the image and likeness of the perfect heavenly pattern to the pattern), but we are also confessing to the completion of the work of restoration.

1 Cor. 15:53b	"…this mortal must put on immortality."

Eph. 4:13	"**Till we all come** in the unity of the faith, and of the knowledge of the Son of God, **unto a perfect man, unto the measure of the stature of the fulness of Christ:**"
Col. 3:10	"And have put on the **new man**, which is renewed in knowledge after the **image of him that created him**."

To the original:

Gen. 1:27a	"So **God created man in his own image**."

And that the body of Yeshua is that perfect temple that was in heaven which Moses could only see the back side of.

In other words, this earthly tabernacle of clay is molded into the fullness of the image of that perfect heavenly tabernacle, Yeshua HaMesiach (Jesus the Christ), is to be created again in the image and likeness of God as in the beginning.

There is a law of reproduction. *That* law of reproduction applies to vegetation.

Gen. 1:11	"And God said, Let the earth bring forth grass, the herb yielding seed, and the fruit tree yielding fruit **after his kind**, whose seed is in itself, upon the earth: and it was so."
Gen. 1:12	"And the earth brought forth grass, and herb yielding seed **after his kind**, and the tree yielding fruit, whose seed was in itself, **after his kind**: and God saw that it was good."

Gen. 1:13	"And the evening and the morning were the third day."

We can see by the following verses that to bring forth **after his kind** also applies to animals.

Gen. 1:20	"And God said, Let the waters bring forth abundantly the moving creature that hath life, and fowl that may fly above the earth in the open firmament of heaven."
Gen. 1:21	"And God created great whales, and every living creature that moveth, which the waters brought forth abundantly, **after their kind**, and every winged fowl **after his kind**: and God saw that it was good."
Gen. 1:22	"And God blessed them, saying, **Be fruitful, and multiply**, and fill the waters in the seas, and let fowl multiply in the earth."
Gen. 1:23	"And the evening and the morning were the fifth day."
Gen. 1:24	"And God said, Let the earth bring forth the living creature **after his kind**, cattle, and creeping thing, and beast of the earth **after his kind**: and it was so."
Gen. 1:25	"And God made the beast of the earth **after his kind**, and cattle **after their kind**, and every thing that creepeth

upon the earth **after his kind**: and God saw that it was good."

And that this **same** concept even applies to mankind.

> **Gen. 5:3** "And Adam lived an hundred and thirty years, and begat a son **in his own likeness, after his image**; and called his name Seth."

Therefore, when God created man in His own image, God was keeping His own law that He had already established.

> **Gen. 1:26** "And God said, Let us make man **in our image, after our likeness**: and let them have dominion over the fish of the sea, and over the fowl of the air, and over the cattle, and over all the earth, and over every creeping thing that creepeth upon the earth."

> **Gen. 1:27** "So God created man **in his own image, in the image of God** created he him; **male and female created he them**."

> **Gen. 1:28** "And God blessed **them**, and God said unto **them**, Be fruitful, and multiply, and replenish the earth, and subdue it: and have dominion over the fish of the sea, and over the fowl of the air, and over every living thing that moveth upon the earth."

> **Gen. 1:29** "And God said, Behold, I have given you every herb bearing seed, which is upon the face of all the earth, and

	every tree, in the which is the fruit of a tree yielding seed; to you it shall be for meat."
Gen. 1:30	"And to every beast of the earth, and to every fowl of the air, and to every thing that creepeth upon the earth, wherein there is life, I have given every green herb for meat: and it was so."
Gen. 1:31	"And God saw every thing that he had made, and, behold, it was very good. And the evening and the morning were the sixth day."

We can see, therefore, that God had dominion over everything on the earth (and in the universe), and when He brought forth a son, his son had the same dominion (in the earth). Also, as God is eternal in the original condition, Adam would have lived eternally.

All of the same character and nature (and attributes) that was in God were also in Adam, and Adam, in that original condition/position, had no need for salvation because he was created in a "saved" condition from the beginning. The fall produced characteristics in Adam that were not of God and which were of a fallen nature, not a saved nature. Just as it was God who created man in His own image (**Gen. 1:27**) in the beginning, God describes Himself as:

Rev. 22:13	"I am **Alpha and Omega**, the **beginning and the end**, the **first and the last**."

And in the end, He is:

Rev. 21:22	"And I saw no **temple** therein: for **the Lord God Almighty** and **the Lamb** are the **temple** of it."

Therefore, when Satan used the serpent to cause the fall of the woman, he was literally trying to corrupt the image and likeness that God made to remake it in his own fallen image. Then we can conclude that the Lamb of God was that heavenly temple that was in the beginning (**Gen. 1:26**) and will be in the end (**Rev. 22:17**).

However, the temple that Moses saw in symbolic form when he was in the mountain was not the symbolic form of the Lord Jesus Christ. The proof of this is because the veil in the temple that Moses saw would eventually have to be removed (**2 Cor. 3:14–16**), and therefore, was not part of the **eternal** pattern. This was probably the reason why Moses was still not satisfied and asked to see God in His real (eternal) form (not symbolically) and did see Him from behind; it was only then that he saw the manifestation of God in human form (in the fullness of His glory and majesty).

Therefore, when the fullness of the restoration of all things comes, man will be once again as he was in the beginning—saved, eternal, and with full dominion over the earth (**Dan. 7:27**). It also means that when it is done, it will be the **exclusive** work of God to again create man in His image and likeness. Just as man did not help God to create himself in the beginning, then neither does God need anything else from us but humility (the incense of heaven) and surrender (as dust of the earth) in order for Him to do the work of restoration in the end.

What did the symbols that Moses saw in the mountain signify?

It was the condition of mankind after the fall that was in great need of restoration. It is for this reason that we have been given all of these symbols in order to teach us the spiritual pattern of heavenly things and how they apply to us today. We needed to know about the dragon cherubim that was in the veil and the details of how to overcome for that veil to be removed from our minds. It is the incense of humility that conquers the dragon (because he cannot humble himself) and brings the heart into a condition of total surrender and circumcision of heart to be entirely converted to the Lord so that He can remove the veil and the temple filled with the Shekinah.

PART 4
The Outer Court

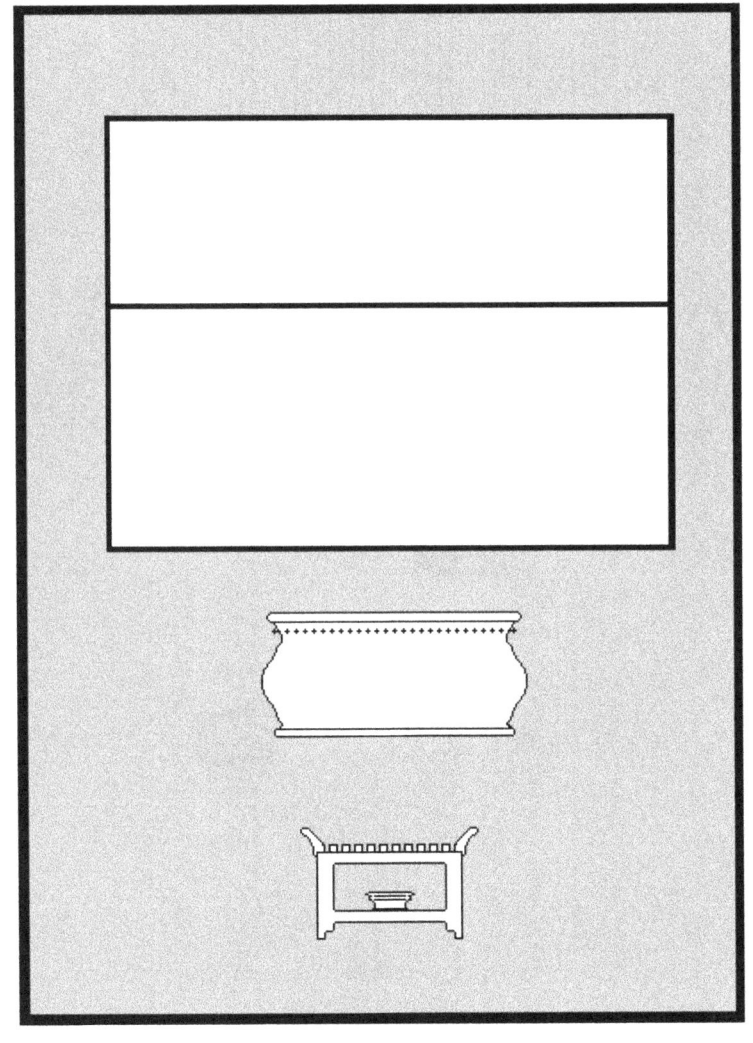

Drawing #27

Drawing #28

CHAPTER 23

The Basket and Wave Offerings

Introduction to the Outer Court

In order to correctly understand the application of the Scriptures to the Outer Court (our bodies) and for it to not be misunderstood as legalism or religiosity, it must be understood that everything necessary to overcome the fallen condition that is in the flesh and to be fully restored to the original image and likeness of God can ONLY be provided by the very life (that is in the blood, the Holy Spirit) of God permanently abiding in us (**John 1:4**; **Acts 20:28**). The presence of *that* life must be permanent and not just an anointing that comes and goes (**John 7:39**).

Sadly, many people mistake the *anointing* of the Holy Spirit for the *baptism* of the Holy Spirit. To be baptized in the Holy Spirit is different than being baptized in water. Baptism in water is being completely immersed, but then we have to leave the water in order to breathe. However, when we are immersed (baptized) in the Holy Spirit, we are to *never* leave that complete immersion (**Acts 17:28**); to leave that complete immersion is to begin the process of death. This is true because *that* life (of God, **Acts 20:28**) becomes *our* life, and it is *that* life which joins us together with Him and makes us to be part of His family and to be able (**John 1:12**) to transition (as true "Hebrews." See Chapter Six the section on **"The Context for the Covenant"**) from just being a bride (that is only promised *unto* marriage) into being the Wife of the Lamb (**Rev. 19:7-9**).

Also, it is *only* by the supernatural power of *that* life continually dwelling in us that we can obediently walk in a way that manifests every jot and tittle of the Word in and through our flesh. Every attempt to be obedient without it being the expression of *that* life will fail.

Rev. 19:7 "Let us be glad and rejoice, and give honour to him: for the **marriage** of the Lamb is come, and his **wife** hath made herself ready."

Rev. 19:8 "And to her was granted that she should be arrayed in fine linen, clean and white: for the fine linen is the righteousness of saints."

Rev. 19:9 "And he saith unto me, Write, Blessed are they which are called unto the **marriage** supper of the Lamb. And he saith unto me, These are the true sayings of God."

The Feast of Tabernacles (**Lev. 23:33–43**) was symbolic of the wedding supper of the Lamb (**Rev. 19:7–9**). It was in the Feast of Tabernacles that all of Israel gathered together around **the** Tabernacle/Temple to celebrate the feast. They were to make booths or tabernacles for each of their families around the Tabernacle/Temple. Because each believer is a temple of the Holy Spirit (**1 Cor. 3:16**), each time that they gather together in the place that God has appointed for them to worship Him (**Heb. 10:25**), it is a rehearsal of the Feast of Tabernacles and the wedding supper of the Lamb. In the moment that is appointed by God (**1 Thess. 4:15-17**), they will all be gathered for the wedding supper of the Lamb, the real and GREAT Feast of Tabernacles.

In *that* GREAT Feast of Tabernacles, all of the temples/tabernacles where He has made His habitation throughout history will be gathered together around THE perfect Heavenly Tabernacle that He IS. It is the revelation of the manifestation of the great truth of the reality that was symbolized by the Tabernacle/Temple and the Feast of Tabernacles, which was the Old Testament basis for the Apostle Paul's teaching about the "catching away" of the Church.

It is here that we are going to briefly consider a detail about the high priests' garment that we have not mentioned before.

Exo. 28:2 "And thou shalt make holy garments for Aaron thy brother **for glory and for beauty**."

1 Chr. 16:29 "Give unto the LORD the glory due unto his name: bring an offering, and come before him: **worship the LORD in the beauty of holiness**."

Exo. 28:33 "And beneath upon the hem of it thou shalt make pomegranates of blue, and of purple, and of scarlet, round about the hem thereof; and bells of gold between them round about."

Exo. 28:34 "A **golden bell** and a **pomegranate**, a **golden bell** and a **pomegranate**, upon the hem of the robe round about."

Exo. 28:35 "And it shall be upon Aaron to minister: and his **sound** shall be **heard** when he goeth in unto the holy place before the LORD, and when he cometh out, **that he die not**."

Therefore, the sounding of the bells that were part of the hem of the garments of the High Priest proclaimed the **beauty of holiness** as the priests went into the Holy of Holies to put the blood upon the Mercy Seat.

> **Heb. 12:14** "**Follow** peace with all men, **and holiness, without which no man shall see the Lord**."
>
> **Heb. 12:15** "Looking diligently lest any man fail of the grace of God; lest any root of bitterness springing up trouble you, and thereby many be defiled."
>
> **Heb. 12:16** "Lest there be any fornicator, or profane person, as Esau, who for one morsel of meat sold his birthright."

It might be asked why this detail was left for a deeper discussion about the Outer Court (see also the "covering" in Chapter Six the section on **"The Context for the Covenant"**). It is because the bells sounded with every **step** that the high priest made. That sounding of the bells is a parallel of when Moses had to take off his shoes to **walk** carefully (holy) in the presence of God (**Exo. 3:5**). The sounding of the bells are a sign of a holy **walk** in the presence of a Holy God that is ONLY possible by the Holy Spirit, without which—instead of blessing because of the wrong approach—there may come a curse, and even death (**1 Cor. 11:28–32**).

> **Exo. 28:35** "And it shall be upon Aaron to minister: and his sound shall be heard when he goeth in unto the holy place before the LORD, and when he cometh out, **that he die not**."

When the **Eph. 4:11** priesthood are entering into the Holy of Holies, the **Exo. 28:35** and **Exo. 19:19** sound takes the form that is found in **Eze. 9:4, Joel 2:13,17,** and **Rom. 8:22–27,** sighing and crying that fulfills **Josh. 3:6,8,13–17** symbolic pattern with the burden of the Covenant of God (**Josh. 3:3,6,13,15,17, 4:10,16,18**) upon their hearts.

The next detail about the garment was the fringed borders.

> **Num. 15:37** "And the LORD spake unto Moses, saying,"
>
> **Num. 15:38** "Speak unto the children of Israel, and bid them that they make them **fringes in the borders of their garments** throughout their generations, and that they **put upon the fringe of the borders a ribband of blue**."
>
> **Num. 15:39** "And it shall be unto you for a **fringe**, that ye may look upon it, and remember all the commandments of the LORD, and do them; and that ye seek not after your own heart and your own eyes, after which ye use to go a whoring."
>
> **Num. 15:40** "**That ye may remember, and do all my commandments, and be holy unto your God.**"
>
> **Num. 15:41** "I am the LORD your God, which brought you out of the land of Egypt, to be your God: I am the LORD your God."

Another item about the high priest's clothing was the golden plate that he was to wear upon his forehead.

> **Exo. 28:36** "And thou shalt make **a plate of pure gold**, and grave upon it, like the engravings of a signet, **HOLINESS TO THE LORD**."
>
> **Exo. 28:37** "And thou shalt put it on a blue lace, that it may be upon the mitre; upon the forefront of the mitre it shall be."
>
> **Exo. 28:38** "And it shall be upon Aaron's forehead, that Aaron may bear the iniquity of the holy things, which the children of Israel shall hallow in all their holy gifts; **and it shall be always upon his forehead**, that they may be accepted before the LORD."

Even the **blue lace** that was used to bind the plate of gold to the mitre that the high priest wore symbolized holiness. We can see this same thing symbolized in the **blue ribbon** that all of the people were commanded to put upon the **fringes** in the border of their garments (**Num. 15:38–40**).

The Promise of the Father

The Lord Jesus spoke to the apostles about "the promise of the Father."

> **Luke 24:49** "And, behold, I send the **promise of my Father** upon you: but tarry ye in the city of Jerusalem, until ye be endued with power from on high."

Acts 1:4 "And, being assembled together with them, commanded them that they should not depart from Jerusalem, but wait for the **promise of the Father**, which, saith he, ye have heard of me."

Acts 2:33 "Therefore being by the right hand of God exalted, and having received of the **Father the promise of the Holy Ghost**, he hath shed forth this, which ye now see and hear."

What was the promise of the Father?

Jer. 31:31 "Behold, the days come, saith the LORD, that I will make a **new covenant** with the house of Israel, and with the house of Judah."

Jer. 31:32 "Not according to the covenant that I made with their fathers in the day that I took them by the hand to bring them out of the land of Egypt; which my covenant they brake, **although I was an husband unto them**, saith the LORD."

Jer. 31:33 "But this shall be the **covenant** that I will make with the house of Israel; After those days, saith the LORD, I will put my law in their **inward parts**, and write it in their **hearts**; and will be their God, and they shall be my people."

Heb. 8:10 "For this is the **covenant** that I will make with the house of Israel after those days, saith the Lord; I will put my laws into their **mind**, and write them in their **hearts**: and I will be to them a God, and they shall be to me a people."

Heb. 10:16 "This is the **covenant** that I will make with them after those days, saith the Lord, I will put my laws into their **hearts**, and in their **minds** will I write them."

Heb. 10:17 "And their sins and iniquities will I remember no more."

The heart and mind (inward parts) are the two porches that constitute the Sanctuary, the Inner Man, the tent within the tent (of the Outer Court).

Joel 2:28 "And it shall come to pass afterward, that I will **pour out my spirit** upon all **flesh**; and your sons and your daughters shall prophesy, your old men shall dream dreams, your young men shall see visions."

Joel 2:29 "And also upon the servants and upon the handmaids in those days will I pour out my spirit."

It was the promise of a new (marriage, **Jer. 31:32**) covenant in which the law (descriptions of the character of God) would be written (in hearts and minds) in the sanctuary of the temples that we are, by the Holy Spirit (the life that was in the blood), to then be made manifest in and through our flesh (the Outer Court, **Luke 24:49**) by the power of **His** Life in us as living epistles (**2 Cor. 3:3**), to be seen and read of all men (**2 Cor. 3:2**) as testimonies to and for His Glory (**Isa. 43:10,12, 44:8**; **2 Cor. 3:2–3**).

> **Luke 24:49** "And behold, I send forth the promise of my Father upon you: but tarry ye in the city, until ye be **clothed** with power from on high." (ASV)

That witness of the glory, power, might, and majesty of the invisible God is made visible for all to see by *all* three porches (heart, mind, **and** body) of these temples that we are, being filled with the glory of His presence (Shekinah) so much that even our flesh (Outer Court) is clothed upon (**Gen. 3:21**; **John 1:14**) with the skin of **our** sacrifice and can manifest **His** obedience with signs following (power from on High). The greatest expression of healing (**Isa. 53:5**) in our flesh is:

> **1 Cor. 15:51** "Behold, I tell you a mystery: We all shall not sleep, but we shall all be **changed**."
>
> **1 Cor. 15:52** "in a moment, in the twinkling of an eye, at the last trump: for the trumpet shall sound, and the dead shall be raised incorruptible, **and we shall be changed**."
>
> **1 Cor. 15:53** "**For this corruptible must put on incorruption, and this mortal must put on immortality**."
>
> **1 Cor. 15:54** "But when this corruptible shall have put on incorruption, and this mortal shall have put on immortality, then

shall come to pass the saying that is written, **Death is swallowed up in victory**."

2 Cor. 5:1 "For we know that if the earthly house of our tabernacle be dissolved, we have a building from God, a house not made with hands, eternal, in the heavens."

2 Cor. 5:2 "For verily in this we groan, longing to be **clothed** upon with our habitation which is from heaven."

2 Cor. 5:3 "if so be that being **clothed** we shall not be found naked."

2 Cor. 5:4 "For indeed we that are in this tabernacle do groan, being burdened; not for that we would be unclothed, but that we would be **clothed** upon, **that what is mortal may be swallowed up of life**."

Kings and Priests

Part of the promise that the Lord made to make us to be kings and priests (**Rev. 1:6, 5:10**) and a kingdom of priests (**Exo. 19:5–6**) is the commandment for kings to write a copy of the Law of God and to read from it EVERY day.

Deut. 17:14 When thou art come unto the land which the LORD thy God giveth thee, and shalt possess it, and shalt dwell therein, and shalt say, I will set a king over me, like as all the nations that are about me;

Deut. 17:15   Thou shalt in any wise set him king over thee, whom the LORD thy God shall choose: one from among thy brethren shalt thou set king over thee: thou mayest not set a stranger over thee, which is not thy brother.

Deut. 17:16   But he shall not multiply horses to himself, nor cause the people to return to Egypt, to the end that he should multiply horses: forasmuch as the LORD hath said unto you, Ye shall henceforth return no more that way.

Deut. 17:17   Neither shall he multiply wives to himself, that his heart turn not away: neither shall he greatly multiply to himself silver and gold.

Deut. 17:18   And it shall be, when he sitteth upon the throne of his kingdom, that **he shall write him a copy of this law in a book out of that which is before the priests the Levites**:

Deut. 17:19   And it shall be with him, and **he shall read therein all the days of his life**: that he may learn to fear the LORD his God, to **keep** all the words of this law and these statutes, to **do** them:

> **Deut. 17:20** **That his heart be not lifted up above his brethren**, and that he **turn not aside** from the commandment, to the right hand, or to the left: to the end that he may prolong his days in his kingdom, he, and his children, in the midst of Israel.

The commandment included the incense of humility (**v. 20**) and a holy walk (of obedience, **v. 19–20**). These are necessary parts of becoming kings and priests. A portion of the responsibility that every individual and family has as temples of the Holy Spirit is to read the Bible EVERY day with an attitude of humility to be obedient.

People who truly are of faith will not look upon the weakness of their own flesh or of their own abilities as an excuse to disobey.

People of faith will humbly keep their attention focused upon the author of their faith, to receive the power that is necessary to walk upon (higher than) the waters (**Isa. 55:6–11**; **Matt. 14:29**; **Mal. 4:2–3**).

The Basket and the Wave Offerings

Every time the Bible mentions wave and heave offerings, the use of the **basket** is also implied.

Basket: **Exo. 29:3,23,32; Lev. 8:2,26, 8:31; Num. 6:15,17,19; Deut. 26:2,4, 28:5, 28:17.**

Wave: **Exo. 29:24,26–27; Lev. 7:30,34, 8:27,29, 9:21, 10:14–15, 14:12,21,24, 23:11–12, 23:15,17,20; Num. 5:25, 6:20, 18:11,18.**

Heave: **Exo. 9:8,10,22–23, 10:21–22, 16:4, 17:14, 20:4,11,22, 24:10, 29:27–28, 31:17, 32:13; Lev. 7:14,32,34, 10:14–15, 26:19, 6:20; Num. 15:19–21, 18:8,11,19,24,26–30,32, 31:29,41; Deut. 1:10,28, 2:25, 3:24, 4:11,19,26,32,36,39, 5:8, 7:24,**

9:1,14, 10:14,22, 11:11,17,21, 12:6,11,17, 17:3, 25:19, 26:15, 28:12,23–24,62, 29:20, 30:4,12,19, 31:28, 32:1,40, 33:13,26,28.

The reason for this is because the only detail that was provided by God to bring the shewbread and incense from the Holy Place into the Outer Court and the wave and heave offerings from the Outer Court into the Holy Place was the basket.

When searching the root meaning of the word *basket*, we find that the same word in Hebrew can be interpreted into English as various other words, depending upon the context that it is used in. A basket, cage, pot, kettle, cauldron, or mandrakes. Used to contain love offerings or (mandrake, summer fruit, figs) sweet smell that acts as an aphrodisiac to excite or stimulate.

In the temple, the basket was used to carry the consecrated bread (with incense, **Lev. 24:7**; **Num. 7:14–86**) from the Holy Place to the Outer Court to be offered with burnt offerings of the flesh of sacrificial animals upon the altar and to bring flesh offerings from the altar into the Holy Place to be presented to God by being waved or lifted up (heaved) before the Inner Veil, before being consumed (eaten, **Exo. 29:32–33**) in the Holy Presence. In all cases, the bread and the flesh had to be burnt or cooked upon the altar for burnt offerings in the Outer Court and accompanied with the Holy Incense so that the cloud of smoke could rise up as a sweet smelling aroma before the Lord.

Lev. 24:5	"And thou shalt take **fine flour**, and bake **twelve cakes** thereof: two tenth deals shall be in one cake."
Lev. 24:6	"And thou shalt set them in two rows, six on a row, upon the pure table before the LORD."
Lev. 24:7	"And thou shalt **put pure frankincense upon each row**, that it may be on the bread for a **memorial**, even

	an offering made by fire unto the LORD."
Lev. 24:8	"**Every sabbath he shall set it in order** before the LORD continually, being taken from the children of Israel by an **everlasting covenant**."
Lev. 24:9	"And it shall be Aaron's and his sons'; and they shall eat it in the holy place: for it is most holy unto him of the offerings of the LORD made by fire by a **perpetual statute**."

Notice neither the flesh nor the meat (bread) offering *alone* could produce the sweet aroma before the Lord. Both of them had to be accompanied with the Holy Incense (**frank**incense literally means the *true* incense) in order to be the sweet aroma before the Lord. All of our acts of obedience must be done in humility (incense) and presented in humility before the Lord as a love *offering* in order to stimulate Him to respond with supernatural empowerment to make it acceptable in His presence (remember, the power of the life that is in the blood works *through* the incense of humility).

There is a difference between an offering and a sacrifice. A sacrifice is a payment for an offence that was committed; an offering is done by freewill out of love. Both can be either received or rejected. There was a promise to receive the offering *IF* it was accompanied with incense that the blood was working through. If the offering was not properly presented with incense, then it was rejected, possibly with fatal consequences.

The "proper" presentation had to *only* be with fire that was kindled by God Himself, in the correct place, by the correct person and correct sequence, using instruments of brass (in the Outer Court, symbolic of judgment) or gold (in the Sanctuary, symbolic of divine inspiration).

The basket was made out of supple willow branches or bulrushes that were woven together while green and then allowed to dry or stiffen in order to give them a more solid form. The basket was not a box (made out of hard wood that was not "woven" together). The following is a list of the application of the Hebrew word for *basket* and what it was used for.

Gen. 30:14–16—mandrakes

Gen. 40:16–18—baskets

Exo. 29:3—basket, unleavened wheat bread, wafers, and cakes tempered with oil, bullock, two rams (**Exo. 29:22–34**)

Lev. 8:2—basket, bullock, two rams, unleavened bread (**Lev. 8:22-32**)

Num. 6:15–19—basket, unleavened bread, wafers, and cakes mingled with oil, ram shoulder drink offerings

Deut. 26:2–15—basket, firstfruits, tithing

Deut. 28:5,17—basket, blessing, cursing

Jdgs. 6:19—basket, kid, unleavened cakes

1 Sam. 2:14—kettle, flesh

2Kin 10:7—baskets, heads

2 Chr. 35:13—caldrons, passover lamb

Job 41:20—pot

Psa. 81:6—**pots**

Sol. 7:13—**mandrakes**, all manner of pleasant fruits, new and old

Jer. 5:27—**cage**, birds

Jer. 6:9—**baskets**, grapes

Jer. 24:1–2—**baskets**, good figs, bad figs

Amos 8:1–2—**basket**, summer fruit

Please remember that there is a parallel of use between the golden censer (used exclusively in the Sanctuary that passed between the Holy Place and the Holy of Holies) and the basket (that passed back and forth between the Holy Place and the Outer Court).

The basket was the **only** instrument that entered into the Sanctuary that was not either made out of gold or covered with gold. **Both** the golden censer **and** the basket are symbolic of attitudes, and **both** carried incense during the use of the golden censer, and the basket while taking the bread and frankincense to the Outer Court. Even though there was no incense in the basket other than that which was in the smoke that flavored the flesh of the wave offering, when the wave offering was brought into the Holy Place, it was brought into the continual aroma of incense that came from the altar for incense and that filled the entire Tabernacle and, even more so, the Sanctuary.

After being waved before the inner veil, some of the offerings were eaten inside of the Holy Place (**Lev. 24:7**), and some of them were taken back (in the basket) to the Outer Court to be burnt upon the altar. Even the offerings that were to be eaten in the Holy Place, if they were not entirely consumed, they had to be taken (again in the basket) back to the Outer Court to be burnt upon the altar (**Exo. 29:34**) before the sun rose in the morning.

The Passover Lamb

Exo. 12:10   "And ye shall **let nothing of it remain until the morning**; and that which remaineth of it until the morning ye shall burn with fire."

Num. 9:11   "The fourteenth day of the second month at even they shall keep it, and eat it with unleavened bread and bitter herbs."

Num. 9:12   "They shall **leave none of it unto the morning**, nor break any bone of it: according to all the ordinances of the passover they shall keep it."

Deut. 16:4   "And there shall be no leavened bread seen with thee in all thy coast seven days; **neither shall there any thing of the flesh, which thou sacrificedst the first day at even, remain all night until the morning**."

The Manna

Exo. 16:19   "And Moses said, Let no man **leave of it till the morning**."

In this, we can see a parallel between four different things: manna, the Passover lamb, sacrifices, and how the first three point to the fourth—the Lamb of God, our Passover (**1 Cor. 5:7**).

Exo. 23:18   "Thou shalt not offer the blood of my sacrifice with leavened bread;

neither shall the fat of my sacrifice remain until the morning."

Exo. 29:34 "And if ought of the flesh of the consecrations, or of the bread, **remain unto the morning**, then thou shalt burn the remainder with fire: it shall not be eaten, because it is holy."

Exo. 34:25 "Thou shalt not offer the blood of my sacrifice with leaven; neither shall the sacrifice of the feast of the passover be **left unto the morning**."

Lev. 7:11 "And this is the law of the sacrifice of peace offerings, which he shall offer unto the LORD."

Lev. 7:12 "If he offer it for a thanksgiving, then he shall offer with the sacrifice of thanksgiving unleavened cakes mingled with oil, and unleavened wafers anointed with oil, and cakes mingled with oil, of fine flour, fried."

Lev. 7:13 "Besides the cakes, he shall offer for his offering leavened bread with the sacrifice of thanksgiving of his peace offerings."

Lev. 7:14 "And of it he shall offer one out of the whole oblation for an heave offering unto the LORD, and it shall be the priest's that sprinkleth the blood of the peace offerings."

Lev. 7:15 "And the flesh of the sacrifice of his peace offerings for thanksgiving shall be eaten **the same day** that it is offered; **he shall not leave any of it until the morning**."

Lev. 7:16 "But if the sacrifice of his offering be a vow, or a voluntary offering, it shall be eaten **the same day** that he offereth his sacrifice: and on the morrow also the remainder of it shall be eaten."

Lev. 7:17 **"But the remainder of the flesh of the sacrifice on the third day shall be burnt with fire."**

Lev. 7:18 "And if any of the flesh of the sacrifice of his peace offerings be eaten at all on the third day, it shall not be accepted, neither shall it be imputed unto him that offereth it: it shall be an abomination, and the soul that eateth of it shall bear his iniquity."

Why was it not permitted to leave any of the sacrifices until the morning?

Lam. 3:22 "It is of the LORD'S mercies that we are not consumed, because **his compassions fail not**."

Lam. 3:23 "**They are new every morning**: great is thy faithfulness."

The Lord Jesus Christ is our Passover Lamb.

1 Cor. 5:7 "Purge out therefore the old leaven, that ye may be a new lump, as ye are unleavened. For even **Christ our passover** is sacrificed for us."

He is also the true bread (manna) that came down from heaven.

John 6:30 "They said therefore unto him, What sign shewest thou then, that we may see, and believe thee? what dost thou work?"

John 6:31 "Our fathers did eat **manna** in the desert; as it is written, He gave them **bread from heaven** to eat."

John 6:32 "Then Jesus said unto them, Verily, verily, I say unto you, Moses gave you not that **bread from heaven**; but my Father giveth you the **true bread from heaven**."

John 6:33 "For **the bread of God is he which cometh down from heaven, and giveth life unto the world**."

John 6:34 "Then said they unto him, Lord, evermore give us **this bread**."

John 6:35 "And Jesus said unto them, **I am the bread of life**: he that cometh to me shall never hunger; and he that believeth on me shall never thirst."

John 6:36 "But I said unto you, That ye also have seen me, and believe not."

John 6:37	"All that the Father giveth me shall come to me; and him that cometh to me I will in no wise cast out."
John 6:38	"For **I came down from heaven**, not to do mine own will, but the will of him that sent me."
John 6:39	"And this is the Father's will which hath sent me, that of all which he hath given me I should lose nothing, but should raise it up again at the last day."
John 6:40	"And this is the will of him that sent me, that every one which seeth the Son, and believeth on him, may have everlasting life: and I will raise him up at the last day."
John 6:41	"The Jews then murmured at him, because he said, I am the bread which came down from heaven."
John 6:42	"And they said, Is not this Jesus, the son of Joseph, whose father and mother we know? **how is it then that he saith, I came down from heaven?**"
John 6:43	"Jesus therefore answered and said unto them, Murmur not among yourselves."
John 6:44	"No man can come to me, except the Father which hath sent me draw

	him: and I will raise him up at the last day."
John 6:45	"It is written in the prophets, And they shall be all taught of God. Every man therefore that hath heard, and hath learned of the Father, cometh unto me."
John 6:46	"Not that any man hath seen the Father, save he which is of God, he hath seen the Father."
John 6:47	"Verily, verily, I say unto you, He that believeth on me hath everlasting life."
John 6:48	**"I am that bread of life."**
John 6:49	"Your fathers did eat **manna** in the wilderness, and are dead."
John 6:50	**"This is the bread which cometh down from heaven, that a man may eat thereof, and not die."**
John 6:51	**"I am the living bread which came down from heaven**: if any man eat of this **bread**, he shall live for ever: and the **bread** that I will give is my flesh, which I will give for the life of the world."
John 6:52	"The Jews therefore strove among themselves, saying, How can this man give us his flesh to eat?"

John 6:53	"Then Jesus said unto them, Verily, verily, I say unto you, Except ye eat the flesh of the Son of man, and drink his blood, ye have no life in you."
John 6:54	"Whoso eateth my flesh, and drinketh my blood, hath eternal life; and I will raise him up at the last day."
John 6:55	"For my flesh is meat indeed, and my blood is drink indeed."
John 6:56	"He that eateth my flesh, and drinketh my blood, dwelleth in me, and I in him."
John 6:57	"As the living Father hath sent me, and I live by the Father: so he that eateth me, even he shall live by me."
John 6:58	**"This is that bread which came down from heaven**: not as your fathers did eat manna, and are dead: **he that eateth of this bread shall live for ever."**

Because it *only* by the power of **His** life (**Gen. 9:4; Lev. 17:11,14; Deut. 12:23**) in us that we are able to offer unto God the fruits of obedience (Outer Court symbolic of our flesh), and we cannot justify today's failures by yesterday's obedience; we must humbly implore and trust in His faithfulness to offer a new sacrifice (of obedience) to Him **every day**.

Rom. 12:1	"I beseech you therefore, brethren, by the mercies of God, that ye pres-

	ent your **bodies** a living sacrifice, holy, acceptable unto God, which is your reasonable service."
Rom. 12:2	"And be not conformed to this world: but be ye transformed by the renewing of your **mind**, that ye may prove what is that good, and acceptable, and perfect, will of God."

The Outer Court and the Sanctuary working together to present a living sacrifice in holiness unto God in the Outer Court in a way that is acceptable unto Him. In *that* place of divine surrender and obedience, He promised that He would meet with us, and once we have *that* encounter, we will *never* be the same as before. It is *then* that His glory and character is made visible (Outer Court, our flesh, bodies) for others to see (**2 Cor. 3:2–3**). We do the surrender and the obedience it implies by the manifestation of the power of His Life in us; however, the obedience cannot be hidden (**Matt. 5:14–16**) in the same way that Moses could not completely hide the light that shone from his face and could only cover it a little with a veil.

The intensity of the divine light of God (**John 1:4**) in the inner man (symbolized by the Sanctuary) can only be *partially* hidden by the veil of our flesh (**Heb. 10:20–22**).

Drawing #29

CHAPTER 24

The Sea of Brass and Washing

Exo. 30:18 "Thou shalt also make a laver of **brass**, and his foot also of **brass**, to **wash** withal: and thou shalt put it between the tabernacle of the congregation and the altar, and thou shalt put water therein."

Exo. 30:19 "For Aaron and his sons shall **wash** their hands and their feet thereat."

Exo. 30:20 "When they go into the tabernacle of the congregation, they shall **wash** with water, that they die not; or when they come near to the altar to minister, to burn offering made by fire unto the LORD."

Exo. 30:21 "So they shall **wash** their hands and their feet, **that they die not**: and it shall be a statute for ever to them, even to him and to his seed throughout their generations."

2 Chr. 4:6 "He made also ten lavers, and put five on the right hand, and five on the left, to **wash** in them: such things as they offered for the burnt offering they **washed** in them; but the sea was for the priests to **wash** in."

When Solomon built the Temple, he made lavers to wash the sacrifices in, but the sea of brass was for the priests to wash in so that the blood that was upon the sacrifices would not contaminate the water that the priests washed themselves with.

The Washing of the Priest

Exo. 29:4 "And Aaron and his sons thou shalt bring unto the door of the tabernacle of the congregation, and shalt **wash** them with water."

Exo. 40:12 "And thou shalt bring Aaron and his sons unto the door of the tabernacle of the congregation, and **wash** them with water."

Exo. 40:30 "And he set the laver between the tent of the congregation and the altar, and put water there, to **wash** withal."

Exo. 40:31 "And Moses and Aaron and his sons **washed** their hands and their feet thereat."

Exo. 40:32 "When they went into the tent of the congregation, and when they came near unto the altar, they **washed**; as the LORD commanded Moses."

Num. 8:6	"Take the Levites from among the children of Israel, and **cleanse** them."
Num. 8:7	"And thus shalt thou do unto them, to **cleanse** them: Sprinkle water of purifying upon them, and let them shave all their flesh, and let them **wash** their clothes, and so make themselves clean."
Num. 19:7	"Then the priest shall **wash** his clothes, and he shall **bathe** his flesh in water, and afterward he shall come into the camp, and the priest shall be unclean until the even."
Num. 19:8	"And he that burneth her shall **wash** his clothes in water, and **bathe** his flesh in water, and shall be unclean until the even."
Num. 19:9	"And a man that is clean shall gather up the ashes of the heifer, and lay them up without the camp in a clean place, and it shall be kept for the congregation of the children of Israel for a **water of separation**: it is a purification for sin."
Num. 19:10	"And he that gathereth the ashes of the heifer shall **wash** his clothes, and be unclean until the even: and it shall be unto the children of Israel, and unto the stranger that sojourneth among them, for a statute for ever."

Num. 19:21 "And it shall be a perpetual statute unto them, that he that sprinkleth the **water of separation** shall **wash** his clothes; and he that toucheth the **water of separation** shall be unclean until even."

The Washing of Sacrifices

Exo. 29:17 "And thou shalt cut the ram in pieces, and **wash** the inwards of him, and his legs, and put them unto his pieces, and unto his head."

Lev. 1:13 "But he shall **wash** the inwards and the legs with water: and the priest shall bring it all, and burn it upon the altar: it is a burnt sacrifice, an offering made by fire, of a sweet savour unto the LORD."

Lev. 9:14 "And he did **wash** the inwards and the legs, and burnt them upon the burnt offering on the altar."

When both the symbols of priest and sacrifice came together in the same person, then all of the above scriptures were fulfilled at one time.

Matt. 3:13 "Then cometh Jesus from Galilee to Jordan unto John, to be baptized of him."

Matt. 3:14 "But John forbad him, saying, I have need to be baptized of thee, and comest thou to me?"

> **Matt. 3:15** "And Jesus answering said unto him, Suffer it to be so now: for thus it becometh us to fulfil all righteousness. Then he suffered him."

How was *all* righteousness fulfilled? It is because in *that* baptism, *both* the high priest *and* the sacrifice were washed at the *same* time.

Some people say that they want to be baptized like the Lord Jesus Christ was—NO ONE can be baptized like the Lord Jesus was, because (as Emmanuel) He was sinless and had no need to repent of His sins (which He didn't have).

The baptism that John the Baptist did was for repentance (of sin).

> **Matt. 3:11** "I indeed baptize you with water unto **repentance**: but he that cometh after me is mightier than I, whose shoes I am not worthy to bear: he shall baptize you with the Holy Ghost, and with fire."
>
> **Matt. 3:12** "Whose fan is in his hand, and he will thoroughly purge his floor, and gather his wheat into the garner; but he will burn up the chaff with unquenchable fire."

The baptism that the Apostles did was for repentance, for remission of sins, and to receive the baptism/gift of the Holy Ghost (the promise of the Father).

> **Luke 24:49** "And, behold, I send **the promise of my Father** upon you: but tarry ye in the city of Jerusalem, until ye be endued with power from on high."

Acts 1:4	"And, being assembled together with them, commanded them that they should not depart from Jerusalem, but wait for **the promise of the Father**, which, saith he, ye have heard of me."
Acts 1:5	"For John truly baptized with water; but ye shall be **baptized with the Holy Ghost** not many days hence."
Acts 2:38	"Then Peter said unto them, **Repent**, and be baptized every one of you in the name of Jesus Christ for the **remission** of sins, and ye shall receive the **gift** of the Holy Ghost."

But the Lord Jesus Christ was unlike any other man that was ever born upon the face of the earth, because He was the sinless Lamb of God that (with the courage of the Lion of the Tribe of Judah) paid the price (as a lamb) to be able to take the seven-sealed book of redemption and to open it.

Rev. 5:1	"And I saw in the right hand of him that sat on the throne a book written within and on the backside, sealed with seven seals."
Rev. 5:2	"And I saw a strong angel proclaiming with a loud voice, Who is worthy to open the book, and to loose the seals thereof?"
Rev. 5:3	"And **no man in heaven, nor in earth, neither under the earth,** was

	able to open the book, neither to look thereon."
Rev. 5:4	"And I wept much, because **no man was found worthy to open and to read the book, neither to look thereon**."
Rev. 5:5	"And one of the elders saith unto me, Weep not: **behold, the Lion of the tribe of Juda, the Root of David, hath prevailed to open the book, and to loose the seven seals thereof**."
Rev. 5:6	"And I beheld, and, lo, in the midst of the throne and of the four beasts, and in the midst of the elders, stood a **Lamb as it had been slain**, having seven horns and seven eyes, which are the seven Spirits of God sent forth into all the earth."
Rev. 5:7	"And **he came and took the book** out of the right hand of him that sat upon the throne."

The Washing of the Water by the Word

Eph. 5:25	"Husbands, love your wives, even as Christ also loved the church, and gave himself for it."
Eph. 5:26	"That he might sanctify and cleanse it with the **washing of water by the word**."

Eph. 5:27	"That he might present it to himself a glorious church, not having spot, or wrinkle, or any such thing; but that it should be holy and without blemish."
Tit. 3:4	"But after that the kindness and love of God our Saviour toward man appeared."
Tit. 3:5	"Not by works of righteousness which we have done, **but according to his mercy he saved us, by the washing of regeneration, and renewing of the Holy Ghost**."
Tit. 3:6	"Which he shed on us abundantly through Jesus Christ our Saviour."
Tit. 3:7	"That being justified by his grace, we should be made heirs according to the hope of eternal life."
Heb. 10:22	"Let us draw near with a true heart in full assurance of faith, having our hearts sprinkled from an evil conscience, **and our bodies washed with pure water**."
John 15:3	"Now ye are **clean** through the **word** which I have spoken unto you."

The question is not so much one of *what* the Word is as it is a question of *who* the Word is, and we find the answer in the following verses.

John 1:1   "In the beginning was the Word, and the Word was with God, and **the Word was God**."

John 1:14   "And **the Word was made flesh, and dwelt among us**, (and we beheld his glory, the glory as of the only begotten of the Father,) full of grace and truth."

Matt. 1:18 "Now the birth of Jesus Christ was on this wise: When as his mother Mary was espoused to Joseph, before they came together, she was found with child of the Holy Ghost."

Matt. 1:19 "Then Joseph her husband, being a just man, and not willing to make her a publick example, was minded to put her away privily."

Matt. 1:20 "But while he thought on these things, behold, the angel of the Lord appeared unto him in a dream, saying, Joseph, thou son of David, fear not to take unto thee Mary thy wife: for that which is conceived in her is of the Holy Ghost."

Matt. 1:21 "And she shall bring forth a son, and thou shalt call his name JESUS: for he shall save his people from their sins."

Matt. 1:22	"Now all this was done, that it might be fulfilled which was spoken of the Lord by the prophet, saying."
Matt. 1:23	"Behold, a virgin shall be with child, and shall bring forth a son, **and they shall call his name Emmanuel, which being interpreted is, God with us**."

If we try to produce obedience without it being the exclusive result of the power of **His** life, producing **His** obedience in us, we will certainly fail, and the resulting failed obedience will not be an acceptable sacrifice unto God. But there is a true obedience that flows from the power of His mercies and faithfulness to manifest **His** life (in power) in us every day as we humbly (incense) yield to His Lordship (attitudes of humility symbolized in the golden censer and the basket).

John 15:1	"I am the true vine, and my Father is the husbandman."
John 15:2	"Every branch in me that beareth not fruit he taketh away: and every branch that beareth fruit, he purgeth it, that it may bring forth more fruit."
John 15:3	"**Now ye are clean through the word which I have spoken unto you.**"
John 15:4	"**Abide in me, and I in you. As the branch cannot bear fruit of itself, except it abide in the vine; no more can ye, except ye abide in me.**"

John 15:5	"I am the vine, ye are the branches: He that abideth in me, and I in him, the same bringeth forth much fruit: **for without me ye can do nothing.**"
John 15:6	"If a man abide not in me, he is cast forth as a branch, and is withered; and men gather them, and cast them into the fire, and they are burned."
John 15:7	"If ye abide in me, and my words abide in you, ye shall ask what ye will, and it shall be done unto you."
John 15:8	"**Herein is my Father glorified, that ye bear much fruit; so shall ye be my disciples**."

CHAPTER 25

Change of Garments and the Anointing Oil

Every time that the priests moved in either direction between the Sanctuary and the Outer Court, they had to change garments.

Going from the Holy Place to the Outer Court

Lev. 16:23	"And Aaron shall come into the tabernacle of the congregation, and shall **put off** the linen garments, which he put on when he went into the holy place, and shall leave them there."
Lev. 16:24	"And he shall wash his flesh with water in the holy place, and **put on** his garments, and come forth, and offer his burnt offering, and the burnt offering of the people, and make an atonement for himself, and for the people."
Eze. 44:19	"And when they go forth into the utter court, even into the utter court to the people, they shall **put off** their garments wherein they ministered,

and lay them in the holy chambers, and they shall **put on** other garments; and **they shall not sanctify the people with their garments**."

Going from the Outer Court into the Sanctuary

Eze. 44:17 "And it shall come to pass, that when they enter in at the gates of the **inner court**, they shall be clothed with linen garments; and no wool shall come upon them, whiles they minister in the gates of the inner court, and within."

Eze. 44:18 "They shall have linen bonnets upon their heads, and shall have linen breeches upon their loins; they shall not gird themselves with any thing that causeth sweat."

After they were correctly dressed for the porch that they were going into, they also had to be anointed.

The Anointing Oil

Exo. 30:22 "Moreover the LORD spake unto Moses, saying,"

Exo. 30:23 "Take thou also unto thee principal spices, of pure myrrh five hundred shekels, and of sweet cinnamon half so much, even two hundred and fifty shekels, and of sweet calamus two hundred and fifty shekels."

Exo. 30:24	"And of cassia five hundred shekels, after the shekel of the sanctuary, and of oil olive an hin."
Exo. 30:25	"And **thou shalt make it an oil of holy ointment**, an ointment compound after the art of the apothecary: it shall be an **holy anointing oil**."
Exo. 30:26	"And thou shalt anoint the tabernacle of the congregation therewith, and the ark of the testimony."
Exo. 30:27	"And the table and all his vessels, and the candlestick and his vessels, and the altar of incense."
Exo. 30:28	"And the altar of burnt offering with all his vessels, and the laver and his foot."
Exo. 30:29	"And thou shalt sanctify them, that they may be most holy: whatsoever toucheth them shall be holy."
Exo. 30:30	"**And thou shalt anoint Aaron and his sons, and consecrate them, that they may minister unto me in the priest's office**."
Exo. 30:31	"And thou shalt speak unto the children of Israel, saying, This shall be an **holy anointing oil** unto me throughout your generations."

Exo. 30:32	"Upon man's flesh shall it not be poured, neither shall ye make any other like it, after the composition of it: it is holy, and it shall be holy unto you."
Exo. 30:33	"Whosoever compoundeth any like it, or whosoever putteth any of it upon a stranger, shall even be cut off from his people."
Exo. 30:34	"And the LORD said unto Moses, Take unto thee sweet spices, stacte, and onycha, and galbanum; these sweet spices with pure frankincense: of each shall there be a like weight."
Exo. 30:35	"And thou shalt make it a perfume, a confection after the art of the apothecary, tempered together, pure and holy."
Exo. 30:36	"And thou shalt beat some of it very small, and put of it before the testimony in the tabernacle of the congregation, where I will meet with thee: it shall be unto you most holy."
Exo. 30:37	"And as for the perfume which thou shalt make, ye shall not make to yourselves according to the composition thereof: it shall be unto thee holy for the LORD."

| Exo. 30:38 | "Whosoever shall make like unto that, to smell thereto, shall even be cut off from his people." |

The washing of the priests was also part of the process of the change of garments and anointing while the priests were moving between the sanctuary and the Outer Court. Please see the previous chapter for the washing.

How the Change of Clothing Relates to Us

| Isa. 64:6 | "But we are all as an unclean thing, **and all our righteousnesses are as filthy rags**; and we all do fade as a leaf; and our iniquities, like the wind, have taken us away." |

Any and every attempt to define righteousness outside of the context of it being the natural and automatic product of the very life of God (**John 1:4**) obediently manifesting itself in and through us is NOT acceptable to God. This sets the context for the related scriptures that follow, and because of this, it is understood that the righteousness that we should be hungering and thirsting for is that of God and not our own righteousness without Him.

| Matt. 5:6 | "Blessed are they which do hunger and thirst after righteousness: for they shall be filled." |

Now we can understand that being "filled" is a reference to the scripture.

| Isa. 6:1 | "In the year that king Uzziah died I saw also the Lord sitting upon a throne, high and lifted up, and **his train filled the temple**." |

Isa. 6:2	"Above it stood the seraphims: each one had six wings; with twain he covered his face, and with twain he covered his feet, and with twain he did fly."
Isa. 6:3	"And one cried unto another, and said, Holy, holy, holy, is the LORD of hosts: the whole earth is **full of his glory**."
Isa. 6:4	"And the posts of the door moved at the voice of him that cried, and **the house was filled with smoke**."

The righteousness of God (**Rev. 19:8**), His train or garments fill ("fill" in **Matt. 5:6**) the temple (**1 Cor. 3:16**), and we are the temple (**Matt. 12:45**; **Luke 11:26**; **John 14:17**; **Rom. 8:9**; **Rom. 8:11**; **1 Cor. 3:16**; **Jas. 4:5**; **1 John 3:24**; **1 John 4:13**) for the dwelling place of the Holy Spirit (Hebrew: Ruach HaKodesh, Spirit of Holiness). Even the Seraphims that were created to dwell in the fire, who have six wings (**Isa. 6:2**; **Rev. 4:8**), are constantly in a state of humility (**Isa. 6:4,** smoke/incense) before God. Therefore, when **Isa. 6:4** mentions that the "posts of the door moved," it is a reference to:

Isa. 66:1	"Thus saith the LORD, The heaven is my throne, and the earth is my footstool: where is the house that ye build unto me? and where is the place of my rest?"
Isa. 66:2	"For all those things hath mine hand made, and all those things have been, saith the LORD: but to this man will I look, even to him that

is poor and of a contrite spirit, and **trembleth at my word**."

Isa. 66:5 "Hear the word of the LORD, **ye that tremble at his word**; Your brethren that hated you, that cast you out for my name's sake, said, Let the LORD be glorified: but he shall appear to your joy, and they shall be ashamed."

Isa. 66:6 "A voice of noise from the city, a voice from the temple, a voice of the LORD that rendereth recompence to his enemies."

Also in **Isa. 6:4,** when it says "and the house was filled with smoke," it is a reference to His house that (we are) will be filled with the smoke of the incense of humility as we can see by the following several scriptures.

Isa. 56:7 "Even them will I bring to my holy mountain, and make them joyful in my **house of prayer**: their burnt offerings and their sacrifices shall be accepted upon mine altar; for **mine house shall be called an house of prayer** for all people."

Matt. 21:13 "And said unto them, It is written, **My house shall be called the house of prayer**; but ye have made it a den of thieves."

Mar 11:17 "And he taught, saying unto them, Is it not written, **My house shall be**

> **called of all nations the house of prayer**? but ye have made it a den of thieves."

Luke 19:46 "Saying unto them, It is written, **My house is the house of prayer**: but ye have made it a den of thieves."

Notice that prayer is one of the primary expressions through which the incense of humility is expressed. Therefore, if we are the dwelling place, the temples for His habitation, the place where He has put His name, filled with His righteousness and His humility, it becomes the house of prayer; then His eyes will be open day and night toward **us** to hear **our** prayers.

2 Chr. 6:20 "That thine **eyes may be open upon this house day and night, upon the place whereof thou hast said that thou wouldest put thy name there**; to hearken unto the prayer which thy servant prayeth toward this place."

But the key to being all of those things is the incense of humility that fills our prayers and identifies our prayers as the "prayers of the saints" and servants of the Most High God.

Rev. 5:8 "And when he had taken the book, the four beasts and four and twenty elders fell down before the Lamb, having every one of them harps, and golden vials full of **odours**, which are the prayers of saints."

The Greek word for *odours* in **Rev. 5:8** (*thumiama*) is the same word that is the word *incense* in **Rev. 8:3–4** and is used in the singular tense.

> **Rev. 8:3** "And another angel came and stood at the altar, having a golden censer; and there was given unto him much **incense**, that he should offer it with the **prayers of all saints** upon the golden altar which was before the throne."
>
> **Rev. 8:4** "And the **smoke** of the **incense**, which came with the **prayers of the saints**, ascended up before God out of the angel's hand."
>
> **Rev. 8:5** "And the angel took the censer, and filled it with fire of the altar, and cast it into the earth: and there were voices, and thunderings, and lightnings, and an earthquake."

Therefore, in Rev. 5:8, we must compare the plural of "vials" with the plural of "prayers" to conclude that the vials are the prayers which are identified as "the prayers of the saints" because of being filled with the (singular) incense of humility. It all works together to bring us to the marriage of the Lamb and to clothe us with the wedding garments of His righteousness.

> **Rev. 19:7** "Let us be glad and rejoice, and give honour to him: for the **marriage of the Lamb** is come, **and his wife hath made herself ready**."
>
> **Rev. 19:8** "And to her was granted that she should be arrayed in **fine linen, clean and white: for the fine linen is the righteousness of saints**."

Now we can see that "the righteousness of saints" is **not** THEIR righteousness without Him, but rather, it is His righteousness that He clothes her (them) with because of her coming into the special relationship with Him of marriage. This also shows us how the following verses, instead of contradicting each other, they work together to give deeper meaning.

> **Isa. 42:8** "I am the LORD: that is my name: and **my glory will I not give to another**, neither my praise to graven images."
>
> **Isa. 48:11** "For mine own sake, even for mine own sake, will I do it: for how should my name be polluted? and **I will not give my glory unto another**."

Together with:

> **Eph. 5:25** "Husbands, love your wives, even as Christ also loved the church, and gave himself for it."
>
> **Eph. 5:26** "That he might sanctify and cleanse it with the **washing** of water by the word."
>
> **Eph. 5:27** "That he might present it to himself a **glorious** church, not having spot, or wrinkle, or any such thing; but that it should be holy and without blemish."
>
> **Eph. 5:32** "This is a great mystery: but I speak concerning Christ and the church."

It is no longer a mystery or a contradiction, because He is not giving His glory to another. He is simply clothing His Wife (as part of Himself. **Gen. 2:24**; **Matt. 19:5**) with His righteousness and glory, because she has become one with Him in marriage by the "washing of water by the word," and it is anointed with power (**Gen. 3:24**, "flaming sword") to bring into manifestation the "purpose" that it was sent for (**Isa. 55:11**).

All of those who fall for the trick and lie of the devil—to automatically consider every mention of "obedience" and "holiness" as legalism and religiosity and not as the natural and automatic expression of the very life of God in us—are refusing to come to the marriage of the LAMB and judge themselves "sea (**Gen. 1:2**; **Joel 2:28**; **Rev. 17:1,15**) of **brass**" to be unworthy of that privileged relationship. They are refusing both the washing and the clothing without which the anointing will not remain. Without the incense of humility to submit ourselves to the washing of the waters by the Word and to be clothed with His righteousness, we will not receive the covering of the Shekinah (glory of the presence of God) permanently filling the temple that we are. Without the incense, there will be no glory and no wedding. To reject the supernaturally expressed obedience of the very life of the Lamb of God in and through us is apostasy (divorce) instead of marriage.

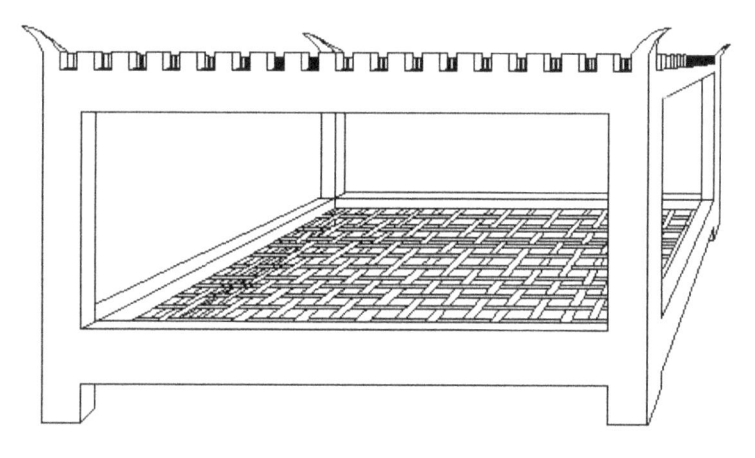

Drawing #30

CHAPTER 26

Burnt Offerings

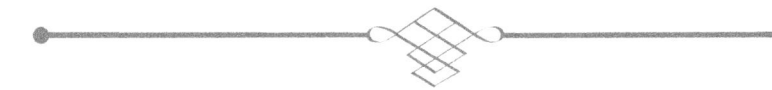

Burnt offerings cannot happen without fire. The fire was to never go out upon the altar.

> **Lev. 6:9** Command Aaron and his sons, saying, This is the law of the burnt offering: It is the burnt offering, because of the burning upon the altar all night unto the morning, **and the fire of the altar shall be burning in it.**
>
> **Lev. 6:12** And **the fire upon the altar shall be burning in it; it shall not be put out**: and the priest shall burn wood on it every morning, and lay the burnt offering in order upon it; and he shall burn thereon the fat of the peace offerings.
>
> **Lev. 6:13** **The fire shall ever be burning upon the altar; it shall never go out.**

The fire must be that true fire that is sent by God.

> **Lev. 9:23** And Moses and Aaron went into the tabernacle of the congregation,

and came out, and blessed the people: **and the glory of the LORD appeared unto all the people**.

Lev. 9:24 **And there came a fire out from before the LORD, and consumed upon the altar the burnt offering and the fat**: which when all the people saw, they shouted, and fell on their faces.

1 Chr. 21:26 And David built there an altar unto the LORD, and offered burnt offerings and peace offerings, and called upon the LORD; **and he answered him from heaven by fire upon the altar of burnt offering**.

1 Kings 18:36 And it came to pass at the time of the offering of the evening sacrifice, that Elijah the prophet came near, and said, LORD God of Abraham, Isaac, and of Israel, let it be known this day that thou art God in Israel, and that I am thy servant, and that I have done all these things at thy word.

1 Kings 18:37 Hear me, O LORD, hear me, that this people may know that thou art the LORD God, and that thou hast turned their heart back again.

1 Kings 18:38 **Then the fire of the LORD fell, and consumed the burnt sacrifice, and the wood, and the stones, and**

> the dust, and licked up the water that was in the trench.

1 Kings 18:39 And when all the people saw it, they fell on their faces: and they said, The LORD, he is the God; the LORD, he is the God.

If the fire is kindled by the hand of man by carnal exuberance upon any altar, then it is rejected by God.

Lev. 10:1 And Nadab and Abihu, the sons of Aaron, took either of them his censer, and put fire therein, and put incense thereon, and offered **strange fire** before the LORD, which he commanded them not.

Lev. 10:2 And there went out fire from the LORD, and devoured them, and they died before the LORD.

Lev. 10:3 Then Moses said unto Aaron, This is it that the LORD spake, saying, **I will be sanctified in them that come nigh me, and before all the people I will be glorified**. And Aaron held his peace.

Num. 3:4 **And Nadab and Abihu died before the LORD**, when they offered **strange fire** before the LORD, in the wilderness of Sinai, **and they had no children**: and Eleazar and Ithamar ministered in the priest's office in the sight of Aaron their father.

Num. 26:61   **And Nadab and Abihu died**, when they offered **strange fire** before the LORD.

God will send the true fire when the approach is correct with the incense of humility. Any other approach, in any other attitude, is rejected (Cain's altar, **Gen. 4:3–5**). This is one of the primary reasons why the fires of revival cease to move, because God **will** be sanctified in them that come near unto Him, and the only acceptable way for Him to be sanctified comes through the incense of humility. In this, we can see that the way that God had respect to Abel's sacrifice is that He answered by fire. There is coming a revival that will be unlike any other revival that has ever come before.

Isa. 57:15   For thus saith the high and lofty One that **inhabiteth eternity**, whose name is Holy; I **dwell** in the high and holy place, **with him** also that is of a **contrite** and **humble spirit**, to **revive** the spirit of the humble, and to **revive** the heart of the contrite ones.

The word *contrite* in **Isa. 57:15** literally means "ground up" as in a grinding mill. There **will** be a people that will receive a revival that will take them to dwell with Him in eternity. The secret is, how long are they willing to remain contrite and humble? The revival will only last as long as the approach remains acceptable before God in contrition and with the incense of humility. Remember, the incense had to accompany the showbread from off of the golden table in the Holy Place, to be burnt together with the flesh of the burnt offering in the Outer Court in order for the sacrifice to be acceptable unto God. Any offering (in the Outer Court of our flesh) that is offered without the showbread (The Word of God) and the incense of humility that produces obedience (see Table 1) will cause the revival fires to go out.

> **Mic 6:8** He hath shewed thee, O man, what is good; and what doth the LORD require of thee, but to **do justly**, and to **love mercy**, and to **walk humbly with thy God**?

To **do justly** in the sight of God is not legalism. It is the natural and automatic manifestation of the power of His Life in us expressing His character, and He does not break any jot or tittle of His own law. To **love mercy** is to judge righteous judgment (see Chapters 10–13) for salvation and not for condemnation. To **walk humbly with God** is a walk that is in subjection and obedience to Him as our Sovereign Lord and King (see Table 1).

The Different Types of Burnt Offerings

1) Sin Offerings
   A) For the Nation/World: goat, and Lamb (see Chapter 7)
   B) For the Family/Tribe: bullock (see Chapter 7)
   C) Individual: bullock, goat, lamb, or dove
2) Peace Offerings
3) Freewill Offerings
4) Red heifer ashes for purification and separation (see Chapter 27)

God is the consuming fire.

> **Deut. 4:24** For the LORD thy God is a **consuming fire**, even a jealous God.

> **Deut. 9:3** Understand therefore this day, that the LORD thy God is he which

goeth over before thee; as a **consuming fire** he shall destroy them, and he shall bring them down before thy face: so shalt thou drive them out, and destroy them quickly, as the LORD hath said unto thee.

Heb. 12:29 For our God is a **consuming fire**.

He makes our hearts to be His throne.

Luke 24:32 And they said one to another, Did not our **heart burn** within us, while he talked with us by the way, and while he opened to us the scriptures?

He was beginning to fulfill the **Jer. 31:31–33** promise of the Father in them.

Luke 24:45 Then opened he their understanding, that they might understand the scriptures.

CHAPTER 27

The Red Heifer and the Water of Purification

Every time that the pillar of fire moved, the Tabernacle had to be moved also. Each of the families of the Levites had their specific tasks that were assigned by God for them to do in the process of moving the Tabernacle. Once the pillar of fire stopped in a new location, the task of setting up the Tabernacle began.

After all of the details of setting up the Tabernacle were finished, but before the sacrifices could begin again, the Tabernacle, all of its furnishings, and utensils had to be purified by being sprinkled with the water of purification. The water of purification had two ingredients that it consisted of. The first is the water that flowed from the rock that followed them.

> **1 Cor. 10:1** "Moreover, brethren, I would not that ye should be ignorant, how that all our fathers were under the cloud, and all passed through the sea."

> **1 Cor. 10:2** "And were all baptized unto Moses in the cloud and in the sea."

> **1 Cor. 10:3** "And did all eat the same spiritual meat."

> **1 Cor. 10:4** "And did all drink the same spiritual drink: for they drank of that spiritual Rock **that followed them**: and that Rock was Christ."

Therefore, the Rock of Horeb from which flowed the water for all of Israel was symbolic of the Lord Jesus Christ. But even in the natural, every time that Israel camped in a new location, they did not have to go in search of water. They knew that if they went the same direction from the camp and the same distance, they would find water. It was this water that flowed from the rock, which they used to drink, bathe, water their flocks, and fulfill the various washings of the priests and sacrifices, and for the water of purification.

In the spiritual, it is the same. Once we learn the proper approach to God and enter into His presence, then all that we have to do is follow the same directions with the same effort and we will find the same blessing as the first time. However, if we do something that takes us away from His camp, it may cost us a little more effort to come back to the fountain of living waters. That is where the application of the second ingredient applies.

The second ingredient was the ashes of the red heifer.

> **Num. 19:1** "And the LORD spake unto Moses and unto Aaron, saying."

> **Num. 19:2** "This is the ordinance of the law which the LORD hath commanded, saying, Speak unto the children of Israel, that they bring thee a **red heifer without spot, wherein is no blemish, and upon which never came yoke**."

> **Num. 19:3** "And ye shall give **her** unto Eleazar the priest, that he may bring **her**

forth without the camp, and one shall slay **her** before his face."

Num. 19:4 "And Eleazar the priest shall take of **her** blood with his finger, and sprinkle of **her** blood directly before the tabernacle of the congregation seven times."

Num. 19:5 "And one shall burn the **heifer** in his sight; **her** skin, and **her** flesh, and **her** blood, with **her** dung, shall he burn."

Num. 19:6 "And the priest shall take cedar wood, and hyssop, and scarlet, and cast it into the midst of the burning of the **heifer**."

Num. 19:7 "Then the priest shall wash his clothes, and he shall bathe his flesh in water, and afterward he shall come into the camp, and the priest shall be unclean until the even."

Num. 19:8 "And he that burneth **her** shall wash his clothes in water, and bathe his flesh in water, and shall be unclean until the even."

Num. 19:9 "And a man that is clean shall gather up the ashes of the **heifer**, and lay them up without the camp in a clean place, and it shall be kept for the congregation of the children of

Israel for a **water of separation**: it is a **purification** for sin."

Num. 19:10 "And he that gathereth the ashes of the **heifer** shall wash his clothes, and be unclean until the even: and it shall be unto the children of Israel, and unto the stranger that sojourneth among them, for a statute for ever."

Num. 19:11 "He that toucheth the dead body of any man shall be unclean seven days."

Num. 19:12 "He shall **purify** himself with it on the third day, and on the seventh day he shall be clean: but if he **purify** not himself the third day, then the seventh day he shall not be clean."

Num. 19:13 "Whosoever toucheth the dead body of any man that is dead, and **purifieth** not himself, defileth the tabernacle of the LORD; and that soul shall be cut off from Israel: because the **water of separation** was not sprinkled upon him, he shall be unclean; his uncleanness is yet upon him."

Num. 19:14 "This is the law, when a man dieth in a tent: all that come into the tent, and all that is in the tent, shall be unclean seven days."

Num. 19:15	"And every open vessel, which hath no covering bound upon it, is unclean."
Num. 19:16	"And whosoever toucheth one that is slain with a sword in the open fields, or a dead body, or a bone of a man, or a grave, shall be unclean seven days."
Num. 19:17	"And for an unclean person they shall take of the ashes of the burnt **heifer** of **purification** for sin, and running water shall be put thereto in a vessel."
Num. 19:18	"And a clean person shall take hyssop, and dip it in the water, and sprinkle it upon the tent, and upon all the vessels, and upon the persons that were there, and upon him that touched a bone, or one slain, or one dead, or a grave."
Num. 19:19	"And the clean person shall sprinkle upon the unclean on the third day, and on the seventh day: and on the seventh day he shall **purify** himself, and wash his clothes, and bathe himself in water, and shall be clean at even."
Num. 19:20	"But the man that shall be unclean, and shall not **purify** himself, that soul shall be cut off from among the congregation, because he hath defiled the sanctuary of the LORD:

	the **water of separation** hath not been sprinkled upon him; he is unclean."
Num. 19:21	"And it shall be a **perpetual statute** unto them, that he that sprinkleth **the water of separation** shall wash his clothes; and he that toucheth the **water of separation** shall be unclean until even."
Num. 19:22	"And whatsoever the unclean person toucheth shall be unclean; and the soul that toucheth it shall be unclean until even."
Heb. 9:13	"For if the blood of bulls and of goats, **and the ashes of an heifer** sprinkling the unclean, sanctifieth to the **purifying** of the flesh."
Heb. 9:14	"**How much more shall the blood of Christ, who through the eternal Spirit** offered himself without spot to God, **purge your conscience from dead works to serve the living God?**"

The heifer had to be entirely red, without defect, or any other color than red in its hair, horns, or hooves. And because it was to be a female, it was symbolic of the church (**Eph. 5:32**). It also shows that the entire church that becomes the wife of the Lamb (**Rev. 19:7–9**) will have ALL of her dead works burned up and consumed by fire (**Gen. 3:24**; **Deut. 4:24**; **Heb. 12:29**), to have access to the Tree of Life who is also The Lamb of God and the Husband/Head (**Eph. 1:22**; **5:23**; **Col. 1:18**) of the Elect Church, to live with Him and to serve Him throughout eternity (**Isa. 57:15**).

CHAPTER 28

Examining the Sacrifice

1 Cor. 11:28 "But let a man **examine himself**, and so let him eat of that bread, and drink of that cup."

1 Cor. 11:29 "For he that eateth and drinketh unworthily, eateth and drinketh damnation to himself, not discerning the Lord's body."

1 Cor. 11:30 "For this cause many are weak and sickly among you, and many sleep."

1 Cor. 11:31 "For if we would **judge ourselves**, we should not be judged."

1 Cor. 11:32 "But when we are judged, we are chastened of the Lord, that we should not be condemned with the world."

2 Cor. 13:5 "**Examine yourselves**, whether ye be in the faith; prove your own selves. Know ye not your own selves, how that Jesus Christ is in you, except ye be reprobates?"

Jas. 1:22	"But be ye doers of the word, and not hearers only, deceiving your own selves."
Jas. 1:23	"For if any be a hearer of the word, and not a doer, he is like unto a man beholding his natural face in a glass."
Jas. 1:24	"For he beholdeth himself, and goeth his way, and straightway forgetteth what manner of man he was."
Jas. 1:25	"But whoso **looketh into** the perfect **law of liberty**, and continueth therein, he being not a forgetful hearer, but a doer of the work, this man shall be blessed in his deed."
Jas. 2:12	"So speak ye, and so do, as they that shall be judged by the **law of liberty**."
Jas. 2:13	"For he shall have judgment without mercy, that hath shewed no mercy; and **mercy rejoiceth against judgment**."
Psa. 26:2	"**Examine me, O LORD, and prove me; try my reins and my heart**."
John 5:26	"For as the Father hath life in himself; so hath he given to the Son to have life in himself."

John 5:27	"And hath given him authority to execute judgment also, because he is the Son of man."
John 5:28	"Marvel not at this: for the hour is coming, in the which all that are in the graves shall hear his voice."
John 5:29	"And shall come forth; they that have done good, unto the resurrection of life; and they that have done evil, unto the resurrection of damnation."
John 5:30	"I can of mine own self do nothing: as I hear, I judge: and my judgment is just; because I seek not mine own will, but the will of the Father which hath sent me."

It is done by the washing of the water by the (Person) of the Word.

John 1:1	"In the beginning was the Word, and the Word was with God, and the Word was God."
John 1:4	"In him was life; and the life was the light of men."
John 1:14	"And the Word was made flesh, and dwelt among us, (and we beheld his glory, the glory as of the only begotten of the Father,) full of grace and truth."

Eph. 5:26 "That he might sanctify and cleanse it with the washing of water by the word."

Eph. 5:27 "That he might present it to himself a glorious church, not having spot, or wrinkle, or any such thing; but that it should be holy and without blemish."

Because it is NOT just a dead letter, but the living and anointed Word of God in power to STILL make Himself manifest in flesh and, in particular, the redeemed flesh of the glorious church that becomes the Wife of the Lamb also is one with Him in marriage.

Therefore, we now have access back to THE Tree of Life through the **flaming sword** of the anointed (fire, **Deut. 4:24; Heb. 12:29**) and living Word (sword, **Eph. 6:17**) of God (**Gen. 3:24**) who by Himself has provided for us access back to Himself (**Gen. 3:24; Col. 1:20; Rev. 22:2,14**).

EPILOGUE

The image restored, perfection on display from the eternal to the eternal.

Gen. 49:10	"The sceptre shall not depart from Judah, nor a lawgiver from between his feet, until **Shiloh** come; and unto him shall the gathering of the people be."
Isa. 53:10	"Yet it pleased the LORD to bruise him; he hath put him to grief: when thou shalt make his soul an offering for sin, he shall see his seed, he shall prolong his days, and **the pleasure of the LORD shall prosper in his hand**."
Isa. 55:10	"For as the rain cometh down, and the snow from heaven, and returneth not thither, but watereth the earth, and maketh it bring forth and bud, that it may give seed to the sower, and bread to the eater."
Isa. 55:11	"**So shall my word be that goeth forth out of my mouth**: it shall not return unto me void, but it shall

accomplish that which I please, and **it shall prosper in the thing whereto I sent it**."

Exo. 15:3 "**The LORD is a man of war**: the LORD is his name."

Isa. 42:13 "The LORD shall go forth as a mighty man, he shall stir up jealousy **like a man of war**: he shall cry, yea, roar; **he shall prevail against his enemies**."

1 Thess. 5:23 "And the very God of peace sanctify you wholly; and I pray God your whole **spirit** and **soul** and **body** be preserved blameless unto the coming of our Lord Jesus Christ."

1 Thess. 5:24 "**Faithful is he that calleth you, who also will do it.**"

A key detail to understanding God and His purposes is to understand several details about His unchangeableness and that He is eternal.

God is perfect, and because He is perfect, He is also eternal. Anything that has any imperfection in it by definition cannot be eternal, because the imperfection is entropy, and entropy will cause eventual collapse and destruction.

The opposite is also true; if something is eternal, by definition it must also be perfect. Understanding this detail helps us to understand the scriptures better. If there are details in the scriptures that speak about the beginning that are lacking, we can look at what they say about the end to help us to fill in the missing pieces. If there are details about the end that are lacking, we can look at the beginning to help us to fill in the missing pieces. The reason for this is that

God does not change, because any change away from perfection is a change toward entropy and destruction.

The same perfection that existed before there was war in heaven is the same perfection that will be after all things are restored.

It is for this reason we can consider some of the following scriptures as an epilogue.

Psa. 90:2 "Before the mountains were brought forth, or ever thou hadst formed the earth and the world, even from everlasting to everlasting, thou art God."

Matt. 25:34 "Then shall the King say unto them on his right hand, **Come, ye blessed of my Father, inherit the kingdom prepared for you from the foundation of the world.**"

John 17:5 "And now, O Father, **glorify thou me with thine own self with the glory which I had with thee before the world was.**"

John 17:24 "Father, I will that they also, whom thou hast given me, be with me where I am; that they may behold my glory, which thou hast given me: for **thou lovedst me before the foundation of the world.**"

1 Cor. 2:7 "But we speak the wisdom of God in a mystery, even the hidden wisdom, which **God ordained before the world unto our glory.**"

Eph. 1:4	"According **as he hath chosen us in him before the foundation of the world**, that we should be holy and without blame before him in love."
2 Tim. 1:9	"Who hath saved us, and called us with an holy calling, not according to our works, but according to his own purpose and grace, **which was given us in Christ Jesus before the world began**."
Tit. 1:2	"In hope of eternal life, which God, that cannot lie, **promised before the world began**."
Heb. 4:3	"For we which have believed do enter into rest, as he said, As I have sworn in my wrath, if they shall enter into my rest: although **the works were finished from the foundation of the world**."
1 Pet. 1:18	"Forasmuch as ye know that ye were not redeemed with corruptible things, as silver and gold, from your vain conversation received by tradition from your fathers."
1 Pet. 1:19	"But with the precious blood of Christ, as of a lamb without blemish and without spot."
1 Pet. 1:20	"Who verily was **foreordained before the foundation of the world**,

> **Rev. 13:8** "And all that dwell upon the earth shall worship him, whose names are not **written in the book of life of the Lamb slain from the foundation of the world**."
>
> **Rev. 17:8** "The beast that thou sawest was, and is not; and shall ascend out of the bottomless pit, and go into perdition: and they that dwell on the earth shall wonder, whose names were not **written in the book of life from the foundation of the world**, when they behold the beast that was, and is not, and yet is."

Just as there are some whose names are not written in the Lamb's book of life, there are others whose names **are** written in the Lamb's book of life from the foundation of the world. Because they were there from the beginning. They **will** be there still in the end.

> **John 17:1** "These words spake Jesus, and lifted up his eyes to heaven, and said, Father, the hour is come; glorify thy Son, that thy Son also may glorify thee."
>
> **John 17:2** "As thou hast given him power over all flesh, **that he should give eternal life to as many as thou hast given him**."

John 17:3	"And this is life eternal, that they might know thee the only true God, and Jesus Christ, whom thou hast sent."
John 17:4	"I have glorified thee on the earth: I have finished the work which thou gavest me to do."
John 17:5	"And now, O Father, **glorify thou me with thine own self with the glory which I had with thee before the world was**."
John 17:6	"I have manifested thy name unto the men which thou gavest me out of the world: **thine they were, and thou gavest them me**; and they have kept thy word."
John 17:7	"Now they have known that all things whatsoever thou hast given me are of thee."
John 17:8	"For I have given unto them the words which thou gavest me; and they have received them, and have known surely that I came out from thee, and they have believed that thou didst send me."
John 17:9	"I pray for them: I pray not for the world, **but for them which thou hast given me; for they are thine**."

John 17:10 "And all mine are thine, and thine are mine; and I am glorified in them."

John 17:11 "And now I am no more in the world, but these are in the world, and I come to thee. Holy Father, **keep through thine own name those whom thou hast given me, that they may be one, as we are**."

John 17:12 "While I was with them in the world, I kept them in thy name: **those that thou gavest me I have kept, and none of them is lost**, but the son of perdition; that the scripture might be fulfilled."

John 17:13 "And now come I to thee; and these things I speak in the world, that they might have my joy fulfilled in themselves."

John 17:14 "I have given them thy word; and the world hath hated them, because they are not of the world, even as I am not of the world."

John 17:15 "I pray not that thou shouldest take them out of the world, but that thou shouldest keep them from the evil."

John 17:16 "They are not of the world, even as I am not of the world."

John 17:17 "Sanctify them through thy truth: thy word is truth."

John 17:18	"As thou hast sent me into the world, even so have I also sent them into the world.
John 17:19	"And for their sakes I sanctify myself, that they also might be sanctified through the truth."
John 17:20	"Neither pray I for these alone, but for them also which shall believe on me through their word."
John 17:21	"**That they all may be one; as thou, Father, art in me, and I in thee**, **that they also may be one in us: that the world may believe that thou hast sent me.**"
John 17:22	"**And the glory which thou gavest me I have given them; that they may be one, even as we are one.**"
John 17:23	"**I in them, and thou in me, that they may be made perfect in one**; and that the world may know that thou hast sent me, and hast loved them, as thou hast loved me."
John 17:24	"Father, **I will that they also, whom thou hast given me, be with me where I am; that they may behold my glory, which thou hast given me: for thou lovedst me before the foundation of the world.**"

John 17:25 "O righteous Father, the world hath not known thee: but I have known thee, and these have known that thou hast sent me.

John 17:26 "**And I have declared unto them thy name, and will declare it: that the love wherewith thou hast loved me may be in them, and I in them**."

The Throne Established

Rev. 4:5 "And **out of the throne proceeded** lightnings and **thunderings** and voices: and there were seven lamps of fire burning before the throne, which are the seven Spirits of God."

When the book of Revelations speaks about "thunder," it is speaking about the sound of the voice of God. However, in the verse above, not only do we see that it is the voice of God, but we also see that the voice of God (thunder) comes from within the throne. When we understand that the throne of God is in the heart, then the following scripture makes much more sense.

Matt. 12:34 "O generation of vipers, how can ye, being evil, speak good things? **for out of the abundance of the heart the mouth speaketh**."

Luke 6:45 "A good man out of the good treasure of his heart bringeth forth that which is good; and an evil man out of the evil treasure of his heart bringeth forth that which is evil: **for of**

the abundance of the heart his mouth speaketh."

If THE King is seated on His throne in our hearts, and as the scriptures say, He is a consuming fire (**Deut. 4:24, 9:3; Heb. 12:29**), then we can understand the following scripture more completely.

Dan. 7:9 "I beheld till the thrones were cast down, and the Ancient of days did sit, whose garment was white as snow, and the hair of his head like the pure wool: **his throne was like the fiery flame**, and his wheels as burning fire."

Dan. 7:10 "**A fiery stream issued and came forth from before him**: thousand thousands ministered unto him, and ten thousand times ten thousand stood before him: the judgment was set, **and the books were opened**."

The thrones are cast down as in "humbling" (not destroyed) so that they can be established for THE Ancient of Days to be seated. Because He is a consuming fire, when He is seated in His throne in hearts, "his throne was like the fiery flame;" the following scripture takes more meaning.

Luke 24:32 "And they said one to another, **Did not our heart burn within us,** while he talked with us by the way, and while he opened to us the scriptures?"

Those that have Him seated on the throne of their hearts, when they speak, the words that come forth are from the "throne that is as a fiery flame" and are "a fiery stream" that comes forth from before Him. Then when it says that "the books were opened," the following scripture applies.

> **2 Cor. 3:2** "Ye are our epistle written in our hearts, **known and read of all men**."
>
> **2 Cor. 3:3** "Forasmuch as **ye are manifestly declared to be the epistle of Christ** ministered by us, **written** not with ink, but **with the Spirit of the living God**; not in tables of stone, but **in fleshy tables of the heart**."

And they become the promise of the New Covenant (**Jer. 31:31–33**) made manifest and open for all to see.

The Seven Thunders

We have seen that the names for the seven lamps in the Holy Place of the mind are called faith, virtue, knowledge, temperance, patience, godliness, and brotherly kindness, and that they are sealed, approved or capped off by agape—divine love. As long as those attributes of the personality traits of God do not perfectly reflect His image and likeness, they cannot receive His seal of approval. But when those virtues mature to the place where even God can give His witness and testimony that they reflect Him, He gives a seal of His approval upon them.

How does He place His seal of approval upon the virtues of His character traits? By speaking or pronouncing it. Where does that pronouncement come from? It comes from within His throne where He is seated. This is NOT something that man can superficially acquire for himself. If it truly is God that has given the seal of His witness and testimony upon the virtues, then there will also be supernatural signs that follow, because He is supernatural. Because He speaks His seal of approval upon each of the seven virtues, there are seven times that He speaks that approval, and each time that He speaks His seal of approval, it thunders.

Rev. 10:1	"And I saw another mighty angel come down from heaven, clothed with a cloud: and a rainbow was upon his head, and his face was as it were the sun, and his feet as pillars of fire."
Rev. 10:2	"And he had in his hand a little book open: and he set his right foot upon the sea, and his left foot on the earth."
Rev. 10:3	"And cried with a loud voice, as when a lion roareth: and when he had cried, **seven thunders uttered their voices**."
Rev. 10:4	"**And when the seven thunders had uttered their voices**, I was about to write: and I heard a voice from heaven saying unto me, Seal up those things which the **seven thunders** uttered, and write them not."
Rev. 10:5	"And the angel which I saw stand upon the sea and upon the earth lifted up his hand to heaven."
Rev. 10:6	"And sware by him that liveth for ever and ever, who created heaven, and the things that therein are, and the earth, and the things that therein are, and the sea, and the things

	which are therein, that there should be time no longer."
Rev. 10:7	"But in the days of the voice of the seventh angel, when he shall begin to sound, the mystery of God should be finished, as he hath declared to his servants the prophets."

Notice that the seven thunders are NOT the virtues; they are the **seal of approval** that God gives as a witness and testimony that the virtues have matured to the point that they display His image and likeness again. This sealing happens just before we receive the change (transformation) in our mortal bodies.

APPENDIX 1

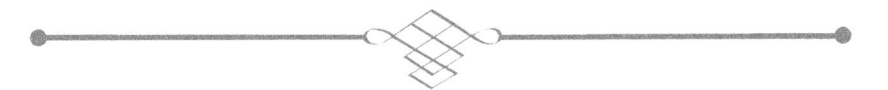

Understanding the Law

In order to understand how the Apostle Paul spoke about "The Law," it is necessary to understand that besides speaking about natural laws and secular laws, he spoke about three basic types of spiritual laws and how they interact with each other.

2 Tim. 2:15 "Study to shew thyself approved unto God, a workman that needeth not to be ashamed, rightly dividing the word of truth."

In order to "rightly divide" the Word of Truth, we must correctly discern which of the various types of "law" it is that the Apostle was talking about in every location where he used the word.

The following is an example of why the topic of "The Law" is so confusing to many people.

Note: Not a complete list.

Old Testament

Law of truth	**Mal. 2:6**
Law of mother	**Prov. 1:8, 6:20**
Law of the wise	**Prov. 13:14**
Law of kindness	**Prov. 31:26**
Law of Moses	**Mal. 4:4**
	Dan. 9:11,13
	Neh. 8:1

	Ezr. 3:2, 7:6
Law of the Lord	**Ezr. 7:10**
	Psa. 1:2, 19:7
	Isa. 5:24, 30:9
	Jer. 8:8, 44:23
	Amos 2:4
Law of God	**Ezr. 7:12,14,21,26**
	Neh. 8:8, 10:28–29
	Psa. 37:31, 81:4, 119:1
	Isa. 1:10
	Hos. 4:6
Law of the house	**Eze. 43:12**
Law is light	**Prov. 6:23**

New Testament

Law of the Jews	**Acts 25:8**
Law	**Rom. 7:21,23**
Law of works	**Rom. 3:27**
Law of faith	**Rom. 3:27**
Law of husband	**Rom. 7:2**
Law of God	**Rom. 7:23**
Law in members of the body	**Rom. 7:23**
Law of sin	**Rom. 7:23, 8:2**
Law of Spirit of life in Christ	**Rom. 8:2**
Law of righteousness	**Rom. 9:31**
Law of Moses	**Luke 2:22, 24:44**
	John 7:23
	Acts 15:5, 13:39
	Acts 28:23
	1 Cor. 9:9
Law of Christ	**Gal. 6:2**
Law of liberty	**Jas. 1:25, 2:12**
Royal Law	**Jas. 2:8**

Law of the Lord	**Luke 2:23,24,39**
Law is holy	**Rom. 7:12**
Law is spiritual	**Rom. 7:14**
Law is good	**Rom. 7:16**
	1 Tim. 1:8
Under the Law to Christ	**1 Cor. 9:21**
Curse of the Law	**Gal. 3:13**
Law schoolmaster	**Gal. 3:24**
Law Fulfilled	**Gal. 5:14**
Law shadow of good to come	**Heb. 10:1**
By Law purged w/blood	**Heb. 9:22**
Sin—transgression of the Law	**1 John 3:4**
Worship contrary to Law	**Acts 18:13**
Gamaliel—doctor of the Law	**Acts 5:34**
The Law and the Prophets	**Matt. 7:12**
Law prophesied until John	**Matt. 11:13**
	Luke 16:16
Hang all the Law	**Matt. 22:40**
Weightier Matter of the Law	**Matt. 23:23**

Foundations

1) Grace does NOT eliminate the need for obedience.
2) Not everything that is done **IN** the flesh is done **BY** the flesh (legalism); it is possible that things can be done **IN** the flesh **BY** the Spirit (holiness). This is what is meant by "walk in the Spirit and you will not fulfill the lusts of the flesh" (**Gal. 5:16**).
3) ONLY the obedience that is done **IN** the flesh **BY** the Spirit is an obedience that is 100 percent acceptable to God (holiness), because it is His Own obedience.
4) ANY and ALL attempts to produce obedience **IN** the flesh **BY** the flesh **alone** (legalism) will fail, but we should still

offer to God the very best of our efforts while waiting for Him to anoint us with power (His life) from on high to be able to produce the obedience **IN** our flesh **BY** the Spirit (holiness).

5) If we take an attitude that we can produce the obedience by our own abilities **alone** (legalism), then by **that attitude** we call God a liar when He said that "without Him we can do NOTHING" (**John 15:5**).

6) ALL attempts to be obedient MUST be done with the recognition of our **absolute dependence** upon God to send His supernatural empowerment upon it to make it acceptable before Him. The problem of "legalism" is NOT a problem with "obedience;" rather, it is a problem with WHO it is that does it and HOW the obedience is being done. If it is being attempted without it being Him doing it, then it will fail.

7) BUT WITH God, ALL things are possible, including walking perfect (holy) before Him (**Matt. 19:26; Mark 9:23, 10:27, 14:36; Luke 18:27; Matt. 5:48; 1 Pet. 1:15**).

8) Not even Jesus was perfect in the sight of fallen man. He was crucified under the accusation of blaspheming against God (**Matt. 9:2, 26:65; Mark 2:7, 14:64; Luke 5:21, 22:65; John 10:33,36; Acts 6:13–14**) and the Temple (**Matt. 26:61, 27:20; Mark 14:58, 15:29**) and making Himself to be God (**John 10:33**). The Lord Jesus was not a man trying to make Himself to be God. He was God who made Himself man (**Acts 20:28; 1 Cor. 2:8**), Immanuel/Emmanuel (**Isa. 7:14, 8:8; Matt. 1:23**).

9) As God is fulfilling His "New Covenant" promise (**Jer. 31:31–33; Heb. 8:10, 10:16; Rom. 2:15; 2 Cor. 3:2–3, 7–8; Heb. 12:23; Rev. 2:17, 14:1**) of writing His Law in our hearts and minds (circumcision of heart, **Lev. 26:41; Deut. 30:6; Jer. 6:10, 9:26; Eze. 44:7,9; Acts 7:51; Rom. 2:25–29; Php. 3:3; Col. 2:11**), we should also ask Him to send His power from on high (**Luke 24:49**) so that it can

be made manifest in and through our flesh (by the power of His life) because only THAT testimony (His) is the saltiness (**Matt. 5:13; Mark 9:50; Luke 14:34; Col. 4:6**) that can bring others to Him. In this way, all three porches of these temples of the Holy Spirit that we are can be filled with His glory—heart, mind, **and** body.

10) There is BOTH a true Grace AND a false Grace. Once we understand the Law, we can discern the difference between the two and avoid the snares of the enemy by false Grace (**1 Kings 3:9; Eze. 44:23; Mal. 3:18**).

11) It is the attributes of the manifest life of the Father in His children that identifies them as being His children.

12) The Law of God was not given by God for Him to have an excuse to bludgeon mankind with it when they fail to keep it by their own abilities (without Him). It was lovingly given as descriptions of how His character behaves itself in different situations so that we can have a positive and concise guideline to identify that we are on the right path (righteousness) instead of having to rely upon our own (fallen) whim. True children of God love their Abba so much that they want to joyously be just like Him (**Exo. 20:6; Deut. 5:10, 7:9, 11;1,22, 19:9, 30:16; Josh. 22:5; Dan. 9:4; John 14:15,23, 15:10; 1 John 5:2–3**). Because of this, obedience becomes the loving joy of the children of God expressing their passionate love for their heavenly Father and the humble submission of His adoring wife to His will. As such, we will seek the way to receive the necessary power to be obedient instead of reasons to justify disobedience. Justifying disobedience carnally is the tactic of the enemy that he uses to try to prevent the manifestation of the glorious church without spot or wrinkle or any such thing (**Eph. 5:27**).

The Three Spiritual Laws

1) **The Law of God**
   A) Unchangeable, eternal (**Mal. 3:6; Gen. 17:7,13,19; Lev. 24:8; Num. 25:13; 2 Sam. 23:5; 1 Chr. 16:17; Psa. 105:10; Isa. 24:5, 55:3, 61:8; Jer. 32:40; Eze. 16:60, 37:26; Heb. 13:20**)
   B) Sharper than a two-edged sword (**Heb. 4:12; Deut. 30:19**), and the edges are:
      I) Blessing for obedience (**Deut. 28:1–14**)
      II) Cursing for disobedience (**Deut. 28:15–68**)
   C) EVERYONE will have to deal with this law sooner or later (**Rom. 14:10; 2 Cor. 5:10**)

2) **The Law of Sin and Death**
   A) Came into effect when Adam fell in sin (**1 Cor. 15:22**);
   B) Produced separation from God (**Eph. 2:12**);
   C) Without God, we can do nothing (**John 15:5**);
   D) ONLY disobedience to Law #1 is possible under this law;
   E) It is only possible to receive (#1, B, II) the curse because of disobedience.

3) **The Law of Liberty and of the Spirit (a.k.a. True Grace)**
   A) Came into effect in the cross of Jesus;
   B) Restores fellowship between man and God (**Eph. 2:19**);
   C) With God, **all** things are possible (**Matt. 19:26; Mar 10:27**);
   D) Obedience to Law #1 is not only possible; when we yield to Him, His obedience in us becomes unstoppable;
   E) It is only possible to receive (#1, B, I) the blessing because of obedience;
   F) Sets us free from Law #2 (**Rom. 8:2**) and the results that it causes Law #1 to produce the curse; we are NOT liberated from obedience and the blessing of Law #1, because we are being created anew in His image and likeness.

By understanding these three spiritual laws AND their **interactions,** we can read the books of Galatians and Romans and they make perfect sense; whereas without this understanding, the things that they say about the Law can and almost certainly will be misunderstood.

We can also see that true Grace saves us from the penalty of the Law (Law #1, B, II) by the power that it (Grace—Law #3) has to produce the supernatural obedience that is the manifestation of the life of God in us (**John 1:4**). At no time is any jot or tittle of the Law of God (Law #1) nullified, ignored, annulled, or eliminated.

Because God is a just and loving God, He will not reward the obedient with the payment of the disobedient. Obedience will be as easy as our willingness to humble ourselves and submit ourselves to God makes it to be, and obedience will be as difficult as our insistence upon our rebellion makes it to be.

1 Pet. 5:2 "Feed the flock of God which is among you, taking the oversight thereof, not by **constraint**, but willingly; not for filthy lucre, but of a **ready mind**."

1 Pet. 5:3 "Neither as being lords over God's heritage, but being **ensamples** to the flock."

1 Pet. 5:4 "And when the chief Shepherd shall appear, ye shall receive a crown of glory that fadeth not away."

1 Pet. 5:5 "Likewise, ye younger, submit yourselves unto the elder. Yea, all of you be subject one to another, and **be clothed with humility: for God resisteth the proud, and giveth grace to the humble**."

1 Pet. 5:6   **"Humble yourselves therefore under the mighty hand of God, that he may exalt you in due time."**

If, therefore, we are setting the stage for the "Final Harvest," and that revival will be a combination of every God-sent revival that has come before **and more** (manifested spoken Word), then we must have new wineskins that are big enough and supple enough to contain both the volume and the potency of this season's new wine.

The ONLY kind of wineskin that is big enough and supple enough to contain the new wine (finishing anointing) for the final harvest is LAMB SKIN (**Gen. 3:21; Rom. 13:14**). And THE Lamb is humble (**Matt. 11:29**). The study of the Three Laws and their interactions are part of the **New Wineskin** (doctrine that gives place to the supernatural manifestation of the very Life of God).

Note: We have access to grace, forgiveness of sins, redemption, and restoration by the blood of the Lord Jesus Christ. The way that grace rescues us from the penalty of disobedience to the Law of God is by bringing us to obedience. God is not unjust to give the payment of disobedience to those that are obedient. However, it is not unjust for God to bless the disobedient in an attempt to draw (invite) them to obedience, but if they do not come to obedience, sooner or later the curse will come.

Matt. 5:43   "Ye have heard that it hath been said, Thou shalt love thy neighbour, and hate thine enemy."

Matt. 5:44   "But I say unto you, Love your enemies, bless them that curse you, do good to them that hate you, and pray for them which despitefully use you, and persecute you."

Matt. 5:45   "That ye may be the children of your Father which is in heaven: for **he**

maketh his sun to rise on the evil and on the good, and sendeth rain on the just and on the unjust."

What is the payment of disobedience? It is always good to follow (be obedient to) the ways of the Lord. Disobedience to the Law of God is called sin.

Rom. 7:12 "Wherefore the **law** is holy, and the commandment holy, and just, and **good**."

Rom. 7:16 "If then I do that which I would not, I consent unto the **law** that it is **good**."

Rom. 7:21 "I find then a **law**, that, when I would do **good**, evil is present with me."

1 Tim. 1:8 "But we know that the **law** is **good**, if a man use it lawfully."

Jas. 4:17 "Therefore to him that knoweth to do **good**, and doeth it not, to him it is sin."

1 John 3:4 "Whosoever committeth sin transgresseth also the law: for **sin is the transgression of the law**."

1 John 3:5 "And ye know that he was manifested to take away our sins; and in him is no sin."

1 John 3:6 "Whosoever abideth in him sinneth not: whosoever sinneth hath not seen him, neither known him."

Rom. 6:22 "**But now being made free from sin**, and become servants to God, ye have your **fruit** unto holiness, and the end everlasting life."

We have been made free from disobedience, and the fruit of holiness (obedience) is eternal life and blessing.

Rom. 6:23 "**For the wages of sin is death**; but the gift of God is eternal life through Jesus Christ our Lord."

2 Chr. 7:14 "If my people, which are called by my name, shall humble themselves, and pray, and seek my face, **and turn from their wicked ways**; then will I hear from heaven, and will forgive their sin, and will heal their land."

Wicked ways are any way that is not God's way. What is necessary? To humble ourselves before God.

Deut. 28:9 "The LORD shall establish thee an holy people unto himself, as he hath sworn unto thee, if thou shalt keep the commandments of the LORD thy God, and walk in his ways."

Deut. 28:10 "And all people of the earth shall see that thou art called by the name of the LORD; and they shall be afraid of thee."

Deut. 28:11 "And the LORD shall make thee plenteous in goods, in the fruit of thy body, and in the fruit of thy cat-

	tle, and in the fruit of thy ground, in the land which the LORD sware unto thy fathers to give thee."
Deut. 28:12	"The LORD shall open unto thee his good treasure, the heaven to give the rain unto thy land in his season, and to bless all the work of thine hand: and thou shalt lend unto many nations, and thou shalt not borrow."
Deut. 28:13	"And the LORD shall make thee the head, and not the tail; and thou shalt be above only, and thou shalt not be beneath; if that thou hearken unto the commandments of the LORD thy God, which I command thee this day, to observe and to do them."
Deut. 28:14	"And thou shalt not go aside from any of the words which I command thee this day, to the right hand, or to the left, to go after other gods to serve them."

All true obedience that is acceptable in the sight of God is the **exclusive** product and expression (manifestation) of the power of His life. It flows naturally and automatically from the heart (the Holy of Holies), and because of true humility and subjection/surrender to Him (in the Holy Place/our minds, **Rom. 12:2**), it makes obedience to be easy (**Matt. 11:28–30**). As long as obedience to the Word of God is difficult, we still need to surrender more.

Obedience will be as difficult as our rebellion makes it to be, and obedience will be as easy as our humility and surrender makes it to be. But there **will be** a glorious church without spot or wrinkle or any such thing. **That** church will be the living proof that it **is** possible to walk perfect in the sight of God and that His blood has enough power to bring into manifestation every jot and tittle of His Word, even in flesh that was born in sin but that has been redeemed.

Finally, we MUST understand everything that the Apostle Paul said about "law" in a way that DOES NOT make him to be disobedient to the commandment that the Lord Jesus gave:

Matt. 5:17 **"Think not that I am come to destroy the law, or the prophets**: I am not come to destroy, but to fulfil."

Matt. 5:18 "For verily I say unto you, Till heaven and earth pass, one jot or one tittle shall in no wise pass from the law, till all be fulfilled."

Matt. 5:19 "**Whosoever** therefore shall break one of these least commandments, and shall teach men so, he shall be called the least in the kingdom of heaven: but whosoever shall do and teach them, the same shall be called great in the kingdom of heaven."

Just as the first Adam was male and female, so also the second Adam (The Son of Man) has BOTH male and female attributes, and **Matt. 5:18–19** must be fulfilled in the female attribute (the elect, chosen, and married Church).

Matt. 24:14 "And this gospel of the kingdom shall be preached in all the world for a witness unto all nations; and **then** shall the end come."

Matt. 24:27	"For as the lightning cometh out of the east, and shineth even unto the west; so shall also the coming of the Son of man be."
Matt. 24:30	"And then shall appear the sign of the Son of man in heaven: and then shall all the tribes of the earth mourn, and they shall see the Son of man coming in the clouds of heaven with power and great glory."
Matt. 24:37	"But as the days of Noe were, so shall also the coming of the Son of man be."
Matt. 24:39	"And knew not until the flood came, and took them all away; so shall also the coming of the Son of man be."

APPENDIX 2

The Birthright

The Birthright and the Kinsman Redeemer (**Appendix 3**) are intimately related. The Birthright is the biblical evidence that when man fell into sin, NOT ALL of the power and authority that God gave him was lost. The portion of the power and authority that was not lost was generally passed down through the firstborn son of each generation. The only exceptions were based upon the firstborn son not demonstrating the necessary character to be able to manifest the power and authority in a way that manifested the character of God and that brings glory, praise, and honor to Him.

The Kinsman Redeemer is the unfolding story of the plan of God to restore back to mankind everything that was lost when man fell into sin and the restoration of the necessary Godly character to be able to manifest that power and authority in the correct (Godly) way.

There are three general responsibilities that the Birthright carried with it:

1) The responsibility to set the example and standards for Godly morality;
2) The responsibility to set the example and standards for worshipping God;
3) The responsibility to set the example and standards for conducting both private and public business in a Godly way.

A great mistake that many people make is thinking that these three responsibilities are part of Jewish or Semitic customs. In fact, these three responsibilities are the expressions of the character and nature of God and how He behaves or manifests His character. They are the examples of God identifying Himself with humanity in and through the firstborn son of each generation to instruct mankind on how to behave and conduct the details of life in a way that will bring the "shalom" of God into manifestation for His glory.

The Hebrew word *shalom* does not just mean "peace" as many people think. The word *shalom* means peace and prosperity in EVERY aspect of life, in health, business, worship, emotions, and character—NOT to the (limited) extent that we are capable of receiving (alone), but to the extent that God is able to pour out upon us as we walk with Him in His ways. To refuse the walk with God in His ways is to limit that impartation and opens the door for the enemy to come into our lives and manifest his purposes to steal, kill, and destroy.

> **John 10:10** "The thief cometh not, but for to steal, and to kill, and to destroy: I am come that they might have life, and that they might have it more abundantly."

If we do not know what rights and responsibilities come along with the Birthright (the power and authority that still remain for us), then we can easily be deceived into allowing the enemy to rob us of the blessings that they bring. We also will not know how to walk (with God) in a way that brings us to inherit the even greater blessings that accompany being restored (by The Kinsman Redeemer) back to the fullness of the original position that God had for us in the beginning. Also, the enemy can deceive us into not moving in the authority that still pertains to us as children of God.

Sadly, part of the lie of the enemy is to think about the obedience that is implied in walking with God in His ways as legalism or religiosity. IF we attempt to do it by our own abilities alone (without God), then that is what it **would** be. However, if we enter into that obedience because of it being the exclusive manifestation of His Life working in and through us, then it is the manifestation of the living reality that the life of God is in us.

This is a paradigm shift that many people find difficult to make, because the only way that they have been accustomed to looking at obedience to God has been in the way that the enemy has provided for them—to steal, kill, and destroy in their lives, instead of the limitless abundance of life that God, in fact, has for us. But once we experience the reality of our life being immersed in the life of God, THEN the obedience simply becomes HIM expressing who He IS in us.

When God created Adam, He created him to have power and authority over the earth and everything that was on the earth (**Gen. 1:26–27**). Because that power and authority was given to a son of God, it can ONLY be possessed by children of God and NOT by any other created being. It is for this reason that even though man fell into sin, the fallen cherub, the dragon could NOT inherit in a direct way the power and authority that was lost. Part of the capabilities of that authority was expressed by the Lord Jesus Christ (the second Adam, **1 Cor. 15:45–49**) when he stopped the storm (**Mark 4:35–41**), created bread and fish (**Matt. 14:13–21, 15:29–39**), spoke to the fig tree (**Matt. 21:18–20**), and when He spoke about faith (**Matt. 21:21; Luke 17:6**). It is important to recognize that **not all** of that power and authority was lost when man fell in sin (**Gen. 3**), because ONLY sons of God can truly wield or possess that power and authority. It is for this reason that if the devil does not have human vessels that he can **deceive** into doing his will, he is almost totally powerless.

Rev. 20:1 "And I saw an angel come down from heaven, having the key of the bottomless pit and a great **chain** in his hand."

Rev. 20:2 "And he laid hold on the dragon, that old serpent, which is the Devil, and Satan, and bound him a thousand years."

| **Rev. 20:3** | "And cast him into the bottomless pit, and shut him up, and set a seal upon him, that he should **deceive** the nations **no more**, **till** the thousand years should be fulfilled: and after that he must be loosed a little season." |

If absolutely all of that power and authority was lost in the fall, then there could be no Birthright. However, we know that the scripture speaks about the Birthright that generally was passed down to the firstborn son in each generation. Therefore, not all of the power and authority that Adam had fell into the hands of the devil, because the devil is not a man or a son of God. The Antichrist will be a man that surrenders as completely to the devil as the saints surrender to God in order for them to become the glorious church without spot or wrinkle. The Lord Jesus is the second Adam, the first **born** of the Father (Adam was **not born**; he was **created**. The Lord Jesus Christ was **both** created **and** born), and the inheritor of the **fullness** of the Birthright.

Therefore, the list of the descendants of Cain in **Gen. 4:16–24** is a genealogy. **Genesis chapter 5** is not a genealogy but a description that traces the firstborn sons to follow the birthright from Adam to Noah. **Gen. 9:18–29** and **chapter 10** is the genealogy of Noah, and **Gen. 11:10–32** again takes up the trail of the birthright from Shem to Abraham.

In general, the Birthright consisted of three kinds of authority. The first was the authority to establish the standards for moral conduct. The second was the authority to establish the manner and standards for worshipping God. The third was the authority to establish the standards for conducting business (both personal and public). It is because of the profound responsibilities that accompany these three kinds of authority that the Birthright was not passed down to the firstborn son **if** he demonstrated some type of serious character flaw.

Two examples of this are Esau who despised the Birthright and considered it lightly by selling it for a bowl of food (**Gen. 25:31–34**; **Heb. 12:16**), and Reuben who went to bed with one of his father's concubines (**Gen. 35:22**; **1 Chr. 5:1–2**). Also, the birthright passed down to the firstborn son of a freeborn wife and not to the son of a slave or concubine. This is evidenced by Ishmael and Dan. The origin of this detail is found in:

Gen. 15:3 "And Abram said, Behold, to me thou hast given no seed: and, lo, one born in my house is mine heir."

Gen. 15:4 "And, behold, the word of the LORD came unto him, saying, This shall not be thine heir; but he that shall come forth out of **thine own bowels** shall be thine heir."

The organs that surround the womb are the bowels. God said that the heir of Abraham would come forth from **his own bowels**. This could ONLY be fulfilled by a legitimate wife, because when a man and a woman are married in the sight of God, they become ONE FLESH. That is **not** something that a slave could fulfill and is evidenced by:

Gen. 22:2 "And he said, Take now thy son, thine **only** son Isaac, whom thou lovest, and get thee into the land of Moriah; and offer him there for a burnt offering upon one of the mountains which I will tell thee of."

Gen. 22:12 "And he said, Lay not thine hand upon the lad, neither do thou any thing unto him: for now I know that thou fearest God, seeing thou hast not withheld thy son, thine **only** son from me."

Gen. 22:16 "And said, By myself have I sworn, saith the LORD, for because thou hast done this thing, and hast not withheld thy son, thine **only** son."

Therefore, the ONLY son that God counted as being the fulfillment of the promise was Isaac and NOT Ishmael. This is exactly what the Apostle Paul explained.

Rom. 9:8 "That is, They which are the children of the flesh, these are not the children of God: but the children of the promise are counted for the seed."

Rom. 9:9 "For this is the word of promise, At this time will I come, and **Sara shall have a son**."

Which was the fulfillment of:

Gen. 17:19 "And God said, **Sarah thy wife shall bear thee a son indeed**; and thou shalt call his name Isaac: and I will establish my covenant with him for an everlasting covenant, and with his seed after him."

Gen. 17:21 "But my covenant will I establish with Isaac, which **Sarah shall bear unto thee** at this set time in the next year."

Gen. 18:10	"And he said, I will certainly return unto thee according to the time of life; and, lo, **Sarah thy wife shall have a son**. And Sarah heard it in the tent door, which was behind him."
Gen. 18:14	"Is any thing too hard for the LORD? At the time appointed I will return unto thee, according to the time of life, and **Sarah shall have a son**."
Gen. 21:1	"And the LORD visited Sarah as he had said, and the LORD did unto Sarah as he had spoken."
Gen. 21:2	"For Sarah conceived, and bare Abraham a son in his old age, at the set time of which God had spoken to him."
Gen. 21:3	"And Abraham called the name of his son that was born unto him, whom Sarah bare to him, Isaac."
Gen. 21:4	"And Abraham circumcised his son Isaac being eight days old, as God had commanded him."
Gen. 21:5	"And Abraham was an hundred years old, when his son Isaac was born unto him."
Gal. 4:22	"For it is written, that Abraham had two sons, the one by a bondmaid, the other by a freewoman."

Gal. 4:23	"But he who was of the bondwoman was born after the flesh; but he of the freewoman was by promise."
Gal. 4:28	"Now we, brethren, as Isaac was, are the children of promise."
Gal. 4:29	"But as then he that was born after the flesh persecuted him that was born after the Spirit, even so it is now."
Gal. 4:30	"Nevertheless what saith the scripture? Cast out the bondwoman and her son: for the son of the bondwoman shall not be heir with the son of the freewoman."
Gal. 4:31	"So then, brethren, we are not children of the bondwoman, but of the free."
Heb. 11:9	"By faith he sojourned in the land of promise, as in a strange country, dwelling in tabernacles with Isaac and Jacob, the heirs with him of the same promise."

Therefore, we can see that the Birthright generally passed to the firstborn son, and also that the inheritance was ONLY to the firstborn son of a legitimate wife and not the firstborn son of a slave. It is important to remember this detail as we consider the next condition for inheriting the Birthright—Reuben, Dan., Gad and Joseph.

Jacob had twelve sons and one daughter (**Gen. 29:32–35, 30:5–24, 35:18**) through four different women; two were legitimate wives, and two were slaves. The first born son through each woman was as follows:

Reuben by Leah (**Gen. 29:32**).
Dan by Bilha the slave (**Gen. 30:5**).
Gad by Zilpah the slave (**Gen. 30:11**).
Joseph by Rachel (**Gen. 30:24**).

Reuben would have had the Birthright because of being the firstborn son of a legitimate wife, but as a result of his adultery with Bilha (**Gen. 35:22**), he lost his Birthright (**1 Chr. 5:1**). Because of the previously established pattern with Ishmael and Isaac, the Birthright could not be passed to either Dan or Gad, because they were the sons of slaves. This was a superseding detail that was above the fact that they were firstborn sons and older than Joseph. This is the major reason that Joseph was hated by his brothers; they were all older than him (except for Benjamin), some of them were firstborn sons but of slaves, and one of them was also the firstborn of a legitimate wife but committed adultery—Reuben.

Gen. 37:3	"Now Israel loved Joseph more than all his children, because he was the son of his old age: and he made him a coat of many colours."
Gen. 37:4	"And when his brethren saw that their father loved him more than all his brethren, they hated him, and could not speak peaceably unto him."

Not only did Jacob love Joseph because he was the son of his old age, but ALSO because Jacob loved the Birthright, and the Birthright fell upon Joseph. Joseph's brothers hated him because he was the favorite son of Jacob, also because even though he was younger than them, he inherited the Birthright, and because he was spiritual and they were carnal.

> **Gen. 37:5** "And Joseph dreamed a dream, and he told it his brethren: and they hated him yet the more."

Because of his (Reuben's) remorse about his adultery and with the recognition that he had legitimately lost the Birthright, he demonstrated the least hatred toward Joseph and several times attempted to deliver Joseph out of the hands of his brothers (**Gen. 37:21–22, 29–30**). This same detail was demonstrated by Reuben many years later.

> **Gen. 42:22** "And Reuben answered them, saying, Spake I not unto you, saying, Do not sin against the child; and ye would not hear? therefore, behold, also his blood is required."

> **Gen. 42:37** "And Reuben spake unto his father, saying, Slay my two sons, if I bring him not to thee: deliver him into my hand, and I will bring him to thee again."

The next detail that shows how that the Birthright could be lost is shown in the interaction between Esau and Jacob, specifically the bowl of pottage. First of all, Esau began to display failures in his character.

> **Gen. 26:34** "And Esau was forty years old when he took to wife Judith the daughter of Beeri the Hittite, and Bashemath the daughter of Elon the Hittite."

> **Gen. 26:35** "Which were a grief of mind unto Isaac and to Rebekah."

Next, Esau despised the Birthright. How did Esau despise the Birthright?

Gen. 25:28	"And Isaac loved Esau, because he did eat of his venison: but Rebekah loved Jacob."
Gen. 25:29	"And Jacob sod pottage: and Esau came from the field, and he was faint."
Gen. 25:30	"And Esau said to Jacob, Feed me, I pray thee, with that same red pottage; for I am faint: therefore was his name called Edom."
Gen. 25:31	"And Jacob said, Sell me this day thy birthright."
Gen. 25:32	"And Esau said, Behold, I am at the point to die: and what profit shall this birthright do to me?"
Gen. 25:33	"And Jacob said, Swear to me this day; and he sware unto him: and **he sold his birthright unto Jacob**."
Gen. 25:34	"Then Jacob gave Esau bread and pottage of lentiles; and he did eat and drink, and rose up, and went his way: **thus** Esau **despised his birthright**."

It is here that we must recognize an important point—the Birthright was **legitimately sold**; not just part of it, but ALL of it. The Birthright does NOT only consist of a natural inheritance, but

ALSO it consists of a spiritual blessing. Most people accuse Jacob of stealing the Birthright and the blessing from Esau when, in fact, Esau sold it ALL to Jacob and THEN tried to steal back the spiritual blessing from Jacob. All that Jacob did was to ensure that Esau did not steal back the spiritual blessing portion of the Birthright that Esau had already sold to him.

Notice there is NOT EVEN ONE place where God said that Jacob stole the Birthright. The ONLY one that made that accusation against Jacob was Esau, and he (Esau) was demonstratibly carnal through despising the Birthright and selling it for a bowl of pottage. This very detail is a scriptural prophecy and warning to us today that explains a small aspect about the "hour of temptation."

> **Rev. 3:10** "Because thou hast kept the word of my patience, I also will keep thee from the **hour of temptation, which shall come upon all the world, to try them that dwell upon the earth**."

When empty promises of financial blessings come without anything being said about walking in righteousness with God, we must recognize that we are being tried to see if we will sell our Birthright, like Esau, or if we will love it (the spiritual blessing of our Birthright) above everything else, including our lives in the flesh. As the scripture says:

> **Matt. 6:33** "But seek ye **first** the kingdom of God, and his righteousness; and all these things shall be added unto you."
>
> **Luke 14:26** "If any man come to me, and hate not his father, and mother, and wife, and children, and brethren, and sisters, yea, and **his own life also**, he cannot be my disciple."

Luke 14:27 "And whosoever doth not bear his cross, and come after me, cannot be my disciple."

John 12:24 "Verily, verily, I say unto you, Except a corn of wheat fall into the ground and die, it abideth alone: but if it die, it bringeth forth much fruit."

John 12:25 **"He that loveth his life shall lose it; and he that hateth his life in this world shall keep it unto life eternal**."

John 12:26 "If any man serve me, let him follow me; and where I am, there shall also my servant be: if any man serve me, him will my Father honour."

How is it possible to lose our lives while we yet live? To be "living" sacrifices (**Rom. 12:1**) and not die? It is ONLY possible by our life being completely immersed in the very life of God who is the very fountain of life. As we remain in that baptism, then we can move into every detail of restoration and Birthright.

APPENDIX 3

The Kinsman Redeemer

Jesus, the second Adam, the first **born** of the Father, is the only one that was **entirely** innocent of sin that came into the world **through birth** and who had a Spirit of life within Him that is compatible with both God and man. Therefore, He was/is the only one that was qualified to do the work of the sacrificial Lamb, the Kinsman Redeemer, and the ultimate high priest.

Rev. 5:1 "And I saw in the right hand of him that sat on the throne a book written within and on the backside, sealed with seven seals."

Rev. 5:2 "And I saw a strong angel proclaiming with a loud voice, **Who is worthy** to open the book, and to loose the seals thereof?"

Rev. 5:3 "**And no man in heaven, nor in earth, neither under the earth, was able to open the book, neither to look thereon.**"

Rev. 5:4 "And I wept much, because **no man was found worthy to open and to read the book, neither to look thereon.**"

Rev. 5:5 "And one of the elders saith unto me, Weep not: behold, the **Lion** of the tribe of Juda, the Root of David, hath prevailed to open the book, and to loose the seven seals thereof."

Rev. 5:6 "And I beheld, and, lo, in the midst of the throne and of the four beasts, and in the midst of the elders, stood a **Lamb** as it had been slain, having seven horns and seven eyes, which are the seven Spirits of God sent forth into all the earth."

Rev. 5:7 "And he came and took the book out of the right hand of him that sat upon the throne."

Rev. 5:8 "And when he had taken the book, the four beasts and four and twenty elders fell down before the Lamb, having every one of them harps, and golden vials full of odours, which are the prayers of saints."

Rev. 5:9 "And they sung a new song, saying, **Thou art worthy to take the book, and to open the seals thereof: for thou wast slain, and hast redeemed us to God by thy blood out of every kindred, and tongue, and people, and nation**."

Rev. 5:10 "And hast made us unto our God kings and priests: and we shall reign on the earth."

Rev. 5:11 "And I beheld, and I heard the voice of many angels round about the throne and the beasts and the elders: and the number of them was ten thousand times ten thousand, and thousands of thousands."

Rev. 5:12 "Saying with a loud voice, **Worthy is the Lamb** that was slain to receive power, and riches, and wisdom, and strength, and honour, and glory, and blessing."

Rev. 5:13 "And every creature which is in heaven, and on the earth, and under the earth, and such as are in the sea, and all that are in them, heard I saying, Blessing, and honour, and glory, and power, be unto him that sitteth upon the throne, and unto the Lamb for ever and ever."

Rev. 5:14 "And the four beasts said, Amen. And the four and twenty elders fell down and worshipped him that liveth for ever and ever."

After the flesh, the Lord Jesus is Brother to Adam (the only other entirely created human being). Therefore, when He did the work of Kinsman Redeemer, it was Adam (the man) that He redeemed, and because Adam (the man) stood in the breach for Adam (the woman, see **Gen. 5:1–2,** "their name") she was also redeemed, and all of the children of faith that they would have engendered were also redeemed.

The Law of the Kinsman redeemer is found in:

Lev. 25:25 "If thy brother be waxen poor, and hath sold away some of his possession, and if any of his kin come to **redeem** it, then shall he **redeem** that which his brother sold."

Lev. 25:26 "And if the man have none to **redeem** it, and himself be able to **redeem** it."

Lev. 25:27 "Then let him count the years of the sale thereof, and **restore** the overplus unto the man to whom he sold it; that he may return unto his possession."

Lev. 25:28 "But if he be not able to **restore** it to him, then that which is sold shall remain in the hand of him that hath bought it until the year of jubile: and in the jubile it shall go out, and he shall return unto his possession."

Lev. 25:29 "And if a man sell a dwelling house in a walled city, then he may **redeem** it within a whole year after it is sold; within a full year may he **redeem** it."

Lev. 25:30 "And if it be not **redeemed** within the space of a full year, then the house that is in the walled city shall be established for ever to him that bought it throughout his generations: it shall not go out in the jubile."

Lev. 25:31   "But the houses of the villages which have no wall round about them shall be counted as the fields of the country: they may be **redeemed**, and they shall go out in the jubile."

Lev. 25:32   "Notwithstanding the cities of the Levites, and the houses of the cities of their possession, may the Levites **redeem** at any time."

Lev. 25:33   "And if a man purchase of the Levites, then the house that was sold, and the city of his possession, shall go out in the year of jubile: for the houses of the cities of the Levites are their possession among the children of Israel."

Lev. 25:34   "But the field of the suburbs of their cities may not be sold; for it is their perpetual possession."

Lev. 25:35   "And if thy brother be waxen poor, and fallen in decay with thee; then thou shalt **relieve** him: yea, though he be a stranger, or a sojourner; that he may live with thee."

Lev. 25:36   "Take thou no usury of him, or increase: but fear thy God; that thy brother may live with thee."

Lev. 25:37   "Thou shalt not give him thy money upon usury, nor lend him thy victuals for increase."

Lev. 25:38 "I am the LORD your God, which brought you forth out of the land of Egypt, to give you the land of Canaan, and to be your God."

Lev. 25:39 "And if thy brother that dwelleth by thee be waxen poor, and be sold unto thee; thou shalt not compel him to serve as a bondservant."

Lev. 25:40 "But as an hired servant, and as a sojourner, he shall be with thee, and shall serve thee unto the year of jubile."

Lev. 25:41 "And then shall he depart from thee, both he and his children with him, and shall return unto his own family, and unto the possession of his fathers shall he return."

Lev. 25:42 "For they are my servants, which I brought forth out of the land of Egypt: they shall not be sold as bondmen."

Lev. 25:43 "Thou shalt not rule over him with rigour; but shalt fear thy God."

Lev. 25:44 "Both thy bondmen, and thy bondmaids, which thou shalt have, shall be of the heathen that are round about you; of them shall ye buy bondmen and bondmaids."

Lev. 25:45 "Moreover of the children of the strangers that do sojourn among you, of them shall ye buy, and of their families that are with you, which they begat in your land: and they shall be your possession."

Lev. 25:46 "And ye shall take them as an inheritance for your children after you, to inherit them for a possession; they shall be your bondmen for ever: but over your brethren the children of Israel, ye shall not rule one over another with rigour."

Lev. 25:47 "And if a sojourner or stranger wax rich by thee, and thy brother that dwelleth by him wax poor, and sell himself unto the stranger or sojourner by thee, or to the stock of the stranger's family."

Lev. 25:48 "After that he is sold he may be **redeemed** again; one of his brethren may **redeem** him."

Lev. 25:49 "Either his **uncle**, or his **uncle's son**, may **redeem** him, or **any that is nigh of kin** unto him of his family may **redeem** him; or if he be able, he may **redeem** himself."

Lev. 25:50 "And he shall reckon with him that bought him from the year that he was sold to him unto the year of jubile: and the price of his sale shall be according unto the number of

	years, according to the time of an hired servant shall it be with him."
Lev. 25:51	"If there be yet many years behind, according unto them he shall give again the price of his **redemption** out of the money that he was bought for."
Lev. 25:52	"And if there remain but few years unto the year of jubile, then he shall count with him, and according unto his years shall he give him again the price of his **redemption**."
Lev. 25:53	"And as a yearly hired servant shall he be with him: and the other shall not rule with rigour over him in thy sight."
Lev. 25:54	"And if he be not **redeemed** in these years, then he shall go out in the year of jubile, both he, and his children with him."
Lev. 25:55	"For unto me the children of Israel are servants; they are my servants whom I brought forth out of the land of Egypt: I am the LORD your God."
Lev. 27:1	"And the LORD spake unto Moses, saying."
Lev. 27:2	"Speak unto the children of Israel, and say unto them, When a man

shall make a singular vow, the persons shall be for the LORD by thy estimation."

Lev. 27:3 "And thy estimation shall be of the male from twenty years old even unto sixty years old, even thy estimation shall be fifty shekels of silver, after the shekel of the sanctuary."

Lev. 27:4 "And if it be a female, then thy estimation shall be thirty shekels."

Lev. 27:5 "And if it be from five years old even unto twenty years old, then thy estimation shall be of the male twenty shekels, and for the female ten shekels."

Lev. 27:6 "And if it be from a month old even unto five years old, then thy estimation shall be of the male five shekels of silver, and for the female thy estimation shall be three shekels of silver."

Lev. 27:7 "And if it be from sixty years old and above; if it be a male, then thy estimation shall be fifteen shekels, and for the female ten shekels."

Lev. 27:8 "But if he be poorer than thy estimation, then he shall present himself before the priest, and the priest shall value him; according to his ability that vowed shall the priest value him."

Lev. 27:9 "And if it be a beast, whereof men bring an offering unto the LORD, all that any man giveth of such unto the LORD shall be holy."

Lev. 27:10 "He shall not alter it, nor change it, a good for a bad, or a bad for a good: and if he shall at all change beast for beast, then it and the exchange thereof shall be holy."

Lev. 27:11 "And if it be any unclean beast, of which they do not offer a sacrifice unto the LORD, then he shall present the beast before the priest."

Lev. 27:12 "And the priest shall value it, whether it be good or bad: as thou valuest it, who art the priest, so shall it be."

Lev. 27:13 "But if he will at all **redeem** it, then he shall add a fifth part thereof unto thy estimation."

Lev. 27:14 "And when a man shall sanctify his house to be holy unto the LORD, then the priest shall estimate it, whether it be good or bad: as the priest shall estimate it, so shall it stand."

Lev. 27:15 "And if he that sanctified it will **redeem** his house, then he shall add the fifth part of the money of thy estimation unto it, and it shall be his."

Lev. 27:16 "And if a man shall sanctify unto the LORD some part of a field of his possession, then thy estimation shall be according to the seed thereof: an homer of barley seed shall be valued at fifty shekels of silver."

Lev. 27:17 "If he sanctify his field from the year of jubile, according to thy estimation it shall stand."

Lev. 27:18 "But if he sanctify his field after the jubile, then the priest shall reckon unto him the money according to the years that remain, even unto the year of the jubile, and it shall be abated from thy estimation."

Lev. 27:19 "And if he that sanctified the field will in any wise **redeem** it, then he shall add the fifth part of the money of thy estimation unto it, and it shall be assured to him."

Lev. 27:20 "And if he will not **redeem** the field, or if he have sold the field to another man, it shall not be **redeemed** any more."

Lev. 27:21 "But the field, when it goeth out in the jubile, shall be holy unto the LORD, as a field devoted; the possession thereof shall be the priest's."

Lev. 27:22 "And if a man sanctify unto the LORD a field which he hath

	bought, which is not of the fields of his possession."
Lev. 27:23	"Then the priest shall reckon unto him the worth of thy estimation, even unto the year of the jubile: and he shall give thine estimation in that day, as a holy thing unto the LORD."
Lev. 27:24	"In the year of the jubile the field shall return unto him of whom it was bought, even to him to whom the possession of the land did belong."
Lev. 27:25	"And all thy estimations shall be according to the shekel of the sanctuary: twenty gerahs shall be the shekel."
Lev. 27:26	"Only the firstling of the beasts, which should be the LORD'S firstling, no man shall sanctify it; whether it be ox, or sheep: it is the LORD'S."
Lev. 27:27	"And if it be of an unclean beast, then he shall **redeem** it according to thine estimation, and shall add a fifth part of it thereto: or if it be not **redeemed**, then it shall be sold according to thy estimation."
Lev. 27:28	"Notwithstanding no devoted thing, that a man shall devote unto the LORD of all that he hath, both

of man and beast, and of the field of his possession, shall be sold or **redeemed**: every devoted thing is most holy unto the LORD."

Lev. 27:29 "None devoted, which shall be devoted of men, shall be **redeemed**; but shall surely be put to death."

Lev. 27:30 "And all the tithe of the land, whether of the seed of the land, or of the fruit of the tree, is the LORD'S: it is holy unto the LORD."

Lev. 27:31 "And if a man will at all **redeem** ought of his tithes, he shall add thereto the fifth part thereof."

Lev. 27:32 "And concerning the tithe of the herd, or of the flock, even of whatsoever passeth under the rod, the tenth shall be holy unto the LORD."

Lev. 27:33 "He shall not search whether it be good or bad, neither shall he change it: and if he change it at all, then both it and the change thereof shall be holy; it shall not be **redeemed**."

Lev. 27:34 "These are the commandments, which the LORD commanded Moses for the children of Israel in mount Sinai."

We can see that **Leviticus** chapters **25** and **27** speak about the details of redemption and show how it relates to the Jubilee year. It also identifies who can redeem (only a near kinsman), what can be redeemed, and the cost of redemption. These chapters also identify that the type of metal that the redemption price is made out of is silver. Therefore, silver is identified as being symbolic of redemption. This has a great symbolic significance in the following two scripture passages in **Genesis chapter 37** and in **Matthew chapters 26 and 27**.

> **Gen. 37:2** These are the generations of Jacob. **Joseph, being seventeen years old**, was feeding the flock with his brethren; and the lad was with the sons of Bilhah, and with the sons of Zilpah, his father's wives: and Joseph brought unto his father their evil report.
>
> **Gen. 37:26** And Judah said unto his brethren, What profit is it if we slay our brother, and conceal his blood?
>
> **Gen. 37:27** Come, and let us sell him to the Ishmeelites, and let not our hand be upon him; for he is our brother and our flesh. And his brethren were content.
>
> **Gen. 37:28** Then there passed by Midianites merchantmen; and they drew and lifted up Joseph out of the pit, and sold Joseph to the Ishmeelites for **twenty pieces of silver**: and they brought Joseph into Egypt.

Therefore, **Gen. 37:2** and **26–28** are the foundation for **Lev. 27:7,** because Joseph was about seventeen years old (**Lev. 27:5** "from five years old even unto twenty years old") and was sold for twenty pieces of silver. However, when the Lord Jesus was sold for thirty pieces of silver:

> **Matt. 26:15** And said unto them, What will ye give me, and I will deliver him unto you? And they covenanted with him for **thirty pieces of silver**.
>
> **Matt. 27:3** Then Judas, which had betrayed him, when he saw that he was condemned, repented himself, and brought again the **thirty pieces of silver** to the chief priests and elders,
>
> **Matt. 27:5** And he cast down the **pieces of silver** in the temple, and departed, and went and hanged himself.
>
> **Matt. 27:6** And the chief priests took the **silver pieces**, and said, It is not lawful for to put them into the treasury, because it is the price of blood.
>
> **Matt. 27:9** Then was fulfilled that which was spoken by Jeremy the prophet, saying, And they took the **thirty pieces of silver, the price of him that was valued**, whom they of the children of Israel did value;

And when we compare it with:

> **Lev. 27:3** And thy estimation shall be of the **male from twenty years old even unto sixty years old**, even thy esti-

mation shall be **fifty shekels of silver**, after the shekel of the sanctuary.

Lev. 27:4 And if it be a **female**, then thy estimation shall be **thirty shekels**.

When the Lord Jesus was sold for thirty pieces of silver, even **that** detail was an attempt to insult him by selling him for the price of a woman instead of a man. However, in this, we can see the greatness of God to turn even the insults of man into something that He can use for His glory. How? Because the Lord Jesus was sold, not for His own redemption, but to redeem the Bride, and because of this, He was sold for thirty pieces (the redemption price of a woman) of silver instead of fifty. It was the price of redemption, to redeem the Bride so that she could bear His name by becoming (**Rev. 19:7–9**) the Wife of the Lamb and the Queen of the Lion of the Tribe of Judah—THE KING!

We can see this work of Kinsman Redeemer being played out in the Book of Ruth. Boaz paid the price to redeem the inheritance of his Jewish near kinswoman (Naomi), and when he did, he got a gentile wife (Ruth).

In the same way, the Lord Jesus Christ paid the price of redemption, not just for Israel, but also for "whosoever will" from every nation, people, and tongue as long as they have the same faith as Abraham (see the very end of **chapter 10**).

However, the Lord Jesus Christ, after the flesh (as a created being), was ONLY near kinsman to ONE other person, and that was Adam. When the price of redemption was paid for Adam, then because Adam stood in the gap between a Holy God and his fallen wife (**Rom. 5:14**), she was also included in the redemption with him. Not only were Adam and his wife redeemed, but **all** of those who would have been born of them by faith without the "touch" that was spoken about in **Genesis 3:3**. THAT is where the "whosoever will" and the faith-seed of Abraham are identified as the manifestation of the original will of God for the commandment (**Gen. 1:28**), to be fruitful and multiply but without the **Gen. 3:3** "touch."

APPENDIX 4

God Being Misunderstood

Understanding Adam
(The Man Adam Was NOT the Great Transgressor)

Adam was a Prophet—**Matt. 19:3–6; Gen. 2:23–24.**
Adam the son of God—**Luke 3:38.**
Adam was not deceived—**1 Tim. 2:14.**
Adam saw and understood what had happened when his wife came to him in a fallen condition and he was still in the original image and likeness of God.
Adam set the pattern for redemption—**Rom. 5:14.**
God gave witness to the correctness of Adam's choice by fulfilling the same pattern in Emmanuel and by the curse not touching him in a direct way—**Gen. 3:17-19.**
The Lord Jesus fulfilled the pattern that was established in Adam—**Rom. 5:14.**

Jacob Became a Prince With God—Gen. 32:28
(The Difference Between a Purchase and a Theft)

See the end of Appendix 2 about the sale of the Birthright for a bowl of pottage. It was Esau that falsely accused Jacob of stealing the birthright, but God NEVER said it about Jacob

The Scriptural Passage

Notice in **Gen. 25:23**, God Himself prophesied, even before Jacob and Esau were born that "the elder shall serve the younger."

Gen. 25:21 "And Isaac intreated the LORD for his wife, because she was barren: and the LORD was intreated of him, and Rebekah his wife conceived."

Gen. 25:22 "And the children struggled together within her; and she said, If it be so, why am I thus? And she went to enquire of the LORD."

Gen. 25:23 "And the LORD said unto her, Two nations are in thy womb, and two manner of people shall be separated from thy bowels; and the one people shall be stronger than the other people; **and the elder shall serve the younger**."

Gen. 25:24 "And when her days to be delivered were fulfilled, behold, there were twins in her womb."

Gen. 25:25 "And the first came out red, all over like an hairy garment; and they called his name Esau."

Gen. 25:26 "And after that came his brother out, and his hand took hold on Esau's heel; and his name was called Jacob: and Isaac was threescore years old when she bare them."

Gen. 25:27	"And the boys grew: and Esau was a cunning hunter, a man of the field; and Jacob was a plain man, dwelling in tents."
Gen. 25:28	"And Isaac loved Esau, because he did eat of his venison: but Rebekah loved Jacob."
Gen. 25:29	"And Jacob sod pottage: and Esau came from the field, and he was faint."
Gen. 25:30	"And Esau said to Jacob, Feed me, I pray thee, with that same red pottage; for I am faint: therefore was his name called Edom."
Gen. 25:31	"And Jacob said, **Sell me this day thy birthright**."
Gen. 25:32	"And Esau said, Behold, I am at the point to die: and what profit shall this birthright do to me?"
Gen. 25:33	"And Jacob said, **Swear to me this day; and he sware unto him: and he sold his birthright unto Jacob**."
Gen. 25:34	"Then Jacob gave Esau bread and pottage of lentiles; and he did eat and drink, and rose up, and went his way: **thus Esau despised his birthright**."

Esau despised the birthright. He was not forced to sell it against his will, and the blessing is part of the birthright. Therefore, the blessing was SOLD at the **same** time as the rest of the birthright, and God knew that it would be that way before they were even born.

Gen. 26:34 "And Esau was forty years old when he took to wife Judith the daughter of Beeri the Hittite, and Bashemath the daughter of Elon the Hittite."

Gen. 26:35 **"Which were a grief of mind unto Isaac and to Rebekah."**

God allowed Isaac to go blind so that Jacob could retain the blessing portion of the Birthright that he had already legally purchased.

Gen. 27:1 "And it came to pass, that when Isaac was old, **and his eyes were dim, so that he could not see**, he called Esau his eldest son, and said unto him, My son: and he said unto him, Behold, here am I."

Gen. 27:2 "And he said, Behold now, I am old, I know not the day of my death."

Gen. 27:3 "Now therefore take, I pray thee, thy weapons, thy quiver and thy bow, and go out to the field, and take me some venison."

Gen. 27:4 "And make me savoury meat, such as I love, and bring it to me, that I may eat; **that my soul may bless thee before I die**."

Gen. 27:5	"And Rebekah heard when Isaac spake to Esau his son. And Esau went to the field to hunt for venison, and to bring it."
Gen. 27:6	"And Rebekah spake unto Jacob her son, saying, Behold, I heard thy father speak unto Esau thy brother, saying."
Gen. 27:7	"Bring me venison, and make me savoury meat, that I may eat, **and bless thee before the LORD before my death**."
Gen. 27:8	"Now therefore, my son, obey my voice according to that which I command thee."
Gen. 27:9	"Go now to the flock, and fetch me from thence two good kids of the goats; and I will make them savoury meat for thy father, such as he loveth."
Gen. 27:10	"And thou shalt bring it to thy father, that he may eat, and **that he may bless thee before his death**."
Gen. 27:11	"And Jacob said to Rebekah his mother, Behold, Esau my brother is a hairy man, and I am a smooth man."
Gen. 27:12	"My father peradventure will feel me, and I shall seem to him as a

	deceiver; and I shall bring a curse upon me, and not a blessing."
Gen. 27:13	"And his mother said unto him, Upon me be thy curse, my son: only obey my voice, and go fetch me them."
Gen. 27:14	"And he went, and fetched, and brought them to his mother: and his mother made savoury meat, such as his father loved."
Gen. 27:15	"And Rebekah took goodly raiment of her eldest son Esau, which were with her in the house, and put them upon Jacob her younger son."
Gen. 27:16	"And she put the skins of the kids of the goats upon his hands, and upon the smooth of his neck."
Gen. 27:17	"And she gave the savoury meat and the bread, which she had prepared, into the hand of her son Jacob."
Gen. 27:18	"And he came unto his father, and said, My father: and he said, Here am I; who art thou, my son?"
Gen. 27:19	"And Jacob said unto his father, I am Esau thy firstborn; I have done according as thou badest me: arise, I pray thee, sit and eat of my venison, **that thy soul may bless me**."

Gen. 27:20	"And Isaac said unto his son, How is it that thou hast found it so quickly, my son? And he said, Because the LORD thy God brought it to me."
Gen. 27:21	"And Isaac said unto Jacob, Come near, I pray thee, that I may feel thee, my son, whether thou be my very son Esau or not."
Gen. 27:22	"And Jacob went near unto Isaac his father; and he felt him, and said, The voice is Jacob's voice, but the hands are the hands of Esau."
Gen. 27:23	"And he discerned him not, because his hands were hairy, as his brother Esau's hands: **so he blessed him**."
Gen. 27:24	"And he said, Art thou my very son Esau? And he said, I am."
Gen. 27:25	"And he said, Bring it near to me, and I will eat of my son's venison, **that my soul may bless thee**. And he brought it near to him, and he did eat: and he brought him wine, and he drank."
Gen. 27:26	"And his father Isaac said unto him, Come near now, and kiss me, my son."
Gen. 27:27	"And he came near, and kissed him: and he smelled the smell of his raiment, and blessed him, and said,

See, the smell of my son is as the smell of a field which the LORD hath blessed."

Gen. 27:28 **"Therefore God give thee of the dew of heaven, and the fatness of the earth, and plenty of corn and wine."**

Gen. 27:29 **"Let people serve thee, and nations bow down to thee: be lord over thy brethren, and let thy mother's sons bow down to thee: cursed be every one that curseth thee, and blessed be he that blesseth thee."**

Gen. 27:30 "And it came to pass, as soon as Isaac had **made an end of blessing Jacob**, and Jacob was yet scarce gone out from the presence of Isaac his father, that Esau his brother came in from his hunting."

Gen. 27:31 "And he also had made savoury meat, and brought it unto his father, and said unto his father, Let my father arise, and eat of his son's venison, **that thy soul may bless me**."

Gen. 27:32 "And Isaac his father said unto him, Who art thou? And he said, I am thy son, thy firstborn Esau."

Gen. 27:33 "And Isaac trembled very exceedingly, and said, Who? where is he that hath taken venison, and brought it me, and I have eaten of all before thou camest, **and have blessed him? yea, and he shall be blessed**."

Gen. 27:34 "And when Esau heard the words of his father, he cried with a great and exceeding bitter cry, and said unto his father, **Bless me, even me also**, O my father."

Gen. 27:35 "And he said, Thy brother came with subtilty, **and hath taken away thy blessing**."

Gen. 27:36 "And he said, Is not he rightly named Jacob? **for he hath supplanted me these two times: he took away my birthright; and, behold, now he hath taken away my blessing**. And he said, **Hast thou not reserved a blessing for me**?"

Gen. 27:37 "And Isaac answered and said unto Esau, Behold, **I have made him thy lord, and all his brethren have I given to him for servants; and with corn and wine have I sustained him**: and what shall I do now unto thee, my son?"

Gen. 27:38 "And Esau said unto his father, **Hast thou but one blessing, my father? bless me, even me also**, O my father. And Esau lifted up his voice, and wept."

Gen. 27:39 "And Isaac his father answered and said unto him, **Behold, thy dwelling shall be the fatness of the earth, and of the dew of heaven from above.**"

Gen. 27:40 "**And by thy sword shalt thou live, and shalt serve thy brother; and it shall come to pass when thou shalt have the dominion, that thou shalt break his yoke from off thy neck.**"

Gen. 27:41 "**And Esau hated Jacob because of the blessing wherewith his father blessed him**: and Esau said in his heart, The days of mourning for my father are at hand; then will I slay my brother Jacob."

Gen. 27:42 "**And these words of Esau her elder son were told to Rebekah: and she sent and called Jacob her younger son, and said unto him, Behold, thy brother Esau, as touching thee, doth comfort himself, purposing to kill thee.**"

Gen. 27:43 "Now therefore, my son, obey my voice; and arise, **flee thou to Laban my brother** to Haran."

Gen. 27:44 "**And tarry with him a few days, until thy brother's fury turn away.**"

Gen. 27:45 "Until thy brother's anger turn away from thee, and he forget that which thou hast done to him: then I will send, and fetch thee from thence: why should I be deprived also of you both in one day?"

Gen. 27:46 "And Rebekah said to Isaac, **I am weary of my life because of the daughters of Heth**: if Jacob take a wife of the daughters of Heth, such as these which are of the daughters of the land, what good shall my life do me?"

Gen. 28:1 **"And Isaac called Jacob, and blessed him, and charged him, and said unto him, Thou shalt not take a wife of the daughters of Canaan."**

Gen. 28:2 "Arise, go to Padanaram, to the house of Bethuel thy mother's father; and take thee a wife from thence of the daughters of Laban thy mother's brother."

Gen. 28:3 "And God Almighty bless thee, and make thee fruitful, and multiply thee, that thou mayest be a multitude of people."

Gen. 28:4 "And give thee the blessing of Abraham, to thee, and to thy seed with thee; that thou mayest inherit the land wherein thou art a stranger, which God gave unto Abraham."

Gen. 28:5	**"And Isaac sent away Jacob: and he went to Padanaram unto Laban**, son of Bethuel the Syrian, the brother of Rebekah, Jacob's and Esau's mother."
Gen. 28:6	**"When Esau saw that Isaac had blessed Jacob, and sent him away to Padanaram, to take him a wife from thence; and that as he blessed him he gave him a charge, saying, Thou shalt not take a wife of the daughters of Canaan."**
Gen. 28:7	"And that Jacob obeyed his father and his mother, and was gone to Padanaram."
Gen. 28:8	**"And Esau seeing that the daughters of Canaan pleased not Isaac his father."**
Gen. 28:9	**"Then went Esau unto Ishmael, and took unto the wives which he had Mahalath the daughter of Ishmael Abraham's son, the sister of Nebajoth, to be his wife."**
Gen. 28:10	"And Jacob went out from Beersheba, and went toward Haran."
Gen. 29:1	"Then Jacob went on his journey, and came into the land of the people of the east."

Gen. 29:2 "And he looked, and behold a well in the field, and, lo, there were three flocks of sheep lying by it; for out of that well they watered the flocks: and a great stone was upon the well's mouth."

Gen. 29:3 "And thither were all the flocks gathered: and they rolled the stone from the well's mouth, and watered the sheep, and put the stone again upon the well's mouth in his place."

Gen. 29:4 "And Jacob said unto them, My brethren, whence be ye? And they said, Of Haran are we."

Gen. 29:5 "And he said unto them, Know ye Laban the son of Nahor? And they said, We know him."

Gen. 29:6 "And he said unto them, Is he well? And they said, He is well: and, behold, Rachel his daughter cometh with the sheep."

Gen. 29:7 "And he said, Lo, it is yet high day, neither is it time that the cattle should be gathered together: water ye the sheep, and go and feed them."

Gen. 29:8 "And they said, We cannot, until all the flocks be gathered together, and till they roll the stone from the well's mouth; then we water the sheep."

Gen. 29:9	"And while he yet spake with them, Rachel came with her father's sheep: for she kept them."
Gen. 29:10	"And it came to pass, when Jacob saw Rachel the daughter of Laban his mother's brother, and the sheep of Laban his mother's brother, that Jacob went near, and rolled the stone from the well's mouth, and watered the flock of Laban his mother's brother."
Gen. 29:11	"And Jacob kissed Rachel, and lifted up his voice, and wept."
Gen. 29:12	"And Jacob told Rachel that he was her father's brother, and that he was Rebekah's son: and she ran and told her father."
Gen. 29:13	"And it came to pass, when Laban heard the tidings of Jacob his sister's son, that he ran to meet him, and embraced him, and kissed him, and brought him to his house. And he told Laban all these things."
Gen. 29:14	"And Laban said to him, Surely thou art my bone and my flesh. And he abode with him the space of a month."
Gen. 29:15	"And Laban said unto Jacob, Because thou art my brother, shouldest thou

                    therefore serve me for nought? tell me, what shall thy wages be?"

Gen. 29:16   "And Laban had two daughters: the name of the elder was Leah, and the name of the younger was Rachel."

Gen. 29:17   "Leah was tender eyed; but Rachel was beautiful and well favoured."

Gen. 29:18   "And Jacob loved Rachel; and said, I will serve thee seven years for Rachel thy younger daughter."

Gen. 29:19   "And Laban said, It is better that I give her to thee, than that I should give her to another man: abide with me."

Gen. 29:20   "And Jacob served seven years for Rachel; and they seemed unto him but a few days, for the love he had to her."

Respecting the Election of God
(Honoring Ministerial Gifts According to God's Expectations)

Amos 3:7   "Surely the Lord GOD will do nothing, but he revealeth his **secret** unto his **servants** the **prophets**."

Notice the "secret" is singular but "servants" and "prophets" are plural. God has a plan for salvation, the details of which He reveals to His servants the prophets. There is not just one prophet that receives the complete revelation, but various prophets, each of which receive a portion of the revelation according to the divine election of God. The plan of God is so great that no single prophet can contain it all (except the Lord Jesus, Emmanuel). Because of this, God carefully prepares His prophets and molds their character until He can use them to reveal the portion of His plan that He created them for. This means two things.

First, in order to understand the plan of God more completely, they will have to be humble enough to listen to each other.

Second, even though others may vainly imagine that because of their education or eloquence they are able to present the revelation better than the one that God chose to reveal it to, just because they imagine it does NOT mean that it is true. But God created, molded, and chose the vessel that He did for His own purposes, and though man may try, he cannot improve upon God's purposes.

A prime example of this is John the Baptist. He came out of the desert, dressed in a way that could hardly be considered as appropriate for the forerunner of The King of kings and The Lord of lords. But he was the vessel that God prepared for that purpose, and no one else could fulfill that purpose in the way that God wanted it to be done.

Jer. 23:30   "Therefore, behold, I am **against** the prophets, saith the LORD, that **steal** my words every one from his neighbour."

When God reveals a part of His plan to a prophet, there are many details surrounding the central theme of the revelation that accompany it. The revelation is not complete without taking these details into consideration. Many times, when the revelation is being presented to others, a key phrase may be used to symbolize the revelation. An example of this could be "a virgin will give birth to a son." However, there are many other details that surround this key phrase that are necessary to more fully understand the true significance of the revelation. Such as his name will be called Wonderful, Counselor, The Mighty God, The Everlasting Father, The Prince of Peace. These details must accompany the key phrase in order to understand what God is saying.

If some other prophet uses the key phrase in relation with the revelation that God has given to him, and even if that connection is completely correct but the connection does not in some way include the other necessary details, then confusion or even error can come in. There are two ways that this connection can be made.

The first is a way that does not show as much respect to the divine election of God in creating and using the prophet that He gave the revelation to. This is if the second prophet begins to expound upon "the virgin that will conceive" as though he is the one that God gave the revelation to.

The second way gives fuller reverence and respect to God's election, and that is if the second prophet says, "the prophet Isaiah said."

Then if the listener asks about it, the second prophet replies with, "Go ask Isaiah, he's the one that God gave the revelation to, and no one else can explain it quite like he can."

This is the basis of why we give scriptural references as we are speaking, because it provides the opportunity for the listener to go back to the source (original vessel chosen by God to give the revelation) of the reference that we are using, and thereby get a fuller idea of what God is talking about. Doing this also shows reverence and respect to God's election, demonstrates humility because of our not presenting it as something given directly to ourselves, and shows that we know the true source of supernatural faith as found in the following scripture.

> **Rom. 10:17** "So then **faith** cometh by hearing, and hearing by the **word** of God."

When prophets make reference to the revelations that were given to other prophets and neglect to inform people of where they got that information from, they are failing to respect God's election. But God wants us to not only recognize **when** He speaks and the **fullness** of meaning of what he said, but also to respect the **vessel** that He chose to speak through.

1 Chr. 16:22	"Saying, **Touch not** mine anointed, and do my prophets no **harm**."
Acts 3:22	"For Moses truly said unto the fathers, A prophet shall the Lord your God raise up unto you of your brethren, like unto me; him shall ye **hear in all things** whatsoever he shall say unto you."
Matt. 10:41	"He that **receiveth** a prophet in the name of a prophet shall receive a prophet's **reward**; and he that **receiveth** a righteous man in the name of a righteous man shall receive a righteous man's **reward**."

Some may question that by neglecting to make reference to a prophet that any harm comes to that prophet. Consider the following scripture:

1 Cor. 9:14	"Even so hath the Lord **ordained** that they which preach the gospel should **live** of the gospel."

It is part of God's plan for the ministers that serve Him, that they should also be sustained by His provision. The provision that God has provided for His ministers is that of tithes and offerings. It was customary in ancient times that whenever someone came to inquire the word of the Lord from a prophet (seer) that they would bring a gift (**1 Sam. 9:7-10**; **2 Kings 8:8–9**). This was in recognition of the very practical fact that the prophets also must eat and that they also have a right to have a family and home and that they have a charge from God to constantly labor in the Word of God.

Because of respecting this reality, the people were blessed. When one prophet neglects to tell where he received prophetic words from (other than when it was directly revealed to himself from God), then he is denying sustenance to the other prophet and, as such, is doing him harm in a very real way. This is because people will not know who to go to in order to receive the surrounding details from the vessel that God chose to reveal it through. It is because of this that God said:

Jer. 23:30 "Therefore, behold, I am **against** the prophets, saith the LORD, that **steal** my words every one from his neighbour."

Stealing the word of God from the mouth of another prophet, therefore, is neglecting to give reference to the person that they received that portion of their revelation from. And because it does harm in very real ways both to the first prophet and also to the people, God is against those that do such. If the prophets (and other ministers) want a greater blessing from the Lord upon their ministries and entire lives, then they need to become faithful to show respect to the vessels that God chooses to reveal His Word to. This need is every bit as necessary as the need for people to give their tithes and offerings, because they are intimately connected.

However, this concept has several more aspects than the one already mentioned and also a comprehensive view that takes all of these aspects into account. As stated in the beginning of this appendix article, the prophets must listen to each other in order to get the fuller picture of what God is doing. This requires that they be willing to humble themselves first before God and, second, with each other. If this is done, then the scripture can be fulfilled that says:

Prov. 27:17 "Iron sharpeneth iron; so a man **sharpeneth** the countenance of his **friend**."

And the exactness of the word of God through the prophets together with its application for the day and season that we are living in can be refined. Please note that this refining must always remain true to every jot and tittle of the word of God that has already been revealed until that time. Even if a group of prophets come to an agreement, if any detail of that agreement does not conform to the word of God that has already been given, then at the very least, **that detail** must be either discarded or changed until it **does** come into complete agreement with the Word (**2 Pet. 1:20**).

By the prophets listening to what God is revealing through other prophets and by them being humble before God, they begin to put on display the attributes that God wants them to exemplify to the other ministries. Those attributes are a demonstration in living reality of how God can knit their ministries together to work in harmony with each other to bring the delivering power of God's truth to the body of Christ.

John 8:32	"And ye shall know the **truth**, and the **truth** shall make you **free**."
John 14:6	"Jesus saith unto him, **I am** the way, the **truth**, and the life: no man cometh unto the Father, but by me."
Rom. 16:25	"Now to him that is of power to stablish you according to my gospel, and the **preaching of Jesus Christ**, according to the revelation of the mystery, which was kept secret since the world began."
Eph. 4:11-12	"And he gave some, apostles; and some, prophets; and some, evangelists; and some, pastors and teachers; For the perfecting of the saints, for **the work of the ministry**, for the **edifying of the body** of Christ."

It must be recognized that each one of these ministries are also members of the same body that they are called to edify. Even though this statement may seem to be obvious, there are implications that are not as recognized when it comes to its practical application. In the same manner that the whole body of Christ needs to hear each one of these five types of ministry, this need also exists, even among the ministries themselves. It is no mere coincidence that there are five basic food groups of natural food, and there are five types of ministries that prepare spiritual food to be served in the house of God.

> **Eph. 4:11** "And he gave some, **apostles**; and some, **prophets**; and some, **evangelists**; and some, **pastors** and **teachers**."

The preaching ministries are not all (only) pastors. Even though it is possible for a pastor, apostle, evangelist, or teacher to have a **gift** of prophecy, there is a great difference between the **gift** of prophecy and the prophetic **ministry**. In the same manner, even though prophets, evangelists, pastors, and teachers may have great organizational skills, there is a great difference between being able to organize programs, and the ministry of an apostle which is called of God to harmonize and coordinate the interactions of ministers for the benefit of the entire body of Christ and to align them with the vision that God gives to the prophets. It is ONLY through this alignment with the prophetic vision (which comes through the Prophets) that they will know how to be prepared for things that will shortly come to pass.

> **Mal. 3:6** "For I am the LORD, **I change not**; therefore ye sons of Jacob are not consumed."
>
> **Mal. 3:7** "Even from the days of your fathers ye are gone away from mine ordinances, and have not kept them.

Return unto me, and I will return unto you, saith the LORD of hosts. But ye said, Wherein shall we return?"

Mal. 3:8 "Will a man rob God? Yet ye have robbed me. But ye say, Wherein have we robbed thee? In tithes and offerings."

Mal. 3:9 "Ye are cursed with a curse: for ye have robbed me, even this whole nation."

Mal. 3:10 "Bring ye **all the tithes** into the storehouse, **that there may be meat in mine house**, and prove me now herewith, saith the LORD of hosts, if I will not open you the windows of heaven, and pour you out a blessing, that there shall not be room enough to receive it."

Mal. 3:11 "And I will rebuke the devourer for your sakes, and he shall not destroy the fruits of your ground; neither shall your vine cast her fruit before the time in the field, saith the LORD of hosts."

Mal. 3:12 "And all nations shall call you blessed: for ye shall be a delightsome land, saith the LORD of hosts."

Just as our bodies need a balanced diet to be healthy, so also the body of Christ needs a balanced diet of spiritual food in order to be healthy. Just because there are different food groups, all of the food groups combine together to make a single meal. Part of Satan's plan to destroy (bring sickness and death) the body of Christ is to eliminate as many of the different ministries as he can or to keep them as separated as possible. By doing this, he can bring on sickness, decay, and death in the body.

For many hundreds of years, the recognition of the need for the entirety of the ministries has been eroded. This is one of the major reasons why the body of Christ as a whole has not been more victorious. This diabolical plan takes two primary forms as it relates to the function of the ministries together as a whole. The first is to try to remove as many of them as possible, and the second is to keep them separated. The enemy has ingeniously woven both of these forms together and combined it together with the love of money.

1 Tim. 6:10 "For the **love** of money is the root of all evil: while some coveted after, they have erred from the faith, and pierced themselves through with many sorrows."

Notice that the only vessels that God uses to provide spiritual food in His house are not just only pastors, but there are five types of ministries that God wants to work together in harmony for His service. Just as with natural food, the body of Christ needs a balanced diet. If all five types of food are eaten, then the body will be full of vigor and able to fulfill the work that is required of it. If any one of the food groups is neglected, then sooner or later weakness, sickness, and even death will come. If more than one of the food groups are neglected, then the results will come more quickly and be more severe.

For all too long, the ministries of the prophets and apostles have been considered as no longer being needed or even existing. Satanic influence has tried to take the teaching ministry, rename it with the title of theologian, and set it up to take the place of prophets. But God did not promise to reveal His secret to theologians (or teachers, **except through** the vision that God imparts through the prophets). He promised to reveal it to prophets. In the same manner, the enemy has tried to take the ministry of pastors and rename it with the title of archbishop or cardinal and set it to take the place of apostles and deny the true operation of the ministry of the apostles, all at the same time as claiming to be an "apostolic" church.

This is the subtle way that these ministries (apostles and prophets) have been removed from functioning in the body of Christ. However, even though these ministries are being restored back to their rightful operation, the enemy is still nullifying the majority of the benefit that they can have for the body by keeping the ministries separated.

Today, we have apostles that are **pastoring** their own churches, prophets **pastoring** their own churches, evangelists and teachers **pastoring** their own churches **separately** and in a way that God never intended. While there is nothing wrong with each of these ministries being the senior minister in their own church, this is almost exclusively done without the recognition that God wants **all** of these ministries to be in operation in **each** local congregation.

This is so that every local congregation can have a properly balanced spiritual diet and so that they can be the spiritual powerhouses that God intends for them to be.

The key to understanding this is found in:

> **Mal. 3:10** "Bring ye **all the tithes** into the storehouse, **that there may be meat in mine house**, and prove me now herewith, saith the LORD of hosts, if I will not open you the windows of heaven, and pour you out a blessing, that there shall not be room enough to receive it."

In this, we can see that the purpose of the tithes is specifically to provide for the sustenance of the ministries, all five types of them working **together** in **harmony** and **not** competing against each other.

If, therefore, the entirety of the tithes of the local congregation is consumed by only one type of these ministries, and an **equitable** distribution is not made to the others, then that ministry has failed to recognize the harmonious functioning that God desires there to be of all of these ministries working together and has failed to provide the necessary balanced spiritual diet for the local body to have the fullness of spiritual health. Any local congregation that has even fifty faithful tithe-giving members is capable of supporting a fully functioning five-fold ministerial staff and for those ministers to each live at the same average standard of living as the congregation.

How can this "equitable" distribution be scripturally proven?

First, consider that four of the five ministries that God has ordained are largely travelling ministries, namely apostles, prophets, evangelists, and teachers, and then by comparing this detail to the following scripture.

Deut. 18:6	"And if a Levite come from any of thy gates out of all Israel, where he sojourned, and come with all the desire of his mind unto the place which the LORD shall choose."
Deut. 18:7	"Then he shall minister in the name of the LORD his God, as all his brethren the Levites do, which stand there before the LORD."
Deut. 18:8	"They shall have **like portions** to eat, beside that which cometh of the sale of his patrimony."

The entire process for implementing these things in the body of Christ begins with the prophets humbling themselves before God and respecting God's election in whom He chooses to reveal specific attributes of His secret to; and then working together harmoniously so that God can display the power of His truth in action. As the apostles begin to catch the vision from the prophets, they will begin to coordinate the efforts of the body to put God's plan into effect but, once again, through humbling themselves before God. As all of this begins to be made manifest—the will of God will be done in earth as it is in heaven. The results of this will be:

Eph. 4:12 "For the **perfecting** of the saints, for the **work** of the ministry, for the **edifying** of the body of Christ."

Eph. 4:13 "Till we all come in the **unity** of the faith, and of the **knowledge** of the Son of God, unto a perfect man, unto the **measure** of the stature of the **fulness** of Christ."

Eph. 4:14 "That we henceforth be no more children, tossed to and fro, and carried about with every wind of doctrine, by the sleight of men, and cunning craftiness, whereby they lie in wait to deceive."

Eph. 4:15 "But **speaking** the truth in love, may **grow** up into him in all things, which is the head, even Christ."

Eph. 4:16 "From whom the whole body fitly joined together and compacted by that which every joint **supplieth**, according to the **effectual working** in the measure of every part, **maketh**

increase of the body unto the **edifying** of itself **in love**."

Also notice that in **Eph. 4:12,** the scriptures say "for the work of the ministry" and that the word *ministry* is used in the singular tense and NOT in the plural. In order for the ministry of the Lamb to be completely expressed to the Wife of the Lamb, **all five** spiritual food groups are **required**.

APPENDIX 5

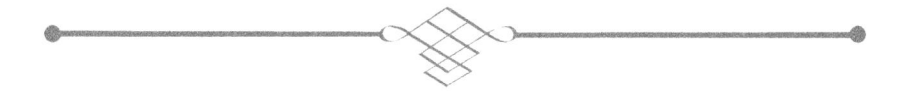

The Son of Man

In order to fully understand what the biblical term of "Son of Man" means, it is necessary to understand some other foundational truths about God, Adam, and the original plan that God had for them. You might say…Adam-them?

Gen. 5:1 "This is the book of the generations of Adam. In the day that God created man, in the likeness of God made he him."

Gen. 5:2 "Male and female created he **them**; and blessed **them**, and called **their** name Adam, in the day when **they** were created."

It should not be a great surprise, after all:

Gen. 1:26 "And God said, Let **us** make man in **our** image, after **our** likeness: and let **them** have dominion over the fish of the sea, and over the fowl of the air, and over the cattle, and over all the earth, and over every creeping thing that creepeth upon the earth."

Gen. 1:27 "So God created man in his own image, in the image of God created he him; male **and** female created he **them**."

And God proved that He is:

Rev. 22:13 "I am **Alpha** and **Omega**, the **beginning** and the **end**, the **first** and the **last**."

When the SAME **one** that spoke together in the beginning (**Gen. 1:26–27**) also spoke together in the end (**Rev. 22:17**).

Rev. 22:17 "And **the Spirit and the bride say, Come**. And let him that heareth say, Come. And let him that is athirst come. And whosoever will, let him take the water of life freely."

This SAME concept is mentioned various times throughout the scriptures.

Matt. 19:3 "The Pharisees also came unto him, tempting him, and saying unto him, Is it lawful for a man to put away his wife for every cause?"

Matt. 19:4 "And he answered and said unto them, Have ye not read, that **he which made them at the beginning** made them male and female."

Matt. 19:5 "**And said, For this cause shall a man leave father and mother, and**

	shall cleave to his wife: and they twain shall be one flesh?"
Matt. 19:6	"Wherefore they are no more twain, but one flesh. What therefore God hath joined together, let not man put asunder."
Matt. 19:7	"They say unto him, Why did Moses then command to give a writing of divorcement, and to put her away?"
Matt. 19:8	"He saith unto them, Moses because of the hardness of your hearts suffered you to put away your wives: **but from the beginning it was not so**."
Gen. 2:23	"**And Adam said**, This is now bone of my bones, and flesh of my flesh: she shall be called Woman, because she was taken out of Man."
Gen. 2:24	**"Therefore shall a man leave his father and his mother, and shall cleave unto his wife: and they shall be one flesh."**

The Lord Jesus said that it was God who spoke the words of **Matt. 19:5**, but the first time that they were spoken, they came out of the mouth of Adam. All of these scriptures together help us to understand:

1) Who and what God is;
2) Who and what Adam was;
3) What the original plan of God was for them;

4) What the original was that established the pattern for "the Son of Man."

A few more details to help complete the picture:
In the beginning, God established the law of reproduction.

Gen. 1:11 "And God said, Let the earth bring forth grass, the herb yielding seed, and the fruit tree yielding fruit **after his kind**, whose seed is in itself, upon the earth: and it was so."

Gen. 1:12 "And the earth brought forth grass, and herb yielding seed **after his kind**, and the tree yielding fruit, whose seed was in itself, **after his kind**: and God saw that it was good."

Gen. 1:20 "And God said, Let the waters bring forth abundantly the moving creature that hath life, and fowl that may fly above the earth in the open firmament of heaven."

Gen. 1:21 "And God created great whales, and every living creature that moveth, which the waters brought forth abundantly, **after their kind**, and every winged fowl **after his kind**: and God saw that it was good."

Gen. 1:24 "And God said, Let the earth bring forth the living creature after his kind, cattle, and creeping thing, and beast of the earth after his kind: and it was so."

> **Gen. 1:25** "And God made the beast of the earth **after his kind**, and cattle **after their kind**, and every thing that creepeth upon the earth **after his kind**: and God saw that it was good."

Eight times in Genesis chapter 1, we see the term "after his/their kind" repeated. However, it should also be noted that each kind of life ALSO had a distinct MANNER to bring forth.

When it came time for God to bring forth after HIS kind **and** manner, He spoke the creative Word, and Adam (male and female) was created.

Therefore, the original **manner** that God had for Adam to bring forth in the beginning was by the spoken creative Word. That commandment was given in:

> **Gen. 1:28** "And God blessed **them**, and God said unto **them, Be fruitful, and multiply**, and replenish the earth, and subdue it: and have dominion over the fish of the sea, and over the fowl of the air, and over every living thing that moveth upon the earth."

But there was ALSO given a further detail about HOW to multiply that many people overlook.

> **Gen. 3:2** "And the woman said unto the serpent, We may eat of the fruit of the trees of the garden."

> **Gen. 3:3** "But of the fruit of the tree which is in the midst of the garden, God hath said, Ye shall not eat of it, **neither shall ye touch it**, lest ye die."

The Hebrew word for "touch" in **verse 3** is *nawgah,* and in this verse, it literally means "to lie with a woman" as in to have sexual relations. How were they to "be fruitful and multiple" without "touching to have sexual relations?" It is ONLY possible if the "being fruitful and multiplying" is done by the spoken creative Word.

It should be noted that at the moment that the **Gen. 1:28** commandment was given, man was still only in the form of a spirit, and only later was that spirit put into flesh (**Gen. 2:7**). This is the VERY way that the Second Adam came into the world—without a sexual touch. If the fall had never happened, then EVERY person that would have been born into the world would have been born of a virgin with ALL of the purity, character, and nature (sinlessness) that was in the Lord Jesus Christ.

Even though "being fruitful and multiplying" by sex was NOT in the original plan of God, Adam—while he was still in the image and likeness of God and when he saw the fallen condition of his wife as she came to him after being defiled by the serpent—chose to accept her back to himself, and he consecrated the secondary way of multiplying as being "honorable" and "undefiled" (**Heb. 13:4**) as long as it is ONLY done in the holy state of matrimony.

This same thing was mentioned by the Lord Jesus Christ in:

Matt. 19:7	"They say unto him, Why did Moses then command to give a writing of divorcement, and to put her away?"
Matt. 19:8	"He saith unto them, Moses because of the hardness of your hearts suffered you to put away your wives: **but from the beginning it was not so.**"

However, in the end, when all things are restored back to how it was in the beginning, that secondary way will be done away with, because everything will be restored to the perfect original condition, will, and purpose that God intended.

We can also see that the First Adam set the pattern that the Second Adam fulfilled.

>**Rom. 5:14** "Nevertheless death reigned from Adam to Moses, even over them that had not sinned after the similitude of Adam's transgression, **who is the figure of him that was to come**."

We KNOW that the Second Adam did not transgress. How was it that the First Adam transgressed and STILL was the FIGURE of the Second Adam?

Simple, we only have to remember **Gen. 5:2**.

>**Gen. 5:2** "Male and female created he them; and blessed them, **and called their name Adam**, in the day when they were created."

It was not the Lord Jesus that was in the fallen condition, it was US (as Bride). Just as the scripture also says about the First Adam and his wife:

>**1 Tim. 2:14** "And Adam was **not deceived**, but the woman **being deceived** was in the transgression."

Therefore, the First Adam (the man) is NOT the part that fell; it was the female part of Adam that fell, and the First Adam did the same for his wife that the Second Adam did for us—he willingly surrendered himself to death in order to stand in the gap between a Holy God and his fallen wife.

>**Rom. 8:19** "For the earnest expectation of the creature waiteth for the manifestation of the sons of God."

Rom. 8:20	**"For the creature was made subject to vanity, not willingly, but by reason of him who hath subjected the same in hope**."
Rom. 8:21	"Because the creature itself also shall be delivered from the bondage of corruption into the glorious liberty of the children of God."

It was the First Adam that subjected the creation to vanity, but what was the hope that he had? That hope was that God would send a redeemer to redeem the fallen condition of his wife, himself, and of the entirety of the fallen creation in the earth. That hope that the First Adam had was not just something superficial; it was based upon the prophetic vision that he had because of his being a prophet, just as the Second Adam was also a prophet, and much more than just one of the prophets—the Second Adam was the very God of the prophets made manifest in flesh, Immanuel.

From all of this, we can see that the term of "Son of Man," when it is used as a title, is referring to something FAR greater than only "prophet." It is referring to the COMPLETE image and likeness of God (BOTH male **and** female).

The tendency that many people have is to focus on ONLY the male part of the Son of Man, BUT for the "Son of Man" to be **fully** manifested, the female portion must ALSO be made manifest in a fully restored condition, because ONLY through **that** manifestation can it be proven that He did, in fact, have the power to redeem **and** restore.

Why is all of this talk about "Son of Man" so important? It is important because of the words that the Lord Jesus Christ spoke about it.

Matt. 10:23	"But when they persecute you in this city, flee ye into another: for verily I say unto you, Ye shall not have gone

over the cities of Israel, till the **Son of man** be come."

Matt. 16:27 "For the **Son of man** shall come in the glory of his Father with his angels; and then he shall reward every man according to his works."

Matt. 19:28 "And Jesus said unto them, Verily I say unto you, That ye which have followed me, in the regeneration when the **Son of man** shall sit in the throne of his glory, ye also shall sit upon twelve thrones, judging the twelve tribes of Israel."

Matt. 24:27 "For as the lightning cometh out of the east, and shineth even unto the west; so shall also the coming of the **Son of man** be."

Matt. 24:30 "And then shall appear the sign of the **Son of man** in heaven: and then shall all the tribes of the earth mourn, and they shall see the **Son of man** coming in the clouds of heaven with power and great glory."

Matt. 24:37 "But as the days of Noe were, so shall also the coming of the **Son of man** be."

Matt. 24:39 "And knew not until the flood came, and took them all away; so shall also the coming of the **Son of man** be."

Matt. 24:44	"Therefore be ye also ready: for in such an hour as ye think not the **Son of man** cometh."
Matt. 25:13	"Watch therefore, for ye know neither the day nor the hour wherein the **Son of man** cometh."
Matt. 25:31	"When the **Son of man** shall come in his glory, and all the holy angels with him, then shall he sit upon the throne of his glory."
Matt. 26:64	"Jesus saith unto him, Thou hast said: nevertheless I say unto you, Hereafter shall ye see the **Son of man** sitting on the right hand of power, and coming in the clouds of heaven."
Mark 8:38	"Whosoever therefore shall be ashamed of me and of my words in this adulterous and sinful generation; of him also shall the **Son of man** be ashamed, when he cometh in the glory of his Father with the holy angels."
Mark 10:45	"For even the **Son of man** came not to be ministered unto, but to minister, and to give his life a ransom for many."
Mark 13:26	"And then shall they see the **Son of man** coming in the clouds with great power and glory."

Mark 13:34   "For the **Son of man** is as a man taking a far journey, who left his house, and gave authority to his servants, and to every man his work, and commanded the porter to watch."

Mark 14:62   "And Jesus said, I am: and ye shall see the **Son of man** sitting on the right hand of power, and coming in the clouds of heaven."

Luke 6:22   "Blessed are ye, when men shall hate you, and when they shall separate you from their company, and shall reproach you, and cast out your name as evil, for the **Son of man**'s sake."

Luke 9:26   "For whosoever shall be ashamed of me and of my words, of him shall the **Son of man** be ashamed, when he shall come in his own glory, and in his Father's, and of the holy angels."

Luke 12:8   "Also I say unto you, Whosoever shall confess me before men, him shall the **Son of man** also confess before the angels of God."

Luke 12:10   "And whosoever shall speak a word against the **Son of man**, it shall be forgiven him: but unto him that blasphemeth against the Holy Ghost it shall not be forgiven."

Luke 12:40	"Be ye therefore ready also: for the **Son of man** cometh at an hour when ye think not."
Luke 17:22	"And he said unto the disciples, The days will come, when ye shall desire to see one of the days of the **Son of man**, and ye shall not see it."
Luke 17:24	"For as the lightning, that lighteneth out of the one part under heaven, shineth unto the other part under heaven; so shall also the **Son of man** be in his day."
Luke 17:26	"And as it was in the days of Noe, so shall it be also in the days of the **Son of man**."
Luke 17:30	"Even thus shall it be in the day when the **Son of man** is revealed."
Luke 18:8	"I tell you that he will avenge them speedily. Nevertheless when the **Son of man** cometh, shall he find faith on the earth?"
Luke 21:27	"And then shall they see the **Son of man** coming in a cloud with power and great glory."
Luke 21:36	"Watch ye therefore, and pray always, that ye may be accounted worthy to escape all these things that shall come to pass, and to stand before the **Son of man**."

Luke 22:69	"Hereafter shall the **Son of man** sit on the right hand of the power of God."
John 1:51	"And he saith unto him, Verily, verily, I say unto you, Hereafter ye shall see heaven open, and the angels of God ascending and descending upon the **Son of man**."

In the following verse, we find an interesting detail:

John 3:13	"And no man hath ascended up to heaven, but he that came down from heaven, even the **Son of man** which **is in heaven**."

He spoke present tense about the Son of man (Himself) which **IS** in heaven. This shows us an important detail: the Lord Jesus Christ was/is the dwelling place of God. Even though He was on the earth, He was STILL in heaven, because God was dwelling in Him; and wherever God is, there is heaven also. It is in this manner that even though **we** are still on the earth, we **can** be seated together with Him **in heavenly places**.

Eph. 1:3	"Blessed be the God and Father of our Lord Jesus Christ, who hath blessed us with all spiritual blessings **in heavenly places** in Christ."
Eph. 2:6	"And hath raised us up together, and made us sit together **in heavenly places** in Christ Jesus."
Eph. 3:10	"To the intent that now unto the principalities and powers **in heav-**

enly places might be known by the church the manifold wisdom of God."

This is a great mystery that ONLY the ones who have made their hearts to be His throne can know and understand. However, it is a requirement in order to fulfill the portion of the Lord's prayer for His will to be done **in earth** as it is in heaven, because when our hearts have become His throne and He is seated on His throne, heaven has come down into earth, the earth of our bodies as His temples.

John 3:14	"And as Moses lifted up the serpent in the wilderness, even so must the **Son of man** be lifted up."
John 5:27	"And hath given him authority to execute judgment also, because he is the **Son of man**."
John 6:27	"Labour not for the meat which perisheth, but for that meat which endureth unto everlasting life, which the **Son of man** shall give unto you: for him hath God the Father sealed."
John 6:53	"Then Jesus said unto them, Verily, verily, I say unto you, Except ye eat the flesh of the **Son of man**, and drink his blood, ye have no life in you."
John 6:62	"What and if ye shall see the **Son of man** ascend up where he was before?"

John 12:23	And Jesus answered them, saying, The hour is come, that the **Son of man** should be glorified."
John 12:34	"The people answered him, We have heard out of the law that Christ abideth for ever: and how sayest thou, The **Son of man** must be lifted up? who is this **Son of man**?"
John 13:31	"Therefore, when he was gone out, Jesus said, Now is the **Son of man** glorified, and God is glorified in him."

Therefore, in order to understand Bible prophecy and the necessary preparation for the coming of the Lord, it is necessary to understand about "the Son of man," because it is a key to understanding the purposes of God.

In the Old Testament, the term "Son of man:"

Is used 197 times in the KJV Bible.
Is used 108 times in the Old Testament.
Is used 15 times in the OT outside of the book of Ezekiel.
Is used 93 times in the book of Ezekiel.
Is used at least 20 times as a **title**. Indicated in the KJV with an upper case "S" in the word *Son* (**Eze. 2:1,3, 3:1,3,4,10, 4:16, 8:5,6,8,12, 11:2, 23:36, 37:3,11, 40:4, 43:7,18, 44:5, 47:6**).
Is used 32 times as a **description**. Indicated in the KJV with a lower case "s" in the word *son* (**Eze. 2:6, 2:8, 3:25, 4:1, 5:1, 7:2, 8:15, 8:17, 11:4, 12:3, 13:17, 20:4, 20:27, 21:6, 21:12, 21:14, 21:19, 21:28, 22:2, 24:25, 27:2, 33:7, 33:10, 33:12, 33:30, 36:1, 37:9, 37:16, 38:14, 39:1, 39:17, 43:10**).

Is used 41 times at the beginning of a sentence. Since the first letter in every sentence is upper case, it is impossible to use the above standard to identify the usage, **except** through the context.

In the New Testament the term "Son of man:"

Is used 89 times in 85 verses.
Is used four times outside of the "Gospels."
Is used only once in the New Testament in **Heb. 2:6** as a description.
Is always used as a title by the Lord Jesus when referring to Himself.

Therefore, the New Testament use of the term "Son of man" is the parallel of the Old Testament Book of Ezekiel's use of the term "Son of man" **as a title**.

From this, we can conclude that the New Testament Greek "*hweeos Anthropos*" is the same as the Old Testament Hebrew "*ben Adam*" when it is used **as a title** and is a reference to the promised Son (**Gen. 1:28**, **3:15,21**) that was to come without a sexual touch (**Gen. 3:3**) to be the Kinsman Redeemer (the faith anchor of Adam's hope, **Rom. 8:20**) that was to restore all of the faith seed of God back to the original relationship and condition that was in the beginning before the fall (the Lamb slain from the foundation of the world, **Rev. 13:8**).

From this, we can also see that the male part of the image and likeness of God was manifested in the Second Adam when He came to redeem His people (**Matt. 1:21**), and the female part of the image and likeness of God is made manifest in the female part of the Second Adam (**Eph. 5:25–27**) as He mentioned in **Matt. 5:17–19** when He makes a people to be kings and priests (**Rev. 1:6, 5:10**).

As such, the manifestation of the Son of man in the end times is the same as the manifestation of the Sons of God (**John 1:12**; **Rom. 8:14,19**; **Gal. 4:6**; **Php. 2:15**; **Heb. 12:7**; **1 John 3:1–2**), and it happens in a people that as a Bride that is able to become the Wife of the Lamb (**Rev. 19:7–9**) and become one **in** Him.

This sets an entirely different paradigm for the interpretation of end-time prophecy and the fulfillment of the Word that has been spoken. It speaks about a people that humble themselves so completely to God that He is the one that fulfills His Word in them by the power of His life that lives in them to put Him on display so that the works that He did, we will do also.

> **John 14:12** "Verily, verily, I say unto you, He that believeth on me, **the works that I do shall he do also**; and greater works than these shall he do; because I go unto my Father."

APPENDIX 6

Understanding the Timepiece of God

There are many people that believe that Israel is the timepiece of God, and rightly so. However, just as with a clock, if you don't know how to read the hands of the clock, then you still do not know what time it is. The timepiece of God is presented in **Numbers chapter 2**. When the camping order was established, the principal tribes that were placed on each side of the tabernacle are as follows:

On the **East** side: **Judah, Num. 2:3**, Banner: Lion, **Gen. 49:9.**
On the **South** side: **Reuben, Num. 2:10**, Banner: Ox (as strength), **Gen. 49:3.**
In the **midst** of the camp around the Tabernacle: Levi, **Num. 1:47, 2:17,33, 3:12,41,45, 8:14,18, 18:23–26; Deut. 18:1.**
On the **West** side: **Ephraim, Num. 2:18**, Banner: Man, **Gen.**
On the **North** side: **Dan, Num. 2:25**, Banner: Serpent, **Gen. 49:16–17.**

These principal tribes in their camping order are effectively the hands on the clock or timepiece of God. When the camping order was established, God placed them in order **beginning** on the **East** side of the Tabernacle and then proceeded in a **clockwise** direction to **end** up on the **North** side.

The **East** is the **beginning** of the procession of the timepiece of God, and the **North** is the **end** of the procession. **North**, therefore, is symbolic of the **end times**. In Bible prophecy, if the term "end times" is inserted in the place of the word "**north**," the prophecy reads almost like reading the headlines in today's newspapers. This is a key to understanding the time and season in which we are living and in identifying that we are indeed living in the "end times" (**north**). The tribe of Judah on the East was the beginning of the timepiece marking time with the Lion of the Tribe of Judah, the Lamb of God (**Rev. 5:5–6**), beginning the procession.

The set order of camping is when the beginning of the timepiece was established. Now to consider the end of the timepiece which is revealed, primarily, in **Revelations chapter 7**.

Rev. 7:3   Saying, Hurt not the earth, neither the sea, nor the trees, till we have **sealed** the servants of our God in their foreheads.

Rev. 7:4   "And I heard the number of them which were **sealed**: and there were **sealed** an hundred and forty and four thousand of all the tribes of the children of Israel."

Rev. 7:5   "Of the tribe of **Juda** were **sealed** twelve thousand. Of the tribe of **Reuben** were sealed twelve thousand. Of the tribe of **Gad** were **sealed** twelve thousand."

Rev. 7:6   "Of the tribe of **Aser** were **sealed** twelve thousand. Of the tribe of **Nepthalim** were **sealed** twelve thousand. Of the tribe of **Manasses** were **sealed** twelve thousand."

Rev. 7:7   "Of the tribe of **Simeon** were **sealed** twelve thousand. Of the tribe of

	Levi were **sealed** twelve thousand. Of the tribe of **Issachar** were sealed twelve thousand."
Rev. 7:8	"Of the tribe of **Zabulon** were sealed twelve thousand. Of the tribe of **Joseph** were **sealed** twelve thousand. Of the tribe of **Benjamin** were **sealed** twelve thousand."

When comparing **Numbers chapter 2** with **Revelations chapter 7,** many people have noted some differences. First is that the tribes of Dan and Ephraim are not mentioned in **Revelations chapter 7**. However, each of them are not mentioned for two entirely different reasons.

Num. 2;	**Rev 7**
Dan	*missing*
Judah	Juda
Reuben	Ruben
Gad	Gad
Asher	Aser
Naphtali	Nepthalim
Manasseh	Manasses (**Joseph**)
Simeon	Simeon
Levi (no inheritance)	Levi (inheritance in the place of Dan.)
Issachar	Issachar
Zebulun	Zabulon
Ephraim	**Joseph**
Benjamin	Benjamin

The tribe of Ephraim is not mentioned because it is represented in Joseph and in combination with the tribe on Manasses. It is actually the fulfillment of the two following scriptures that Joseph would have a double portion because of having the Birthright.

Gen. 48:22	"Moreover I have given to thee **one portion above thy brethren**, which I took out of the hand of the Amorite with my sword and with my bow."
Eze. 47:13	"Thus saith the Lord GOD; This shall be the border, whereby ye shall inherit the land according to the twelve tribes of Israel: **Joseph shall have two portions**."

We can see this representation of Ephraim in Joseph further demonstrated in:

Eze. 37:16	"Moreover, thou son of man, take thee one **stick**, and **write** upon it, For Judah, and for the children of Israel his companions: then take another **stick**, and **write upon it, For Joseph, the stick of Ephraim**, and for all the house of Israel his companions."
Eze. 37:19	"Say unto them, Thus saith the Lord GOD; Behold, I will take **the stick of Joseph, which is in the hand of Ephraim**, and the tribes of Israel his fellows, and will put them with him, even with the **stick** of Judah, and make them one **stick**, and they shall be one in mine hand."

We can see a similar event that happened where names were written upon "sticks" or "rods."

Num. 17:1	"And the LORD spake unto Moses, saying,"

Num. 17:2	"Speak unto the children of Israel, and take of every one of them a **rod** according to the house of their fathers, of all their princes according to the house of their fathers twelve **rods**: **write** thou every man's name upon his **rod**."
Num. 17:3	"And thou shalt write **Aaron**'s name upon the **rod** of **Levi**: for one rod shall be for the head of the house of their fathers."
Num. 17:4	"And thou shalt lay them up in the tabernacle of the congregation before the testimony, where I will meet with you."
Num. 17:5	"And it shall come to pass, that the man's **rod**, whom I shall choose, shall blossom: and I will make to cease from me the murmurings of the children of Israel, whereby they murmur against you."
Num. 17:6	"And Moses spake unto the children of Israel, and every one of their princes gave him a **rod** apiece, for each prince one, according to their fathers' houses, even twelve **rods**: and the **rod** of Aaron was among their **rods**."
Num. 17:7	"And Moses laid up the **rods** before the LORD in the tabernacle of witness."

Num. 17:8 "And it came to pass, that on the morrow Moses went into the tabernacle of witness; and, behold, the **rod** of Aaron for the house of Levi was budded, and brought forth buds, and bloomed blossoms, and yielded almonds."

Num. 17:9 "And Moses brought out all the **rods** from before the LORD unto all the children of Israel: and they looked, and took every man his **rod**."

Num. 17:10 "And the LORD said unto Moses, Bring Aaron's **rod** again before the testimony, to be kept for a token against the rebels; and thou shalt quite take away their murmurings from me, that they die not."

Num. 17:11 "And Moses did so: as the LORD commanded him, so did he."

In order to understand why the tribe of Dan was omitted, it is necessary to understand how the birth order of the patriarchs, the Birthright, and the commandment about idolatry all work together. Please refer to **Appendix 2** about the Birthright and specifically that the firstborn sons of slave women were not even considered to inherit the Birthright. Then consider the following birth-order table.

Birth Order	Father	Wife	Slave Name	Ref
1	**Jacob**	**Leah**	**Reuben**	Gen 29:32
2	Jacob	Leah	Simeon	Gen 29:33
3	Jacob	Leah	Levi	Gen 29:34
4	Jacob	Leah	Judah	Gen 29:35
5	Jacob	Rachel	**BilhaDan**	Gen 30:5-6
6	Jacob	Rachel	BilhaNaphtali	Gen 30:7-8
7	Jacob	Leah	**ZilpahGad**	Gen 30:9-11
8	Jacob	Leah	ZilpahAsher	Gen 30:12-13
9	Jacob	Leah	Issachar	Gen 30:17-18
10	Jacob	Leah	Zebulun	Gen 30:19-20
	Jacob	Leah	Dinah	Gen 30:21
11	**Jacob**	**Rachel**	**Joseph**	Gen 30:22-24
12	Israel	Rachel	Benjamin	Gen 35:16-18
13	Joseph	Asenath	Manasseh	Gen 41:51
14	Joseph	Asenath	Ephraim	Gen 41:52

Notice that Dan was the first one that was born of a slave woman and his tribal banner was the serpent (**Gen. 49:17**). Many people mistakenly think that the symbol on the banner of the tribe of Dan was the eagle and they base that belief upon the order in which the different types of cherubim are mentioned in the Bible. However, they have to do that contrary to the biblical witness that the symbols for all of the other tribes are also specified in **Genesis chapter 49** at the same time that the symbol of serpent was identified for the tribe of Dan.

The question must be asked: what tribe does the eagle represent? The answer is found by identifying the tribe that was inserted to have an inheritance together with the other tribes in the end and that did not have the same kind of an inheritance with them in the beginning. That tribe is the Tribe of Levi.

The next detail that is necessary to understand why the tribe of Dan was missing in **Revelations chapter 7** is the law about idolatry.

Deut. 29:9 "Keep therefore the words of this covenant, and do them, that ye may prosper in all that ye do."

Deut. 29:10 "Ye stand this day all of you before the LORD your God; your captains of your tribes, your elders, and your officers, with all the men of Israel."

Deut. 29:11 "Your little ones, your wives, and thy stranger that is in thy camp, from the hewer of thy wood unto the drawer of thy water."

Deut. 29:12 "That thou shouldest enter into covenant with the LORD thy God, and into his oath, which the LORD thy God maketh with thee this day."

Deut. 29:13 "That he may establish thee to day for a people unto himself, and that he may be unto thee a God, as he hath said unto thee, and as he hath sworn unto thy fathers, to Abraham, to Isaac, and to Jacob."

Deut. 29:14 "Neither with you only do I make this covenant and this oath."

Deut. 29:15 "But with him that standeth here with us this day before the LORD our God, and also with him that is not here with us this day."

Deut. 29:16	"(For ye know how we have dwelt in the land of Egypt; and how we came through the nations which ye passed by."
Deut. 29:17	"And ye have seen their abominations, and their idols, wood and stone, silver and gold, which were among them:"
Deut. 29:18	**"Lest there should be among you man**, or woman, or family, **or tribe, whose heart turneth away this day from the LORD our God, to go and serve the gods of these nations**; lest there should be among you a root that beareth gall and wormwood."
Deut. 29:19	"And it come to pass, when he heareth the words of this curse, that he bless himself in his heart, saying, I shall have peace, though I walk in the imagination of mine heart, to add drunkenness to thirst."
Deut. 29:20	"The LORD will not spare him, but then the anger of the LORD and his jealousy shall smoke against that man, and all the curses that are written in this book shall lie upon him, **and the LORD shall blot out his name from under heaven**."

The Tribe of Dan fell into idolatry according to:

Amos 8:14 "They that swear by the sin of Samaria, and say, Thy **g**od, **O Dan.**, liveth; and, The manner of Beersheba liveth; **even they shall fall, and never rise up again.**"

The last mention of the Tribe of Dan in the Bible is in **Amos 8:14**. Why was it the last mention of the Tribe of Dan? Because they fell into idolatry (**Amos 8:14**, lowercase "god ") as a tribe (**Deut. 29:18**) and God blotted out their name (**Deut. 29:20**) and they never rose again (**Amos 8:14**).

The Tribe of Levi did not have an inheritance in **Numbers chapter 2**, but they are given an inheritance among the other tribes in **Revelations chapter 7** in the place of the tribe of Dan.

BOTH the Tribe of Dan being cut off and the Tribe of Levi taking his place happen in the north at the end of time. It symbolizes that there will be two types of churches on the **north**, one that will go into apostasy (divorce) and one that will become kings and priests (Levites, **Rev. 1:6**, **5:10**) before God. Those two churches are also symbolized by the Great Harlot and by the Wife of the Lamb. It is also symbolized by the easily forgotten fact that the symbol for the end of time (north) is **NOT** just any kind of an eagle; it is a "flying eagle."

Rev. 4:6 "And before the throne there was a sea of glass like unto crystal: and in the midst of the throne, and round about the throne, were four beasts full of eyes before and behind."

Rev. 4:7 "And the first beast was like a lion, and the second beast like a calf, and the third beast had a face as a man, and the fourth beast was like a **flying eagle**."

THE INCENSE AND THE GLORY

This detail demonstrates that not only will there be a glorious church without spot or wrinkle or any such thing (**Eph. 5:27**) in the end that becomes kings and **priests** (Levites, **Rev. 1:6**, **5:10**), but also that the same church will meet Him in the air (**1 Thess. 4:17**).

That church will also fulfill the expressed desire of God in:

Exo. 19:6 "And ye shall be unto me a **kingdom of priests, and an holy nation**. These are the words which thou shalt speak unto the children of Israel."

ABOUT THE AUTHOR

James D. Sargent spent over thirty years intensively studying about prophecy and revival and how the Bible relates to current events. He began to notice recurring patterns that help to identify the necessary requirements for revivals that leave a permanent impression in human history.

The Lord Jesus said in **Luke 6:43–45** that a man can be known by that which comes forth from the abundance of his heart. This book proceeded from that which has been sown into his heart by the Word of God. He trusts that it will be a blessing to every reader. If you want to know about the author, read the book.

CPSIA information can be obtained
at www.ICGtesting.com
Printed in the USA
BVHW070800240619
551796BV00001B/16/P

9 781645 156970